Angelo de Gubernatis

Zoological Mythology

The Legends of Animals

Angelo de Gubernatis

Zoological Mythology
The Legends of Animals

ISBN/EAN: 9783744660051

Printed in Europe, USA, Canada, Australia, Japan

Cover: Foto ©Andreas Hilbeck / pixelio.de

More available books at **www.hansebooks.com**

ZOOLOGICAL MYTHOLOGY

OR

THE LEGENDS OF ANIMALS

BY

ANGELO DE GUBERNATIS

PROFESSOR OF SANSKRIT AND COMPARATIVE LITERATURE IN THE ISTITUTO DI STUDII SUPERIORI E DI PERFEZIONAMENTO, AT FLORENCE
FOREIGN MEMBER OF THE ROYAL INSTITUTE OF PHILOLOGY AND ETHNOGRAPHY OF THE DUTCH INDIES

IN TWO VOLUMES

VOL. II.

LONDON
TRÜBNER & CO., 60 PATERNOSTER ROW
1872

Detroit: Reissued by Singing Tree Press, Book Tower, 1968

CONTENTS.

Part First.

THE ANIMALS OF THE EARTH.

(Continued.)

PAGE

CHAPTER V.

THE HOG, THE WILD BOAR, AND THE HEDGEHOG, 1

CHAPTER VI.

THE DOG, 17

CHAPTER VII.

THE CAT, THE WEASEL, THE MOUSE, THE MOLE, THE SNAIL, THE ICHNEUMON, THE SCORPION, THE ANT, THE LOCUST, AND THE GRASSHOPPER, ... 41

CHAPTER VIII.

THE HARE, THE RABBIT, THE ERMINE, AND THE BEAVER, . 76

CHAPTER IX.

THE ANTELOPE, THE STAG, THE DEER, AND THE GAZELLE, . 83

CHAPTER X.

THE ELEPHANT, . 91

CHAPTER XI.

THE MONKEY AND THE BEAR, . 96

CHAPTER XII.

THE FOX, THE JACKAL, AND THE WOLF, ... 121

PAGE

CHAPTER XIII.

THE LION, THE TIGER, THE LEOPARD, THE PANTHER, AND THE CHAMELEON, ... 153

CHAPTER XIV.

THE SPIDER, 162

Part Second.

THE ANIMALS OF THE AIR.

CHAPTER I.

BIRDS, . 167

CHAPTER II.

THE HAWK, THE EAGLE, THE VULTURE, THE PHŒNIX, THE HARPY, THE STRIX, THE BAT, THE GRIFFON, AND THE SIREN, ... 180

CHAPTER III.

THE WREN, THE BEETLE, AND THE FIREFLY, 207

CHAPTER IV.

THE BEE, THE WASP, THE FLY, THE GNAT, THE MOSQUITO, THE HORSEFLY, AND THE CICADA, ... 215

CHAPTER V.

THE CUCKOO, THE HERON, THE HEATHCOCK, THE PARTRIDGE, THE NIGHTINGALE, THE SWALLOW, THE SPARROW, AND THE HOOPOE, ... 225

CHAPTER VI.

THE OWL, THE CROW, THE MAGPIE, AND THE STORK, . . 243

CHAPTER VII.

THE WOODPECKER AND THE MARTIN, . . . 264

CHAPTER VIII.

THE LARK AND THE QUAIL, ... 273

PAGE

CHAPTER IX.

The Cock and the Hen, 279

CHAPTER X.

The Dove, the Duck, the Goose, and the Swan, 294

CHAPTER XI.

The Parrot, . 320

CHAPTER XII.

The Peacock, . 323

Part Third.

THE ANIMALS OF THE WATER.

CHAPTER I.

Fishes, and particularly the Pike, the Sacred Fish or Fish of St Peter, the Carp, the Melwel, the Herring, the Eel, the Little Goldfish, the Sea-Urchin, the Little Perch, the Bream, the Dolphin, and the Whale, 329

CHAPTER II.

The Crab, 354

CHAPTER III.

The Tortoise, 360

CHAPTER IV.

The Frog, the Lacerta Viridis, and the Toad, 371

CHAPTER V.

The Serpent and the Aquatic Monster, . 388

Conclusion, . 421

ZOOLOGICAL MYTHOLOGY;

OR

THE LEGENDS OF ANIMALS.

First Part.

THE ANIMALS OF THE EARTH.

CHAPTER V.

THE HOG, THE WILD BOAR, AND THE HEDGEHOG.

SUMMARY.

The hog as a hero disguise.—The disguises of the hero and of the heroine.—Ghoshâ, the leprous maiden.—The moon in the well.—Apâlâ cured by Indras.—Apâlâ has the dress of a hog.—Godhâ, the persecuted maiden in a hog's dress.—The hogs eat the apples in the maiden's stead.—The meretricious Circe and the hogs.—Porcus and upodaras.—The wild boar god in India and in Persia.—Tydœus, the wild boar.—The wild boar of Erymanthos.—The wild boar of Meleagros.—The Vedic monster wild boar.—The dog and the pig.—Puloman, the wild boar, burned.—The hog in the fire.—The hog cheats the wolf.—The astute hedgehog.—The hegehog, the wild boar, and the hog are presages of water.—The porcupine and its quills; the comb and the dense forest.—The ears and the heart of the wild boar.—The wild boar and the hog at Christmas.—The devil a wild boar.—The heroes killed by the wild boar.—The tusk of the wild boar now life-giving, now deadly; the dead man's tooth.—The hero asleep; the hero become a eunuch; the lettuce-eunuch eaten by Adonis, prior to his being killed by the wild boar.

The hog, as well as the wild boar, is another disguise of the solar hero in the night—another of the forms very often assumed by the sun, as a mythical hero, in the darkness or clouds. He adopts this form in order sometimes to hide himself from his persecutors, sometimes to exterminate them, and sometimes on account of a divine or demoniacal malediction. This form is sometimes a dark and demoniacal guise assumed by the hero; on which account the poem of *Hyndla*, in the *Edda*, calls the hog a hero's animal. Often, however, it represents the demon himself. When the solar hero enters the domain of evening, the form he had of a handsome youth or splendid prince disappears; but he himself, as a general rule, does not die along with it; he only passes into another, an uglier, and a monstrous form. The black bull, the black horse, the grey horse, the hump-backed horse, the ass, and the goat, are all forms of the same disguise with which we are already acquainted. The thousand-bellied Indras, who has lost his testicles; Arǵunas, who disguises himself as a eunuch; Indras, Vishṇus, Zeus, Achilleüs, Odin, Thor, Helgi, and many other mythical heroes, who disguise themselves as women; and the numerous beautiful heroines who, in mythology and tradition, disguise themselves as bearded men, are all ancient forms under which was represented the passage of either the sun or the aurora of evening into the darkness, cloud, ocean, forest, grotto, or hell of night. The hero lamed, blinded, bound, drowned, or buried in a wood, can be understood when referred respectively to the sun which is thrown down the mountain-side, which is lost in the darkness, which is held fast by the fetters of the darkness, which plunges into the ocean of night, or which hides itself from our sight in the nocturnal forest. The illumined and illuminating sun, when it ceases to shine in the dark night, becomes devoid of sight, devoid of intelligence, and stupid. The handsome solar hero becomes ugly when, with the night, his splendour ceases; the strong, red, healthy, solar hero, who pales and grows dark in the night, becomes ill. We still say in Italy that the sun is ill when we see it lose its brightness, and, as it were, grow pale.

In the 117th hymn of the first book of the *Ṛigvedas*, the Açvinâu cure the leprous daughter of Kakshîvant, Ghoshâ, who is growing old without a husband in her father's house, and find her a husband; the Açvinâu deliver the aurora from the darkness of night, and marry her.[1]

In the eightieth hymn of the eighth book of the *Ṛigvedas*, the same myth occurs again with relation to Indras, and in a more complete form. We have already remarked, in the first book of the *Ṛigvedas*, the maiden Apâlâ who descends from the mountain to draw water, and draws up the somas (ambrosia, or else the moon, whence, as it seems to me, the origin of the double Italian proverb, "Pescare, or mostrare la luna nel pozzo," to fish up, or show the moon in the well, which was afterwards corrupted to indicate one who says, or narrates, what is untrue or impossible), and takes it to Indras, the well-known drinker of ambrosia (here identified with the moon, or somas). Indras, contented with the maiden, consents, as she is ugly and deformed, to pass over the three heavenly stations, that is, to pass over his father's head, her vast breast and her bosom.[2] In the last strophe of the hymn quoted above, Indras makes a luminous robe,

---

[1] Cfr. the chapter on the Duck, the Goose, the Swan, and the Dove.

[2] Imâni trîni vishtapâ tânîndra vi rohaya çiras tatasyorvarâm âd idam ma upodare.

a skin of the sun, for Apâlâ, who has been thrice purified, by the wheel, by the chariot itself, and by the rudder of Indras's chariot.[1] And the same myth occurs once more in a clearer and more complete form in a legend of the *Bṛihaddevatâ*. Apâlâ beseeches Indras, loved by her, to make for her a beautiful and perfect (faultless, unimpeachable) skin. Indras, hearing her voice, passes over her with wheel, chariot, and rudder; by three efforts, he takes off her ugly skin. Apâlâ then appears in a beautiful one. In the skin thus stript off there was a bristle (çalyakaḥ); above, it had a hirsute appearance; below, it resembled the skin of a lizard.[2] The bristle or thorn upon the skin of Apâlâ is naturally suggestive of the hedgehog, the porcupine, the wild boar, and the bristly hog. The aurora, as the Vedic hymn sings, shines only at the sight of her husband; thus Apâlâ, of the ugly or

---

[1] Khe rathasya khe 'nasaḥ khe yugasya çatakrato apâlâm indra trish pûtvy akṛinoḥ sûryatvaćam.

[2] Sulomâm anavadyâñgîṁ kuru mâṁ çakra sutvaćâm
Tasyâs tad vaćanam çrutvâ prîtas tena purandaraḥ
Rathaćhidreṇa tâm indraḥ çakaṭasya yugasya ća
Prakshipya niçćakarsha tris tataḥ sâ sutvaćâ 'bhavat
Tasyâṁ tvaći vyapetâyâm sarvasyâṁ çalyako 'bhavat
Uttarâ tv abhavad godhâ krikalâças tvag uttamâ.

Godhâ seems to signify he who has the form of a hair (*go*, among its other meanings, has that of hair). As an animal, the dictionaries also recognise in the godhâ a lizard. But perhaps we may also translate it by toad or frog; we could thus also understand the fable of the frog which aspires to equal the ox. I observe, moreover, to exemplify the ease with which we can pass from the ox to the frog, and from the frog to the lizard, how in the Russian story of *Afanassieff*, ii. 23, a beautiful princess is hidden in a frog; in Tuscan and Piedmontese stories and in Sicilian superstitions, in a toad. In the stories of the *Pentamerone*, the good fairy is a *lacerta cornuta* (a horned lizard). Ghoshâ, too, has for its equivalent in Sanskṛit, karkaṭaçṛiñgî, which means a horned shrimp. In other varieties the young prince is a he-goat or a dragon.

the hog's skin, and Ghoshâ, the leprous maiden, become splendid and healthy by the grace of their husband. Thus Cinderella, or she who has a dress of the colour of ashes, or of a grey or dark colour, like the sky of night (in Russian stories Cinderella is called Cernushka, which means little black one, as well as little dirty one), appears exceedingly beautiful only when she finds herself in the prince's ball-room, or in church, in candlelight, and near the prince: the aurora is beautiful only when the sun is near.

In the twenty-eighth story of the sixth book of *Afanassieff*, the maiden persecuted by her father and would-be seducer, who wishes to marry her, because he thinks her as beautiful as her mother (the evening aurora is as beautiful as the morning aurora), covers herself with a hog's skin, which she takes off only when she marries a young prince.[1] In another story of White Russia,[2] we have, instead, the son of a king persecuted by his father, who is constrained to quit his father's house with a cloak made of a pig's skin. In an unpublished story of the Monferrato, the contents of which Dr Ferraro has communicated to me, the girl persecuted by her step-mother is condemned to eat in one night an interminable number of apples; by means of two hog's bristles, she calls up a whole legion of pigs, who eat the apples in her stead.

As to the rudder of Indras's chariot in the lower bosom of Apâlâ, it would seem to me to have a phallic signification. Indras may have cured Apâlâ by marrying her, as the Açvinâu, by means of a husband, cured the leprous Ghoshâ, who was growing old in her father's house. In the tenth story of the *Pentamerone*, the king

[1] For the persecuted maiden in connection with the hog or hogs, cfr. also the *Pentamerone*, iii. 10.

[2] *Afanassieff*, v. 38.

of Roccaforte marries an old woman, believing he is espousing a young one. He throws her out of the window, but she is arrested in her fall by a tree, to which she clings; the fairies pass by, and make her young again, as well as beautiful and rich, and tie up her hair with a golden ribbon. The aged sister of the old woman who has grown young again (the night) goes to the barber, thinking that the same result may be attained simply by having her skin removed, and is flayed alive. For the myth of the two sisters, night and aurora, the black maiden and she who disguises herself in black, in grey, or the colour of ashes, consult also the *Pentamerone*, ii. 2. According to the Italian belief, the hog is dedicated to St Anthony, and a St Anthony is also celebrated as the protector of weddings, like the Scandinavian Thor, to whom the hog is sacred. The hog symbolises fat; and therefore, in the sixteenth Esthonian story, the hog is eaten at weddings.

The companions of Odysseus, transformed by the meretricious enchantress Circe, with the help of poisonous herbs, into filthy hogs, care only to gratify their bodily appetites, whence Horace, in the second of the first book of the *Epistolæ*—

> "Sirenum voces, et Circes pocula nosti,
> Quæ si cum sociis stultus cupidusque bibisset
> Sub domina meretrice fuisset turpis et excors
> Vixisset canis immundus, vel amica luto Sus."

The hog, as one of the most libidinous of animals, is sacred to Venus; for this reason, according to the Pythagorian doctrines, lustful men are transformed into hogs, and the expression "pig" is applied to a man given over to every species of lust. In Varro[1] we read:—"Nuptiarum initio, antiqui reges ac sublimes viri in Hetruria in

[1] *De Re Rustica*, ii. 4.

conjuctione nuptiali nova nupta et novus maritus primum porcum immolànt; prisci quoque Latini et etiam Græci in Italia idem fecisse videntur, nam et nostræ mulieres, maximæ nutrices naturam, qua fœminæ sunt, in virginibus appellant porcum, et græce choiron, significantes esse dignum insigni nuptiarum." The rudder of Indras, which passes over the upodaras (or lower bosom) of Apâlâ, is illustrated by this passage in Varro.

As to the wild boar, its character is generally demoniacal; but the reason why the Hindoo gods were invested with this form was in a great degree due to equivocation in language. The word *vishṇus* means he who penetrates; on account of its sharp tusks, in a Vedic hymn,[1] the wild boar is called vishṇus, or the penetrator. Hence, probably, by the same analogy, in another hymn, Rudras, the father of the Marutas, the winds, is invoked as a red, hirsute, horrid, celestial wild boar,[2] and the Marutas are invoked when the thunderbolts are seen in the form of wild boars running out from the iron teeth and golden wheels;[3] that is, carried by the chariot of the Marutas, the winds, who also are said to have tongues of fire, and eyes like the sun.[4] Vishṇus himself, in the *Ṛigvedas*, at the instigation of Indras, brings a hundred oxen, the

[1] *Ṛigv.* i. 61, 7.

[2] Divo varâham arusham kapardinaṁ tveshaṁ rûpaṁ namasâ ni hvayâmahe; *Ṛigv.* i. 114, 5.

[3] Paçyan hiraṇyaćakrân ayodaṅshṭrâu vidhâvato varâhân; *Ṛigv.* i. 88, 5.

[4] Agniǵiḥvâ manavaḥ sûraćakshasaḥ; *Ṛigv.* i. 89, 7.—In the *Edda*, the chariot of Frey is drawn by a hog. The head of the mythical hog is luminous. In the twenty-eighth story of the second book of *Afanassieff*, Ivan Durák obtains from the two young heroes, who miraculously appear to him, three marvellous gifts, *i.e.*, the hog with golden bristles, the buck with golden horns and tail, and the horse with mane and tail also of gold.

milky gruel, and the destroying wild boar.[1] Therefore Indras himself loves the shape of a wild boar, which, in the *Avesta*, is his *alter ego*. / Verethraghnas assumes the same form. We know that the sun (sometimes the moon), in the form of a ram or he-goat, thrusts and pushes against the cloud, or the darkness, until he pierces it with his golden horns; and so Vishṇus, the penetrator, with his sharp golden tusks (thunderbolts, lunar horns, and solar rays), puts forth such great strength in the darkness and the cloud that he bursts through both, and comes forth luminous and victorious. According to the Pâuranic traditions, Vishṇus, in his third incarnation, when killing the demon Hiraṇyâkshas (or him of the golden eye), drew forth or delivered the earth from the waters (or from the ocean of the damp and gloomy night of the winter).[2] According to the *Râmâyaṇam*,[3]

---

[1] Viçvet tâ vishṇur âbharad urukramas tveshitaḥ çatam mahishân kshîrapâkam odanaṁ varâham indra emusham; *Ṛigv.* viii. 66, 10.—In the Thebaid of Statius (v. 487), Tydœus, too, is dressed in the spoils of a wild boar—

"Terribiles contra setis, ac dente recurvo,
Tydea per latos humeros ambire laborant
Exuviæ, Calydonis honos."

[2] According to other fables, the three persons of the Trinity at one time disputed as to who had the pre-eminence. Brahmân, who, from the summit of the lotus where he was seated, saw nothing in the universe, believed himself the first of creatures. He descended into the stem of the lotus, and finding at last Nârâyaṇas (Vishṇus) asleep, he asked him who he was. "I am the first-born," replied Vishṇus; Brahmân disputed this title and dared even to attack him. But during the struggle, Mahâdeva (Çiva) threw himself between them, crying, "It is I who am the first-born. Nevertheless I will recognise as my superior him who is able to see the summit of my head or the sole of my feet." Vishṇus (as hidden or infernal moon), transforming himself into a wild boar, pierced through the ground and penetrated to the infernal regions, where he saw the feet of Mahâdeva. The latter, on his return, saluted him as the first-born of the gods; Bournouf, *L'Inde Française*. [3] ii. 119.

Indras took the form of a wild boar immediately after his birth.

The Arcadian wild boar of Mount Erymanthüs is familiar to the reader. Hêraklês killed it in his third labour, in the same way as Vishṇus in the third of his incarnations became a wild boar; Ovid describes him very elegantly in the eighth book of the *Metamorphoses*—

> "Sanguine et igne micant oculi, riget horrida cervix;
> Et setæ densis similes hastilibus horrent.
> Stantque velut vallum, velut alta hastilia setæ,
> Fervida cum rauco latos stridore per armos
> Spuma fluit, dentes æquantur dentibus Indis,
> Fulmen ab ore venit frondes afflatibus ardent."

The wild boar of Meleagros is a variety of this very monster; it is, therefore, not without reason that when Hêraklês goes to the infernal regions, all the shades flee before him, except those of Meleagros and Medusa. Meleagros and Hêraklês resemble each other, are identified with each other; as to Medusa, we must not forget that the head of the Gorgon was represented upon the ægis of Zeus, that Gorgon is one of the names given to Pallas, and that the Gorgons, and especially Medusa, are connected with the garden of the Hesperîdes, where the golden apples grow which Hêraklês loves.

In the sixty-first hymn of the first book of the *Ṛigvedas*, the god, after having eaten and drunk well, kills, with the weapon stolen from the celestial blacksmith Tvashṭar, the monster wild boar, who steals that which is destined for the gods.[1] In the ninety-ninth hymn of the tenth book of the *Ṛigvedas*, Tritas (the third brother), by the strength which he has received from

[1] Asyed u mâtuḥ savaneshu sadyo mahah pitum papivâń ćarv annâ mushâyad vishṇuḥ paćataṁ sahîyâm vidhyad varâhaṁ tiro adrim astâ; str. 7.

Indras, kills the monster wild boar.[1] In the *Tâittiriya Brâhmaṇam*, we find another very interesting passage. The wild boar keeps guard over the treasure of the demons, which is enclosed within seven mountains. Indras, with the sacred herb, succeeds in opening the seven mountains, kills the wild boar, and, in consequence, discovers the treasure.[2] In the fifty-fifth hymn of the seventh book of the *Ṛigvedas*, the hog and the dog lacerate and tear each other to pieces in turns;[3] the dog and the pig are found in strife again in the Æsopian fable.

In the *Mahâbhâratam*,[4] Puloman assumes the form of a wild boar to carry off the wife of Bhṛigus; she prematurely gives birth to Ćyavanas, who, to avenge his mother, burns the wild boar to ashes. The thunderbolt tears through the cloud, the sun's ray (or the lunar horn) breaks through the darkness. In the popular Tuscan story, the stupid Pimpi kills the hog, by teasing and tormenting it with the tongs, which he has made red-hot in the fire. In the ninth of the Sicilian stories collected by Laura Gonzenbach, the girl Zafarana, throwing three hog's bristles upon the burning embers, causes the old prince, her husband, to become young and handsome again; it is ever the same lucid myth (a variety of Apâlâ). Thus, in the first Esthonian story, the prince, by eating pork (or in the night forest), acquires the faculty of under-

[1] Asya trito nv oǵasâ vṛidhâno vipâ varâham ayoagrayâ han; str. 6.

[2] Varahoyam vamamoshaḥ saptanâm girîṇâm parastâd vittam vedyam asurânâm vibharti, sa darbhapiṅǵûlam (piṅgalam?) uddhṛitya, sapta girîn bhittvâ tam ahanniti, already quoted by Wilson, *Ṛigv. San.* i. 164.—Cfr. the chapter on the Woodpecker.

[3] Tvam sûkarasya dardṛihi tava dardartu sûkarah; str. 4.—The dog in relation with the hog occurs again in the two Latin proverbs: "Canis peccatum sus dependit," and "Aliter catuli longe olent, aliter sues."

[4] i. 893.

standing the language of birds; the hero acquires malice, if he has it not already; he becomes cunning, if he was previously stupid; we therefore also find in a story of *Afanassieff*,[1] the wolf cheated, first by the dog, then by the goat, and finally by the hog, who nearly drowns him. The wolf wishes to eat the hog's little ones; the hog requests him to wait under a bridge, where there is no water, whilst he goes, as he promises, in the meantime to wash the young porkers; the wolf waits, and the hog goes to let off the water, which, as it passes under the bridge, puts the wolf's life in danger. Hence the belief noticed by Aristotle, that the hog is a match for the wolf, and the corresponding Greek fables. This prudence is found carried to the highest degree in the hedgehog. The Arabs are accustomed to say that the champion of truth must have the courage of the cock, the scrutiny of the hen, the heart of the lion, the rush of the wild boar, the cunning of the fox, the prudence of the hedgehog, the swiftness of the wolf, the resignation of the dog, and the complexion of the naguir.[2] A verse attributed to Archilokos says:—

"Poll' oid' alôpêx, all' echinos en mega,"

which passed into the proverb: "One knavery of the hedgehog is worth more than many of the fox." In the *Âitarey. Br.*,[3] the hedgehog is said to be born of the talon of the rapacious hawk. In the Æsopian fables, the wolf comes upon a hedgehog, and congratulates himself upon his good luck; but the hedgehog defends itself. The wolf flatters it and beseeches it to lay down its arms, but it answers that it is imprudent to do so

[1] iv. 13.
[2] Daumas, *La Vie Arabe*, xv.
[3] iii. 3, 26.

while the danger of fighting remains. Hence the common belief that the wolf is afraid of the hedgehog; hence the proverb, "It is very easy to find the hedgehog, but very difficult to hold it." In a fable of Abstemius, the hedgehog appears as an enemy, not only of the wolf, but also of the serpent; it pricks the viper which has taken refuge in its den. Then the viper begs it to go out, but it answers, "Let him go out who cannot stay." The hedgehog has the appearance of a little wild boar; and as an enemy of the wolf and of the serpent, it appears to me to combine in one the dwarf Vishṇus and the wild boar Vishṇus, the exterminator of monsters, who, as we know, almost always assume, in Hindoo mythology, the form of a wolf or a serpent. And inasmuch as Vishṇus, like Indras, is a thundering and rain-giving god, in his character of sun in the cloud, or nightly and autumnal moon, the hedgehog, too, is believed to presage wind and rain. The wild boar, when dreamed of, is, according to Artemidoros, quoted by Aldrovandi,[1] an omen of tempest and rain deluge. To this, refers also the fable spoken of by Ælianos and Pliny concerning the hogs carried off by the pirates, which make the ship sink. The cloud-hogs are evidently represented by this myth.

The porcupine seems to be an intermediate form between the hedgehog and the wild boar. According to the popular belief, the ashes of a dead porcupine are, when scattered on the head, an excellent remedy against baldness, and a hair-restorative. And inasmuch as it is difficult to make the porcupine's quills fall, I read in Aldrovandi,[2] that women "Ad discriminandos capillos, ut illos conservent illæsos, aculeis potius hystricum, quam acubus utuntur." This information derived from

[1] Cfr. Aldrovandi, *De Quadrup. Digit. Viv.* ii. [2] *Ibid.*

Aldrovandi is interesting, as enabling us to understand a not uncommon circumstance in Russian stories. The hero and heroine who flee from the monster that pursues them have received from a good magician or a good fairy the gift of a comb, of such a nature that when thrown on the ground it makes a dense thicket or impenetrable forest arise, which arrests the pursuer's progress.[1] This is a reminiscence of the porcupine with the thick-set quills, of the bristly wild boar, of the gloomy night or cloud itself, of the horned moon, which hides the fugitive solar hero and heroine from the sight of the pursuer.

Notwithstanding this, the hog and the wild boar generally play in Indo-European tradition a part resembling that of the scape-goat and of the ass *souffre-douleur.* In the *Pańćatantram,* the ears and the heart of the credulous ass, torn by the lion, are eaten. In Babrios, the *rôle* of the ass is sustained by the stag (which is often in myths a variation of the foolish hero). In the *Gesta Romanorum,*[2] the wild boar loses, by his silliness, first one ear, then the other, then his tail; at last he is killed, and his heart eaten by the cook. In Germany, it is the custom, as it formerly was in England, to serve up at dinner on Christmas Day an ornamented boar's head, no doubt as a symbol of the gloomy monster of lunar winter killed at the winter solstice, after which the days grow always longer and brighter. For the same reason, the common people in Germany often go to sleep

[1] Cfr. *Afanassieff,* v. 28.

[2] lxxxiii., quoted by Benfey in his Einleitung to the *Pańćatantram.* —The fable is taken from the thirtieth of Avianus, where the wild boar loses his two ears and is then eaten, but the cook (who represents in tradition the cunning hero) has taken its heart to eat it:—

> "Sed cum consumpti dominus cor quæreret Apri
> Impatiens, fertur (cor) rapuisse coquus."

on Christmas Day in the pig-sty, hoping to dream there; this dream is a presage of good luck. The new sun is born in the sty of the winter hog; even the Christian Redeemer was born in a stable, but instead of the hog it was the ass, its mythical equivalent, that occupied it. For this reason, too, the devil often assumes in German superstition the form of a monstrous boar, which the hero kills.[1] The wild boar is also described as an *aversier* (or demon) in the romance of *Garin le Loherain*[2]—

"Voiés quel aversier,
Grant a le dent fors de la gueule un piet
Mult fu hardis qui a cop l'atendié."

The author of *Loci Communes* says that Ferquhar II., king of Scotland, was killed by a wild boar; other writers tell us, on the contrary, that his death was caused by a wolf; but we already know how, in the myth, wolf and wild boar are sometimes equivalent the one to the other.

In the same way as Vishṇus changed himself into a wild boar, and the hog was sacred to the Scandinavian Mars, so was the wild boar sacred to the Roman and Hellenic Mars; and even Mars himself assumed the shape of a monstrous lunar wild boar in order to kill the young Adonis, beloved of Venus. There is no god or saint so perfect but has once in his life committed a fault, as there is not a demon so wicked as not to have done good at least once. The adversaries exchange parts. In Servius, it is with a wild boar's tusk that the bark is cut off the tree in which Myrrha, pregnant with

---

[1] In Du Cange, too, "*aper* significat diabolum; Papias M. S. Bitur. Ex illo Scripturæ: 'Singularis aper egressus est de silva.'"—Cfr. also Uhland's *Schriften zur Geschichte der Dichtung und Sage*, iii. 141, *et seq.*

[2] ii. 220, *et seq.*, quoted by Uhland.

Adonis after her incest with her father, shuts herself up (we have above seen, on the contrary, Indras who opens with an herb the hiding-place of the wild boar, in order to kill it). We here have again the incestuous father, the girl in the wooden dress, the forest, the penetrating tusk of the wild boar which bursts through the forest of night, and enables the young hero to come forth, whom he kills in the evening out of jealousy. In the ancient popular belief of Sweden, too, the wild boar kills the sun whilst he is asleep in a cavern and his horses grazing. Notice, moreover, the double character of the tusk of the nocturnal lunar wild boar; in the morning it is a life-giving tusk, which enables the solar hero to be born; in the evening it is a death-dealing one; the wild boar is alive during the night, and the darkness is split open by the white tooth of the living wild boar. The lunar wild boar or hog is sacrificed,—it is killed at morn, in the nuptials of the solar hero. The tooth of this dead wild boar, in the evening, causes the death of the young hero or heroine, or else transforms them into wild beasts. In popular fairy tales the witch, feigning a wish to comb the head of the hero or the heroine, thrusts into his or her head now a large pin, now a dead man's tooth, and thus deprives them of life or human form. This is a reminiscence of the tusk of the cloudy, nocturnal, or wintry wild boar who kills the sun, or metamorphoses him, or puts him to sleep.

To represent the evening sun asleep, a curious particular is offered us in the myth of Adonis. It is well-known that doctors attribute to the lettuce a soporific virtue, not dissimilar to that of the poppy. Now, it is interesting to read in *Nikandros Kolophonios*, quoted by Aldrovandi, that Adonis was struck by the wild boar after having eaten a lettuce. Ibykos, a Pythagorean poet, calls the lettuce by the name of eunuch, as it is that which puts to sleep, which renders stupid and impotent; Adonis who has eaten the lettuce is therefore taken from Venus by the lunar wild boar, being eunuch and incapable. The solar hero falls asleep in the night, and becomes a eunuch, like the Hindoo Arǵunas, when he is hidden; and otherwise, the sun becomes the moon.

CHAPTER VI.

THE DOG.

SUMMARY.

Why the myth of the dog is difficult of interpretation.—*Entre chien et loup.*—The dog and the moon.—The bitch Saramâ; her double aspect in the Vedâs and in the *Râmâyaṇam;* messenger, consoler, and infernal being.—The dog and the purple; the dog and the meat; the dog and its shadow; the fearless hero and his shadow; the black monster; the fear of Indras.—The two Vedic dogs; Sârameyas and Hermês.—The favourite dog of Saramâ; the dog that steals during the sacrifice; the form of a dog to expiate crimes committed in former states of existence; relative Hindoo, Pythagorean and Christian beliefs.—The dog Yamas.—The dog demon that barks, with the long bitter tongue.—The red bitch towards morning a beautiful maiden during the night.—The intestines of the dog eaten.—The hawk that carries honey and the sterile woman.—Dog and woodpecker.—The dog carries the bones of the witch's daughter.—The dog-messenger brings news of the hero.—The nurse-bitch.—The dog and his collar; the dog tied up; the hero becomes a dog.—The dog helps the hero.—The branch of the apple-tree opens the door.—The dog tears the devil in pieces.—The two sons of Ivan think themselves dog's sons.—The intestines of the fish given to be eaten by the bitch.—Ivan the son of the bitch, the very strong hero, goes to the infernal regions.—Dioscuri, Kerberos, funereal purifying dogs of the Persians; the penitent dog; the two dogs equivalent to the two Açvinâu.—The luminous children transformed into puppies; relative legends; the maiden whose hands have been cut off obtains golden hands; branches of trees, hands, sons born of a tree; the myth compared and explained in the Vedic hymns, with the example of Hiraṇyahastas; the word *vadhrimatî.*—The demoniacal dog.—The strength of the mythical dog.—Monstrous dogs.—The dog Sirius.—To swear by the dog or by the wolf.—A dog is always born among wolves.—The dog dreamed of.—Double appearance of the dog; the stories of the king of the assassins and of the magician with seven heads.—St Vitus invoked in Sicily whilst a dog is being tied up.—The dog of the shepherd behaves like a wolf among the sheep.—The dog as an instrument of chastisement; the expressions to lead the dog and the ignominious punishment of carrying the dog.—The dogs that tear in pieces; the death caused by the dog prognosticated; the dogs Sirius and Kerberos igneous and pestilential; the incendiary dog of St Dominic, the inventor of pyres for burning heretics, and the dog of the infected San Rocco.

THE myth of the dog is one of those of which the interpretation is more delicate. As the common dog stays upon the doorstep of the house, so is the mythical dog generally found at the gate of the sky, morning and evening, in connection with the two Açvinâu. It was a fugitive phenomenon of but an instant's duration which determined the formation of the principal myth of the dog. When this moment is past, the myth changes its nature. I have already referred to the French expression, "entre chien et loup," as used to denote the twilight;[1] the dog precedes by one instant the evening twilight, and follows by one instant that of morning: it is, in a word, the twilight at its most luminous moment. Inasmuch as it watches at the gates of night, it is usually a funereal, infernal, and formidable animal; inasmuch as it guards the gates of day, it is generally represented as a propitious one; and as we

[1] Leukophôs; a verse of Vilkelmus Brito defines it in a Latin strophe given in Du Cange—

"Tempore quo neque nox neque lux sed utrumque videtur;"

and further on—

"Interque *canem distare lupumque.*"

According to Pliny and Solinus, the shadow of the hyena makes the dog dumb, *i.e.*, the night disperses the twilight; the moon vanishes.

have seen that, of the two Açvinâu, one is in especial relation with the moon, and the other with the sun, so, of the two dogs of mythology, one is especially lunar; and the other especially solar. Between these two dogs we find the bitch their mother, who, if I am not mistaken, represents now the wandering moon of heaven, the guiding moon that illumines the path of the hero and heroine, now the thunderbolt that tears the cloud, and opens up the hiding-place of the cows or waters. We have, therefore, thus far three mythical dogs. One, menacing, is found by the solar hero in the evening at the western gates of heaven; the second, the more active, helps him in the forest of night, where he is hunting, guides him in danger, and shows him the lurking-places of his enemies whilst he is in the cloud or darkness; the third, in the morning, is quiet, and found by the hero when he comes out of the gloomy region, towards the eastern sky.

Let us now examine briefly these three forms in Hindoo mythology. I have said that the mythical bitch appears to me sometimes to represent the moon, and sometimes the thunderbolt. In India, this bitch is named Saramâ, properly she who walks, who runs or flows. We are accustomed to say of the dog that it barks at the moon, which the popular proverb connects with robbers. The dog that barks at the moon,[1] is perhaps the same dog that barks to show that robbers are near. In the 108th hymn of the tenth book of the *Ṛigvedas,* we have a dramatic scene between the misers or thieves (the Paṇayas) and the bitch Saramâ, the messenger of Indras, who wishes for their treasures.[2] In order to come to

[1] The dog was sacred to the huntress Diana, whom we know to be the moon, hence the Latin proverb, "Delia nota canibus."

[2] Indrasya dûtir ishitâ ćarâmi maha ićhantî paṇayo nidhîn vaḥ; str. 2.

them, she traverses the waters of the Rasâ (a river of hell); the treasure that is hidden in the mountain consists of cows, horses, and various riches; the Paṇayas wish Saramâ to stay with them as their sister, and to enjoy the cows along with them; Saramâ answers that she does not recognise their brotherhood, inasmuch as she is already the sister of Indras, and the terrible Añgirasas.[1] In the sixty-second hymn of the first book, the bitch Saramâ discovers the cows hidden in the rock, and receives in recompense from Indras and the Añgirasas nourishment for her offspring; then men cry out, and the cows bellow.[2] Going towards the sun, in the path of the sun, Saramâ finds the cows.[3] When Indras splits the mountain open, Saramâ shows him first the waters.[4] Having previously seen the fissure in the mountain, she showed the way. The first she guided rapidly, the band of the noisy ones having previously heard the noise.[5] This noise may refer either to the waters, the sounding rivers (nadâs, nadîs), or the lowing cows (gavas). Now, this bitch that discovers the hiding-places, inasmuch as she breaks through the darkness of night, seems to be the moon; inasmuch as she breaks through the cloud, she seems to be the thunderbolt. The secret of this

[1] Rasâyâ ataram payâṅsi; str. 2.—Ayaṁ nidhiḥ sarame adribudhno gobhir açvebhir vasubhir nyṛishṭaḥ; str. 7.—Svasâraṁ tvâ kṛiṇavâi mâ punar gâ apa te gavâṁ subhage bhaǵâma; str. 9.—Nâhaṁ veda bhrâtṛitvaṁ no svasṛitvam indro vidur añgirasaç ćaghorâḥ; str. 10.

[2] Indrasyâñgirasâm ćeshṭâu vidat saramâ tanayâya dhâsim bṛihaspatir bhinad adrim vidad gâḥ sam usriyâbhir vâvaçanta naraḥ; str. 3.

[3] Ṛitaṁ yatî saramâ gâ avindat.—Ṛitasya pathâ saramâ vidad gâh; *Ṛigv.* v. 45, 7, 8.

[4] Apo yad adrim puruhûta dardar âvir bhuvat saramâ pûrvyaṁ te; *Ṛigv.* iv. 16, 8.

[5] Vidad yadî saramâ rugṇam adrer mahi pâthaḥ pûrvyaṁ sadhryak kaḥ agraṁ nayat supady aksharâṇâm aćhâ ravam prathamâ ǵânatî gât; *Ṛigv.* iii. 31, 6.

equivoque lies in the root *sar*. In the *Ṛigvedas*, we have seen Saramâ disdaining to pass for the sister of the thieves or the monsters; in the *Râmâyaṇam*,[1] the wife of one of the monsters, of the very brother of Râvaṇas the robber, is called Saramâ, and takes, instead of the monster's part, that of Râmas and Sîtâ the ravished wife. We have already several times seen the moon as a beneficent cow, as a good fairy, or as the Madonna. Saramâ (of which Suramâ, another benignant rakshasî, is probably only an incorrect form[2]), the consoler of Sîtâ, who announces prophetically her approaching deliverance by her husband Râmas, appears to me in the light of another impersonation of the moon. It is on this account that Sîtâ[3] praises Saramâ as a twin-sister of hers (sahodarâ), affectionate, and capable of traversing the heavens, and penetrating into the watery infernal regions (rasâtalam).[4] The benignant sister of Sîtâ can only be another luminous being; she is the good sister whom the maiden of the Russian story, persecuted by her incestuous father, in *Afanassieff*, finds in the subterranean world, where she is consoled and assisted in escaping from the power of the witch; she is the moon. The moon is the luminous form of the gloomy sky of night, or of the funereal and infernal region; whilst its two luminous barriers in that sky, in the east and in the west, are morning and evening aurora; the luminous forms of the cloudy sky are lightning and thunderbolts. And it is from one of these luminous mythical forms that the Greeks, according to Pollux, quoted by Aldrovandi, made of the dog the inventor of purple, which the dog of Hêraklês was the first to bite.

[1] vi. 9. [2] v. 62. [3] vi. 10.
[4] Cfr. the Vedic text above quoted.

The dog of the Æsopian fable,[1] with meat in its mouth, is a variation of this myth. The red sky of evening appears purple in the morning, and in the evening as the meat that the dog lets fall into the waters of the ocean of night. In the *Pańćatantram*, we have instead the lion of evening (the evening sun), who, seeing in the fountain (or in the ocean of night) another lion (now the moon, now his own shadow, the night, or the cloud), throws himself into the water to tear him to pieces, and perishes in it. The hare (the moon) is the animal which allures the famished lion of evening to perish in the waters.

The two sons of the bitch Saramâ preserve several of their mother's characteristics. Now they are spoken of together as Sârameyâu; now they are mentioned together, but distinct from one another; now one alone of them, the most legitimate, by the name of Sârameyas, whose identity with the Greek Hermês or Hermeias has already been proved by Professor Kuhn. Saramâ in connection with the Paṇayas, merchants or thieves, and Saramâ as the

---

[1] In the *Tuti-Name*, instead of the dog with the bone or piece of meat, we have the fox. The dog who sees his shadow in the water; the fearless hero who, in Tuscan stories, dies when he sees his own shadow; the black monster (the shadow) who, in numerous stories, presents himself instead of the real hero to espouse the beautiful princess, carry our thoughts back to Indras, who, in the *Ṛigvedas*, after having defeated the monster, flees away over the rivers, upon seeing something which is probably the shadow of Vṛitras, killed by him, or his own shadow. In the *Âitar. Brâhm.* iii. 2, 15, 16, 20, this flight of Indras is also recorded, and it is added, that Indras hides himself, and that the Pitaras (*i.e.*, the souls of the departed) find him again. Indras thinks that he has killed Vṛitras, but really has not killed him; then the gods abandon him; the Marutas alone (as dogs friendly to the bitch Saramâ) remain faithful to him. The monster killed by Indras in the morning rises again at eve. According to other Vedic accounts, Indras is obliged to flee, stung by remorse, having committed a brâhmanicide.

divine messenger, gives us the key to the legend of Mercury, god of thieves and merchants, and messenger of the gods.

In a Vedic hymn we find described with great clearness the two dogs that guard the gates of hell, the monsters' dwelling, or the kingdom of the dead. It prays for one departed, "that he may be able to pass safely beyond the two dogs, sons of Saramâ, having four eyes, spotted, who occupy the right path, and to come to the benignant Manes" (for there are also the malignant ones, or Durvidatrâḥ); these dogs are called "the very fierce guardians, who watch the road, observing men, have vast nostrils, are long-winded, and very strong, the messengers of Yamas;" they are invoked "that they may cause to enjoy the sight of the sun, and give a happy life."[1] But the *Ṛigvedas* itself already shows us the two sons of the bitch Saramâ, as the two who look in turns (one after the other), whom Indras must put to sleep.[2] One, however, of the two sons of Saramâ is especially invoked and feared, the Sârameyas *par excellence.* The Vedic hymn speaks of him as he who returns (punaḥsaras), and represents him as "luminous, with reddish teeth, that shine like spears, in the well-rooted gums," and implores him to sleep, or "to bark only at the robber, or at the thief, not at the singers of hymns in honour of Indras."[3] The bitch Saramâ is passionately fond of her

---

[1] Ati drava sârameyâu çvânâu ćatarakshâu çabalâu sâdhunâ pathâ athâ pitṛînt suvidatrâṇ upehi—Yâu te çvânâu yama rakshitârâu ćaturakshâu pathirakshî nṛićakshasâu—Urûṇasâv asutṛipâ udumbalâu yamasya dûtâu ćarato ǵanâṅ anu—Tâv asmabhyaṁ dṛiçaye sûryâya punar dâtâm asum adyeha bhadram; *Ṛigv.* x. 14, 10–12.

[2] Ni shvâpaya mithûdṛiçâu; *Ṛigv.* i. 29, 3.—The Petropolitan Dictionary explains the word *mith.* by "abwechselend sichtbar."

[3] Yad arǵuna sarameya dataḥ piçaṅga yaćhase vîva bhrâǵanta ṛishṭaya upa srakveshu bapsato ni shu svapa; stenaṁ râya sârameya taskaraṁ vâ punaḥsara stotrîn indrasya râyasi kim asmân dućhunâyase ni shu svapa; *Ṛigv.* vii. 55, 2, 3.

son; in recompense for her discovery of the cows of Indras, she demands nourishment for her son, which nourishment the commentator explains to be the milk of the liberated cows; the first rays of the morning sun and the last rays of the evening sun drink the milk of the dawn or silvery twilight. In the *Mahâbhâratam*,[1] the bitch Saramâ curses King Ǵanameǵayas, because his three brothers, when attending the sacrifice, maltreated and flogged the dog Sârameyas, who had also gone there, although he had neither touched with his tongue nor desired with his eyes the oblations destined to the gods (as, on the contrary, the white dog did, who, in the sacrifice of Dion, near Athens, stole part of the victim, whence the name of Künosargês was given to that place). The same legend occurs again, slightly modified, in the seventh book of the *Râmâyaṇam*.[2] Râmas sends Lakshmaṇas, his brother, to see whether there are any disputes to be settled in the kingdom; Lakshmaṇas returns, saying that the whole kingdom is at peace. Râmas sends him again; he sees a dog erect on the doorstep of the palace, barking. The name of this dog is Sârameyas. Râmas enables him to enter the palace. The dog complains that he has been beaten without just cause by a Brâhman. The Brâhman is called, appears, confesses his fault, and awaits his punishment. The dog Sârameyas proposes as his punishment that the Brâhman should take a wife (the usual proverbial satire against wives), and become head of a family in the very place where he himself had supported the same dignity prior to assuming the shape of a dog. After this the dog Sârameyas, who remembers his previous states of existence, returns to do penitence at Benares, whence he had come.

---

[1] i. 657, 666.

[2] Canto 62.

Therefore the dog and the Kerberos are also a form into which the hero of the myth passes. The Hindoo and Pythagorean religious beliefs both teach that metempsychosis is a means of expiation; the curse of the offended deity is now a vengeance now a chastisement for an error that the hero or some one of his relations has committed, and which has provoked the deity's indignation.[1]

Sometimes the deity himself assumes the form of a dog in order to put the hero's virtue to the proof, as in the last book of the *Mahâbhâratam*, where the god Yamas becomes a dog, and follows Yudhishṭhiras (the son of Yamas), who regards him with such affection, that when invited to mount into the chariot of the gods, he refuses to do so, unless his faithful dog is allowed to accompany him.

Sometimes, however, the shape of a dog or bitch (as it is easy to pass from Yamas, the god of hell in the form of a dog, to the dog-fiend) is a real and specific form of a demon. The *Ṛigvedas* speaks of the dog-demons bent upon tormenting Indras, who is requested to kill the monster in the form of an owl, a bat, a dog, a wolf, a great bird, a vulture;[2] it invokes the Açvinâu to destroy on every side the barking dogs;[3] it solicits

[1] Thus Hecuba, the wife of Priam, after having suffered cruel tribulation as a woman, in Ovid—

> "Perdidit infelix hominis post omnia formam
> Externasque novo latratu terruit auras."

In the *Breviarium Romanum*, too, in the offices of the dead, God is besought not to consign to the beasts (ne tradas bestiis, &c.) the souls of His servants.

[2] Eta u tye patayanti çvayâtava indram dipsanti dipsavo 'dâbhyam —Ulukayâtuṁ çuçulûkayâtuṁ ǵahi çvayâtum uta kokayâtum suparṇayâtum gridhrayâtuṁ dṛishadeva pra mṛiṇa raksha indra; *Ṛigv.* vii. 104, 20, 22.

[3] Ǵambhayatam abhito râyataḥ; *Ṛigv.* i. 182, 4.

the friends to destroy the long-tongued and avaricious dog (in the old Italian chronicle of Giov. Morelli, misers are called Cani del danaro, dogs of money), as the Bhrigavas have killed the monster Makhas.[1] And the skin of the red bitch is another monstrous form in which is dressed every morning (as the aurora in the morning sky), in the twenty-third Mongol story, the beautiful maiden who is in the power of the prince of the dragons ; she (as moon) is beautiful maiden only at night ; towards day she becomes a red bitch (the moon gives up her place to the aurora) ; the youth who has married her wishes to burn this bitch's skin, but the maiden disappears ; the sun overtakes the aurora, and he disappears with the moon. We have already seen this myth.

In the eighteenth hymn of the fourth book of the *Ṛigvedas*, the thirteenth strophe seems to me to contain an interesting particular. A devotee complains as follows : —"In my misery I had the intestines of the dog cooked ; I found among the gods no consoler ; I saw my wife sterile ; the hawk brought honey to me."[2] Here we find the dog in connection with a bird.[3] In the twenty-

[1] Apa çvânaṁ çnathishṭana sakhâyo dîrghağihvyam—Apa çvânam arâdhasam hatâ makhaṁ na bhṛigavaḥ ; *Ṛigv.* ix. 101, 1, 13.

[2] Avartyâ çuna ântrâṇi peće na deveshu vivide marḍitâram apaçyaṁ ğâyâm amahîyamânâm adhâ me çyeno madhv â ğabhâra ; *Ṛigv.* iv. 18, 13. The bird who brings honey has evidently here a phallical meaning, as also the intestine, the part that is inside of now the dog, now the fish, and now the ass (all of which are phallical symbols), desired as a delicacy by the women of fairy tales, must be equivalent to the *madhu* brought by the bird.

[3] In the fifth story of the fourth book of the *Pentamerone*, the bird does the same that a dog does in the third story of the third book ; the bird brings a knife, the dog brings a bone, and the imprisoned princess, by means of this knife and bone, is enabled to make a hole in the prison, and to free herself.

fifth story of the fourth book of *Afanassieff*, we find the woodpecker that brings food and drink to its friend the dog, and avenges him after his death. In the forty-first story of the fourth book, the dog is killed by the old witch, because he carries in a sack the bones of her wicked daughter, who has been devoured by the head of a mare. In the twentieth story of the fifth book, we have the dog in the capacity of a messenger employed by the beautiful girl whom the serpent has married; he carries to her father a letter that she has written, and brings his answer back to her. In the legend of St Peter, the dog serves as a messenger between Peter and Simon the magician; in the legend of San Rocco, the dog of our Lord takes bread to the saint, alone and ill under a tree. The name of Cyrus's nurse, according to Textor, was Küna, whence Cyrus might have been nourished, like Asklêpios, with the milk of a dog. I have already said that the story of the dog is connected with the myth of the Açvinâu, or, what is the same thing, with that of the horse; horse and dog are considered in the light of coursers: the horse bears the hero, and the dog usually takes news of the hero to his friends, as the bitch Saramâ, the messenger of the gods, does in the *Ṛigvedas.*[1] The hero who assumes the shape of a horse cautions his father, when he sells him to the devil, not to give up the bridle to the buyer. In the twenty-second story of the fifth book of *Afanassieff*, the young man transforms himself into a dog, and lets his father sell him to a great lord, who is the devil in disguise, but tells him not to give up the collar.[2] The

[1] In the *Pentamerone*, i. 7, the enchanted bitch brings to the princess news of the young hero.

[2] In the seventh Esthonian story, the man with the black horse binds three dogs tightly; if they get loose, no one will be able to keep them back.—In the *Edda*, Thrymer, the prince of the giants, keeps the grey dogs bound with golden chains.

gentleman buys the dog for two hundred roubles, but insists upon having the collar too, calling the old man a thief upon the latter refusing to consign it into his hands. The old man, in his distraction, gives it up; the dog is thus in the power of the lord, that is, of the devil. But on the road, a hare (the moon) passes by; the gentleman lets the dog pursue it, and loses sight of it; the dog again assumes the shape of a hero, and rejoins his father. In the same story, the young man adopts, the second time, the form of a bird (we shall see the Açvinâu as swans and doves in the chapter on the swan, the goose, and the dove), and the third time that of a horse. In the twenty-eighth story of the fifth book, a horse, a dog, and an apple-tree are born of the dead bull who protects Ivan and Mary fleeing in the forest from the bear. Riding on the horse, and accompanied by the dog, Ivan goes to the chase. The first day he captures a wolf's whelp alive, and carries it home; the second day he takes a young bear; the third day he returns to the chase, and forgets the dog; then the six-headed serpent, in the shape of a handsome youth, carries off his sister, and shuts the dog up under lock and key, throwing the key into the lake. Ivan returns, and, by the advice of a fairy, he breaks a twig off the apple-tree, and strikes with it the bolt of the door which encloses the dog; the dog is thus set at liberty, and Ivan lets dog, wolf, and bear loose upon the serpent, who is torn in pieces by them, and recovers his sister. In the fiftieth story of the fifth book, the dog of a warrior-hero tears the devil, who presents himself first in the form of a bull, and then in that of a bear, to prevent the wedding of the hero taking place. In the fifty-second story of the sixth book, the dogs which Ivan Tzarević has received from two fairies, together with a wolf's whelp, a bear's, and a lion's cub, tear the monster serpent to pieces. The two dogs carry us back to the myth of the Açvinâu. In the fifty-third story of the sixth book, the monster cuts Ivan's head off. Ivan has two sons, who believe themselves to be of canine descent; they ask their mother to be permitted to go and resuscitate their father. An old man gives them a root, which, when rubbed on Ivan's body, will bring him to life again; they take it, and use it as directed. Ivan is resuscitated, and the monster dies. Finally, in the fifty-fourth story of the fifth book of *Afanassieff*, we learn how the sons of the dog are born, and their mode of birth is analogous to that mentioned in the Vedic hymn. A king who has no sons has a fish with golden fins; he orders it to be cooked, and to be given to the queen to eat. The intestines of the fish (the phallos) are thrown to the bitch, the bones are gnawed by the cook, and the meat is eaten by the queen. To the bitch, the cook, and the queen a son is born at the same time. The three sons are all called Ivan, and are regarded as three brothers; but the strongest (he who accomplishes the most difficult enterprises) is Ivan the son of the bitch, who goes under ground into the kingdom of the monsters (as of the two Dioscuri, one descends into hell, like the two funereal dogs, light-coloured and white, of the Avesta, which are in perfect accordance with the Vedic *Sârameyâu*[1]). In

[1] Einen gelblichen Hund mit vier Augen oder einen weissen mit gelben Ohren; *Vendidad*, viii. 41, *et seq.*, Spiegel's version. And Anquetil, describing the *Baraschnon no schabé*, represents the purifying dog as follows:—"Le Mobed prend le bâton à neuf nœuds, entre dans les Keischs et attache la cuillère de fer au neuvième nœud. L'impur entre aussi dans les Keischs. On y amène un chien; et si c'est une femme que l'on purifie, comme elle doit être nue, c'est aussi une femme qui tient le chien. L'impur ayant la main droite sur sa tête et la gauche sur le chien, passe successivement sur les six premières pierres et s'y lave avec l'urine que lui donne le Mobed."—In the *Kâtyây. Sû.*

the same story, besides the three brother-heroes, three heroic horses are brought forth by the three mares that have drunk the water in which the fish was washed before being cooked; in other European variations, and in the Russian stories themselves, therefore, we sometimes have, instead of the bitch's son, the son of the mare (or the cow). The two Açvinâu are now two horses, now two dogs, now a dog and a horse (now a bull and a lion).[1] Ivan Tzarević, whom the horse and the dog save from danger, is the same as the Vedic hero, the sun, whom the Açvinâu save from many dangers.

In the Russian stories, as well as in the Italian ones, the witch substitutes for one, two, or three sons of the prince, who have stars on their forehead, and were born of the princess in her husband's absence, one, two, or three puppies. In these same stories, the hand of the persecuted princess is cut off. In the thirteenth story of the third book of *Afanassieff*,[2] the witch sister-in-law accuses her husband's sister of imaginary crimes in his presence. The brother cuts her hands off; she wanders into the forest; she comes out again only after the lapse of several years; a young merchant becomes enamoured of her, and marries her. During her husband's absence,

---

the question is seriously discussed whether a dog, who was seen to fast on the fourteenth day of the month, did so on account of religious penitence.—Cfr. Muir's *Sanskṛit Texts*, i. 365.

[1] Dog and horse, with bites and kicks, kill the monster doe and free the two brother-heroes in the *Pentamerone*, i. 9.

[2] Cfr. also the sixth of the third book.—In the second story of the third book of the *Pentamerone*, the sister herself cuts off her own hands, of which her brother, who wishes to marry her, is enamoured. —Cfr. the *Mediæval Legends of Santa Uliva*, annotated by Professor Alessandro d'Ancona, Pisa, Nistri, 1863; and the *Figlia del Re di Dacia*, illustrated by Professor Alessandro Wesselofski, Pisa, Nistri, 1866, besides the thirty-first of the stories of the Brothers Grimm.

she gives birth to a child whose body is all of gold, effigies of stars, moon, and sun covering it. His parents write to their son, telling him the news; but the witch sister-in-law abstracts the letter (as in the myth of Bellerophôn), and forges another, which announces, on the contrary, that a monster, half dog and half bear, is born. The husband writes back, bidding them wait until he returns to see with his own eyes his new-born son. The witch intercepts this letter also, and changes it for another, in which he orders his young wife to be sent away. The young woman, without hands, wanders about with her boy. The boy falls into a fountain; she weeps; an old man tells her to throw the stumps of her arms into the fountain; she obeys, her hands return, and she recovers her boy again. She finds her husband; and no sooner does she uncover the child in his sight, than all the room shines with light (asviatilo).

In a Servian story,[1] the father of the maiden whose hands had been cut off by the witch, her mother-in-law, causes, by means of the ashes of three burned hairs from the tail of the black stallion and that of the white mare, golden hands to grow on the maiden's arms. The apple-tree, with golden branches, which we have already mentioned, is the same as this girl who comes out of the forest (or wooden chest) with golden hands. From the branches it is easy to pass to the hands of gold, to the fair-haired son who comes out of the trunk.[2] The idea of a youth as the branch of a tree has been rendered poetical by Shakspeare, who makes the Duchess of Gloster say of the seven sons of Edward—

[1] The thirty-third of the collection of Karadzik, quoted by Professor Wesselofsky in his introduction to the story of the *Figlia del Re di Dacia*.

[2] Cfr. my little essay on the *Albero di Natale*.

"Edward's seven sons, whereof thyself art one,
Were as seven phials of his sacred blood,
Or seven fair branches springing from one root."[1]

In Hindoo myths, the hand of Savitar having been cut off, one of gold is given to him, whence the epithet he enjoys of Hiraṇyahastas, or he who has a golden hand. But in the 116th and 117th hymns of the first book we find a more interesting datum. The branch is the hand of the tree; the branch is the son who detaches himself from the maternal trunk of the tree; the golden son is the same as the golden branch, the golden hand of the tree. The mother who obtains a golden hand is the same as the mother who has Hiraṇyahastas—*i.e.*, Golden-hand—for her son. The Vedic hymn says that the Açvinâu gave Golden-hand as a son to the Vadhrimatî.[2] The word *vadhrimatî* is equivocal. The Petropolitan Dictionary interprets it only as she who has a eunuch, or one who is castrated, for her husband, but the proper sense of the word is she who has something cut off, she who has, that is, the maimed arm, as in the fairy tale, for which reason she is given a golden hand. As the wife of a eunuch, the Vedic woman, therefore, receives from the Açvinâu a son with a golden hand; as having an imperfect arm, she receives only a golden hand, as in the 116th hymn of the first book, the same Açvinâu give to Viçpalâ, who had lost his own in battle, an iron leg.[1]

[1] *King Richard II.*, act. i. scene 2.

[2] Çrutaṁ tać ćhâsur iva vadhrimat yâ hiraṇyahastam açvinâv adattam; *Ṛigv.* i. 116, 13.—Hiraṇyahastam açvinâ rarâṇâ putraṁ narâ vadhrimatyâ adattam; i. 117, 24.—The dog in connection with a man's hand is mentioned in the Latin works of Petrarch, when speaking of Vespasian, who considered as a good omen the incident of a dog bringing a man's hand into the refectory.

[3] Sadyo gañghâm âyasîm viçpalâyai dhane hite sartave praty adhattam; str. 15.

The *Ṛigvedas*, therefore, already contains in its germ the very popular subject of the man or woman without hands, in same way as we have already found in it, in embryo, the legends of the lame man, the blind man or woman, the ugly and the disguised woman.

But to return to the dog. Besides his agility[1] in running, his strength holds a prominent place in the myth. The Kerberos shows an extraordinary strength in rending his enemies. In the Russian stories the dog is the hero's strength, and is associated with the wolf, the bear, and the lion. In popular stories, now terrible lions and now dreadful dogs are found guarding the gate of the monster's dwelling. The monk of San Gallo, in Du Cange, says that the "canes germanici" are so agile and ferocious, that they suffice alone to hunt tigers and lions; the same fable is repeated in Du Cange of the dogs of Albania, which are so great and fierce, "ut tauros premant et leones perimant." The enormous chained dog, painted on the left side of the entrance of Roman houses, near the porter's room; the motto *cave canem;* the expiations made in Greece and at Rome (whence the names "Canaria Hospitia" and "Porta Catularia," where a dog was immolated to appease the fury of the Canicula, and whence the verse of Ovid—

> "Pro cane sidereo canis hic imponitur aræ,")

at the time of the Canicula or of the Canis Sirius, to

[1] It is perhaps for this reason that the Hungarians give to their dogs names of rivers, as being runners; but it is also said that they do so from their belief that a dog which bears the name of a river or piece of water never goes mad, especially if he be a white dog, inasmuch as the Hungarians consider the red dog and the black or spotted one as diabolical shapes. In Tuscany, when a Christian's tooth is taken out, it must be hidden carefully, that the dogs may not find it and eat it; here dog and devil are assimilated.

conjure away the evils which he brings along with the summer heat, in connection with the *sol leo*, and the corresponding festival of the killing of the dog (künophontis), besides the barking dogs that appear in the groin of Scylla,[1] are all records of the mythical dog of hell. The dog, as a domestic animal, has been confounded with the savage brute which generally represents the monster. The dog is scarcely distinguishable from the wolf in the twilight. In Du Cange we read that in the Middle Ages it was the custom to swear now by the dog now by the wolf.[2] In the country round Arezzo, in Tuscany, it is believed that when a she-wolf brings forth her young ones, a dog is always found among them, which, if it were allowed to live, would exterminate all the wolves. But the she-wolf, knowing this, no sooner perceives the dog-wolf than she drowns it when she takes the wolves to drink.[3] In the district of

[1] Scylla laves her groin in a fountain, the waters of which the enchantress Circe has corrupted, upon which monstrous dogs appear in her body, whence Ovid—

"Scylla venit mediaque tenus descenderat alvo,
Cum sua fœdari latrantibus inguina monstris
Aspicit, ac primo non credens corporis illas
Esse sui partes, refugitque, abiitque timetque
Ora proterva canum."

[2] Hæc lucem accipiunt ab Joinville in Hist. S. Ludovici, dum fœdera inter Imp. Joannem Vatatzem et Comanorum Principem inita recenset, eaque firmata ebibito alterius invicem sanguine, hacque adhibita ceremonia, quam sic enarrat: "Et ancore firent-ils autre chose. Car ils firent passer un chien entre nos gens et eux, et découpèrent tout le chien à leurs espées, disans que ainsy fussent-ils découpez s'ils failloient l'un à l'autre."—Cfr. in Du Cange the expression "cerebrare canem."

[3] In a fable of Abstemius, a shepherd's dog eats one of the sheep every day, instead of watching over the flock. The shepherd kills him, saying, that he prefers the wolf, a declared enemy, to the dog, a false friend. This uncertainty and confusion between the dog and the

Florence, it is believed that the wolf, as well as the dog, when it happens to be the subject of a dream, is (as

---

wolf explains the double nature of the dog; to prove which I shall refer to two unpublished Italian stories: the first, which I heard from the mouth of a peasant-woman of Fucecchio, shows the bitch in the capacity of the monster's spy; the second was narrated a few years ago by a Piedmontese bandit to a peasant-woman who had shown hospitality to him, at Capellanuova, near Cavour in Piedmont. The first story is called *The King of the Assassins*, and is as follows:—

There was once a widow with three daughters who worked as seamstresses. They sit upon a terrace; a handsome lord passes and marries the eldest; he takes her to his castle in the middle of a wood, after having told her that he is the chief of the assassins. He gives her a she-puppy and says, "This will be your companion; if you treat her well, it is as if you treated me well." Taking her into the palace, he shows her all the rooms, and gives her all the keys; of four rooms, however, which he indicates, there are two which she must not enter; if she does so, evil will befall her. The chief of the assassins spends one day at home and then three away. During his absence she maltreats the puppy, and gives her scarcely anything to eat; then she lets herself be overcome by curiosity, and goes to see what there is in the two rooms, followed by the puppy. She sees in one room heads of dead people, and in the other tongues, ears, &c., hung up. This sight fills her with terror. The chief of the assassins returns and asks the bitch whether she has been well treated; she makes signs to the contrary, and informs her master that his wife has been in the forbidden rooms. He cuts off her head, and goes to find the second sister, whom he induces to come to him by under invitation to visit his wife; she undergoes the same miserable fate. Then he goes to take the third sister, and tells her who he is; she answers, "It is better thus, for I shall no longer be afraid of thieves." She gives the bitch soup, caresses her, and makes herself loved by her; the king of the assassins is contented, and the puppy leads a happy life. After a month, while he is out and the puppy amusing itself in the garden, she enters the two rooms, finds her two sisters, and goes into the other rooms, where there are ointments to fasten on limbs that have been cut off, and ointments to bring the dead to life. Having resuscitated her sisters, and given them food, she hides them in two great jars, furnished with breathing holes, and asks her husband to take them as a present to her mother, warning him not to look into the jars, as she will see him.

in Terence) a prognostic of sickness or death, especially if the dog is dreamt of as running after or trying to bite

---

He takes them, and when he tries to look in, he hears, as he had been forewarned, not one voice, but two whispering from within them, "My love, I see you." Terrified at this, he gives up the two jars at once to the mother. Meanwhile his wife has killed the bitch in boiling oil; she then brings all the dead men and women to life, amongst whom there is Carlino, the son of a king of France, who marries her. Upon the return of the king of the assassins he perceives the treachery, and vows revenge; going to Paris, he has a golden pillar constructed in which a man can be concealed without any aperture being visible, and bribes an old woman of the palace to lay on the prince's pillow a leaf of paper which will put him and all his servants to sleep as soon as he reclines on it. Shutting himself up in the pillar, he has it carried before the palace; the queen wishes to possess it, and insists upon having it at the foot of her bed. Night comes; the prince puts his head upon the leaf, and he and his servants are at once thrown into a deep sleep. The assassin steps out of the pillar, threatens to put the princess to death, and goes into the kitchen to fill a copper with oil, in which to boil her. Meanwhile she calls her husband to help her, but in vain; she rings the bell, but no one answers; the king of the assassins returns and drags her out of bed; she catches hold of the prince's head, and thus draws it off the paper; the prince and his servants awake, and the enchanter is burnt alive.

The second story is called *The Magician of the Seven Heads*, and was narrated to me by the peasant-woman in the following terms:—

An old man and woman have two children, Giacomo and Carolina. Giacomo looks after three sheep. A hunter passes and asks for them; Giacomo gives them, and receives in reward three dogs, Throttle-iron, Run-like-the-wind, and Pass-everywhere, besides a whistle. The father refuses to keep Giacomo at home; he goes away with his three dogs, of which the first carries bread, the second viands, and the third wine. He comes to a magician's palace and is well received. Bringing his sister, the magician falls in love with her and wishes to marry her; but to this end the brother must be weakened by the abstraction of his dogs. His sister feigns illness and asks for flour; the miller demands a dog for the flour, and Giacomo yields it for love of his sister; in a similar manner the other two dogs are wheedled away from him. The magician tries to strangle Giacomo, but the latter blows his whistle, and the dogs appear and kill the magician and the one. In Horace (*Ad Galatheam*) it is an evil omen to meet with a pregnant bitch—

> "Impios parræ præcinentis omen
> Ducat et prœgnans canis."

In Sicily, St Vitus is prayed to that he may keep the dogs chained—

> "Santu Vitu, Santu Vitu,
> Io tri voti vi lu dicu:
> Va', chiamativi a lu cani
> Ca mi voli muzzicari."

And when tying the dog up, they say—

> "Santu Vitu,
> Beddu e pulitu,
> Anghi di cira
> E di ferru filatu;
> Pi lu nuomu di Maria
> Ligu stu cani
> Ch' aju avanti a mia."

---

sister. Giacomo goes away with the three dogs, and comes to a city which is in mourning because the king's daughter is to be devoured by the seven-headed magician. Giacomo, by means of the three dogs, kills the monster; the grateful princess puts the hem of her robe round Throttle-iron's neck and promises to marry Giacomo. The latter, who is in mourning for his sister, asks for a year and a day; but before going he cuts the seven tongues of the magician off and takes them with him. The maiden returns to the palace. The chimney-sweeper forces her to recognise him as her deliverer; the king, her father, consents to his marrying her; the princess, however, stipulates to be allowed to wait for a year and a day, which is accorded. At the expiration of the appointed time, Giacomo returns, and hears that the princess is going to be married. He sends Throttle-iron to strike the chimney-sweeper (the black man, the Saracen, the Turk, the gipsy, the monster) with his tail, in order that his collar may be remarked; he then presents himself as the real deliverer of the princess, and demands that the magician's heads be brought; as the tongues are wanting, the trick is discovered. The young couple are married, and the chimney-sweeper is burnt.

When the dog is tied up, they add—

"Fermati, cani
Ca t' aju ligatu."[1]

In Italy and Russia, when the dog howls like a wolf, that is, plays the wolf, it forebodes misfortune and death. It is also narrated,[2] that after the alliance between Cæsar, Lepidus, and Antony, dogs howled like wolves.

When one is bitten by a dog[3] in Sicily, a tuft of hair is cut off the dog and plunged into wine with a burning cinder; this wine is given to be drunk by the man who has been bitten. In *Aldrovandi*,[4] I read, on the other hand, that to cure the bite of a mad dog, it is useful to cover the wound with wolf's skin.

The dog is a medium of chastisement. Our Italian expressions, "Menare il cane per l'aia" (to lead the dog about the barn-floor), and "Dare il cane a menare" (to give the dog to be led about), are probably a reminiscence of the ignominious mediæval punishment of Germany of carrying the dog, inflicted upon a noble criminal, and which sometimes preceded his final execution.[5] The

---

[1] Cfr. the *Biblioteca delle Tradizioni Popolari Siciliane*, edited by Gius. Pitrè, ii. canto 811.

[2] In Richardus Dinothus, quoted by Aldrovandi.

[3] From a letter of my friend Pitrè.

[4] *De Quadrup. Dig. Viv.* ii.

[5] Cfr. Du Cange, *s. v.* "canem ferre." The ignominy connected with this punishment has perhaps a phallic signification, the dog and the phallos appear in connection with each other in an unpublished legend maliciously narrated at Santo Stefano di Calcinaia, near Florence, and which asserts that woman was not born of a man, but of a dog. Adam was asleep; the dog carried off one of his ribs; Adam ran after the dog to recover it, but brought back nothing save the dog's tail, which came away in his hand. The tail of the ass, horse, or pig, which is left in the peasant's hand in other burlesque traditions, besides serving as an indication, as the most visible part, to find the lost or fallen animal again, or to return into itself, may perhaps have

punishment of laceration by dogs, which has actually been carried out more than once by the order of earthly tyrants, has its prototype in the well-known myth of Kerberos and the avenging dogs of hell. Thus Pirithoos, who attempts to carry off Persephônê from the infernal king of the Molossians, is torn to pieces by the dog Trikerberos. Euripides, according to the popular tradition, was lacerated in the forest by the avenging dogs of Archelaos. It is told of Domitian, that when an astrologer on one occasion predicted his approaching death, he asked him whether he knew in what way he himself would die; the astrologer answered that he would be devoured by dogs (death by dogs is also predicted in a story of the *Pentamerone*); Domitian, to make the oracle false, ordered him to be killed and burned; but the wind put the flames out, and the dogs approached and devoured the corpse. Boleslaus II., king of Poland, in the legend of St Stanislaus, is torn by his own dogs while wandering in the forest, for having ordered the saint's death. The Vedic monster Çushnas, the pestilential dog Sirius of the summer skies, and the dog Kerberos of the nocturnal hell, vomit flames; they chastise the world, too, with pestilential flames; and the pagan world tries all arts, praying and conjuring, to rid itself of their baleful influences. But this dog is

a meaning analogous to that of the tail of Adam's dog.—I hope the reader will pardon me these frequent repugnant allusions to indecent images; but being obliged to go back to an epoch in which idealism was still in its cradle, while physical life was in all its plenitude of vigour, images were taken in preference from the things of a more sensible nature, and which made a deeper and more abiding impression. It is well known that in the production of the Vedic fire by means of the friction of two sticks, the male and the female are alluded to, so that the grandiose and splendid poetical myth of Prometheus had its origin in the lowest of similitudes.

immortal, or rather it generates children, and returns to fill men with terror in a new, a more direct, and a more earthly form in the Christian world. It is narrated, in fact, that before the birth of St Dominic, the famous inventor of the tortures of the Holy Inquisition (a truly satanic Lucifer), his mother, being pregnant of him, dreamed that she saw a dog carrying a lighted brand about, setting the world on fire. St Dominic truly realised his mother's dream; he was really this incendiary dog; and, therefore, in the pictures that represent him, the dog is always close to him with its lighted brand. Christ is the Prometheus enlarged, purified, and idealised; and St Dominic, the monstrous Vulcan, deteriorated, diminished, and fanaticised, of the Christian Olympus. The dog, sacred in pagan antiquity to the infernal deities, was consecrated to St Dominic the incendiary, and to Rocco, the saint who protects the sick of the plague. The Roman feasts in honour of Vulcan (Volcanalia) fell in the month of August; and the Roman Catholic Church fêtes in the month of August the two saints of the dogs of the fire and the plague, St Dominic and St Rocco.

CHAPTER VII.

THE CAT, THE WEASEL, THE MOUSE, THE MOLE, THE SNAIL, THE ICHNEUMON, THE SCORPION, THE ANT, THE LOCUST, AND THE GRASSHOPPER.

SUMMARY.

Mârǵâras, mârgaras, mṛigas, mṛigâris, mṛigarâǵas.—Nakulas.—Mûsh.—Vamras, vamrî, vaprî, valmîkam, *formica*.—The serpent and the ants.—Indras as an ant; the serpent eaten by the ants.—Vamras drinking, assisted by the Açvinâu.—The grateful ant; the hermit-dwarfs.—Ants' milk.—Ants' legs.—The ant dies when its wings grow; the ants and the treasure.—The ants separate the grains.—The locust and the ant; çarabhas as the moon.—Grasshopper and ant.—Avere il grillo, aver la luna; indovinala, grillo.—Wedding between ant and grasshopper.—Locusts destroyed by fire.—Hippomürmêkes.—The Indian locust that guards honey again.—The scorpion, and its poison absorbed.—The ichneumon, enemy of the serpent.—The weasel.—Galanthis.—The cat with ears of butter.—The cat as a judge.—The lynx.—The penitent cat.—The beneficent cat.—The cat with a golden tail.—Cat and dog as friends; the dog carries the cat; they find the lost ring again.—The new-born son changed for a cat.—The cat that sings and tells tales.—The cat created by the moon; Diana as a cat.—The sacred cat.—The funereal and diabolical cat.—Cat and fox.—The cat hangman.—*Le chat botté.*—*Chatte blanche;* the cat that spins and weaves.—The cat becomes a girl.—The enchanted palace of the cats.—The cats of February; the black cat; the cat dreamed-of.—The cat becomes a witch at seven years of age.—The cat in the sack.—The mewing of the cat.—The cats dispute for souls.—Battle of cats.—The mice that bite their tails or that gnaw the threads of the net.—The mouse in the honey.—The mouse that becomes a maiden; the mouse and the mountain.—The mouse that becomes a tiger.—The souls of the dead pass into mice;

funereal and diabolical mice; superstitions relating to this belief.—The mouse that releases the lion and the elephant from the trap.—Ganeças crushes the mouse; Apollo Smyntheus.—When the cat 's away the mice can dance.—The mouse plays blind-man's-buff with the bear.—The grateful mouse.—The mouse that foresees the future.—Mouse and sparrow, first friends and then enemies.—The batrachomyomachia.—The mouse, the tooth, and the coin.—Hiraṇyakas; the squirrel.—The monster mole; the mole as a gravedigger; the blind mole.—The snail in the popular song; the snail and the serpent; the snail as a funereal animal.

I UNITE in one series several mythical nocturnal animals, which, although really of very different natures, enter into only one order of myths.

They are thieving and hunting animals, and are therefore very aptly placed in the darkness of night (*naktaćârin* is an epithet applied in Sanskṛit both to the cat and the thief), in the nocturnal forest, in connection now with Diana the huntress, or the good fairy the moon, and now with the ugly witch; now appearing as the helpers of the hero, and now as his persecutors.

The etymologies of several Hindoo words may be of some interest to the reader, and may with propriety be adduced here. *Mârǵâras,* the cat, means the cleanser (as the animal that, in fact, cleans itself). Referring to the myth, we know already that one of the principal exactions of the witch is that her step-daughter should comb her hair, or else clean the corn, during the night; and that the good fairy, the Madonna, while she too has her hair combed, scatters gems about, spins, and cleans the corn for the good maiden. The witch of night forces the maiden aurora to separate the luminous wheat of evening from the dark tares of night; the moon with its silvery splendour disperses the shades of night. The *mârǵâras,* or cleanser of the night, the white cat, is the moon. *Araṇyamârǵâras,* or cat of the forest, is the name given to the wild cat, with which the lynx, too, is identified. As a white cat, as the moon, it protects innocent animals; as a black cat, as the dark night, it persecutes them. The cat is a skilful hunter; moreover, it is easy to confound the word *mârģâras* (the cleanser) with the word *mârgaras*, the proper meaning of which is hunter, investigator, he who follows the track, the *mârgas*, or else the enemy of the *mṛigas* (as mṛigâris); the road is the clean part of the land, as the margin is the white or clean part of a book. The hunter may be he that goes on the margin or on the track, or else he that hunts and kills the mṛigas or forest animal. The moon (the huntress Diana) is also called in Sanskṛit *mṛigarâģas*, or king of the forest animals; and, as kings are wont, it sometimes defends its subjects and sometimes eats them. The cat-moon eats the grey mice of the night.

Nakulas is the name given in Sanskṛit to the ichneumon, the enemy of mice, scorpions, and snakes. The word seems to be derived from the root *naç*, *nak* = *necare*, whence nakulas would appear to be the destroyer (of nocturnal mice).

The mouse, *mûsh*, *mûshas*, *mûshakas*, is the thief, the ravisher, whence also its name rat (*a rapiendo*).

The Hindoo names of the ant are *vamras* and *vamrî* (besides *pipîlakas*). *Vamrî* is connected with *vapâ*, *vapram*, *vaprî*, ant-hole, and, by metathesis, *valmîkam* (*i.e.*, appertaining to ants), which has the same meaning. The Latin *formica* unites together the two forms *vamrî* and *valmîkam*. The roots are *vap*, in the sense of to throw, and *vam*, to erupt or to throw out, as the ants do when they erect little mounds of earth.

In the *Mahâbhâratam*, the hole of a serpent is also called by the name of *valmîkam;* from this we can explain the fable of the third book of the *Pańćatantram*, where we have a serpent fighting against ants. He kills many of them, but their number is so interminable that he is at last forced to succumb. Thus, in the mythical Vedic heavens, it is in the shape of a vamras or ant that Indras fights victoriously against the old monster that invades the sky.[1] Nay, more, in the *Pańćatantram*, the ants sting and bite the serpent and kill it; thus Indras (who, as we have just said, is an ant in the cloud or the night) gives to the ants the avaricious serpent, the son of Agrus, dragging it out of its hiding-place.[2] Indras is therefore a variety of the Captain Formicola of the Tuscan fairy tale. Finally, the *Ṛigvedas* offers us yet another curious particular. The two Açvinâu come to assist Vamras (or Indras in his form of an ant, *i.e.*, they come to assist the ant) whilst it is drinking (vamraṁ vipipânam). The ant throws or lifts up little hillocks of earth by biting the ground. The root *vap*, which means to throw, to scatter, has also the sense of to cut, and perhaps to make a hole in. The convex presupposes the concave; and *vam* is related to *vap* (as *somnus* is related to *hüpnos*, to *svapnas*, and to *sopor*). Indras, as an ant, is the wounder, the biter of the serpent. He makes it come out of its den, or vomits it forth (eructat); the two etymological senses are found again in the myth. The weapons with which Indras wounds the serpent are doubtless now the solar rays, and now the thunderbolts. Indras, in the cloud, drinks the somas. The ant drinks, and the Açvinâu, whilst it drinks, come to its help, for no doubt the ant when drinking is in danger of being

[1] Vṛiddhasya ćid vardhato dyâm inakshataḥ stavâno vamro vi ǵaghâna saṁdihaḥ; *Ṛigv.* i. 51, 9.

[2] Vamrîbhiḥ putram agruvo adânaṁ niveçanâd dhariva â ǵabhartha; *Ṛigv.* iv. 19, 9.—Another variation is the hedgehog, which, as we have seen in Chapter V., forces the viper out of its den.

drowned. And this brings us to the story of the grateful animals, in which the young hero finds an ant about to be drowned.

In the twenty-fourth of the Tuscan fairy tales published by me, when the shepherd's son, by a good advice which he has received, determines to do good to every one he meets, he sees on the path an ant-hill, which is about to be destroyed by water; he then makes a bank round it, and thus saves the ants;[1] in their turn the ants pay back the debt. The king of the land demands of the young man, as a condition of receiving his daughter in marriage, that he should separate and sort the different kinds of grain in a granary; up marches Captain Formicola with his army, and accomplishes the stipulated task. In other varieties of the same story, instead of the embankment, we have the leaf that the hero puts under the ant to float it out of the water contained in the footprint of a horse, which again recalls the lotus-leaf on which the Hindoo deity navigates the ocean. This water in which the ant is drowning was afterwards changed into the proverbial ants' milk,[2] which is now used to express an impossibility, but which, when referred to Indras, to the mythical ant, represents the ambrosial and pluvial moisture. In the sixth Sicilian story of Signora Gonzenbach, the boy Giuseppe, having given crumbs of bread to the hungry ants, receives from the king of the ants the present of an ant's leg, in order that he may

[1] The dwarf-hermits, who transport a leaf upon a car, and are about to be drowned in the water contained in the foot-print of a cow, and who curse Indras, who passes smiling without assisting them, in the legend of the *Mahâbhâratam*, are a variety of these same ants.—Cfr. the chapters on the Elephant and on the Fishes, where we have Indras who fears to be submerged.

[2] Fa cunto ca no le mancava lo latto de la formica; *Pentamerone*, i. 8.

use it when required. When he wishes to become an ant, in order to penetrate into the giant's palace, he has only to let the ant's leg fall to the ground, with the words, "I am a Christian, and am becoming an ant," which immediately comes to pass. In the same story Giuseppe procures sheep, in order to attract the serpent by their smell, and induce it to come out of its lurking-place. Here we evidently return to the Vedic subject of the ant Indras, who tempts the serpent to come out in order to give it to the ants. In the eighth story of the fourth book of the *Pentamerone*, the ant shows the third part of the way to the girl Cianna, who is going to search for the mother of time; on the door of her dwelling Cianna will find a serpent biting its tail (the well-known symbol of the cyclical day or year, and of time, in antiquity), and she is to ask the mother of time, on the ant's part, advice as to how the ants can live a hundred years. The mother of time answers to Cianna that the ants will live a hundred years when they can dispense with flying, inasmuch as "quanno la formica vo morire, mette l'ascelle" (*i.e.*, the wings). The ant, grateful for this good advice, shows Cianna and her brothers the place underground where the thieves have deposited their treasure. We also remember the story of the ants who bring grains of barley into the mouth of the royal child Midas, to announce his future wealth. In *Herodotus* (iii.), and in the twelfth book of the stories of *Tzetza*,[1]

[1] *Biblion Istorikon*, xii. 404.—In the *Epist. Presb. Johannis*, we find also:—"In quadam provincia nostra sunt formicæ in magnitudine catulorum, habentes vii. pedes et alas iv. Istæ formicæ ab occasu solis ad ortum morantur sub terra et fodiunt purissimum aurum tota nocte—quærunt victum suum tota die. In nocte autem veniunt homines de cunctis civitatibus ad colligendum ipsum aurum et imponunt elephantibus. Quando formicæ sunt supra terram, nullus ibi audet accedere propter crudelitatem et ferocitatem ipsarum."—Cfr. *infra*.

I find the curious information that there are in India ants as large as foxes, that keep golden treasures in their holes; the grains of wheat are this gold. The morning and evening heavens are sometimes compared to granaries of gold; the ants separate the grain during the night, carrying it from west to east, and purifying it of all that is unclean, or cleansing the sky of the nocturnal shadows. The work assigned every night by the witch to the maiden aurora of evening is done in one night by the black ants of the sky of night. Sometimes the girl meets on the way the good fairy (the moon), who comes to her help; the maiden, assisted by the ants, meets the madonna-moon. But the moon is called also the leaper or hopper, a nocturnal locust; the darkness, the cloud and the dark-coloured earth (in lunar eclipses) are at the same time ant-hills and black ants, that pass over or before the moon; and, therefore, in the race between the ant and the locust, it is said in the fable that the ant won the race. The locust, or *çarabhas*, or *çalabhas*, is presented to us as an improvident animal in two sentences of the first and fourth books of the *Pańćatantram.* The green grasshopper or locust leaps; the fair-haired moon leaps. (I have already noticed in the chapter on the ass how the words *haris* and *harit* mean both green and fair, or yellow; in the second canto of the sixth book of the *Râmâyaṇam,* the monkey Çarabhas is said to inhabit the mountain Ćandras or Mount Moon; Çarabhas, therefore, appears as the moon.) Locust and grasshopper jump (cfr. the Chap. on the hare); hence the ant is not only in connection with the locust, but also with the grasshopper: the Hindoo expression *çarabhas* means both grasshopper (in Sanskṛit, also named *varshakarî*) and locust. In one of the popular songs of the Monferrato collected by Signor Ferraro, we have the wedding of the grasshopper and the ant; the magpie, the mouse, the ortolan, the crow, and the goldfinch bring to the wedding a little cut straw, a cushion, bread, cheese, and wine. In the popular Tuscan songs published by Giuseppe Tigri, I find the word *grilli* (grasshoppers) used in the sense of lovers. In Italian, *grillo* also means caprice, and especially amorous caprice; and *medico grillo* is applied to a foolish doctor.[1] And yet the grasshopper ought to be the diviner *par excellence.* In Italy, when we propose a riddle, we are accustomed to end it with the words "indovinala, grillo" (guess it, grasshopper); this expression perhaps refers to the supposed fool of the popular story, who almost always ends by showing himself wise. The sun enclosed in the cloud and in the gloom of night is generally the fool, but he is at the same time the fool who, in the kingdom of the dead, sees, hears, and learns everything; and the moon, too, personified as a grasshopper or locust, is the supposed fool who, on the contrary, knows, sees, understands, and teaches everything; from the moon are taken prognostics; hence riddles may be proposed to the capricious moon, or the celestial cricket. In Italian, the expressions "aver la luna" (to have the moon), and "avere il grillo" (to have the grasshopper), are equivalent, and mean to suffer from a nervous attack, or the spleen. I also find the wedding between ant and grasshopper in a very popular, but as yet unpublished Tuscan song. The ant asks the grasshopper whether he desires her for his wife, and recommends him, if he does not, to look after his own affairs, that is, to leave her alone. And then the narrative

---

[1] Of this expression a historical origin is given, referring it to a Bolognese doctor of the twelfth century, named Grillo.—Cfr. Fanfani, *Vocabolario dell 'uso Toscano, s. v.* "grillo."

begins. The grasshopper goes into a field of linen; the ant begs for a thread to make herself aprons and shirts for the wedding; then the grasshopper says he wishes to marry her. The grasshopper goes into a field of vetches; the ant asks for ten vetches, to cook four in a stew, and to put six upon the spit for the wedding-dinner. After the wedding, the grasshopper follows the trade of a greengrocer, then that of an innkeeper; but his affairs succeed so badly, that he first puts his own trousers in pawn, and then becomes bankrupt, and beats his wife the ant; at last he dies in misery. Then the ant faints away, throws herself upon the bed, and beats her breast for sorrow with her heel (as ants do when they die).[1] The nuptials of the black ant, the gloom of night,

[1] Here are the words of the song of this curious wedding, which I heard sung at Santo Stefano di Calcinaia, near Florence:—

"Grillo, mio grillo,
Se tu vuoi moglie, dillo;
Se tu n' la vuoi,
Abbada a' fatti tuoi.
Tinfillulilalera
Linfillulilalà.

"Povero grillo, 'n un campo di lino,
La formicuccia gne ne chiese un filo.
D'un filo solo, cosa ne vuoi tu fare?
Grembi e camicie; mi vuo' maritare.
Disse lo grillo:—Ti piglierò io.
La formicuccia:—Son contenta anch' io.
Tinfillul., &c.

"Povero grillo, 'n un campo di ceci;
La formicuccia gne ne chiese dieci
Di dieci soli, cosa ne vuoi tu fare?
Quattro di stufa, e sei li vuo' girare.
Tinfillul., &c.

"Povero grillo facea l'ortolano
L'andava a spasso col ravanello in mano;

with the moon, locust, or grasshopper, take place in the evening; the grasshopper dies, the moon pales, and the black ant, the night, also disappears. In the *Pańćatantram*, the locusts are destroyed by fire. In the so-called letter of Alexander the Great to Olympias,[1] I find the ants scared away by means of fire, whilst they are endeavouring to keep horses and heroes at a distance. These extraordinary ants recall to us the hippomürmêkes of the Greeks, or ants of horses. The ants, the insects of the forest of night, molest the hero and solar horse that traverse it; the black ants of night are dispersed by the solar fire of the morning: this we can understand all the better when Tzetza, quoted before, speaking of the Indian ants, calls them as large as foxes; when Pliny, in the eleventh book of his History, says they are of the colour of a cat, and the size of Egyptian wolves; and when Solinus tells us that they have the shape of a large dog, with lion's feet, with which they dig gold up. Ælianos calls them guardians of gold (tôn chrüsôn

Povero grillo, andava a Pontedera,
Con le vilancie pesava la miseria.
Tinfillul, &c.

"Povero grillo, l'andiede a Monteboni,
Dalla miseria l'impegnò i calzoni;
Povero grillo facea l'oste a Colle,
L'andò fallito e bastonò la moglie.
Tinfillul., &c.

"La formicuccia andò alla festa a il Porto,
Ebbe la nova che il suo grillo era morto
La formicuccia, quando seppe la nova
La cascò in terra, stette svenuta un 'ora.
La formicuccia si buttò su il letto,
Con le calcagna si batteva il petto.
Tinfillul.," &c.

[1] Cfr. Zacher, *Pseudo-Callisthenes*, Halle, 1867.

philattontes). Evidently the ants have already taken here a monstrous and demoniacal aspect. Several other ancient authors have written concerning these Indian ants, including Herodotus, Strabo, Philostratos, and Lucian. I shall only mention here, as bearing on our subject, that, according to Lucian, it is by night that they dig up the gold, and that, according to Pliny, the ants dig up gold in winter (night and winter are often equivalent in mythology). "The Indians, moreover, steal it during summer, whilst the ants stay hidden in their subterranean lurking-places on account of the vapours; however, tempted forth by the smell, they run out, and often cut the Indians in pieces, although they flee away on very swift camels, they are so rapid, ferocious, and desirous of gold."[1] This monster ant, with lion's claws, which Pliny also describes as horned, approaches very closely to the mythical black scorpion of the clouds and the night, the Vedic *Vṛiçćikas*, which, now a very little bird (iyattikâ çakuntikâ), now a very small ichneumon (kushumbhakas, properly the little golden one, perhaps the young morning sun), destroys with its tooth (açmanâ, properly with the biter), absorbing or taking away the poison, as jars take off the water, *i.e.*, the sun's rays dissipate the vapours of the sun enclosed in the cloud or the gloom.[2] Here the ichneumon (viverra ichneumon) appears as the benefactor of the scorpion, rather than as its enemy; it takes its poison away, that is, it frees the sun from the sign of Scorpio, from the vapours which envelope it. The ichneumon is in Sanskṛit called *nakulas*. In the twelfth story of the first book of the *Pańćatantram*, we see it, on the contrary, as the

[1] Pliny, *Hist. Nat.* xi. 31.

[2] Iyattikâ çakuntikâ sakâ ǵaghâsa te visham; *Ṛigv.* i. 191, 11.

declared enemy of the black serpent, which it kills in its den. But inasmuch as the weasel-ichneumon bites venomous animals, it is itself obliged to deliver itself from the venom it has in consequence imbibed. Therefore, in the *Atharvavedas*, mention is already made of the salutary herb with which the nakulas (which is also the name of one of the two sons of the Açvinâu, in the *Mahâbhâratam*) cures himself of the bite of venomous animals, that is, of serpents, scorpions, and monstrous mice, his enemies. The weasel (mustela), which differs but little from the ichneumon, is almost the same in the myths. The weasel, too, as we learn from the ninth book of Aristotle's *History of Animals*, fights against serpents, after having eaten the famous herb called rue, the smell of which is said to be insupportable to serpents. But, as its Latin name tells us, it is no less skilful as a hunter of mice.[1] The reader is doubtless familiar with the Æsopian fable of the weasel which petitions the man for its liberty for the service which it has rendered him by freeing his house from rats ; and with that of Phædrus, of the old weasel which catches mice in the flour-trough by rolling itself in the flour, so that the mice approach, under the impression that it is a solid mass. Plautus's parasite reckons upon a good dinner for himself from having met with a weasel carrying away the whole of a mouse except its feet (auspicio hodie optumo exivi foras ; mustela murem abstulit præter pedes) ; but the expected dinner never appearing, he declares that the presage is false, and pronounces the weasel a prophet only of evil, inasmuch as in one and the same day it changes its place ten times. According to the ninth book of Ovid's *Metamorphoses*, the maid Galanthis was

[1] iv. 1.

changed by the goddess Lucina (the moon) into a weasel, for having told a lie, announcing the birth of Hêraklês before it had taken place :—

> "Strenuitas antiqua manet, nec terga colorem
> Amisêre suum, forma est diversa priori;
> Quæ, quia mendaci parientem juverat ore,
> Ore parit."

The popular superstition which makes the weasel bring forth its young by its mouth, probably had its origin in this fable. From the mouth intemperate words are brought forth. Simonides, in Stobeus, quoted already by Aldrovandi,[1] compares wicked women to weasels. The moon that changes the chattering Galanthis into a weasel appears to be the same as the white moon itself transformed into a white weasel, the moon that explores the nocturnal heaven and discovers all its secrets.

Ants, mice, moles (like serpents), love, on the contrary, to stay hidden, and to keep their secrets concealed. The ichneumon, the weasel, and the cat generally come out of their hiding-places, and chase away whoever is concealed, carrying away from the hiding-places whatever they can. They are both themselves thieves, and hunt other thieves.

It is easy now to pass from the Latin *mustela* to the Sanskṛit cat *mûshakârâtis*, or *mûshikântakṛit*.

In the *Pañćatantram*, the cat Butter-ears (dadhikarṇas), or he of the white ears, who feigns to repent of his crimes, is called upon to act as judge in a dispute pending between the sparrow, kapiñgalas and the hare Quick-walker (sîghragas), who had taken up his quarters in the dwelling of the absent sparrow. Butter-ears solves the question by feigning deafness, and requesting the two

[1] *De Quad. Dig. Viv.* ii.

disputants to come nearer, to confide their arguments in his ears; the hare and the sparrow rely on his good faith, and approach, when the cat clutches and devours them both. In the *Hitopadeças*,[1] we have, instead of the sparrow, the vulture ćaradgavas, which meets with its death in consequence of having shown hospitality to the cat, "of which it knew neither the disposition nor the strength" (aǵńâtakulaçîlasya). In the *Tuti-Name*,[2] we have, instead of the cat, the lynx,[3] that wishes to possess itself of the lion's house, which is guarded by the monkey; it terrifies the lion, and drives it to flight. In the *Anvari-Suhaili*,[4] instead of the cat or lynx, we find represented the leopard. In the *Mahâbhâratam*,[5] we find again the fable of the penitent cat. The cat, by the austerity which it practises on the banks of the Ganges, inspires confidence in the birds, which gather round it to do it honour. After some time, the mice imitate the example of the birds, and put themselves under the cat's protection, that it may defend them. The cat makes its meals upon them every day, by inducing one or two to accompany it

[1] i. 49.

[2] ii. 22.

[3] The forgetfulness of the lynx, as well as of the cat, is proverbial. St Jerome, in the Ep. ad Chrisog.—"Verum tu quod natura lynces insitum habent, ne post tergum respicientes meminerint priorum, et mens perdat quod oculi videre desierint, ita nostræ es necessitudinis penitus oblitus." Thus of the lynx it is said by Ælianos that it covers its urine with sand (like the cat), so that men may not find it, for in seven days the precious stone lyncurion is formed of this urine. The cat that sees by night, the lynx that sees through opaque bodies, the fable of Lynkeus, who, according to Pliny, saw in one day the first and the last moon in the sign of Aries, and the lynx that, according to Apollonios, saw through the earth what was going on in hell, recall to us the moon, the wise and all-seeing fairy of the sky, and the infernal moon.

[4] Quoted by Benfey in the Einleitung to the *Pańćatantram*.

[5] v. 5421–5448.

to the river, and fattens exceedingly fast, whilst the mice diminish every day. Then a wise mouse determines to follow the cat one day when it goes to the river; the cat eats both the mouse that accompanies it and the spy. Upon this the mice discover the trick, and evacuate altogether the post of danger. The penitent cat is already proverbial in the *Code of Manus.*[1] In the *Reineke Fuchs* of Goethe,[2] the cat goes to steal in the priest's house, by the wicked advice of the fox, when every one falls upon him—

> "Sprang er wüthend entschlossen
> Zwischen die Schenkel des Pfaffen und biss und kratzte gefährlich."

The *Roman du Renard,*[3] when the priest is mutilated by the cat, makes his wife exclaim—

> "C'en est fait de nos amours!
> Je suis veuve sans recours!"

In the same *Roman,* when the cat Tibert, the ambassador of King Lion, arrives at Mantpertuis, where the fox reigns, we read—

> "Tibert lui présenta la patte;
> Il fait le saint, il fait la chatte!
> Mais à bon chat, bon rat! Renard aussi le flatte!
> Il s'entend à dorer ses paroles de miel!
> Si l'un est saint, l'autre est hermite;
> Si l'un est chatte, l'autre est mite."

---

[1] "Let no man, apprised of this law, present even water to a priest who acts like a cat;" iv. 192, version of Jones and Graves' *Chamney Haughton,* edited by Percival, Madras, 1863.—In a Russian story quoted by Afanassieff in his observations to the first volume of his stories, the cat Eustachio feigns itself penitent or monk in order to eat the mouse when it passes. It being observed that the cat is too fat for a penitent, it answers that it eats from the duty of preserving its health.

[2] iii. 147, Stuttgart, Cotta, 1857.

[3] Translation by Ch. Potvin, Paris and Brussels, 1861.

In the romance of the fox, the fox endeavours to destroy the cat by inducing it to catch the mice that are in the priest's house. In an unpublished Tuscan story,[1] we have, on the contrary, the fox that invites the mouse to the shop of a butcher who has recently killed a pig. The mouse promises to gnaw the wood till the hole is large enough for the fox to pass through it; the fox eats till it is able to pass, and then goes away; the mouse eats and fattens so much that it can no longer pass; the cat then comes and eats it.

In the thirty-fourth story of the second book of *Afanassieff*, the cat occurs again, as in India, in connection with the sparrow, but not to eat it; on the contrary, they are friends, and twice deliver the young hero from the witch. This is a form of the Açvinâu. In the sixty-seventh story of the sixth book, the two Açvinâu return in the shape respectively of a dog and a cat (now enemies one of the other, as the two mythical brothers often show themselves, and now friends for life and death). A young man buys for a hundred roubles a dog with hanging ears, and for another hundred roubles a cat with a golden tail,[2] both of which he nourishes well. With a hundred roubles more, he acquires the ring of a dead princess, from which thirty boys and a hundred and seventy heroes, who perform every kind of marvel, can come forth at the possessor's will. By means of these wonders, the young

---

[1] From the peasant-woman Uliva Selvi, who told it to me at Antignano, near Leghorn.

[2] Cfr. *Afanassieff*, v. 32, where a cat is bought by a virtuous workman for the price of a kapeika (a small coin), the only price that he had consented to take as a reward for his work; the same cat is bought by the king for three vessels. With another kapeika, earned by other work, the workman delivers the king's daughter from the devil, and subsequently marries her.

man is enabled to wed the king's daughter; but as the latter wishes to ruin him, she makes him drunk, steals his ring, and departs into a far distant kingdom. The Tzar then shuts the youth up in prison; the dog and the cat go to recover the lost ring. When they pass the river, the dog swims and carries the cat upon his back (the blind and the lame, St Christopher and Christ). They come to the place where the princess lives, and enter into her dwelling. They then engage themselves in the service of the cook and the housemaid; the cat, following its natural instinct, gives chase to a mouse, upon which the mouse begs for its life, promising to bring the ring to the cat. The princess sleeps with the ring in her mouth; the mouse puts its tail into her mouth; she spits, the ring comes out, and is taken by the dog and the cat, who deliver the young man, and force the fugitive Tzar's daughter to return to her first abode.

In the following story of *Afanassieff*, when the youngest of the three sisters bears three sons to Ivan Tzarević, her envious elder sisters make the prince believe that she has brought forth a cat, a dog, and a vulgar child. The three real sons are carried off; the princess is blinded and enclosed with her supposed child in a cask, which is thrown into the sea. The cask, however, comes to shore and opens;[1] the supposititious son immediately bathes the princess's eyes with hot water, and she recovers her sight, after which he finds her three luminous sons again, who light up whatever is near them with their splendour, and is again united to her husband. In a Russian variation of the same story, the three sons are changed by the witch into three doves; the princess,

[1] Cfr. analogous subjects in Chapter I., *e.g.*, Emilius the lazy and stupid youth, and the blind woman who recovers her sight.

with her supposed son, is saved from the sea, and takes refuge upon an island, where, perched upon a gold pillar, a wise cat sings ballads and tells stories. The three doves are transformed into handsome youths, whose legs are of silver up to the knee, their chests of gold, their foreheads like the moon, and their sides formed of stars, and recover their father and mother.

Thus far we have seen the cat with white ears, who hunts the hare (or moon), the morning twilight, and the penitent cat who eats mice at the river's side, and which is mythically the same. We have observed that, of the two Açvinâu, one represents especially the sun, and the other the moon; the thieving cat, who is the friend of some thieves and the enemy of others (whence the Hungarian and Tuscan superstition, to the effect that for a good cat to be a skilful thief, it must itself have been stolen; then it is sure to catch mice well), is now the morning twilight, now the moon who gives chase to the mice of the night. According to the Hellenic cosmogony, the sun and the moon created the animals; the sun creating the lion, and the moon the cat. In the fifth book of Ovid's *Metamorphoses*, when the gods fled from the giants, Diana took the form of a cat.[1] In Sicily the cat is sacred to St Martha, and is respected in order not to irritate her: he who kills a cat will be unhappy for seven years. In the ancient German belief, the goddess

[1] Huc quoque terrigenam venisse Typhœa narrat,
Et se mentitis superos celasse figuris;
Duxque gregis, dixit, fit Jupiter; unde recurvis
Nunc quoque formatus Lybis est cum cornibus Ammon
Delius in corvo, proles Semeleia capro
Fele soror Phœbi, nivea Saturnia vacca,
Pisce Venus latuit, Cyllenius ibidis alis.
—v. 325–332.

Freya was drawn by two cats. At present, the cat and the mouse are sacred to the funereal St Gertrude. In the sixty-second story of the sixth book of *Afanassieff*, we have the chattering cat, which the hero Baldak must kill in the territory of the hostile Sultan (that is, in the wintry night). In the eighth story of the fourth book of the *Pentamerone*, we also find a she-cat that plays the part of the ogre's spy; in the tenth story of the *Pentamerone*, and in the first of the *Novelline di Santo Stefano di Calcinaia*, on the contrary, the cat reveals the witch's treachery to the prince. In the twenty-third story of the fourth book of *Afanassieff*, the cat Katofiei appears as the husband of the fox, who passes him off as a burgomaster. United together, they terrify the wolf and the bear,[1] the cat climbing up a tree. In the Æsopian fables, on the contrary, the cat and the fox dispute as to which is the superior animal; the cat makes the dog catch the fox, whilst it itself climbs up a tree. In the third story of the second book of *Afanassieff*, the cat associates with the cock in the search for the bark of trees; it delivers its comrade three times from the fox that had run off with it; the third time, the cat not only liberates the cock, but also eats the four young foxes. In the thirtieth story of the fourth book, the cat Catonaiević, the son of Cato (this name is derived from the equivoque between the words *catus* and *caton;* in French, besides *chat*, we have *chaton*, *chatonique*, &c.), delivers the cock twice from the fox, but the third time the fox eats the poor bird. In a Russian variety of this story, the cat kills the five little foxes and then the fox, after having sung as follows :—

[1] In the eighteenth story of the third book of *Afanassieff* it is in company with the lamb (in the nineteenth, with the he-goat) that the cat terrifies the wolf and the bear.

"The cat walks upon its feet
In red boots;
It wears a sword by its side,
And a stick by its thigh;
It wishes to kill the fox,
And to make its soul perish."[1]

In another variety, the cat and the lamb go to deliver the cock from the fox. The latter has seven daughters. The cat and the lamb allure them by songs to come out, and they kill them one after the other, wounding them in their foreheads; they then kill the fox itself, and so deliver the cock. In the romance of the fox, the cat is the hangman, and ties the fox to the gibbet.

In the third story of the first book, the witch's cat, grateful to the good girl who has given her some ham to eat, teaches her how to escape, and gives her the usual towel which, when thrown on the ground, makes a river appear, and the usual comb which, in like manner, causes an impenetrable forest to arise before the witch who runs after the girl to devour her.

We have already seen the Vedic moon who sews the wedding-robe with a thread that does not break. In the Russian story we have already remarked how the little puppet, to oblige the good maiden, makes a shirt destined for the Tzar, which is so fine that no one else can make the like. In the celebrated tale of the witty Madame d'Aulnoy, *La Chatte Blanche*, we have the white cat

---

[1] "Idiot kot na nagáh,
V krasnih sapagáh;
Nessiot sabliu na plessié;
A paloćku pri bedrié,
Hoćiet lissu parubít,
Ieià dushu zagubít."

Puss-in-boots (le chat botté), helps the third brother in the tale of Perrault.

Blanchette, veiled in black, who inhabits the enchanted palace, rides upon a monkey, speaks, and gives to the young prince, who rides upon a wooden horse (the forest of night), inside an acorn, the most beautiful little dog that ever existed in the world, that he may take it to the king his father—a little dog, "plus beau que la canicule" (evidently the sun itself, which comes out of the golden egg or acorn), which can pass through a ring (the disc of the sun), and then a marvellously painted cloth, which is so fine that it can pass through the eye of a small needle, and is enclosed in a grain of millet, although of the length of "quatre cents aunes" (the eye of the needle, the acorn, the grain of millet, and the ring are equivalent forms to represent the solar disc). This wonderful cat finally herself becomes a beautiful maiden, "Parut comme le soleil qui a été quelque temps enveloppé dans une nue; ses cheveux blonds étaient épars sur ses épaules; ils tombaient par grosses boucles jusqu'à ses pieds. Sa tête était ceinte de fleurs, sa robe, d'une légère gaze blanche, doublée de taffetas couleur de rose." The white cat of night, the white moon, resigns her place in the morning to the rosy aurora; the two phenomena that succeed each other appear to be metamorphoses of the same being. The white cat, with its attendant cats, before becoming a beautiful maiden, invites the prince to assist in a battle which he engages in with the mice. To this we can compare the Æsopian fable of the young man who, in love with a cat, beseeches Venus to transform her into a woman. Venus gratifies him; the youth marries her; but when the bride is in bed (*i.e.*, in the night, when the evening aurora again gives up its place to the moon, or when it meets with the grey mice of night), a mouse passes by, and the woman, who still retains her feline nature, runs after it.

When the sun enters into the night, it finds in the starry heavens an enchanted palace, where either there is not a living soul to be found, or where only the cat-moon moves about. Hence, in my opinion, the origin of the expression that we make use of in Italy to indicate an empty house—"Non vi era neanche un gatto" (there was not even a cat there). The cat is considered the familiar genie of the house. The enchanted palace is always situated either at the summit of a mountain, or in a gloomy forest (like the moon). This palace is the dwelling either of a good fairy, or a good magician, or of a witch, or a serpent-demon, or at least cats. The visit to the house of the cats is the subject of a story which I have heard told, with few variations, in Piedmont and in Tuscany.[1]

We have hitherto seen only the luminous or white cat, the cat-moon and twilight, under a generally benignant aspect. But when the night is without a moon, we have only the black cat in the dense gloom. This black cat then assumes a demoniacal character.

In the Monferrato it is believed that all the cats that wander about the roofs in the month of February are not

[1] In Tuscany the previously mentioned story-teller, Uliva Selvi, at Antignano, near Leghorn, narrated it to me as follows:—A mother has a number of children and no money; a fairy tells her to go to the summit of the mountain, where she will find many enchanted cats in a beautiful palace, who give alms. The woman goes, and a kitten lets her in; she sweeps the rooms, lights the fire, washes the dishes, draws water, makes the beds, and bakes bread for the cats; at last she comes before the king of the cats, who is seated with a crown on his head, and asks for alms. The great cat rings the golden bell with a golden chain, and calls the cats. He learns that the woman has treated them well, and orders them to fill her apron with gold coins (rusponi). The wicked sister of the poor woman also goes to visit the cats, but she maltreats them, and returns home all scratched, and more dead than alive from pain and terror.

really cats, but witches, which one must shoot. For this reason, black cats are kept away from the cradles of children. The same superstition exists in Germany.[1] In Tuscany, it is believed that when a man desires death, the devil passes before his bed in the form of any animal except the lamb, but especially in that of a he-goat, a cock, a hen, or a cat. In the German superstition,[2] the black cat that places itself upon the bed of a sick man announces his approaching death; if it is seen upon a grave, it signifies that the departed is in the devil's power. If one dreams of a black cat at Christmas, it is an omen of some alarming illness during the following year. Aldrovandi, speaking of Stefano Cardano, narrates that, being old and seriously ill, or rather dying, a cat appeared unexpectedly before him, emitted a loud cry, and disappeared. The same Aldrovandi tells us of a cat which scratched the breast of a woman, who, recognising in it a supernatural being, died after the lapse of a few days. In Hungary it is believed that the cat generally becomes a witch from the age of seven years to that of twelve, and that witches ride upon tom-cats, especially black ones; it is, moreover, believed that to deliver the cat from the witch, it is necessary to make upon its skin an incision in the form of a cross. The cat in the bag of proverbs has probably a diabolical allusion. In the tenth story of the *Pentamerone*, when the King of Roccaforte, thinking that he is marrying a beautiful maiden, finds that, on the contrary, he has espoused a hideous veiled old hag (the night), he says, "Questo è peo nce vole a chi accatta la gatta dinto lo sacco." In

---

[1] Cfr. Rochholtz, *Deutscher Glaube und Brauche*, i. 161.

[2] *Ib.*—I find the same belief referred to in the twenty-first Esthonian story of Kreutzwald.

Sicily, when the Rosary is recited for navigators, the mewing of the cat presages a tedious voyage.[1] When the witches in *Macbeth* prepare their evil enchantments against the king, the first witch commences with the words—

"Thrice the brinded cat hath mewed."

In a German belief noticed by Professor Rochholtz, two cats that fight against each other are to a sick man an omen of approaching death. These two cats are probably another form of the children's game in Piedmont and Tuscany, called the game of souls, in which the devil and the angel come to dispute for the soul. Of the two cats, one is probably benignant and the other malignant; they represent perhaps night and twilight. An Irish legend tells us of a combat between cats, in which all the combatants perished, leaving only their tails upon the battlefield. (A similar tradition also exists in Piedmont, but is there, if I am not mistaken, referred to wolves.) Two cats that fight for a mouse, and allow it to escape, are also mentioned in Hindoo tradition.[2]

In the 105th hymn of the first book of the *Ṛigvedas*, and in the thirty-third of the tenth book, a poet says to Indras, "The thought rends me, thy praiser, as mice tear

[1] It is almost universally believed that when the cat cleans itself behind its ears with its wet paw, it presages rain. And yet the Latin proverb says—

"Catus amat pisces, sed aquas intrare recusat;"

and the Hungarian proverb, that the cat does not die in water. It is for this reason, perhaps, that it is said, in a watery autumn the cat is worth little—("The cat of autumn and the woman of spring are not worth much;" *Hung. prov.*)

[2] Polier, *Mythologie des Indes*, ii. 571.

their tails by gnawing at them."[1] But according to another interpretation, instead of "tails," we should read "threads;" in this case, the mice that rend the threads would refer to the fable of the mouse that delivers from the net now the elephant, and now the lion (of which fable I shall endeavour to prove the Vedic antiquity in the next chapter).

The twelfth story of the third book of the *Pańćatantram* is of great mythological interest. From the beak of a hawk (in another Hindoo legend, from two cats that are disputing for it) a mouse takes refuge in the hands of a penitent, whilst he is bathing in the river. The penitent transforms the mouse into a beautiful maiden, and wishes to marry her to the sun; the maiden declines—he is too hot. The penitent next wishes to marry her to the cloud which defeats the sun; the maiden declares it is too dark and cold. He then proposes to give her to the wind which defeats the cloud (in the white *Yaǵurvedas*, the mouse is sacred to the god Rudras, the wind that howls and lightens in the cloud); the maiden refuses—it is too changeful. The penitent now proposes that she should wed the mountain, against which the wind cannot prevail, but the girl says it is too hard; and

[1] Mûsho na çiçnâ vy adanti mâdhyaḥ stotâraṁ te çatakrato; *Ṛigv.* i. 105, 8.—The commentator now interprets *çiçnâ* by *sutrâni*, threads, and now calls the reader's attention to the legend of the mice that lick their tails after plunging them into a vase full of butter, or some other savoury substance; but here *vy adanti* can only mean, they lacerate by biting, as in the preceding strophe we have the thought that tears by biting, as the wolf tears the thirsty wild beast (mâ vyanti âdhyo na tṛishṇaǵam mṛigam).—The mouse in the jar of provisions also occurs in the fable of the mouse and the two penitents in the *Pańća-tantram,* in the Hellenic fable of the son of Minos and of Pasiphäe, who, pursuing a mouse, falls into a jar of honey, in which he is suffocated, until recalled to life by a salutary herb.

finally the penitent asks if she would be willing to part with her affections to the mouse, who alone can make a hole in the mountain; the maiden is satisfied with this last proposal, and is again transformed into a female mouse, in order to be able to wed the male mouse. In this beautiful myth (which is a variation of the other one which we have already mentioned of the cat-maiden that, though transfigured, still retains its instinct as a huntress of mice), the whole revolution of the twenty-four hours of the day is described. The mouse of night appears first; the twilight tries to make it its prey; the night becomes the aurora; the sun presents itself for her husband; the sun is covered by the cloud, and the cloud is scattered by the wind; meanwhile the evening aurora, the girl, appears upon the mountain; the mouse of night again appears, and with her the maiden is confounded. The *Hîtopadeças* contains an interesting variety of the same myth. The mouse falls from the vulture's beak, and is received by a wise man, who changes it into a cat, then, to save it from the dog, into a dog, and finally into a tiger. When the mouse is become a tiger, it thinks of killing the wise man, who, reading its thoughts, transforms it again into a mouse. Here we find described the same circle of daily celestial phenomena. The succession of these phenomena sometimes causes transformations in the myths.

The well-known proverb of the mountain that gives birth to the mouse, refers to the myth contained in the story of the *Pañćatantram*.. We already know that the solar hero enters in the evening with the solar horse into the mountain and becomes stone, and that all the heavens assume the colour of this mountain. From the mountain come forth the mice of night, the shadows of night, to which the cat-moon and the cat-twilight give chase; the thieving propensities of the mice display themselves in the night. In German superstition the souls of the dead assume the forms of mice, and when the head of a house dies, it is said that even the mice of the house abandon it.[1] In general, every apparition of mice is considered a funereal presage; it is on this account that the funereal St Gertrude was represented surrounded by mice. The first witch in *Macbeth*, when she wishes to persecute the merchant who is sailing towards Aleppo, and shipwreck him, that she may avenge herself upon his wife, who had refused to give her some chestnuts, threatens to become like a rat without a tail. In the *Historia Sarmatiæ*, quoted by Aldrovandi, the uncles of King Popelus II., whom, with his wife for accomplice, he murders in secret, and throws into the lake, become mice, and gnaw the king and queen to death. The same death is said to have been the doom of Miçćislaus, the son of the Duke Conrad of Poland, for having wrongfully appropriated the property of widows and orphans; and of Otto, Archbishop of Mainz, for having burned the granary during a famine. Mice are said to have presaged at Rome the first civil war, by gnawing the gold in the temple; and it was, moreover, alleged that a

[1] Den Mäusen pfeifen, heisst den Seelen ein Zeichen geben, um von ihnen abgeholt zu werden; ebenso wie der Rattenfänger zu Hameln die Lockpfeife bläst, auf deren Ton alle Mäuse und Kinder der Stadt mit ihm in den Berg hineinziehen, der sich hinter ihnen zuschliesst. Mäuse sind Seelen. Die Seele des auf der Jagd entschläfenen Königs Guntram kommt schlängleinartig aus seinem Munde hervor, um so in einen nächsten Berg und wieder zurückzulaufen. Der goethe'sche Faust weigert sich dem Tanz mit dem hübschen Hexenmädchen am Blocksberg fortzusetzen:—

"Den mitten im Gesange sprang
Ein rothes Mäuschen ihr aus dem Munde."

—Rochholtz, *Deut. Glaube u. Brauch*, i. 156, 157.

female mouse had given birth in a trap to five male mice, of which she had devoured two. Other prodigies, in which mice were implicated, are mentioned as having taken place at Rome, even in the times of Cato, who was accustomed to make them the butt of his indignant scorn. To a person who told him, for instance, how the mice had gnawed the boots, he answered that this was no miracle; it would have been a miracle if the boots (*caligæ*) had eaten the mice.

The mouse in the fable is sometimes in connection with the elephant and the lion, whom it sometimes insults and despises (as in the *Tuti-Name*),[1] and sometimes comes to help and deliver from their fetters. The meaning of the myth is evident: the elephant and the lion represent here the sun in the darkness; in the evening the mouse of night leaps upon the two heroic animals, which are then old or infirm; in the morning the sun is delivered out of the fetters of the night, and it is supposed that it was the mouse which gnawed the ropes and set at liberty now the elephant, as in the *Pańćatantram*, now the lion, as in the Æsopian fable.

The Hindoo god Gaṇeças, the god of poets, eloquence, and wisdom, is represented with an elephant's head, and his foot crushing a mouse. Thus, among the Greeks, Apollo Smintheus, so called because he had shot the mice that stole the yearly provisions from Krinos, the priest of Apollo himself, was represented with a mouse under him. As the Christian Virgin crushes the serpent of night under her foot, so does the pagan sun-god crush under his feet the mouse of night.

When the cat's away, the mice may play; the shadows of night dance when the moon is absent.

[1] i. 268.

In the fifteenth story of the fifth book of *Afanassieff*, the witch step-mother desires her old husband to lead away his daughter to spin in the forest[1] in a deserted hut. The girl finds a little mouse there, and gives it something to eat. At night the bear comes, and wishes to play with the girl at the game of blind-man's-buff (this very popular game has evidently a mythical origin and meaning; every evening in the sky the sun amuses itself by playing blind-man's-buff; it blinds itself, and runs blind into the night, where it must find again its predestined bride or lost wife, the aurora). The little mouse approaches the maiden, and whispers in her ear, "Maiden, be not afraid; say to him, 'Let us play;' then put out the fire and hide under the stove; I will run and make the little bells ring." (Mice seem to have an especial predilection for the sound of bells. It is well-known how, in the Hellenic fable, the council of mice resolve, to deliver themselves from the cat, to put a bell round its neck; no one, however, undertakes to perform the arduous enterprise.) The bear thinks he is running after the maiden, and runs, on the contrary, after the mouse, which he cannot catch. The bear tires himself out, and congratulating the maiden, says to her, "Thou art my mistress, maiden, in playing at blind-man's-buff; to-morrow morning I will send you a herd of horses and a chariot of goods." (The morning aurora comes out of the forest, delivers herself from the clutches of the bear, from the witch of the night, and appears drawn by horses upon a chariot full of treasure. The myth is a lucid one.)

[1] The mouse that passes over the yarn occurs again in German tradition:—"Gertrudenbuchlein ab: Zwei Mäuschen nagen an einer flachsumwundenen Spindel; eine Spinnerinn sitzt am St Gertrudentag, noch in der Zeit der Zwölften, wo die Geister in Gestalt von Mäusen erscheinen, darf gesponnen werden;" Rochholtz, *ut supra*, i. 158.

In other numerous legends we have the grateful mouse that helps the hero or heroine. In the thirteenth Calmuc story, the mouse, the monkey, and the bear, grateful for having been delivered, from the rogues that tormented them, by the son of the Brahman, come to his help by gnawing and breaking open the chest in which the young man had been enclosed by order of the king; afterwards, with the assistance of the fishes, they help him to recover a lost talisman.

In the fifty-eighth story of the sixth book of *Afanassieff*,[1] the mouse, the war-horse, and the fish silurus, out of gratitude assist the honest workman who has fallen into a marsh, and cleanse him; upon seeing which the princess, that has never laughed, laughs, and thereafter marries the workman. (The young morning sun comes out of the marsh or swamp of night; the aurora, who was at first a dark, wicked, and ugly girl, marries the young sun whom the mouse has delivered out of the mud, as it delivered the lion out of the toils.)

In the fifty-seventh story of the sixth book of *Afanassieff*, it is the mouse that warns Ivan Tzarević to flee from the serpent-witch (the black night) his sister, who is sharpening her teeth to eat him.

In the third story of the first book of *Afanassieff*, the mice help the good maiden, who had given them something to eat, to do what the witch, her step-mother, had commanded.

In the twenty-third story of the fifth book of *Afanassieff*, the mouse and the sparrow appear at first as friends and associates. But one day the sparrow, having found a poppy-seed, thinks it so small that he eats it up

[1] Cfr. *Pentamerone*, iii. 5.—In the story, iv. 1, the grateful mice assist Mineć Aniello to find the lost ring by gnawing the finger on which the magician wears it.

without offering a share to his partner. The mouse hears of it, and is indignant; he breaks the alliance, and declares war against the sparrow. The latter assembles all the birds of the air, and the mouse all the animals of the earth, and a sanguinary battle commences. In a Russian variety of the same story, instead of the sparrow, it is the mouse that breaks the compact. They collect together the provisions against winter, but when, towards the end of the season, they are all but finished, the mouse expels the sparrow, and the sparrow goes to complain to the king of the birds. The king of the birds visits the king of the beasts, and sets forth the complaint of the sparrow; the king of the beasts then calls the mouse to account, who defends himself with such humility and cunning, that he ends by convincing his monarch that the sparrow is in the wrong. Then the two kings declare war against each other, and engage in a formidable struggle, attended with terrible bloodshed on both sides, and which ends in the king of the birds being wounded. (The nocturnal or wintry mouse expels the solar bird of evening or of autumn.)

In the *Batrachomyomachia*, attributed to Homer, the royal mouse Psicharpax (properly ravisher of crumbs), the third son of Troxartes (eat-bread), boasts to Phüsignathos (he who inflates his cheeks), the lord of the frogs, that he does not fear the man, the point of whose finger (akron daktülôn) he has bitten while he was asleep; whilst, on the other hand, he has for his enemies the falcon (which we have already, in the Hindoo story, seen let the mouse fall from its beak) and the cat. The frog, who wishes to entertain the mouse, invites it to get upon his back, to be carried to his royal mansion; at first the mouse is amused with its ride, but when the frog makes it feel the icy water, the poor mouse's heart begins to fail; finally, at the sight of a serpent, the frog forgets its rider and runs away, throwing the mouse head-over-heels into the water to be the prey of the serpent. Then, before expiring, remembering that the gods have an avenging eye, it threatens the frogs with the vengeance of the army of the mice. War is prepared. The mice make themselves good boots with the shells of beans; they cover their cuirasses of bulrushes with the skin of a flayed cat; their shield is the centre knob of the lamps (lüchnôn to mesomphalon, *i.e.*, if I am not mistaken, a fragment of a little lamp of terra-cotta, and, properly speaking, the lower and central part); for a lance they have a needle, and for a helmet a nutshell. The gods are present at the battle as neutrals,—Pallas having declared her unwillingness to help the mice, because they stole the oil from the lamps burning in her honour, and because they had gnawed her peplum, and being equally indifferent to the frogs, because they had once wakened her when returning from war, and when, being tired and weary, she wished to rest. The battle is fiercely fought, and is about to have an unfavourable result for the frogs, when Zeus takes pity upon them; he lightens and hurls his thunderbolts. At last, seeing that the mice do not desist, the gods send a host of crabs, who, biting the tails, the hands, and the feet of the mice, force them to flee. This is undoubtedly the representation of a mythical battle. The frogs, as we shall see, are the clouds; the night meets the cloud; the mouse fights with the frog. Zeus, the thunder-god, to put an end to the struggle, thunders and lightens; at last the retrograde crab makes its appearance; the combatants, frogs and mice, naturally disappear.

The mouse is never conceived otherwise than in connection with the nocturnal darkness, and hence, by extending the myth, in connection also with the darkness of winter, from which light and riches subsequently come forth. In Sicily it is believed that when a child's tooth is taken out, if it be hidden in a hole, the mouse will take it away and bring a coin for the child in compensation. The mouse is dark-coloured, but its teeth and fore-parts are white and luminous. The mouse Hiraṇyakas, or the golden one, in the *Pańćatantram*, is the black or grey mouse of night. It is the red squirrel that, in an Æsopian fable, answers to the query of the fox why it sharpens its teeth when it has nothing to eat, that it does so to be always prepared against its enemies. In the *Edda*, the squirrel runs upon the tree Yggdrasil, and sets the eagle and Nidhögg at discord.

The mole and the snail are of the same nature as the grey mouse. The Hindoo word *âkhus*, or the mole (already spoken of as a demon killed by Indras, in the *Ṛigvedas*[1]), properly signifies the excavator.

In the *Reineke Fuchs* the mole appears as a gravedigger, as the animal that heaves the earth up, and makes ditches underground; it is, in fact, the most skilful of gravediggers, and its black colour and supposed blindness are in perfect accordance with the funereal character assigned to it by mythology. In an apologue of Laurentius, the ass complains to the mole of having no horns, and the monkey of having a short tail; the mole answers them—

> "Quid potestis hanc meam
> Miseram intuentes cœcitatem, hæc conqueri?"

[1] Alâyyasya paraçur nanâça tam â pavasya (pavasva according to Aufrecht's text, and according to the commentator—cfr. Bollensen, Zur Herstellung des Veda, in the *Orient und Occident* of Benfey, ii. 484) deva soma; âkhuṁ ćid eva deva soma; *Ṛigv.* ix. 67, 30.

According to the Hellenic myth, Phineus became a mole because he had, following the advice of his second wife, Idaia, allowed his two sons by his first wife, Cleopatra, to be blinded, and also because he had revealed the secret thoughts of Zeus.[1]

In Du Cange I find that even in the Middle Ages it was the custom on Christmas Eve for children to meet with poles, having straw wrapped round the ends, which they set fire to, and to go round the gardens, near the trees, shouting—

> "Taupes et mulots
> Sortez de nos clos
> Sinon je vous brulerai la barbe et les os."

We find a similar invocation in the seventh story of the second book of the *Pentamerone*. The beautiful girl goes to find maruzze, and threatens the snail to make her mother cut off its horns—

> "Iesce, iesce, corna
> Ca mammata te scorna,
> Te scorna 'ncoppa l'astreco
> Che fa lo figlio mascolo."

In Piedmont, to induce the snail to put its horns out, children are accustomed to sing to it—

> "Lümassa, lümassora,
> Tira fora i to corn,
> Dass no,[2] i vad dal barbé
> E it tje fass taié!"

[1] Cfr. the *Antigonê* of Sophocles, v. 973, *et seq.*

[2] This *dass no* of the Piedmontese means "if not," and is evidently of Germanic origin. The Piedmontese dialect has also taken from the Germanic languages the final negative.—In Germany, children sing to the snails—

> "Schneckhûs, peckhûs,
> Stäk dîn vêr hörner rût,
> Süst schmît ick dî in'n graven
> Da frêten dî de raven."

—Cfr. Kuhn und Schwartz, *N. d. S. M. u. G.*, p. 453.

Sicilian children terrify the snail by informing it that their mother is coming to burn its horns with a candle—

"Nesci li corna ch 'a mamma veni
E t' adduma lu cannileri."

In Tuscany they threaten the white snail (la marinella), telling it to thrust out its little horns to save itself from kicks and blows—

"Chiócciola marinella,
Tira fuori le tue cornella,
E se tu non le tirerai
Calci e pugni tu buscherai."

In Tuscany it is believed, moreover, that in the month of April the snail makes love with the serpents, and is therefore venomous; hence they sing—

"Chi vuol presto morire
Mangi la chiocciola d' aprile."[1]

The snail of popular superstition is demoniacal; hence it is also invoked by children in Germany by the name of the funereal St Gertrude—

"Kuckuck, kuckuck Gerderut
Stäk dîne vêr Horns herut."[2]

---

1 In *Rabelais*, i. 38, when Gargantua has eaten five pilgrims in his salad, another still remains hidden under a leaf of lettuce. His father says to him—"Je crois que c'est là une corne de limasson, ne le mangez point. Pourquoy? dist Gargantua, ilz sont bons tout se moys."

2 Simrock, *Handbuch der Deutschen Mythologie*, 2te Aufl., p. 516.

CHAPTER VIII.

HARE, RABBIT, ERMINE, AND BEAVER.

SUMMARY.

The hare is the moon ; *çaças* and *çaçin*.—The hares at the lake of the moon; the king of the hares in the moon.—The hare and the elephant.—The hare and the lion.—The hare devours the western monster ; the hare devours his mother the mare.—*Mortuo leoni lepores insultant.*—The hare and the eagle.—The hare that guards the cavern of the beasts.—The hare comes out on the 15th of the month and terrifies the wolf.—The hare transformed into the moon by Indras.—Ermine and beaver.—Hare's-foot.—Hare and moon fruitful.—Hare and moon that guide the hero.—*Somnus leporinus.*—The hare and the bear.—The hare and the nuptial procession.—The hare that contains a duck.—The girl riding upon the hare.

The mythical hare is undoubtedly the moon. In Sanskṛit, the *çaças* means properly the leaping one, as well as the hare, the rabbit, and the spots on the moon (the *saltans*), which suggest the figure of a hare. Hence the names of *çaçin*, or furnished with hares, and of *çaçadharas*, *çaçabhṛit*, or he who carries the hare given to the moon. In the first story of the third book of the *Pańćatantram*, the hares dwell upon the shore of the Lake Ćandrasaras, or lake of the moon; and their king, Vigayadattas (the funereal god, the god of death), has for his palace the lunar disc. When the hare speaks to the king of the elephants who crushed the hares (in the same way as we have seen the cow do in Chapter I.), he speaks in the moon's name. The hare makes the elephant believe that the moon is in anger against the elephants because they crush the hares under their feet; then the elephant demands to see the moon, and the hare conducts him to the lake of the moon, where he shows him the moon in the water. Wishing to approach the moon and ask forgiveness, the elephant thrusts his proboscis into the water; the water is agitated, and the reflection of the moon is disturbed, and multiplied a thousand-fold. The hare makes the elephant believe that the moon is still more angry because he has disturbed the water; then the king of the elephants begs for pardon, and goes far away with his subjects; from that day the hares live tranquilly on the shores of the moon-lake, and are no longer crushed under the ponderous feet of their huge companions. The moon rules the night (and the winter), the sun rules the day (and the summer). The moon is cold, the sun is hot. The solar elephant, lion, or bull, goes down at even to drink at the river, at the lake of the nocturnal moon; the hare warns the elephant that if he does not retire, if he continues to crush the hares on the shores of the lake, the moon will take back her cold beams, and then the elephants will die of thirst and excessive heat. The other story of the *Pańćatantram* is a variety of the myth, which we mentioned in the chapter of the dog, of the hare who conducts to his ruin the hungry lion who wishes to eat her, by making him throw himself into a fountain or well. This myth, which is analogous to that of the mouse as the enemy of now the elephant, now the lion, and now the hawk, is already very clearly indicated in the Vedic hymns. In the twenty-eighth hymn of the tenth book of the *Ṛigvedas*, in which the fox comes to visit the western lion (the sick lion[1]), in which we have the lion who falls into the trap[2] (and whom the mouse insults in the evening, and delivers in the morning by gnawing at the ropes which bind it: in the Hellenic proverb it is the hare that draws the lion into the golden net—"elkei lagôs lionta chrüsinô brochô," in the same way as in the *Pańćatantram*, it allures him into the well), and in which the hare devours the western monster[3] (a variety of the Hellenic tradition of the hare brought forth by a mare, and which immediately thereafter devours its mother)—in this hymn we find the germ of several fables of animals of the same cycle. The inferior animal vanquishes the superior one, and upon this peculiarity the whole hymn turns; for this reason, too, in the same hymn, the dog or jackal (canis aureus) assails the wild boar,[4] and the calf defeats the bull.[5] The hare occurs again as the proverbial enemy of the lion (whence the Latin proverb, "Mortuo leoni lepores insultant," or *saltant*; the moon jumps up when the sun dies), in the last book of the *Râmâyaṇam*, where the great king of the monkeys, Bâlin, regards the king of the monsters, Râvaṇas, as a lion does a hare, or as the bird Garuḍasa serpent.[6]

In *Æsop* we find the hare that laughs at its enemy, the dying eagle, because the hunter killed it with an arrow furnished with eagle's feathers. In another Æsopian fable, the rabbit avenges itself upon the eagle which has eaten its young ones,

[1] Lopâçaḥ sinham pratyańćam atsâḥ; *Ṛigv.* x, 28, 4.
[2] Avaruddhaḥ paripadaṁ na sinhaḥ; x. 28, 10.
[3] Çaçah kshuram pratyańćam ǵagâra; x. 28, 9.
[4] Kroshṭâ varâhaṁ nir atakta kakshât; x. 28, 4.
[5] Vatso vṛishabhaṁ çûçuvânaḥ; x. 28, 9.
[6] Sinhaḥ çaçamivâlakshya garuḍo vâ bhuǵaṅgamam; *Râmây.* xxiii.

by rooting up and throwing down the tree upon which the eagle has its nest, so that the eaglets are killed.

In the seventeenth Mongol story, the hare is the guardian of the cavern of the wild beasts (or the moon, the mrigarâĝas and guardian of the forest of night); in the same story an old woman (the old fairy or old Madonna) is substituted for the hare. In the twenty-first Mongol story, the hare sets out on a journey with the lamb, on the fifteenth day of the month, when the moon comes forth, and defends the lamb from the wolf of night, terrifying the latter by telling it that it has received a writing from the god Indras, in which the hare is ordered to bring to Indras a thousand wolves' skins.

In a Buddhist legend, the hare is transfigured by Indras into the moon, because it had freely given him its flesh to eat, when, disguised as a pilgrim, he came up begging for bread. The hare, having nothing else to offer him, threw itself upon the fire, that Indras might appease his hunger.[1]

In the *Avesta* we find the ermine as the king of the animals, and the beaver as the sacred and inviolable animal, in whose skin the pure Ardvîçûra is invested (white and silvery as the white dawn, rosy and golden as the aurora; unless Ardvîçûra, whose diadem is made of a hundred stars, should also be interpreted as denoting the moon, which is now silvery, and now fair and golden). Moreover, for the beaver to represent the moon (the chaste Diana) is in perfect accordance with the reputation it has as a eunuch (castor *a castrando*) in popular

[1] Cfr. *Mémoires sur les Contrées Occidentales*, traduits du Sanscrit par Hiouen Thsang, et du Chinois par St Julien, i. 375.

superstition; whence the words of Cicero concerning beavers,[1] and the verses of Juvenal—

> "Imitatus castora qui se
> Eunuchum ipse facit cupiens evadere damnum
> Testiculorum, adeo medicatum intelliget unguen."[2]

In the twenty-first Esthonian story, a silly husband is called by the name of Hare's-foot. In *Aldrovandi*, on the other hand, Philostratos narrates the case of a woman who had miscarried seven times in the act of child-birth, but who the eighth time brought forth a child, when her husband unexpectedly drew a hare out of his bosom. Although the moon is herself the timid and chaste goddess (or eunuch), she is, as pluvial, the *fæcundatrix*, and famous as presiding over and protecting child-birth; this is why, when the hare-moon, or Lucina, assisted at parturition, it was sure to issue happily. The mythical hare and the moon are constantly identified. It is on this account that in *Pausanias*, the moon-goddess instructs the exiles who are searching for a propitious place to found a city, to build it in a myrtle-grove into which they should see a hare flee for refuge. The moon is the watcher of the sky, that is to say, she sleeps with her eyes open; so also does the hare, whence the *somnus leporinus* became a proverb. In the ninth Esthonian story, the thunder-god is compared to the hare that sleeps with its eyes open; Indras, who transforms the hare into the moon, has already been mentioned; Indras becomes a eunuch in the form of sahasrâkshas, or of the thousand-eyed god

[1] Redimunt ea parte corporis, propter quam maxime expetuntur; *Pro Æmilio Scauro.* It is said that when the beaver is pursued by hunters, it tears off its testicles, as the most precious part for which beavers are hunted, popular medical belief attributing marvellous virtues to beavers' testicles.

[2] xii. 35.

(the starry sky in the night, or the sun in this starry sky); the thousand eyes become one, the *milloculus* becomes *monoculus*, when the moon shines in the evening sky; hence we say now the hundred eyes of Argos, and now simply the eye of Argos—the eye of God.

In a Slavonic tale,[1] the hare laughs at the bear's cubs, and spits upon them; the bear runs after the hare, and in the hunt is decoyed into an intricate jungle, where it is caught. As the lion is unknown in Russia, the bear is substituted for it; the Russian hare allures the bear into the trap, as the Hindoo and Greek one causes the lion to fall into it. This hare which does harm to the solar hero or animal of evening is the same as that which, in the fiftieth story of the fifth book of *Afanassieff*, and in Russian popular tradition, meeting the nuptial car, bodes evil to the wedding, and is of evil omen to the bride and bridegroom. The hare-moon, the chaste protectress of marriages and births, the benefactress of mankind, must not meet the car; if she opposes the wedding (perhaps at evening and in the autumn), or if the hare is crushed or overtaken by the car (as the proverb says), it is a bad presage, not only for the wedded couple, but for all mankind; solar as well as lunar eclipses were always considered sinister omens in popular superstition. In the Russian popular tales we frequently find mention of the hare under a tree, or on a rock in the midst of the sea, where there is a duck, which contains an egg; the yoke of this egg (the solar disc) is a precious stone; when it falls into the hands of the young hero, the monster dies, and he is able to espouse the young princess.[2] The girl of seven years of age,

[1] Cited by Afanassieff in the observations on the first volume of the Russian stories.

[2] Cfr. *Afanassieff*, i. 14, ii. 24, v. 42.

who, to solve in action the riddle proposed by the Tzar, who offers to marry her, rides upon a hare, is a variety of this myth. By the help of the moon, the sun and evening aurora arrive at the region of the morning, find each other, and are married ; the moon is the mediatrix of the mythical nuptials ; the hare which represents it must therefore not only not oppose them, but help them materially ; at evening the moon separates the sun from the aurora ; at morning she unites them again.

CHAPTER IX.

THE ANTELOPE, THE STAG, THE DEER, AND THE GAZELLE.

SUMMARY.

Luminous stag and black stag.—The Marutas drawn by antelopes, and dressed in antelopes' skins.—The stag, the gazelle, and the antelope as forms assumed or created by the demon to ruin several heroes whilst they hunt.—Marîćas.—Indras kills the mṛigas.—The solar hero or heroine transformed into a stag, a gazelle, or an antelope.—Aktaion.—Artemis and the stag.—The stags of the Yggdrasill.—The stag Eikthyrner.—The hind as a nurse.—The hind and the old woman on the 1st of January.—The hind and the snow; the white hind.

THE stag represents the luminous forms that appear in the cloudy or the nocturnal forest; these, therefore, are now lightning and thunderbolts, now the cloud itself from which the lightning and thunderbolts are discharged, now the moon in the gloom of night. The mythical stag is nearly always either entirely luminous or else spotted; when it is black it is of a diabolical nature, and represents the whole sky of night. Sometimes the luminous stag is a form assumed by the demon of the forest to compass the ruin of the hero.

The *Ṛigvedas* represents to us the Marutas, or winds that lighten and thunder in the clouds, as drawn by antelopes. The Marutas "are born shining of themselves, with antelopes, with lances, amid thunder-peals and flashes of lightning."[1] "They have yoked, with a red yoke, the antelopes.[2] The young battalion of the Marutas goes of itself, and has an antelope for its horse."[3] The horses of the Marutas, which we already know to be antelopes, are called winged,[4] and are said to have golden fore-feet.[5] The antelopes of the Marutas are splendid.[6] Nor are the Marutas only carried by antelopes; they also wear upon their shoulders antelopes' skins.[7]

But the antelope, the gazelle, and the stag generally, instead of helping the hero, involve him rather in perplexity and peril. This mythical subject is amplified in numerous Hindoo legends.

In the first scene of Kâlidâsas' *Çakuntalâ*, a black-spotted (kṛishṇasâras) gazelle misleads King Dushyantas.

In the *Mahâbhâratam*,[8] King Parîkshit pursues a gazelle and wounds it (as the god Çivas one day wounded the gazelle of the sacrifice); he then follows its track, but the gazelle flees at sight of him, inasmuch as it has taken the path of heaven in its primitive (*i.e.*, celestial) form. The king loses the track of his prey, and in trying to find it again, brings death upon his head.

In the same *Mahâbhâratam*,[9] King Pandus dies at the

[1] Ye pṛishatîbhir ṛishtibhiḥ sâkaṁ vâçîbhir aṅgibhiḥ—agâyanta svabhânavaḥ; *Ṛigv.* i. 37, 2.

[2] Upo ratheshu pṛishatîr ayugdhvam prashṭir vahati rohitaḥ; i. 39, 6.

[3] Sa hi svasṛit pṛishadaçvo yuvâ gaṇaḥ: i. 87, 4.

[4] Â vidyunmadbhir marutaḥ svarkâi rathebhir yâtha ṛishṭimadbhir açvaparnâiḥ; i. 88, 1.

[5] Açvâir hiraṇyapâṇibhiḥ; viii. 7, 27.

[6] Çubhe sammiçlâḥ pṛishatîr ayukshata; iii. 26, 4.

[7] Aṅseshu etâḥ; *Ṛigv.* i. 166, 10.—Concerning the use of similar skins for dress in India, cfr. the long and instructive note of Professor Max Müller, *Ṛigveda-Sanhita Translated and Explained*, i. 221–223.

[8] i. 1665.

[9] i. 3811, *et seq.*; i. 4585, *et seq.*

moment when he is uniting himself with his wife Mâdrî, because he had one day in the chase transfixed a male gazelle at the instant when it was about to have fruit of its union with a female gazelle.

In the *Vishṇu P.*,[1] King Bharatas, who has abandoned his throne to give himself up entirely to penitence, loses the fruit of his ascetic life, by becoming passionately enamoured of a fawn.

In the *Râmâyaṇam*,[2] Marîćas, who is possessed by a demon, becomes, by order of Râvaṇas, the king of the monsters, a golden stag spotted with silver, having four golden horns adorned with pearls, and a tongue as red as the sun, and tempts Râmas to pursue him in order to procure his silver-spotted skin, for which Sîtâ has expressed a desire, that she might lie down upon it and rest herself. In this way the stag (here an equivalent of the hare) succeeds in separating Râmas from Sîtâ. It then emits a lamentable cry, imitating the voice of Râmas, so as to induce Lakshmaṇas, his brother, to come to his assistance, and leave Sîtâ alone, that Râvaṇas may then be able to carry her off with impunity. Lakshmaṇas leaves her unwillingly, because, perceiving that the stag shines like the constellation of the head of the stag (or gazelle, Mṛigaçiras), he suspects it to be an apparition of Marîćas, who, as a stag, has already caused the ruin of many other princes who have hunted him. The moon, in Sanskṛit, besides the name of Çaçadharas, or who carries the hare, has also that of Mṛigadharas, or who carries the gazelle (or stag). The solar hero loses himself in the forest of night while pursuing the gazelle-moon. A demoniacal gazelle seems to appear even in the *Ṛigvedas*, where Indras fights and

1 ii. 13, translated by Wilson.

2 iii. 40, 48, 49.

kills a monster called Mṛigas. In Germanic tradition there are numerous legends in which the hero who hunts the stag meets with his death or is dragged into hell.[1]

As the moon is a stag or gazelle, and comes after the sun, so it was also sometimes imagined that the solar hero or heroine was transformed into a stag or hind.

In the *Tuti-Name,*[2] a king goes to the chase, kills an antelope, doffs the human form, and disguises himself as an antelope. This mythical disguise can be understood in two ways. The evening sun reflects its rays in the ocean of night, the sun-stag sees its horns reflected in the fountain or lake of night, and admires them. At this fountain sits a beautiful and bewitching siren, the moon; this fountain is the dwelling of the moon; she allures the hero-stag that admires itself in the fountain, and ruins it, or else the stag attracts the hero to the fountain, where it causes him to meet with his death.[3] The stag of the fable, after admiring itself in the fountain, is torn to pieces by the dogs who overtake it in the forest because its horns become entangled in the branches; the solar rays are enveloped in the branches of the nocturnal forest. Aktaion, who, for having seen Artemis (the moon) naked in the bath, is changed into a stag and torn by dogs, is a variety of the same fable. In *Stesichoros,* quoted by Pausanias, Artemis puts a stag's skin round Aktaion and incites the dogs to devour him in order that he may not be able to wed the moon. Sun and moon are brother and sister; the brother, wishing to

[1] Cfr. Simrock, the work quoted before, p. 354.

[2] ii. 258, Rosen's version.

[3] Oft führt der Hirsch nur zu einer schönen Frau am Brunnen; sie ist aber der Unterwelt verwandt und die Verbindung mit ihr an die Bedingung geknüpft, dass die ungleiche Natur des Verbundenen nicht an den Tag gezogen werde.

seduce his sister, meets with his death. A Lithuanian song describes the moon Menas (the Hindoo Manu-s) as the unfaithful husband of the sun (who is a female), being enamoured of Aushrine (the Vedic Usrâ, the morning aurora). The god Perkuns, to avenge the sun, kills the moon. In a Servian song, the moon reproaches his mistress or wife, the morning aurora, on account of her absence. The aurora answers that she travels upon the heights of Belgrade, that is, of the white or the luminous city, in the sky, upon the lofty mountains.

The king in the *Tuti-Name* who assumes the guise of an antelope, appears to be a variety of the solar hero at the moment of the approach of night, or of the ass that invests itself in the lion's skin. But inasmuch as the Indian moon is Mṛigarâgas, or king of the wild animals, no less than the lion, inasmuch as the moon succeeds the sun, one mṛigas another, one lion another, or one stag another, when the solar hero or heroine enters into the night, he or she appears in the form of a luminous stag or hind, no longer as the sun, but as the moon, which, although luminous, penetrates into hell, and is in relation with demons and itself demoniacal.

Artemis (the moon) is represented as a hunting goddess in the act of wounding, with her left hand, an antelope between the horns. To this goddess is also attributed the merit of having overtaken the stags without the help of dogs, perhaps because, sometimes, she is herself a dog, surprising the solar stag of evening. The four stags of Artemis connect themselves in my mind with the four stags that stay round the tree Yggdrasill in the *Edda*, and which come out of the river Häeffing. The stag Eikthyrner which, eating the leaves of the tree Lerad, causes all its waters to flow out, seems, on the other hand, to refer to the sun as it merges and loses its rays in the cloud (the solar stag is also referred to in the *Edda*).

Artemis, who substitutes a hind for Iphigeneia, who was to have been sacrificed, seems to point to the moon-hind as taking the place of the evening aurora. We also recognise the moon in the hind which, according to Ælianos and Diodoros, nourished Telephos, son of Hêraklês (Hêraklês in his fourth labour overtakes the stag with golden horns), who had been exposed in the forest by the order of his grandfather; as well as in that which, according to Justinus, fed with its milk in the forest the nephew of the king of the Tartessians, and afterwards, according to the "Lives of the Saints," the blessed Ægidius, the hermit who lived in the forest. There are numerous mediæval legends which reproduce this circumstance of the young hero abandoned in the forest and nourished now by a goat, now by a hind, the same which afterwards serves as a guide to the royal father in recovering the prince his son, or to the prince-husband in recovering the abandoned princess his bride. It was probably by some such reminiscence of the mythical nourishing hind that, as I read in Du Cange,[1] silver images of stags (cervi argentei) were placed in ancient Christian baptistries.

Among the customs of the primitive Christians condemned by St Augustine, St Maximus of Turin, and other sacred writers, was that of disguising one's self on the 1st of January as a hind or an old woman. The old woman and the hind here evidently represent the witch or ugly woman of winter; and inasmuch as the winter is, like the night, under the moon's influence,

[1] Du Cange adds: "Quoad baptismam, quomodo cervus ad fontes aquarum, summo desiderium perveniendum esse monstraretur."

the disguise of a hind was another way of representing the moon. When the moon or the sun shines, the hind is luminous and generally propitious, the wild goat is beneficent (the wild goat, the deer, and the stag are the same in the myths; the same word, *mṛigas*, serves in India to express the constellation of the gazelle and that of the capricorn or wild goat), and hunts the wolves away from the sleeping hero in the forest.[1] When the sky is dark, the hind, from being luminous, has become black, and, as such, is the most sinister of omens; sometimes, in the midst of the night or of the winter, the beautiful luminous hind, or moon, or sun, disappears, and the black monster of night or of winter remains alone. In the ninth story of the *Pentamerone*, the Huorco (the rakshas or monster) transforms himself into a beautiful hind to allure the young Canneloro, who pursues it in the hope of securing it. But it decoys him into the midst of the forest (of winter), where it causes so much snow to fall, "che pareva che lo cielo cadesse" (the white hind into which the witch transforms the beautiful maiden, in the story of Madame d'Aulnoy, would seem to have the same meaning); then the hind becomes a monster again in order to devour the hero. The period in which the moon is hidden or on the wane, in which the night is dark, was considered ill-omend by the ancient Hindoos, who held, on the other hand, that the time of full moon, or at least of the crescent moon, was propitious. Our country-people have preserved several superstitions relative to a similar belief. In a Rutenian legend, published by Novosielski, the evening star (Lithuanian, *vakerinne;* Slavonic, *večernitza*, the evening aurora) prays its friend

[1] Cfr. Porchat, *Contes Merveilleux*, xiii.

Lunus (the moon is masculine in Slavonic as in Sanskṛit) to wait a little before rising, that they may rise together, and adds, "We shall illumine together sky and earth: the animals will be glad in the fields, and the traveller will bless us on his way."

CHAPTER X.

THE ELEPHANT.

SUMMARY.

The myth of the elephant is entirely Indian.—The Marutas as elephants; Indras as an elephant.—The elephant ridden by Indras and Agnis.—The four elephants that support the world.—Âiravanas and Âiravatas.—The elephant becomes diabolical.—Nâgas and nagas; çriñgiṁ.—The monkeys fight against the elephants.—The elephant in the marsh.—The elephant and the tortoise; war between them.—The eagle, the elephant, and the tortoise.—The bird, the fly, and the frog lure the elephant to his death.—Hermit dwarfs.—Indras and his elephant fall together.

THE whole mythical history of the elephant is confined to India. The strength of his proboscis and tusks, his extraordinary size, the ease with which he carries heavy burdens, his great fecundity in the season of loves, all contributed to his mythical importance, and to his fame as a great ravager of the celestial gloomy or cloudy forest, as an Atlas, a supporter of worlds, and the steed of the pluvial god.

The elephant has a place even in the Vedic heavens.

The Marutas, drawn by antelopes, are compared to wild elephants that level forests;[1] the horns of the antelopes, the tusks of the wild boar, the trunk and tusks of

---

[1] Mṛigâ iva hastinaḥ khâdathâ vanâ yad ârunîshu tavishîr ayugdhvam; *Ṛigv.* i. 64, 7.

the elephant, are of equivalent significance, and are seen in the solar rays, in lightnings and thunderbolts. The pluvial and thundering god Indras is compared to a wild elephant that expends his strength[1]—to a wild elephant that, in the season of loves, is, on all hands, in a constant state of feverish agitation.[2] The god Agnis is invoked to come forth like a formidable king upon an elephant.[3]

The elephant generally represents the sun as it shuts itself up in the cloud or the darkness, or comes out of it, shooting forth rays of light or flashes of lightning (which were also supposed to be caused by the friction on the axle of the wheel of the sun's chariot). The sun, in the four seasons, visits the four quarters of the earth, east and west, south and north; hence, perhaps, the Hindoo conception of four elephants that support the four corners of the earth.[4] Indras, the pluvial god, rides upon an enormous elephant, Âiravatas or Âiravaṇas, the cloud or darkness itself, with its luminous eruptions; âiravatam and âiravatî are also appellations of the lightning. The elephant Âiravaṇas or Âiravatas is one of the first of the progeny of the heavens, begotten of the agitation of the celestial ocean.

It plays a prominent part in the battles of Indras against the monsters; hence Râvaṇas, the monster king of Lañkâ, still bears the scars of the wounds given him by the elephant Airavatas, in the war between the gods and the demons,[5] although this same Râvaṇas boasts of having one day defeated Indras, who rode upon the elephant Âiravaṇas.[6]

But the mythical elephant did not always preserve the character of an animal beloved of the gods; after

[1] Mṛigo na hastî tavishîm ushâṇaḥ; *Ṛigv.* iv. 16, 14.

[2] Dânâ mṛigo na vâraṇaḥ purutrâ ćarathaṁ dadhe; *Ṛigv.* viii. 33, 8.

[3] Yâhi râgevâmavân ibhena; *Ṛigv.* iv. 4, 1.

[4] *Râmây.* i. 42. [5] iii. 36. [6] iii. 47.

other animals were admitted into special favour, it too assumed, in time, a monstrous aspect. The sun hides itself in the cloud, in the cloudy or nocturnal mountain, in the ocean of night, in the autumn or the snowy winter. Hence we have the white elephant (Dhavalas), the malignant killer of wise men (ṛishayas, the solar rays); the wind, father of Hanumant, in the form of a monkey, lacerates him with his claws, and tears out his tusks; the elephant falls like a mountain[1] (the mountain of snow, or white cloud, dissolve themselves; this white elephant and the white mountain, or Dhavalagiris, are the same; the equivoque easily arose between nâgas, elephant, and nagas, mountain and tree; the word *çriñgin*, properly horned, means tree, mountain, and elephant; the wind breaks through and disperses the cloud, and pushes forward the avalanches of snow). Thus it is said that the monkey Sannâdanas was one day victorious over the elephant Âiravatas.[2] (The northern path of the moon is called âiravatapathâ.)

We have already seen the elephant that crushes the hares under his feet on the shores of the moon-lake, and disturbs with his trunk the waters of this lake. In the *Râmâyaṇam*,[3] Bharatas considers it as of a sinister omen his having dreamed of a great elephant fallen into marshy ground. The sun plunges into the ocean of night, and of the autumnal rains.

The elephant near or in the waters is mythically equivalent to the lunar and solar tortoise that dwells on the shores of the lake and sea, or at the bottom of the sea. In the Hindoo cosmogony, it is now the elephant and now the tortoise that supports the weight of the world. For this reason there is rivalry between these two mythical animals.

---

[1] *Râmây.* v. 3. [2] vi. 3. [3] ii. 71.

Therefore the eagle, or king of birds, or the bird Garuḍas, the solar bird, is represented as a mortal enemy now of the serpent, now of the elephant (the word *nâgas* means equally serpent and elephant; Âiravatas is also the name of a monstrous serpent), and now of the tortoise. In the *Râmâyaṇam*,[1] the bird Garuḍas carries into the air an elephant and a tortoise (the relative occidental fables are evidently of Hindoo origin), in order to eat them. The same legend is developed in the *Mahâbhâratam*,[2] where two brothers dispute with each other about the division of their goods, each curses the other, and they become, the one a colossal elephant, and the other a colossal tortoise, and, as such, continue to fight fiercely against each other in a lake, until the gigantic bird Garuḍas (the new sun), takes them both and carries them to the summit of a mountain.

In the fifteenth story of the first book of the *Pańćatantram*, we find birds represented as enemies of the elephant, on account of the ravages it commits, where the bird, the fly, and the frog work the ruin of the elephant; the fly enters into one of the elephant's ears; the bird pecks at its eyes, and blinds it; the frog croaks on the banks of a deep pool; the elephant, impelled by thirst, comes to the pool and is drowned.

The Vedic elephant has a divine nature, being connected with the pluvial Indras; but when Indras fell, to give place to Brahman, Vishṇus, and Çivas, his elephant was also fated to become the prey of the bird of Vishṇus, of the bird Garuḍas (or the sun). In the fable of the *Pańćatantram* quoted above, the elephant brings upon its head the vengeance of the sparrow, because it had rooted up a tree upon which the sparrow had made its nest

[1] iii. 39.

[2] i. 1353, *seq.*

and laid its eggs, which were broken in consequence. The Vishṇuitic legend of the *Mahâbhâratam* relating to the bird Garuḍas, which carries the elephant into the air, offers several other analogous and interesting particulars. The bird Garuḍas flies away with the elephant and the tortoise; on the way, being tired, it rests upon the huge bough of a tree; the bough breaks under the enormous weight. From this bough are suspended, with their heads down, in penitence, several dwarf hermits, born of the hairs of Brahman; then the bird Garuḍas takes in its beak the whole bough, with the little hermits, and carries them up in the air till they succeed in escaping. These hermit dwarfs upon the branch (who remind us of the ants), had one day cursed Indras. Kaçyapas Pragâpatis, wishing one day to make a sacrifice in order to obtain the favour of a son, orders the gods to provide him with wood. Indras, like the four elephants who support the world, places upon his shoulders a whole mountain of wood. Laden with this weight, he meets on the way the hermit dwarfs, who were carrying a leaf in a car, and were in danger of being drowned in a pool of water, the size of the foot-print of a cow. Indras, instead of coming to their assistance, smiles and passes by; the hermit dwarfs, in indignation, pray for the birth of a new Indras; on this account the Indras of birds was born—the bird of Garuḍas, the steed of Vishṇus, which naturally makes war against the steed of Indras, the elephant.

CHAPTER XI.

THE MONKEY AND THE BEAR.

SUMMARY.

Monkey and bear are already associated together in India; Ǵambavant is a great monkey and the king of the bears.—Haris, kapis, kapilâ, kapidhvaǵas; ṛikshas, arkas, ursus, arktos, rakshas; the Great Bear; ṛishayas, harayas.—The Marutas as rivals of Indras; Vishṇus as Indras' rival; the monkeys allied to Vishṇus; the Vedic monster monkey killed by Indras; Haris or Vishṇus.—Harî mother of monkeys and horses.—Bâlin, king of the monkeys, son of Indras, defeated by his brother Sugrîvas, son of the sun.—Hanumant in opposition to Indras; Hanumant son of the wind; Hanumant as the brother of Sugrîvas; Hanumant is the strong brother or companion.—Hanumant flies; he presses the mountain and makes the waters come out of it; he draws the clouds after himself.—The epic monkeys and the Marutas.—The monkey and the water.—The monkeys and the salutary herbs.—The sea-monster draws to itself the shadow of Hanumant and swallows him; Hanumant comes out of the monster's body safe and sound; the mountain Hiraṇyanabhas.—Hanumant makes himself as small as a cat in order to search for Sîtâ; Hanumant proves his power to Sîtâ by making himself as large as a cloud or a mountain; he massacres the monsters with a pillar; Dadhyańć, Hanumant, Samson; Hanumant bound; he sets fire to Lañkâ with his tail.—The monkey sacrificed to cure the burns of horses.—Sîtâ has a weakness for Hanumant.—Dvividas a monster monkey.—The monkey destroys the sparrow's nest.—The monkey draws a king into the jaws of an aquatic monster.—The demoniacal monkey; monkey and fox.—The monkey deceiver.—Sinister omens of the monkey.—The monkey envies the fox's tail.—The stupid monkey.—The bear of the Marutas.—Triçañkus with the skin of a bear; the seven ṛishayas.—Ṛiksharâǵas; the moon as a reputed father.—

Bears and monkeys in the forest of honey; Balarâmas; medvjed; the bear and the honey; Italian proverbs; the bear and the peasant; the deceived bear; the vengeance of the bear; the bear in the sack; the demoniacal bear; the bear and the fox; the monkey and the woodcutter; the bear and the trunk of a tree; the peasant and the gentleman; the death of the athlete Milôn; the bear entangled in the waggon that had fallen into the cistern.—The king bear, monster of the fountain; sons sacrificed to the bear by their father; the young men flee from the bear; the sleep of the bear.—The bear's cub.—The bear and women.—The hero-bear; the heroine she-bear.—The virgin she-bears.—Ursula, ṛikshikâ.—Ivanko Medviedko.—Kalistos.—The bear as a musician.—The quartette of animals.—Bear and monkey.—Bear and ass.—The monkey as a messenger, an intermediate form.

I HERE unite under one heading two animals of very diverse nature and race, but which, from some gross resemblances, probably helped by an equivoque in the language, are closely affiliated in the Hindoo myth. I say Hindoo in particular, because the monkey, which is so common in India, was long unknown to many of the Indo-European nations in their scattered abodes, so that if they had some dim reminiscence of it as connected with that part of Asia where the Âryan mythology took its rise, they soon forgot it when they no longer had under their eyes the animal itself which had suggested the primitive mythical form. But as they held tenaciously by the substance of the myth, they by and by substituted for the original mythical animal, called monkey, in the south the ass, and in the north often the bear. Even in India, where the pre-eminent quality of the monkey was cunning, we already find monkeys and bears associated together. A reddish colour of the skin, want of symmetry and ungainliness of form, strength in hugging with the fore paws or arms, the faculty of climbing, shortness of tail, sensuality, capacity for instruction in dancing and in music, are all characteristics which more or less distinguish and meet in bears as well as in monkeys.

In the *Râmâyaṇam*, the wise Gâmbavant, the Odysseus of the expedition of Lañkâ, is called now king of the bears (ṛikshapârthivaḥ),[1] now great monkey (mahâkapiḥ).[2]

The word *haris* means fair, golden, reddish, sun, and monkey; the word *kapis* (probably, the changeful one) means monkey and sun. In Sanskṛit, the *vidyut* or thunderbolt, the reddish thunderbolt, of the colour of a monkey, is also called *kapilâ*. Arǵunas, the son of Indras, has for insignia the sun or a monkey, whence his name of Kapidhvaǵas.

Professor Kuhn also supposes that the word *ṛikshas*, which means bear and star, is derived from the root *arć* in the sense of to shine (*arkas* is the sun), on account of the reddish colour of the bear's skin.[3] But *ṛikshas* (like ursus and arktos) may also be derived from *rakshas*, the monster (perhaps as a keeper back, a constrictor, arctor); so that the very word which names it supplies the point of transition from the idea of the divine bear to that of the monster bear.

In the *Ṛigvedas*, the Marutas are represented as the most powerful assistants of Indras; but a Vedic hymn

---

[1] *Râmây.* iv. 63.   [2] v. 55.

[3] For the connection between the seven ṛikshas (ṛishayas, wise men, stars, or bears) of the Hindoos and the septemtriones, the seven stars of the she-bear (Arktos, Arkturus), and the Arctic regions, cfr. the interesting discussion of Professor Max Müller, in the second series of his Lectures.—The seven ṛishayas are the same as the seven Añgirasas, the seven harayas, and the Marutas, who are seven (multiplied by three, that is, twenty-one). In the Marutas, as harayas, we have the monkeys. Even the wife of the king of the monkeys is named Târâ, or, properly, the star. Thus there seems to exist between the monkey and the star the same relation as between the bear and the star, a new argument to vindicate the identity of the two animals in mythology.

already shows them in the light of Indras' rivals. The god Vishṇus in the *Ṛigvedas* is usually a sympathetic form of Indras; but in some hymns he already appears as his antagonist. In the preceding chapter we spoke of the Vishṇuitic bird, of the wind, father of Hanumant, and of a monkey, as enemies of Indras' elephant. In Hindoo epic tradition, Vishṇus, personified in Râmas, has the monkeys for his allies. The most luminous and effulgent form of the god is very distinct from his occult and mysterious appearances. Vishṇus, the sun, the solar rays, the moon and the winds that lighten, are an army of golden monkeys to fight the monster. For the same reason the monkey, on the contrary, has in the *Ṛigvedas* a monstrous form; that which was diabolical becomes divine in the lapse of time, and similarly that which was divine, diabolical. In the eighty-sixth hymn of the tenth book of the *Ṛigvedas*, Vishṇus, personified in Kapis (monkey), or Vṛishâkapis (monkey that pours out, pluvial monkey), comes to destroy the sacrifical offerings loved by Indras. Indras, being superior to all, cuts off his head, as he wishes not to be indulgent to an evil-doer.[1] This monkey is probably the pluvial, reddish lightning cloud carried by the wind, which Indras pierces through with his thunderbolt, although these same lightning and thundering clouds, carried by the winds or Marutas (*i.e.*, the Marutas themselves), are usually represented in the *Ṛigvedas* as assisting the supreme deity. A difference having arisen between Vishṇus and Indras, and between the Marutas and Indras, the Marutas took Vishṇus' part, and became monkeys like Vishṇus,—the word *haris*, which is a

[1] Priyâ tashṭâni me kapir vyaktâ vy adûdushat çiro nv asya râvishaṁ na sugaṁ dushkṛite bhuvaṁ viçvasmâd indra uttaraḥ; str. *5*.

favourite name of Vishṇus (now moon, now sun), meaning also monkey. Vishṇus surrounds himself with fair, reddish, or golden monkeys, or with harayas (solar rays or lightning, thunder-striking and thundering clouds), in the same way as the Vedic Indras was drawn by harayas. Râmas *kapirathas* is simply an incarnation of Vishṇus, who usurps the rights of Indras, which last, as we have seen, had lent his harayas to Vishṇus, in order that he might take his three famous steps. Evidently Vishṇus forgot to return the fair-haired ones to his friend; hence from this time the strength of Indras passes almost entirely into Vishṇus, who, in the form of Râmas, helped by the harayas or red-haired ones, *i.e.*, by the monkeys, moves across the Dekhan (a region densely inhabited by monkeys) to the conquest of the isle of Lañkâ. The *Mahâbhâratam* informs us that monkeys and horses had Harî for their mother.[1] The splendid Marutas form the army of Indras, the red-haired monkeys and bears that of Râmas; and the mythical and solar nature of the monkeys and bears of the *Râmâyaṇam* manifests itself several times. The king of the monkeys is a sun-god. The ancient king was named Bâlin, and was the son of Indras (Çakrasûnus). His young brother, Sugrîvas, he who changes his shape at pleasure (kâmarûpas), who, helped by Râmas, usurped his throne, is said to be own child of the sun (bhâskarasyâurasaḥ putraḥsûryanandanah).[2] Here it is evident that the Vedic antagonism between Indras and Vishṇus is reproduced in a zoological and entirely apish form. The old Zeus must give way to the new, the moon to the sun, the evening to the morning sun, the sun of winter to that of spring; the young sun betrays and overthrows the old one. We

[1] i. 2628.

[2] iii. 75.

have already seen that the legend of the two brothers, Bâlin and Sugrîvas, is one of the forms which the myth of the Açvinâu assumes. Râmas, who treacherously kills the old king of the monkeys, Bâlin, is the equivalent of Vishṇus, who hurls his predecessor, Indras, from his throne; and Sugrîvas, the new king of the monkeys, resembles Indras when he promises to find the ravished Sîtâ, in the same way as Vishṇus, in one of his incarnations, finds again the lost Vedâs. And there are other indications in the *Râmâyaṇam*[1] of opposition between Indras and the monkeys who assist Râmas. The great monkey Hanumant, of the reddish colour of gold (hemapiñgalah), has his jaw broken, Indras having struck him with his thunderbolt, and caused him to fall upon a mountain, because, while yet a child, he threw himself off a mountain into the air in order to arrest the course of the sun, whose rays had no effect upon him.[2] (The cloud rises from the mountain and hides the sun, which is unable of itself to disperse it; the tempest comes, and brings flashes of lightning and thunderbolts, which tear the cloud in pieces.)

The whole legend of the monkey Hanumant represents the sun entering into the cloud or darkness, and coming out of it. His father is said to be now the wind, now the elephant of the monkeys[3] (kapikuṅgaras), now keçarin, the long-haired sun, the sun with a mane, the lion sun (whence his name of *keçariṇaḥ putraḥ*). From this point of view, Hanumant would seem to be the brother of Sugrîvas, who is also the offspring of the sun, the strong brother in the legend of the two brothers connected with that of the three; that is to say, we should have now Bâlin, Hanumant, and Sugrîvas

[1] iv. 5. [2] v. 2, vii. 39. [3] v. 3.

brothers, now Râmas, Hanumant, and Lakshamaṇas. The strong brother is between the other two; the sun in the cloud, in the darkness or in the winter, is placed between the evening sun and that of morning, or between the dying sun of autumn and the new one of spring.

Hanumant flies (like the ass); his powers of flight are seated in his sides and his hips, which serve him for wings. Hanumant ascends to the summit of Mount Mahendras, in order to throw himself into the air; whilst he presses the mountain (a real vrishâkapis), he makes the waters gush out of it; when he moves, the trees of the mountain-forest are torn up by their roots, and follow him in the current made by him as he cuts his way through the air (here we meet once more with the mythical forest, the mythical tree that moves of itself like a cloud). The wind in his armpits roars like a cloud (ǵîmûta iva garǵati), and the shadow that he leaves behind him in the air resembles a line of clouds (megharâǵîva vâyuputrânugâminî);[1] he draws the clouds after him.[2] Thus all the epic monkeys of the *Râmâyaṇam* are described in the twentieth canto of the first book by expressions which very closely resemble those applied in the Vedic hymns to the Marutas, as swift as the tempestuous wind (vâyuvegasamâs), changing their shape at pleasure (kâmarûpiṇas), making a noise like clouds, sounding like thunder, battling, hurling mountain-peaks, shaking great uprooted trees, armed with claws and teeth, shaking the mountains, uprooting trees, stirring up the deep waters, crushing the earth with their arms, lifting themselves into the air, making the clouds fall. Thus Bâlin, the king of the monkeys,

[1] *Râmây.* v. 4, v. 5.

[2] v. 55.

comes out of the cavern, as the sun out of the cloud (toyadâdiva bhâskaraḥ).[1]

In the same way as we have seen the harayas, or horses of Indras, the gandharvâs, and the mythical ass in connection with the salutary waters, with the herbs, and with the perfumes, so in the *Râmâyaṇam* it is the monkeys that carry the herbs and the salutary roots of the mountain, that is, of the cloud-mountain or of the mountain of perfumes.

The cloud in which the sun Hanumant travels through the air throws a shadow upon the sea; a sea-monster perceives this shadow, and by it attracts Hanumant to himself. (We have already seen the fearless hero who is misled by his own shadow and lost.) Hanumant is kâmarûpas, like Sugrîvas, and like all the other monkeys, his companions. When he sees that the monster is about to swallow him, he distends and expands his figure out of all measure; the ogress assumes the same gigantic proportions; when she does so, Hanumant (repeating the miracle of his type Haris, or the dwarf Vishṇus), becomes as small as a man's thumb, enters into the vast body of the monster, and comes out on the other side.) Hanumant continues to fly across the ocean, in order to arrive

[1] *Râmây.* iv. 12, v. 6.—The monkey on the sea is also to be found in a Greek apologue, but the subject is somewhat different. A monkey, which during a tempest had been washed from a ship, and tossed about upon the stormy waves under the promontory of Attica, is mistaken by a dolphin for a man; the dolphin, having great affection for the race to which he presumed he belonged, takes him up and carries him towards the shore. But before letting him touch firm ground, he asks him whether he is an Athenian; the monkey answers that he is of illustrious birth; the dolphin asks if he knows the Piræus; the monkey, thinking that it is a man's name, answers that he is a great friend of his; upon which the dolphin, indignant at having been deceived, lets the monkey fall again into the sea.

at the island of Laṅkâ. The ocean takes pity upon him, and, to help him, raises up Mount Hiraṇyanabhas, *i.e.*, of the golden navel, the mountain whence the sun comes out; indeed, Hanumant says[1] that he struck the mountain with his tail, and broke its summit, that shone like the sun, in order to rest upon it. Hanumant then recommences his flight, and finds a new obstacle in the marine monster Siṅhikâ (the mother of Râhus, the eclipse with a serpent's tail, which devours now the sun, now the moon). She also draws to herself the shadow of Hanumant; Hanumant, resorting once more to his former stratagem, becomes small, and enters into her body; but he is no sooner inside than he increases in bulk, swells out, tears her, kills her, and escapes, a feat for which he receives the homage of the birds, who will thenceforth be able to cross the ocean with impunity.[2] When he arrives in Laṅkâ, Hanumant, that he may search for and find Sîtâ by moonlight, becomes as small as a cat (vṛishadaṅçapramâṇas); when he finds her, and offers to carry her away from Laṅkâ, she cannot believe that so small an animal is able to accomplish so great an enterprise; then Hanumant makes himself as tall as a black cloud, as a high mountain; he breaks down the whole forest of açokâs, mounts upon a temple that stands on a thousand columns, claps his hands, and fills all Laṅkâ with the din; he tears from the temple a pillar adorned with gold, and, swinging it around, devotes the monsters to wholesale slaughter.[3] The mythical monkey and the mythical ass resemble each other; hence the analogy between the legend of Dadhyańć (quoted in the second chapter), that of Samson, and that of Hanumant. But the legend of the monkey Hanumant presents another curious re-

[1] *Râmây.* v. 56. [2] v. 8. [3] v. 37.

semblance to that of Samson. Hanumant is bound with cords by Indraǵit, son of Ravaṇas;[1] he could easily free himself, but does not wish to do so. Ravaṇas, to put him to shame, orders his tail to be burned, because the tail is the part most prized by monkeys (kapînâṁ kila lâñgulam ishṭam, whence the fable of the monkey who complains of having no tail). Hanumant's tail is greased and set on fire, and himself thereafter marched in this plight ignominiously through the streets of Lañkâ. But Sîtâ having invoked the favour of the god Agnis, the fire, though it plays round the tail of Hanumant, does not burn it, and Hanumant by this means is able to avenge himself for the insult, by setting fire to and burning to ashes the city of Lañka.[2] (The tail of Hanumant, which sets fire to the city of the monsters, is probably a personification of the rays of the morning or spring sun, which sets fire to the eastern heavens, and destroys the abode of the nocturnal or winter monsters.) The enterprise of the Marutas in the *Ṛigvedas*, and that of the monkey Hanumant in the *Râmâyaṇam*, assume such dimensions that they obscure the fame of both Indras and Râmas; the former without the Marutas, the latter without Hanumant, would be unable to defeat the monsters. Sîtâ perceives this so clearly, that, at the end of the poem, she makes Hanumant such a present that Râmas might well become jealous. Hanumant, however, is an honest and pious cavalier; it suffices him to have

---

1 *Râmây.* v. 56.

2 v. 50.—In the *Pańćatantram*, v. 10, it is said, on the contrary, that monkeys possess the virtue of healing the wounds of horses that have been scalded or burned, as the sun of morning chases the darkness away. According to a variety of this story contained in the *Tuti-Name*, i. 130, the bite of a monkey can be cured only by the blood of the very monkey who had inflicted it.

defended justice in the service of his master, nor does he ask to be recompensed for the hard achievement that he has accomplished. For the rest, a popular Hindoo sentence says that monkeys are not accustomed to weep for themselves;[1] they weep (rodanti) for others. The same is true of the Rudrâs, or winds, that weep in the cloud; they do not lament for themselves; their tears fall upon the ground in beneficent rain that fertilises our fields and tempers the heat of our summers; nevertheless, they themselves afterwards feel, as solar rays, the benefit of weeping, that is, of rain. In the *Râmâyaṇam*, monkeys who die in battle are resuscitated by rain; when the cloud dissolves itself in rain, the fair-haired, the golden ones, the harayas, the sunbeams or monkeys, show themselves again in all their vigour.

We have seen thus far the cloud-monkey, from which the sun emerges, and into which he re-enters. But we have already said more than once that the sun often assumes a monstrous form, when enclosed in the cloud or the darkness. It is thus we explain the divine hero Balarâmas, who, in the *Vishṇu P.*,[2] destroys the demon Dvividas, who had taken the form of a monkey. In the eighteenth story of the first book of the *Pańćatantram*, a monkey, whilst the wind blows and the rain falls, shakes a tree upon which a sparrow has made its nest, and breaks the eggs in pieces. In the tenth story of the fifth book, the king of the monkeys, by means of a crown of pearls, attracts a king of men who had killed monkeys to cure his horses (to which the fire had been communicated by the wool of a ram which the cook had chased away from the kitchen with a burning brand) to a

[1] Ağńatakulaçîle 'pi prîtiṁ kurvanti vânarâḥ âtmârthe ća na rodanti; Böhtlingk, *Indische Sprüche*, 107.

[2] v. 36.

fountain guarded by a monster who devours the king and his suite. In the eleventh story of the same book, a monkey upon a tree is the friend of one of the two crepuscular monsters, and this monster invites it to eat the man; the man, however, retaliates, and fiercely bites its long tail; the monkey then believes this man to be stronger than the monster, and the latter believes the man who holds the monkey by the tail with his teeth to be the monster of the other twilight, *i.e.*, the morning twilight. Here the monkey is confounded with the fox, which is a mythical animal of a specially crepuscular nature, and which also comes to ruin on account of its tail. The reader has already observed how the incendiary monkey-tail of Hanumant corresponds to the tails of the foxes. in the legend of Samson. The Hellenic and Latin proverbs generally regard the monkey as a very cunning animal, so much so that Hercules and the monkey represented the combination of strength and deceit. According to Cardano, a monkey seen in dreams is a presage of deceit. According to Lucian, it was an augury of an unlucky day to meet with a monkey in the early morning. The Spartans considered it an omen of most sinister import that the monkey of the king of the Molossians had upset their urn while they were going to consult the oracle. According to Suetonius, when Nero thought he saw his horse flee, having the shape of a monkey in his hind parts, he believed it to prognosticate death. The monkey, accordingly, was usually conceived of in Greece and at Rome as a cunning and demoniacal animal. The hero in the cloud, in the dark, or in hell, on the other hand, learns wisdom; and just as before this he is only a poor fool, so the monkey, too, is also sometimes represented in the ancient fables of Southern Europe as an animal full of simplicity. In Italy we have a proverb which says that every monkey thinks her young ones beautiful; this refers to the apologue of the monkey that believes her young ones to be the most beautiful animals in the world, because Jove, seeing them one day leaping about, could not refrain from laughing. The fox, in an epigram, laughs at the monkey who craves from him the half of his tail, on the plea that it would disencumber himself of just so much useless appendage, and supply his suitor with the very covering required to protect his all too naked buttocks:—

> "Malo verrat humum quam sit tibi causa decoris,
> Quam tegat immundas res bene munda nates."

In India the analogy between the monkey and the ass, as a stupid animal, is of still more frequent occurrence. In the *Pańćatantram* we have the monkeys who try to warm themselves by the light of the glowworm; a monkey presuming to correct the handiwork of a carpenter, meets with its death by putting its hands into the cleft of a tree trunk, and heedlessly withdrawing the wedge that caused it. In the *Tuti-Name*,[1] we find a variety of the story of the ass and the lyre, *i.e.*, the wise Sâz-Perdâz, who learns from the monkey, assisted by the wind, the way to form musical instruments. (The thundering cloud is the mythical musical instrument *par excellence;* it is the wind that moves it, it is the wind that makes it sound: the hero in the cloud, gandharvas, ass or monkey, is a musician.)

The strong, powerful, and terrible bear of the Marutas,[2] or winds, in the stormy, lightning and thundering cloud, is already mentioned in the Vedic hymn. So the con-

[1] i. 266.

[2] Ṛiksho na vo mârutaḥ çimîvâñ amo dadhro gâuriva bhîmayuḥ *Ṛigv.* v. 56, 3.

stellation of the she-bear[1] seems also to be referred to in them. In the *Râmâyaṇam*,[2] we find in connection with it the legend of King Triçañkus, who, cursed by the sons of Vasishṭhas, becomes a ćandalas, covered with the skin of a bear (ṛikshaćarmanivâsî). Viçvâmitras, the rival of Vasishṭhas, promises to introduce it into heaven, under cover of his own body; but Indras scorns to admit it, and indignantly spurns it, hurling it down heels over head. Viçvâmitras arrests it in its descent as it falls with its head downmost, within the constellation of the seven ṛishayas or wise men, that is to say, in the constellation of the Great Bear. And as the bear is in relation with the polar constellàtion, with the north, the frigid regions, the winter and the stars, so the moon, who rules particularly over the cold night in the icy season, is called in Sanskṛit *ṛiksharâǵas* and *ṛiksheças*, or king of the luminous ones, king of the stars, king of the bears. The king of the bears also takes part in the expedition to Lañka. The king of the bears (here in relation to the moon) is the eunuch, the reputed, father, the St Joseph, of the king of the monkeys, Sugrîvas, who was, on the contrary, really generated in the bosom of the wife of the bear-king, by the magnanimous sun.[3] Led on by the bear or monkey Gâmbavant, the king of the bears (ṛikshapârthivas), the monkeys enter into the forest of the honey (madhuvanam), guarded by the monkey Dadhimukhas (mouth of butter, generated by Somas, the ambrosial god Lunus),[4] and devastate and ransack the forest in order to suck its honey.[5] In the *Vishṇu P.*,[6] even Balarâmas, brother of the god Kṛishnas, makes

1 Amî ya ṛikshâ nihitâsa uććâ; *Ṛigv.* i. 24, 10.
2 *Râmây.* i. 60–62. 3 vi. 46. 4 vi. 6.
5 v. 59. 6 v. 25.

himself drunk with the spirituous liquor contained in the fissure of a tree.

The bear-eater of honey is an extremely popular subject of Russian tradition; the very name of the bear, medv-jed, means in Russian, "he who eats honey" (*miod* is honey, and *iest* to eat; but the form *medv* [medu] is more perfectly equivalent to the Hindoo *madhu* = the sweet honey ambrosia; the bear in the *madhuvanam* corresponds entirely to the medvjed or bear who eats honey of the Russians). In a Slavonic story referred to by Afanassieff in the observations to the first book of the Russian stories, the bear, deceived by the hare, is left shut up in the trunk of a tree. A peasant passes by; the bear begs him to deliver it from this trunk, promising to show him a bee-hive, and beseeching him not to tell any one that a hare had deceived it. The peasant frees the bear; the bear shows the bee-hive, the peasant takes the honey and goes home.[1] The bear goes and

[1] This story, with some variations, was already known in the sixteenth century: "Demetrius Moschovitarum legatus Romam missus, teste Paulo Jovio (quoted by Aldrovandi), narravit proximis annis viciniæ suæ agricolam quærendi mellis causa in prægrandem et cavam arborem superne desiliisse, eumque profundo mellis gurgite collo tenus fuisse immersum et biduo vitam solo melle sustinuisse, cum in illâ solitudine vox agricolæ opem implorantis ad viatorum aures non perveniret. Tandem hic, desperata salute, ursæ beneficio extractus evasit, nam hujus feræ ad mella edenda more humano in arboris civitatem se demittentis, pellem tergoris manibus comprehendit et inde ab ursa subito timore exterrita et retrocedente extractus fuit."—The bear is also celebrated in Kriloff's fables as an eater of honey.—In an apologue of Abstemius, the bear, when searching for honey, is stung by a bee; he avenges himself by destroying the honeycombs, but the swarms of bees fly upon him, and sting and torment him on every side; the bear then complains that by not having known how to support a small evil he had drawn upon himself a very grave one.—The pears of the Italian proverb in connection with the bear also refer to hydromel or to honey. The Italian proverbs are as follows: "Dar le pere in

listens at the door to overhear the conversation. The peasant narrates how he had procured the honey by means of a bear who, following a hare, had been caught in a tree. The bear determines to have its revenge. One day it finds the peasant in the field, and is about to fall upon and rend him,[1] when the fox makes its appearance, shakes its tail, and says to the peasant, "Man, thou hast ingenuity in thy head, and a stick in thy hand." The peasant immediately understands the stratagem. He begs the bear to let him perform his devotions first; and offers, as a devotion, instead of doing penance, to carry the bear, shut up in a sack, three times round the field, after which the bear is to do with him whatever it likes.

---

guardia all' orso" (to give the pears to be guarded by the bear); "Chi divide la pera (or il miele) all' orso ne ha sempre men che parte" (he who divides the pear (or the honey) with the bear, always has less than a part, that is, the bear eats it all), and "L'orso sogna pere" (the bear dreams of pears). To catch the bear is the same as to be inebriated; the bear, in fact, is, in the legends, often inebriated himself with honey, as the Vedic Indras with the ambrosia, and as Balarâmas in the spirituous liquor contained in the fissure of a tree (*Vishṇu-P.* v. 25). The sun in the cloud or in the rainy or wintry season drinks more than necessary. Cfr. also Ralston, *Songs of the Russian People*, p. 182.

[1] In the fifteenth story of *Afanassieff*, the bear revenges himself upon an old man who had cut off one of his paws with a hatchet; the bear makes himself a paw from the wood of a linden-tree, takes the old man and the old woman by surprise in their house and devours them. In the nineteenth story of the fourth book, the bear allies himself with the fox lamed by the peasant, and with the gadfly that the peasant had placed behind the straw, in order to revenge himself upon the peasant, who, promising to cover him with spots like the horse, had struck him here and there on the body with a red-hot axe, so that the bones were left bare. This fable is perhaps connected with the Hindoo superstition that the burns of a horse are cured by means of a monkey. As to the wooden paws, they are doubtless the branches of the cloudy or nocturnal forest. In the *Edda* of Sömund it is said that the Alfes are accustomed to call the trees the beautiful arms; we already know the meaning of the boy with the golden hand.

The bear, proud of being carried by the man,[1] enters into the sack; the man binds it strongly, and then beats it so with his stick that it dies.

The bear, representing usually the luminous one in the darkness, has frequently in Slavonic tradition a demoniacal character,[2] or else that of a fool, like the ass. In the first of the Russian stories, the fox terrifies the bear, and then delivers the peasant from it. (The peasant in popular rustic narratives is almost always a heroic personage, who becomes a wiseacre and a prince.) The peasant cheats his companion, the bear, twice: when they sow turnips together, the peasant reserves for himself whatever grows underground, and leaves to the bear whatever comes out of the earth and appears above; when they sow wheat, the bear, thinking to be very knowing, takes for his own part what grows under, and gives to the peasant what grows above the ground. The peasant is about to be devoured by the bear, when

[1] In the tenth story of the third book of *Afanassieff*, Nadzei, the son of a virgin who is the daughter of a priest, makes himself formidable by cutting down the forest and drawing, without assistance, out of the forest the bear that destroyed the cats.

[2] In a description of the last Sunday of the Roman carnival of the thirteenth century, in Du Cange, *s. v. Carnelevarium*, we read: "Occidunt ursum, occiditur diabolus, id est, temptator nostræ carnis."—In Bohemia it is still the custom at the end of the carnival to bring the bear,—that is, a man disguised as a bear, with straw, who goes round to ask for beer (or hydromel, which takes the place of the mythical honey or ambrosia). The women take the straws to put them into the place where the hens lay their eggs, to make them lay better. In Suabia the straw bear is accused of having killed a blind cat, and therefore condemned, with all formality, to death, after having had, before his death, two priests to console him; on Ash-Wednesday the bear is solemnly buried.—Cfr. Reinsberg von Düringfeld, *Das festliche Jahr.*—The poet Hans Sachs, quoted by Simrock, covers with a bear's skin two old women who are to be presented to the devil.

the fox comes to the rescue.[1] In the first story of the fourth book of *Afanassieff*, the fox goes to pass the winter in the bear's den, and devours all the provision of hens that the bear had laid up. The bear asks what it is eating, and the fox makes him believe that it is taking meat from its own forehead. The bear asks whether it is good, upon which the fox gives him some to taste; the bear then tries also to take meat from his forehead, and dies; thus the fox has enough to eat for a year.

The romance of the fox also presents to us the fox in opposition to the bear, whom he induces to put his paws into the cleft of the trunk of a tree, as happened to the Hindoo monkey of the *Pańćatantram*. In the Russian story,[2] instead of the fox, we have the peasant, and instead of the monkey and the bear, we have the gentleman (who in the poor man's eyes is often a personification of the demon) who is caught by his hands in the fissure of a tree. The peasant revenges himself in this way upon the gentleman who had, after having bought from others a little canary for fifteen roubles, refused to buy from him a large goose for a hundred roubles. The very strong athlete Milôn of Kroton, who in one day used to eat an ox four years old, a legendary hero, is torn to pieces by wild beasts, having been caught by the hands in the crevice of a log which he was splitting. Animal and hero continually alternate in myths. In the fourth story of the fifth book of *Afanassieff*, the peasant meets with his death on account of the funereal and demoniacal storks and the bear. The peasant binds himself to his waggon in order not to fall off; the horse wishes to

[1] Cfr., moreover, *Afanassieff*, ii. 33.—In a popular Norwegian story, the fox makes the bear catch fish with his tail, which is frozen in the water.

[2] *Afanassieff*, v. 2.

drink, and drags the waggon into a well. The bear, being pursued, passes by, falls unexpectedly into the well, becomes involved with the waggon, and, in order to extricate himself, is constrained to drag out waggon, peasant, and all. Soon afterwards the bear, in search of honey, climbs up a tree; another peasant passes, sees the bear upon the tree, and wishing to secure the animal, cuts down the tree; bear and waggon fall down, and the peasant is killed, whilst the bear releases itself and escapes. The bear which is looking for honey and the bear in the well remind us of the *asinus in unguento*, and of the ass in the roses: the ass who is the friend of the gardener or of the priest of Flora and Pomona, in the fable of La Fontaine,[1] has the same signification. In the twenty-eighth story of the fifth book of *Afanassieff*, King Bear lies hidden in a fountain (we have already seen the Hindoo monkey that draws a king into a fountain, into the monster's jaws); a king goes to hunt; feeling thirsty, he wishes to drink at this fountain; the bear clutches him by the beard, and only releases him on condition that he will give up in his stead whatever he has at home without knowing it (this is a variation of the story of Hariçćandras). The king consents, and returning home, learns that twins, named Ivan and Maria, are born to him. To save them from the bear, their father has them lowered into a subterranean cavern, well furnished and very deep, which he supplies with abundant provisions. The twins grow up healthy and strong; the king and queen die, and the bear comes to search for the twins. He finds in the royal palace a pair of scissors, and asks them where the king's sons are; the scissors answer, "Throw me upon the ground in the courtyard;

[1] viii. 10.

where I fall, there search." The scissors fall over the very place under which Ivan and Maria are concealed. The bear opens the ground with his paws, and is about to devour the young brother and sister; they beg for their lives, and the bear spares them, at sight of the abundance of hens and geese provided for them. The bear then resolves to take them into his service; they twice attempt in vain to escape, the first time with the help of a hawk, the second with that of an eagle: at last a bull succeeds in releasing them. Pursued by the bear, they throw down a comb, and an impenetrable forest springs up; the bear lacerates and wounds himself all over in passing through. Ivan then spreads out a towel which makes a lake of fire; at this sight the bear, who is afraid of being burned, who does not like heat, but, on the contrary, prefers cold, goes back.

In the twenty-seventh story of the fifth book of *Afanassieff*, a demoniacal bear with iron hairs, devastates a whole kingdom, devouring all the inhabitants; Ivan Tzarević and Helena Prekrasnaia alone remain; but the king has them placed with provisions upon a high pillar (a new form of Mount Hiraṇyanabhas, whence the sun issues forth, which comes up from the bottom of the sea, and upon which the great monkey Hanumant places himself. The bear is also found in connection with a gem in the *Vishnu P.*[1]) In the *Tuti-Name*,[2] the carpenter teaches two bears to take their food upon a statue which is a perfect image of his companion the miserly goldsmith, who had defrauded him of some money. By means of the bears, whom he represents as the two sons of the goldsmith who had run away from him, he terrifies him. The goldsmith, perceiving the carpen-

[1] iv. 13. [2] i. 6.

ter's craftiness, gives him back his money). The famished bear approaches the pillar. Ivan throws him down some food; the bear, after having eaten, goes to sleep.[1] While he sleeps, Ivan and Helena flee away upon a horse; the bear awakes, overtakes them, brings them back to the pillar, and makes them throw him down some food, after which he again goes to sleep. The young brother and sister then try to escape upon the backs of geese; the bear again wakens, overtakes them, burns the geese, and takes Ivan and Helena back to the pillar. Having a third time supplied the bear with food, it is again overcome by sleep; this time the deliverer comes in the shape of a bull, who blinds the bear with his horns, and throws him into a stream, where he is drowned. In the same story, the demon, wishing to expose Ivan to certain death, sends him to search for the milk of a she-bear.[2] The demon appears again in the form of a bear in the fiftieth story of the fifth book of *Afanassieff*, where the dog of a soldier rends him to pieces. But although the bear is demoniacal, the bear's cub, on the other hand, helps the hero.[3] In the eleventh story of the sixth book

---

[1] Concerning the bear's sleep, it is interesting to read the curious information furnished by Aldrovandi (*De Quadr. Dig. Viv.* i.): "Devorant etiam ursi ineunte hyeme radices nomine nobis adhuc ignotas, quibus per longum temporis spatium cibi cupiditas expletur et somnus conciliatur. Nam in Alpibus Helveticis aiunt, referente Gesnero, vaccarum pastorem eminus vidisse ursum, qui radicem quemdam manibus propriis effossam edebat, et post ursi discessum, illuc se transtulisse; radicemque illam degustasse, qui postmodum tanto somni desiderio affectus est, ut se continere non potuerit, quin in viâ stratus somno frueretur." The bear, as a nocturnal and wintry animal, must of necessity conciliate sleep.

[2] Cfr. *Afanassieff*, vi. 5.—According to Hellenic tradition, Paris and Atalanta were nourished with the milk of a she-bear.

[3] Cfr. *Afanassieff*, v. 27, v. 28.—According to Cardano, to meet with a bear's cub just born indicated a change of fortune for the better.

of *Afanassieff*, a woman who is gathering mushrooms loses herself and enters into the bear's den—the bear takes her to himself. We have already seen the bear that plays at blind-man's-buff with the mouse, thinking that he is playing with the beautiful maiden. The wind Rudras and Æolus, king of the winds, we have already seen, in the first chapter of this book, to be passionately fond of beautiful nymphs. In a Norwegian story (a variation of that of the White Cat), in *Asbiörnsen*, the hero is disguised as a bear, and becomes a beautiful young man by night. His wife, by her indiscreet curiosity, *i.e.*, because she had wished to see him by lamplight, loses him, and her place is taken by the long-nosed princess, until, with the help of a golden apple and a horse, she is able to find her husband again. In the sixth story of the second book of the *Pentamerone*, it is, on the other hand, the girl Pretiosa who, to escape the embraces of her father, goes into the forest disguised as a she-bear. A young prince, the son of the king of the water, becomes enamoured of her, and takes her to the palace. The prince becomes ill for love of the she-bear; she assists him and cures him. While he is kissing her, she becomes a beautiful girl ("la chiù bella cosa de lo Munno"). We learn from two mediæval writings quoted by Du Cange (*s.v. Ursus*), that it was already the custom in the Middle Ages to lead the bear round to make him play indecent games ("Nec turpia joca cum urso vel tornatricibus ante se facere permittat"), and that hairs of a bear stained in some ointment used to be sold, "Tamquam philacteria, ad depellendos morbos, atque, adeo oculorum fascinos amoliendos." The Athenians called she-bears the virgins sacred to the chaste Artemis, the friend of closed places; and to this, it would appear, must also be referred the interesting

Christian legend of the virgin St Ursula,[1] whom Karl Simrock identifies with the demoniacal, funereal, somniferous, death-bringing Holda. Were this identification accepted, Ursula would be, moreover, in close ideal and etymological relation with the Vedic monster Ṛikshikâ.

But to return to the Russian story, the woman who enters into the bear's den unites herself with him, and subsequently gives birth to a son, who is a man down to the waist, and a bear from the waist downwards. His mother, therefore, names him Ivanko-Medviedko (Little John, the son of the bear). This half-man half-bear becomes a cunning animal, and cheats the devil, making him fight with the bear, and persuading him to think that the bear is his middle brother (that is, the strong brother). In a Danish tradition we read of a girl violated by a bear, who gives birth afterwards to a monster. According to the Hellenic myth, the nymph Kalistos, daughter of King Lykaon, violated by Zeus, is changed by Juno or by Artemis into a she-bear, gives birth to Arkas, and, being killed with her son by shepherds, is converted into a star.

The cunning bear appears again as a musician (like the ass) in the seventeenth story of the third book of *Afanassieff*, where he sings so well that he deceives the old shepherdess, and succeeds in carrying off her sheep. In a note to the ninth Esthonian story of Kreutzwald, Herr Löwe observes, that in the Northern languages, the god of thunder and the bear are synonymous. The bear, the monkey, the ass, and the bull (all of which are personifications of the cloud), form a musical quartette in a

[1] Cfr. the work of Schade, *Die Sage von der Heiligen Ursula.* She is also to be found among the *Leggende del Secolo Decimoquarto,* published at Florence by Signor Del Lungo (Barbera, publisher).

fine fable of Kriloff. The bear is made to dance like the monkey,[1] the ass, and the gandharvas, his mythical equivalent. In the same way as the ass's skin chases away fear, the eye of a bear dried and hung upon a child's neck preserves from fear.[2] In the legends of the saints, especially of the hermits, to whom the bear, inspired by God, often gives up his den in obedience to their commands, we read of St Maximin that he transformed a bear into an ass because he had eaten an ass that carried a load.

In the nineteenth fable of the twelfth book of *La Fontaine*, the monkey appears as a messenger of Jove, with the caduceus, to

> "Partager un brin d'herbe entre quelques fourmis;"

while two enormous animals, the elephant and the rhinoceros, are contending for the superiority. The monkey, as Mercury, as an intermediate and mediating form between two heroic similar animals, comes near to the knowing fox, the reddish colour of which (as well as of the bear) it partakes of. It is no longer the pure fair sun of day, and it is not yet the black monster of night; it is too black to be red, and too red to be black; it has

---

1 ". . . il parle, on l'entend, il sait danser, baller
Faire des tours de toute sorte
Passer en des cerceaux."
—*La Fontaine*, *Fables*, ix. 3.

In *La Fontaine*, the monkey is again identified with the ass, as a judge on the tribunal between the wolf and the fox, and afterwards as dressed in the skin of the dead lion. In the fourth fable of the eleventh book, La Fontaine makes the monkey M.A. narrate the story of the *asinus asinum fricat;* in the second fable of the twelfth book the monkey scatters the miser's treasure, as in Hindoo tradition it spoils the sacrificial offerings.

2 Cfr. Aldrovandi, *De Quadr. Dig. Viv.*

all the cunning of the devils, and is acquainted with all the habits of the saints. The monkey, the imitator of man (a Darwinist would say his progenitor), partakes, like man, of the nature of the brutish demon and of the intelligent god.

CHAPTER XII.

THE FOX, THE JACKAL, AND THE WOLF.

SUMMARY.

Lopâças, lopâçikâ.—The jackal takes in Hindoo tradition the place of the fox.—What the fox represents in mythology, and why the jackal is his mythical equivalent.—Double aspect of the mythical fox, in connection with the cock and in connection with the wolf, turned towards the day and towards the night, now friendly, now hostile to the hero.—The fox deceives all the other animals, in order to have all the prey to itself.—The fox is the monster's enemy.—The blue jackal.—The inquisitive jackal.—The avenging jackal.—The astute fox; the woman more cunning than the fox.—The fox's skin.—The buttered tail of the jackal.—The fox eats the honey, the butter, or the cake belonging to the wolf, and then accuses him.—The fox sends the wolf to fish.—The fox eats the woman whom he had promised to bring to life.—The fox as a mourner.—The peasant ungrateful to the fox.—"Cauda de vulpe testatur."—The fox eats the bear; the bird feeds the fox, and afterwards draws it in among the dogs.—Former hospitality is to be forgotten.—The fox as the cat's wife.—The round cheese of the myth is the moon.—The fox steals the fishes.—The fox is of every profession.—The grateful fox enriches the poor hero.—King Fire and Queen Loszna.—The house of the fox and that of the hare.—The fox deceives the cock; the cock deceives the fox.—The fox's tail in the beaks of the chickens.—The fox's malice; the ideal of a prince according to Macchiavelli; fox and serpent.—The fox cheats almost all the animals; it does not, however, succeed in cheating the other foxes, and sometimes not even the lion.—The Catholic Church furnishes new types for the legend of the fox.—Union of the fox with the wolf.—Diverse nature of the wolf.—The red wolf.—The thieving wolf.—The wolf (or the devil) and the fishes; the fish in shallow water.—The dog and the wolf.—

The wolf as a shepherd.—Wolf's belly.—The good wolf and the good maiden.—The son of the wolf understands the language of birds. —The she-wolf as a nurse; she-wolves and strumpets.—Disguises in a wolf's skin.—Wolf-hunter.—The wolf's shadow.—Wolves that chastise in the name of God; sanctified wolves.—The dead wolf; the wolf's skin.—Diabolical wolves.—The white wolf.—Wulfesheofod.—Ysengrin.—The wolf sings psalms.—The cunning of the wolf.—The wolf's tail.—The dwarf in the wolf's body; the dwarf in the wolf's sack.—The she-wolf at Rome.—Dante's she-wolf.

THE fox is scarcely spoken of once in the *Ṛigvedas* by the name of lopâças (alôpêx), as penetrating to the old Western lion; this word (like *lopâkas*, which is interpreted in the Petropolitan Dictionary as "a kind of jackal") seems to mean properly "the destroyer" (according to Professor Weber, *Aasfresser*). The Sanskṛit language also gives us the diminutive *lopâçikâ*, which is interpreted as the female of a jackal and as the fox (vulpecula). The legendary fox, however, is generally represented in Hindoo tradition by the jackal, or *canis aureus* (sṛigâlas, kroshṭar, gomâyus, as a shouter). The fox is the reddish mediatrix between the luminous day and the gloomy night: the crepuscular phenomenon of the heavens taking an animal form, no form seemed more adapted to the purpose than that of the fox or the jackal, on account of their colour and some of their cunning habits: the hour of twilight is the time of uncertainties and of deceits. Professor Weber[1] supposes that all the cunning actions attributed to the jackal in Hindoo fables were taken on loan from the fox of Hellenic fables. We must certainly assign no undue importance to the expressions *vańćakas* and *mṛigadhûrtakas* (the cheater of

[1] Cfr. *Ueber den Zusammenhang indischer Fabeln mit griechischen*, Berlin, Dümmler, 1855.

animals), given in Hindoo lexicons to the jackal, inasmuch as these lexicons are not of very remote antiquity; but at the same time we must confess, that the cunning of the fox has been exaggerated by popular superstition as much as the stupidity of the ass, for a mythical reason, and from tradition, far more than by the observation of exceptional habits in these animals, which could easily be identified in mythology, in which, as I have already observed, some few gross and accidental similarities are enough to cause the same phenomena to be represented by animals of a very different genus. Thus the hairy reddish bodies of the bear and the monkey, and certain postures which they assume in common, are enough to make us understand how they are sometimes substituted for each other in legends; for the same reason, to the monkey and to the bear are attributed some of the enterprises for which the legendary fox is celebrated. How much greater, therefore, must have been the confusion which arose between the *canis vulpes* (the reddish fox) and the *canis aureus* (or jackal), animals which agree in showing themselves towards night, in feeding upon little animals, in having skins of the same colour, who have very bright eyes, and several other zoological characteristics in common?

The legendary fox (or the jackal, which is its mythical equivalent) has, like nearly all mythical figures, a double aspect. As it represents the evening, and as the sun is represented as a bird (the cock), the fox, the proverbial enemy of chickens, is, in the sky too, the robber and devourer of the cock, and as such the natural enemy of the man or hero, who ends by showing himself to be more cunning than it is, and by effecting its ruin. The fox cheats the cock in the evening, and is cheated by the cock in the morning. It is therefore an animal of demoniacal nature, when considered as the devourer or betrayer of the sun (cock, lion, or man), in the form of the red western sky, or of the evening aurora, and as being killed or put to flight by the sun itself (cock, lion, or man), in the form of the red eastern sky, or the morning aurora.[1] We have already seen, in the first chapter of this work, the aurora both as a wise girl and a perverse one; in its animal metamorphosis, the fox reproduces this aspect. But the aurora has not this mythical aspect alone. If, as she is turned towards or against the sun, she is supposed to be the killer of the luminous day in the evening, and to be chased away by the luminous day in the morning, she also, when considered as turning towards or against the night, assumes a heroic and sympathetic aspect, and becomes the friend and assister of the solar hero or animal against the wolf of the darkness of night. In these two mythical aspects is contained and explained all the essential legendary story of the fox, to narrate which, as far as it concerns Western tradition, volumes have already been written. I shall limit myself to culling and summarising from Oriental and Slavonic tradition their chief characteristics, in order to compare them briefly with the most generally known particulars of Western legendary lore; as it seems to me that when I shall have shown the double nature of the fox in mythology, as representing the two auroras, when I shall have proved that the sun is personified now as a hero, now as a cock, and now as a lion, and the night as a wolf, it will be easy to refer to this interpretation the

[1] In a German tradition referred to by Schmidt, *Forschungen*, s. 105, we have the deity who presents himself as a fox to the hunter voluntarily to be sacrificed; the hunter flays him, and the flies and ants eat his flesh. In a Russian story of which I shall give an abridgment, the wolf eats the fox when he sees it without its hairy covering.

immense variety of legendary subjects to which, on account of the smaller proportions to which I have been obliged to reduce this work, I shall be unable to allude.

In the *Mahâbhâratam*,[1] a learned jackal, who has finished his studies, associates with the ichneumon, the mouse, the wolf, and the tiger, but only in order to cheat them all. He makes the tiger kill a gazelle, and then sends all the animals to bathe before eating it. Then, when the tiger returns, he makes him run after the mouse, by representing it as having boasted that it had killed the tiger; he makes the mouse flee, persuading it that the ichneumon has bitten the gazelle, and that its flesh is therefore poisonous; he makes the wolf take to its heels, by informing it that the tiger is coming to devour it; he makes the ichneumon glad to escape, by boasting that he has vanquished the other three animals; then the jackal eats the whole gazelle himself. In the *Pańćatantram*,[2] the jackal cheats, in a similar manner, the lion and the wolf out of their part of a camel; we have already seen how it cheated the lion out of the ass. In the twentieth Mongol story, the fox stirs up discord between the two brothers, bull and lion, who kill each other in consequence.

In the *Râmâyaṇam*,[3] the jackal appears as the hero's friend, inasmuch as by howling, and vomiting fire, he is of sinister omen to the monster Kharas, who prepares to attack Râmas. In the *Khorda-Avesta*, a hero devoured

[1] i. 5566, *et seq.*

[2] i. 16, iv. 2; cfr. also iv. 10, and the chapter on the Hare.—In the story, iii. 14, of the *Pańćatantram*, the jackal cheats the lion who has occupied his cave, by making him roar; and thus assuring himself that the lion is in the cave, he is able to escape.

[3] iii. 29.

by Agra-Mainyu, the god of the monsters, is named Takhmo-urupis, or Takhma-urupa, which means strong fox.

One of the most interesting fables, in a mythological point of view, is that of the jackal who, falling among pigments, comes out blue, or of opaline lustre, and passes himself off as a peacock of the sky. The animals make him their king, but he betrays himself by his voice: hearing other jackals howling, he howls also; upon which the lion, the real king of the beasts, tears him to pieces.[1] This is a variety of the ass dressed in the lion's skin, but yet more so of the crow that takes up and decks itself in the peacock's feathers; the black night shines as an azure sky, as sahasrâkshas (an appellation of Indras and of the peacock, as having a thousand eyes or stars). The evening aurora, the fox, transforms itself into the azure sky of night, until at morn, the deceit being exposed, the lion (*i.e.*, the sun) rends the fox, and disperses the night and the aurora.

The *Pańćatantram* contains two other narratives relating to the legendary jackal—viz., the inquisitive and silly jackal, who, in an attempt to break the skin of a drum to see what is inside, breaks one of his teeth, and who, wishing to eat the string of a bow, has his mouth lacerated and dies;[2] and the vile jackal who, brought up among the lion's cubs, reveals his vulpine nature when he should have thrown himself with the two lions, his adoptive brothers, upon the elephant, but, instead of that,

[1] Cfr. *Pańćatantram*, i. 10; *Tuti-Name*, ii. 146.

[2] i. 2, ii. 3.—In the nineteenth Mongol story, the young man who passes himself off as a hero is ordered to bring to the queen the skin of a certain fox which is indicated to him; on the way the youth loses his bow; returning to look for it, he finds the fox dead close to the bow, which it had tried to bite, and which had struck and killed it.

took to flight.[1] In the *Tuti-Name*,[2] the jackal desires to revenge himself upon the parrots, whom he judges indirectly implicated in the death of his young ones; up comes the lynx, who is astounded that the jackal, celebrated for its craftiness, is unable to devise a way of ruining the parrots. At last the lynx advises him to pretend being lame, and let himself be followed by a hunter as far as the abode of the parrots, at which place he will be able to skulk away, and the hunter, seeing the parrots, will set his nets and catch them.

In the *Tuti-Name* we also find several other particulars relating to the jackal, which will pass into the Russian stories of the fox.

The jackal makes the wolf come out of his den, which the latter had taken possession of, by calling the shepherd.[3] In another place, the cunning fox laughs at the stolid tiger, but the woman proves herself to be more cunning than the fox.[4] It is also in the *Tuti-Name*[5] that we read of a companion of the poor Abdul Meǵid, enamoured of the king's daughter, who teaches him how to enrich himself, or rather to appear rich, in order to wed her. In a much more scientific and interesting variety of this legend, in the Russian stories, it is, on the contrary, the fox who enriches the poor hero. The nineteenth Mongol story, in which the false hero makes his fortune by means of the spoils of a certain designated

[1] iv. 4.

[2] i. 134, 135.

[3] *Tuti-Name*, ii. 125.—In the stories of the same night (the twenty-second) of the *Tuti-Name*, we have the lynx (lupus cervarius) who wishes to take the house of the monkey who occupies the lion's house, and the jackal who runs after the camel's testicles, as in the *Pańćatantram* he runs after those of the bull. In the story, ii. 7, the fox lets his bone fall into the water in order to catch a fish (a variety of the well-known fable of the dog and of the wolf or devil as fisherman).

[4] *Tuti-Name*, ii. 142, 143.

[5] i. 168, *et seq.*

fox, is another intermediate form between the two traditions, the Hindoo and the Russian.

The name of a jackal in the *Pańćatantram* is Dadhipuććhas, which means tail of butter, buttered tail (the aurora is ambrosial).

In the first of the stories of *Afanassieff*, the fox eats the honey belonging to the wolf (which reminds one of the sentence of Plautus, "Sæpe condita luporum fiunt rapinæ vulpium"[1]), and then accuses the wolf of having eaten it himself; the wolf proposes a sort of judgment of God; they are to go together to the sun, and he who pours out honey will be accounted guilty: they go and lie down; the wolf falls asleep, and when the honey comes out of the fox, he pours it upon the wolf, who, when he awakes, confesses his fault. In the first story of the fourth book of *Afanassieff*, the cock and the hen bring ears of corn to the old man and poppies to the old woman; the old couple make a cake of them and put it out to dry.[2] Up come the fox and the wolf and take the cake, but finding that it is not yet dry, the fox proposes going to sleep whilst it is drying. While the wolf sleeps, the fox eats the honey that is in the cake, and puts dung in its place. The wolf awakens, and after him the fox too pretends to waken, and accuses the wolf of having touched the cake; the wolf protests his innocence, and the fox proposes, as a judgment of God, that they shall go to sleep in the sunshine; the wax will come out of

[1] *Querolus*, i. 2.

[2] In the eighteenth story of the fourth book of *Afanassieff*, an extraordinary cake escapes from the house of an old man and woman, and wanders about; it finds the hare, the wolf, and the bear, who all wish to eat it; it sings its story to them all, and is allowed to go; it sings it to the fox, too, but the latter praises the song, and eats the cake, after having made it get upon his back.

him who has eaten the honey.[1] The wolf really goes to sleep, and the fox goes meanwhile to a neighbouring beehive, eats the honey, and throws the honeycombs upon the wolf, who, wakening from his slumbers, confesses his fault, and promises in reparation to give his share of the prey to the fox as soon as he procures any. In the continuation of the story, the fox sends the wolf to fish with his tail (the same as the bone of the dog) in the lake, and, after having made his tail freeze, feigns to be himself ill, and makes the wolf carry him, murmuring on the way the proverb, "He who is beaten carries him who is not beaten." In a variety of the same story, the fox eats the wolf's butter and flour; in another, the fox pretends to be called during the night to act as the rabbit's midwife, and eats the wolf's butter, accusing him afterwards of having eaten it himself; in order to discover the guilty one, they resolve upon trying the judgment by fire, before which the two animals are to go to sleep, and the one from whose skin the butter shall come out, is to be accounted guilty; whilst the wolf is asleep and snoring, the fox upsets the rest of the butter over him. In the seventh story of the fourth book of *Afanassieff*, the fox promises to an old man to bring his wife to life again; he requests him to warm a bath, to bring flour and honey, and then to stand at the door without ever turning round to look at the bath; the old man does so, and the fox washes the old woman and then eats her, leaving nothing but the bones; he then makes a cake of the flour and honey, and eats that too, after which he cries out to the old man to throw the door wide open,

[1] In *Afanassieff*, i. 14, the hero, Theodore, finds some wolves fighting among themselves for a bone, some bees fighting for the honey, and some shrimps fighting for caviare; he makes a just division, and the grateful wolves, bees, and shrimps help him in need.

and escapes. In the first story of the first book, the old man whose wife is dead goes to look for mourners; he finds the bear, who offers to do the weeping, but the old man thinks that he has not a sufficiently good voice; going on, he meets the fox, who also offers to perform the same service, and gives a good proof of his skill in singing (this particular would appear to be more applicable to the crying jackal than to the fox). The old man declares himself perfectly satisfied, and places the cunning beast at the foot of the corpse to sing a lament, whilst he himself goes to make the grave; during the old man's absence, the fox eats everything he finds in the house, and the old woman too. In the ninth story of the fourth book the fable ends otherwise; the fox does his duty as a weeper, and the old man rewards him by the gift of some chickens; the fox, however, demanding more, the old man puts into a sack two dogs and a chicken, and gives it to the fox, who goes out and opens the sack. The dogs run out and pursue him; he takes refuge in his den, but neglects to draw in his tail, which betrays him. "Cauda de vulpe testatur," said also the Latin proverb. In a variety of the first story of the first book, it is as a reward for having released the peasant from the bear that the fox receives a sack containing two hens and a dog. The dog pursues the fox, who takes to his hole, and then asks his feet what they have done; they answer that they ran away; he then asks his eyes and ears, which answer that they saw and heard; finally he asks his tail (here identified with the phallos), which, confused, answers that it put itself between his legs to make him fall. Then the fox, wishing to chastise his tail, puts it out of the hole; the dog, by means of it, drags out the whole fox, and tears him to pieces. In the fourth story of the third book, the fox delivers the peasant from, not the bear, but the wolf; the peasant then cheats him in the same way, by putting dogs into the sack; the fox escapes, and to punish his tail for impeding his flight, leaves it in the dog's mouth, and runs off; afterwards the fox is drowned by falling into a barrel which is being filled with water (the deed of the phallos; cfr. the chapter on the Fishes), and the peasant takes his skin. In another Russian story, recorded by *Afanassieff* in the observations to the first book of his stories, the fox, having delivered the peasant from the bear, asks for his nose in way of recompense, but the peasant terrifies him and puts him to flight. In a Slavonic story referred to in the same observations, the bird makes its nest, of which the fox covets the eggs; the bird informs the dog, who pursues the fox; the latter, betrayed by his tail, holds his usual monologue with his feet, eyes, ears, and tail. In the twenty-second story of the third book, the fox falls with the bear, the wolf, and the hare, into a ditch where there is no water. The four animals are oppressed by hunger, and the fox proposes that each should raise his voice in succession and shout his utmost; he who shouts feeblest will be eaten by the others. The hare's turn comes first, then that of the wolf; bear and fox alone remain. The fox advises the bear to put his paws upon his sides; attempting to sing thus, he dies, and the fox eats him. Being again hungry, and seeing a bird feeding its young, he threatens to kill the young birds unless the parent brings him some food; the bird brings him a hen from the village. The fox afterwards renews his threats, desiring the bird to bring him something to drink; the bird immediately brings him water from the village. Again the fox threatens to kill the young ones if the old bird does not deliver him out of the ditch; the bird throws in billets of wood, and thus succeeds in helping him out. Then the fox desires the bird to make him laugh; the bird invites him to run after it; it then goes towards the village, where it cries out, "Woman, woman, bring me a piece of tallow" (babka, babka, priniessi mnié sala kussók); the dogs hear the cry, come out, and rend the fox. In the twenty-fourth story of the third book, the fox again delivers the peasant from the wolf, whom he had shut up in a sack to save him from the persecution of the hunters. The wolf is no sooner out of danger than he wishes to eat the peasant, saying that "old hospitality is forgotten."[1] The peasant beseeches him to await the judgment of the first passer-by; the first whom they meet is an old mare who has been expelled from the stables on account of her age, after having long served her masters; she finds that the wolf's sentence is just. The peasant begs the wolf to wait for a second passer-by; this is an old black dog who has been expelled from the house after long services, because he can no longer bark; he also approves the wolf's decision. The peasant again begs them to wait for a third and decisive judgment; they meet the fox, who resorts to a well-known stratagem; he affects to doubt that so large an animal as the wolf could get into so small a sack. The wolf, mortified at so unjust a suspicion, wishes to prove that he has told the truth, re-enters into the sack, and is beaten by the peasant till he dies. But the peasant himself then proves ungrateful to the fox, saying, too, that old hospitality is to be forgotten (properly the hospitality of bread and salt, *hlieb-sol*). In the eighth story of the fourth book, the fox brings upon his back to her father and mother a girl who,

---

[1] Cfr. *Lou loup penjat* in the *Contes de l'Armagnac*, collected by Bladé, Paris, 1867, p. 9.

having lost herself in the forest, was weeping upon a tree. The old man and woman, however, are not grateful to the fox; for on the latter asking for a hen in reward, they put him into a sack with a dog; the rest of the story is already known to the reader. In the twenty-third story of the fourth book, the fox marries the cat and puts the bear and the wolf to flight. We have already mentioned the fox of the Russian story who sends the wolf to catch fish in the river with his tail, by which means the tail is frozen off. In a popular Norwegian story, instead of the wolf, it is the bear who is thus cheated by the fox. In a Servian story, we hear of a fox who steals three cheeses off a waggon, and afterwards meets the wolf, who asks where he had found them. The fox answers, in the water (the sky of night). The wolf wishing to fish for cheeses, the fox conducts him to a fountain where the moon is reflected in the water, and points to it as a cheese; he must lap up the water in order to get at it. The wolf laps and laps till the water comes out of his mouth, nose, and ears (probably because he was drowned in the fountain. The wolf, the black monster of night, takes the place of the crow in connection with the cheese (the moon) and the fox; the Servian story itself tells us what the cheese represents[1]). In a Russian story, published in the year 1860, by the Podsniesznik, and quoted in the observations to the first book of the stories of *Afanassieff*, the fox is killed by a peasant whose fish he had stolen; the peasant takes his skin and goes off. Up comes the wolf, and seeing his god-father without a skin, weeps over him

[1] Cfr. the English expression applied to the moon, "made of green cheese;" this is the connection between green and yellow previously mentioned.

according to the prescribed ceremony, and then eats him. We have already seen the fox as a mourner and as a midwife. In the twentieth story of the third book of *Afanassieff*, the fox wishes to work as a blacksmith. In other Russian stories we have the fox-confessor and the fox-physician; finally, the fox as a god-mother is a very popular subject of Russian stories. In a Russian story, published in the fourth number of the Russian *Historical and Juridical Archives of Kalassoff*, the fox appears as a go-between for the marriage of two young men with two princesses. But, above all, the fox is famous for having brought about the wedding of the poor Buhtan Buhtanović and of his *alter ego*, Koszma Skorobagatoi (Cosimo the swiftly-enriched) with the daughter of the Tzar. Buhtan had only five kapeika (twopence in all). The fox has them changed, and asks the Tzar to lend him some bushels to measure the money with. These bushels are each time found too small, and larger ones are demanded, using which, the cunning fox always takes care to leave some small coin at the bottom. The Tzar marvels at the riches of Bùhtan, and the fox then asks for Buhtan the Tzar's daughter to wife. The Tzar wishes first to see the bridegroom. How dress him? The fox then makes Buhtan fall into the mud near the king's palace whilst they are passing over a little bridge. He then goes to the Tzar, relates the misfortune, and begs him to lend him a dress for Buhtan. Buhtan puts it on, and never ceases regarding his changed appearance. The Tzar being astonished at this, the fox hastens to say that Buhtan was never so badly dressed before, and takes the first opportunity of warning him in private against conduct so suspicious. Then, withdrawn from himself, he does nothing but stare at the golden table, which again astonishes the Tzar; this is accounted for by the fox, who explains that in Buhtan's palace similar tables are to be found in the bath-room; meanwhile the fox hints to Buhtan to look more about him. The wedding ceremony is performed and the bride led away. The fox runs on before; but instead of leading them into Buhtan's miserable hut, he takes them to an enchanted palace, after having, by a trick, chased out of it the serpent, the crow, and the cock that inhabited it.[1]—Poor Kuszinka has only one cock and five hens remaining. He takes the fox by surprise whilst he is attempting to eat his hens, but moved by the fox's prayers, releases him. Then the grateful fox promises to transform him into Cosimo the swiftly-enriched. The fox goes into the Tzar's park and meets the wolf, who asks him how he is become so fat; he answers that he has been banqueting at the Tzar's palace. The wolf expresses a desire to go there too, and the fox advises him to invite forty times forty more wolves (that is 1600 wolves). The wolf follows his advice, and brings them all to the Tzar's palace, upon which the fox tells the Tzar that Cosimo the swiftly-enriched sends them to him as a gift. The Tzar marvels at the great riches of Cosimo; the fox uses the same stratagem twice again with the bears and the martens. After this, he asks the Tzar to lend him a silver bushel, pretending that all Cosimo's golden bushels are full of money. The Tzar gives it, and when the fox sends it back, he leaves a few small coins at the bottom, returning it with the request that the Tzar would give his daughter to Cosimo in marriage. The Tzar answers that he must first see the pretender to her hand. The fox then makes Cosimo fall into the water, and arrays him in robes lent by the Tzar, who receives him with

[1] *Afanassieff*, iv. 10.

every honour. After some time, the Tzar signifies his desire of visiting Cosimo's dwelling. The fox goes on before, and finds on the way flocks of sheep, and herds of hogs, cows, horses, and camels. He asks of all the shepherds to whom they belong, and is uniformly answered, "To the serpent-uhlan." The fox orders them to say that they belong to Cosimo the swiftly-enriched, or else they will see King Fire and Queen Loszna,[1] who will burn everything to ashes. He comes to the palace of white stone, where the king serpent-uhlan lives. He terrifies him in the same way, and compels him to take refuge in the trunk of an oak-tree, where he is burnt to death. Cosimo, the swiftly-enriched, becomes Tzar of all the possessions of the uhlan-serpent and enjoys them with his bride.[2] (I need not dwell upon the mythological importance of this story; the serpent consumed by fire is found in the most primitive myths; here the canis-vulpes, the red bitch, the fox seems to play part of the *rôle* of the Vedic messenger-bitch.)

In the first story of *Afanassieff*, the fox chases the hare, instead of the serpent, out of its home. The fox has a house of ice and the hare one of wood. At the arrival of spring, the fox's house melts; then the fox, under the pretext of warming itself, enters the hare's house and sends its occupant away. The hare weeps, and the dogs come to chase the fox away, but it cries

[1] It is here, perhaps, to be remarked that in the Piedmontese dialect lightning is called *loszna*.

[2] *Afanassieff*, iv. 11. In the fourth story of the second book of the *Pentamerone*, instead of a fox, it is the cat that enriches Pippo Gagliufo and runs before him. In the same way as in the Russian stories the man shows himself ungrateful towards the fox, so in the *Pentamerone* the cat ends by cursing the ungrateful Pippo Gagliufo whom she had done good to. In the following story the fox offers herself as companion to the young bride who is looking for her lost husband.

out from its seat by the stove, that when it leaps out, whoever is caught will be torn into a thousand pieces; hearing which, the dogs run away in terror. The bear comes, and then the bull, but the fox terrifies them too. At last the cock comes up with a scythe, and loudly summons it to come out or be cut to pieces. The terrified fox jumps out and the cock cuts it to pieces with the scythe. In another story of Little Russia, mentioned by *Afanassieff* in the observations to the first book of his stories, the fox, on the contrary, is the victim which the hairy goat wishes to expel from its home. Several animals, wolf, lion, and bear, present themselves to help it, but the cock alone succeeds in expelling the intruder. Here the cock appears as the friend of the fox and the enemy of the goat. In the twenty-third story of the third book of *Afanassieff*, the fox defends the sheep against the wolf, who accuses it of having dressed itself in his skin, and brings about the ruin of the wolf by its craftiness. In the third story of the fourth book, the cat and the lamb release the cock from the fox; these contradictions are explained by the double mythical significance which we have attributed above to the fox, and by its double appearance as aurora in the evening and in the morning. In the evening, it generally cheats the hero; in the morning it cheats the monster. In the second story of the fourth book of *Afanassieff*, the fox requests the cock to come down from a tree to confess itself to him. The cock does so, and is about to be eaten by the fox, but it flatters him so much that he lets it escape again. (The solar cock, supposed to be in the fox's power at night, escapes from it and comes forth again in the morning.) The third story of the fourth book gives us the interesting text of the words sung by the fox to deceive the cock:

"Little cock, little cock,
With the golden crest,
With the buttered head,
With the forehead of curdled milk!
Show yourself at the window;
I will give you some gruel
In a red spoon."[1]

The cock, when caught by the fox, invokes the cat's assistance, crying, "Me the fox has carried away; he carried away me, the cock, into the gloomy forest, into distant lands, into foreign lands, into the three times ninth (twenty-seventh) earth, into the thirtieth kingdom; cat Catonaiević, deliver me!"

---

[1] "Pietushók, pietushók,
Zalatói grebeshók,
Másliannaja galovka,
Smiatanij lobók!
Vighliani v oshko;
Dam tebie kashki,
Na krasnoi loszkie."

In an unpublished Tuscan story which I heard related at Antignano near Leghorn, a chicken wishes to go with its father (the cock) into the Maremma to search for food. Its father advises it not to do so for fear of the fox, but the chicken insists upon going; on the way it meets the fox, who is about to eat it, when the chicken beseeches him to let it go into the Maremma, where it will fatten, lay eggs, bring up young chickens, and be able to provide the fox with a much more substantial meal than it now could. The fox consents. The chicken brings up a hundred young ones; when they are grown up, they set out to return home; every fowl carries in its mouth an ear of millet, except the youngest. On the way they meet the fox waiting for them; on seeing all these animals each with a straw in its beak, the astonished fox asks the mother-hen what it is they carry. "All fox's tails," she answers, upon which the fox takes to its heels.—We find the fox's tail in connection with ears of corn in the legend of Samson; the incendiary fox is also found in Ovid's *Fasti*, iv. 705; (from the malice with which the story-teller (a woman) relates the fable, it is probable that the fox's tail has here also a phallic meaning).—In *Sextus Empiricus* we read that a fox's tail hung on the arm of a weak husband is of great use to him.

The knavish actions of the fox, however, are far more celebrated in the West than in the East. A proverb says that, to write all the perfidious knaveries of the fox, all the cloth manufactured at Ghent, turned into parchment, would not be sufficient. This proverb justifies me in saying but little of it, as I am unable to say as much as I should wish. Greeks and Latins are unanimous in celebrating the sagacity and perfidy of the fox. The cynic Macchiavelli, in the eighteenth chapter of the *Principe*, asserts that a good prince must imitate two animals, the fox and the lion, (must, that is to say, have deceit and strength), but especially the fox; and this answers to the sentence attributed by Plutarch (in the *Memorable Sayings of the Greeks*) to Lysander, "Where the lion's skin does not suffice, put on that of the fox." Aristotle, in the ninth book of the *History of Animals*, also considers the fox as the serpent's friend, probably because of the analogy existing between them in respect of perfidiousness, according to another Greek saying, viz., "He who hopes to triumph, must arm himself with the strength of the lion and the prudence of the serpent." A proverbial Latin verse says—

"Vulpes amat fraudem, lupus agnam, fæmina laudem."

There is scarcely an animal which is not deceived by the fox in Greek and Latin fable; the fox alone does not succeed in deceiving the fox. In Æsop, the fox who has lost his tail in a trap endeavours to persuade the other foxes of the uselessness of that appendage; but the latter answer that he would not have given them such advice were he not aware that a tail is a useful member. The fox deceives the ass, giving it up a prey to the lion (as in the *Pańćatantram*); it deceives the hare by offering it as a prey to the dog, who, pursuing the hare, loses both hare and fox;[1] it deceives the goat, by cozening it into the well that it may escape out of it, and then leaving it there to its fate; it cheats in several ways now the cock, now the wolf; and it imposes upon even the powerful king of beasts, whom, however, he sometimes cannot deceive. A graceful apologue of Thomas Morus shows us the counterpart of the Hellenic fable of the fox and the sick lion, that is to say, the sick fox visited by the lion:—

> "Dum jacet angusta vulpes ægrota caverna
> Ante fores blando constitit ore leo.
> Etquid, amica, vale. Cito, me lambente, valebis,
> Nescis in lingua vis mihi quanta mea.
> Lingua tibi medica est, vulpes ait, at nocet illud
> Vicinos, quod habet, tam bona lingua, malos."

But when we come down to the Middle Ages, the fable of the fox develops into such manifoldness, that the study of all the phases in which it unfolds itself ought to be the subject of a special work.[2] Suffice it to notice here that, to popularise in Flanders, and subsequently in France and Germany, the idea of the fox as the type of every species of malice and imposture, it is the priest who, for the most part, is the human impersonation of the masculine Reinart. The *Procession du Renart* is

[1] Thus, in the myth of Kephalos, his dog cannot, by a decree of fate, overtake the fox; but inasmuch as, on the other hand, no one also, by decree of fate, can escape from the dog of Kephalos, dog and fox are both, by the command of Zeus, changed into stone (the two auroras, or dying sun and dying moon).

[2] This work has, on the other hand, been already almost accomplished, as regards the Franco-Germanic part, in the erudite and interesting introduction (pp. 5–163) which Ch. Potvin has prefixed to his translation into verse of the *Roman du Renard*, Paris, Bohné; Bruxelles, Lacroix, 1861. I am told that Professor Schiefner read a discourse two years since at St Petersburg upon the story of the fox, but I do not know whether it has been published.

famous; it was a farce conceived in 1313 by Philippe le Bel, on account of his quarrel with Pope Boniface VIII., and acted by the scholars of Paris. The principal personage was a man disguised in the skin of a fox, and wearing over all a priest's surplice, whose chief industry it was to give chase to chickens. This form of satire, however, directed against the Church, is certainly much older than those times, and goes back to the epoch of the first differences between the Church and the Empire in the eleventh century, at which time two mediæval Latin poems appeared, *Reinardus Vulpes* and *Ysengrimus*; with the schism of England and the Reformation of the sixteenth century, however, *Reinardus Vulpes* decisively became a Romish fox. The finesse and perfection of the satirical poem which S. Naylor, its English translator, calls "the unholy bible of the world," also increased the fox's popularity, and made it yet more proverbial. The principal subjects of the poem existed previously, not only in oral, but also in literary tradition; they were grouped together and put in order, and a more human, more malicious nature was given to the fox, a nature more hypocritical even than before, and more priestly, whence it now more than ever—

"Urbibus et castris regnat et ecclesiis."

Macchiavelli, St Ignazio di Loyola, and St Vincenzo de' Paoli took upon themselves the charge of propagating its type over the whole world.

The wolf is better, when he is a wolf, for then we know at least what he wants; we know that he is our enemy, and are accordingly on our guard; but he, too, sometimes disguises himself, by imposture or magic, as a sheep, a shepherd, a monk, or a penitent, like Ysengrin; and from this point of view resembles not a little his perfidious god-mother the fox; it is well known that amongst the exploits of Reinart there is that of his extra-matrimonial union with the she-wolf.

In the *Ṛigvedas* we already find several interesting mythical data concerning the wolf; he is in it entirely demoniacal, as the exhausted Vṛikas, to which, in a hymn, the Açvinâu give back its strength,[1] seems, as it appears to me, not to be the wolf, but the messenger crow which, during the night, must carry the solar hero.

As in the Zendic *Vendidad*,[2] the souls of good men, when on the way to heaven, are afraid of meeting the wolf, so in the *Ṛigvedas*, the devotee says that once the reddish wolf (which seems to be confounded here with the jackal or the fox) saw him coming on the way, and fled in terror;[3] he invokes the (luminous) night to send the wolf, the robber far away,[4] and the god Pûshan (the sun) to remove the evil wolf, the malignant spirit, from the path of the devotees, the wolf that besieges the roads, thieving, fraudulent, double-dealing.[5] The poet, after having called the enemy Vṛikas, prays, with imprecations, that he may lacerate his own body;[6] and the wild beast, full of witchcraft,[7] which Indras kills, is probably

[1] Vṛikâya ćiǵ ǵasamânâya çaktam; *Ṛigv.* vii. 68, 8.—The grateful wolf and crow are found united to assist Ivan Tzarević in the twenty-fourth story of the second book of *Afanassieff*.

[2] xix. 108, 109.

[3] Aruṇo mâ sakṛid vṛikaḥ pathâ yantam dadarça hi uǵ ǵihîte nićâyya; *Ṛigv.* i. 105, 18.

[4] Yâvayâ vṛikyaṁ vṛikaṁ yavaya stenam ûrmya; *Ṛigv.* x. 127, 6.—A wolf seen in a dream, according to Cardano, announces a robber.

[5] Yo naḥ pûshann agho vṛiko duḥçeva âdideçati apa sma tvam patho ǵahi—Paripanthinam mashîvâṇaṁ huraçćitam—Dvayâvinaḥ; *Ṛigv.* i. 42, 2–4.

[6] Svayaṁ ripus tanvaṁ ririshîshṭa; *Ṛigv.* vi. 51, 6, 7.

[7] Mâyinam mṛigaṁ; *Ṛigv.* i. 80, 7.

a wolf. But, besides this, I think I can find in the *Ṛigvedas* the *lupus piscator* of Russian and Western tradition; (according to Ælianos there were wolves friendly to fishermen near the Palus Mœotis.) In the fifty-sixth hymn of the eighth book, Matsyas (the fish) invokes the Âdityas (that is, the luminous gods) to free him and his from the jaws of the wolf. So in another strophe of the same hymn, we must in reason suppose that it is a fish that speaks when she who has a terrible son (*i.e.*, the mother of the sun) is invoked as protectress from him who in the shallow waters endeavours to kill him.[1] We also find a fish lying in shallow water explicitly mentioned in another hymn;[2] which proves to us the image of the fish without water, which was widely developed in later Hindoo tradition, to have been in the Vedic age already a familiar one. We find the dog as the enemy of the wolf in the Hindoo words *vṛikâris vṛikârâtis*, and *vṛikadançás.* (In the thirteenth story of the fourth book of *Afanassieff*, the wolf wishes to eat the dog; the latter, who feels himself too weak to resist, begs the wolf to bring him something to eat, in order that he may become larger, and be more tender for the wolf's teeth; but when he is in good condition, he acquires strength and makes the wolf run. The enmity of the dog and the wolf was also made popular in the Æsopian fables.)

In the *Râmâyaṇam*,[3] we already meet with the pro-

---

[1] Te na âsno vṛikâṇâm âdityâso mumoćata; *Ṛigv.* viii. 56, 14.—Parshi dîne gabhîra âň ugraputre ǵighâňsataḥ; *Ṛigv.* viii. 56, 11.

[2] Matsyaṁ na dîna udani kshiyantam; *Ṛigv.* x. 68, 8.

[3] iii. 45.—In the twenty-second night of the *Tuti-Name*, the wolf enters, on the contrary, into the house of the jackal; here wolf and jackal are already distinguished in it from one another,—that is, as red wolf and black wolf.

verbial expression of the sheep who do not increase when guarded by the wolf or jackal (rakshayamâṇâ na vardhante meshâ gomâyunâ).

In the *Mahâbhâratam*, the second of the three sons of Kuntî, the strong, terrible, and voracious Bhîmas, is called Wolf's-belly (Vṛikodaras, the solar hero enclosed in the nocturnal or winter darkness). Here the wolf has a heroic and sympathetic form, as in the *Tuti-Name*[1] he, although famished, shows compassion upon a maiden who travels to fulfil a promise; as in the same *Tuti-Name*[2] he helps the lion against the mice, and in the story of Ardschi Bordschi, the boy, son of a wolf, understands the language of wolves, and teaches it to the merchants with whom he lives; like the Russian she-wolf that gives her milk to Ivan Karolievič, in order that he may take it to the witch, his wife, who induced him to fetch it in the hope that he would thereby meet with his death;[3] and like the she-wolf of the fifteenth Esthonian story, who comes up on hearing the cry of a child, and gives its milk to nourish it. The story tells us that the shape of a wolf was assumed by the mother of the child herself, and that when she was alone, she placed her wolf-disguise upon a rock, and appeared as a naked woman to give milk to her child. The husband, informed of this, orders that the rock be heated, so that when the wolf's skin is again placed upon it, it may be burnt, and he may thus be able to recognise and take back to himself his wife. The she-wolf that gives her milk to the twin-brothers, Romulus and Remus, in Latin epic tradition, was no less a woman than the nurse-wolf of the Esthonian story.[4] The German

[1] i. 253. [2] i. 271.

[3] Cfr. *Afanassieff*, vi. 51, v. 27, and v. 28.

[4] It is also said that the nurse of the Latin twins was a strumpet, because *lupæ* or *lupanæ fœminæ* were names given to such women,

hero Wolfdieterich, the wolves who hunt for the hero in Russian stories, sacred to Mars and to Thor as their hunting dogs, have the same benignant nature. (The evening aurora disguises herself in the night with a wolf's skin, nourishes as a she-wolf the new-born solar hero, and in the morning puts down her wolf's skin upon the fiery rock of the East, and finds her husband again.) What Solinus tells us of the Neuri, viz., that they transformed themselves into wolves at stated periods; and what used to be narrated of the Arcadians, to the effect that when they crossed a certain marsh, they became wolves for eight years,—suggests us a new idea of the zoological transformations of the solar hero.[1] In La Fontaine,[2] the shadow of the wolf makes the sheep flee in the evening. As a hero transformed, the wolf has a benignant aspect in legends. According to Baronius, in the year 617, a number of wolves presented themselves

whence also the name of *lupanaria* given to the houses to which they resorted: "Abscondunt spurcas hæc monumenta lupas." Olaus Magnus wrote, that wolves, attracted by smell, attack pregnant women, whence the custom that no pregnant woman should go out unless accompanied by an armed man. The ancients believed that the phallos of the wolf roasted and eaten weakened the Venus.

[1] In the *Legendes et Croyances Superstitieuses de la Creuse*, collected by Bonnafoux, Guéret, 1867, p. 27, we read concerning the loup garou, that the wolf thanks whoever wounds him. It is said that they who are disguised in the skin of the loup garou are condemned souls: "Chaque nuit, ils sont forcés d'aller chercher la maudite peau à un endroit convenu et ils courent ainsi jusqu'à ce qu'ils rencontrent une âme charitable et courageuse qui les délivre en les blessant."

[2] ". . . devant qu'il fût nuit
Il arriva nouvel encombre;
Un loup parut, tout le troupeau s'enfuit
Ce n'était pas un loup, ce n'en était que l'ombre."

The sheep were right, however, to flee. In the *Edda*, the fourth swallow says, "When I see the wolf's ears, I think that the wolf is not far off." The twilight is the shadow or ear of the wolf.

at a monastery, and tore in pieces several friars who entertained heretical opinions. The wolves sent by God tore the sacrilegious thieves of the army of Francesco Maria, Duke of Urbino, who had come to sack the treasure of the holy house of Loreto. A wolf guarded and defended from the wild beasts the head of St Edmund the Martyr, King of England. St Oddo, Abbot of Cluny, assailed in a pilgrimage by foxes, was delivered and escorted by a wolf; thus a wolf showed the way to the beatified Adam, in the same way as, in *Herodotos*, the wolves served as guides to the priests of Ceres. A wolf, having devoured two mares which drew a cart, was forced by St Eustorgius to draw the cart in their stead, and obeyed his orders. St Norbert compelled a wolf, first to let a sheep go after having clutched it, and then to guard the sheep all day without touching them. We read of the youth of the ancient Syracusan hero Hielon that, being at school, a wolf carried off his tablets in order to make him pursue it; no sooner was Hielon out, than the wolf re-entered the school, and massacred the master and the other scholars.

And even after his death the wolf is useful. The ancients believed that a wolf's hide, when put on by one who had been bitten by a mad dog, was a charm against hydrophobia. According to Pliny, wolf's teeth rubbed on the gums of children during teething relieves the pain (which is quite credible, but any other sharp tooth would serve the same purpose, by making the teeth cut sooner). In Sicily it is believed that a wolf's head increases the courage of whoever puts it on. In the province of Girgenti shoes are made of wolf's skin for children whom their parents wish to grow up strong, brave, and pugnacious. The animals themselves that are ridden by persons who wear these shoes are cured of their pain.

The animal *allupatu* (that is, which has once been bitten by a wolf) becomes invulnerable, and never feels any other kind of pain. It is also believed in Sicily that when a wolf's skin is exposed in the open air, it causes drums to break when they are beaten. This superstition reminds us of the fable of the fox that kills itself by breaking the drum or biting the string of a bow; the mythical drum (that is, the cloud) is destroyed when the wolf's skin is taken off. In Æsop's fable, the wolf's skin is recommended by the fox as a cure for the sick lion.

But the wolf of tradition usually has a perverse or diabolical signification; and as the demon is represented now as a master of every species of perfidy and wickedness, and now as a fool, so is the wolf. In the Hellenic myth, Lycaon, King of Arcadia, became a wolf because he had fed upon human flesh. According to Servius, the wolves among the people, called for this reason Hirpini (the Sabine word *hirpus* meaning a wolf), carried off the entrails of the victim sacrificed to Pluto, and therefore brought down a pestilence upon the land. Wolves tore the hero Milôn to pieces in the forest. Wolves are an omen of death; the loup garou of popular French tradition is a diabolical form.[1] In the *Edda*, the two wolves Sköll and Hati wish to take, one the sun and the other the moon; the wolf devours the sun, father of the world, and gives birth to a daughter. He is then killed by Vidarr. Hati precedes the luminous betrothed of the sky; the wolf Fenris, son of the demoniacal Lokis,

[1] Lous loups-garous soun gens coumo nous autes; mès an heyt un countrat dab lou diable, e cado sé soun fourçatz de se cambia en bestios per ana au sabbat e courre touto la neyt. Y a per aco un mouyén de lous goari. Lous cau tira sang pendent qu' an perdut la forme de l'home, e asta leu la reprengon per toutjour; Bladé, *Contes et Proverbes Populaires recueillis en Armagnac*, Paris, 1867, p. 51.

chained by the Ases, bites off the hand that the hero Tyr, as an earnest of the good faith of the Ases, had put into his mouth,[1] when chained to the western gate. Nanna, of the *Pentamerone*, after having travelled over the world, is disguised in the shape of a wolf, and changes in character and in colour, becoming malicious; the three sons of the Finns go to inhabit the Valley of the Wolf, near the Wolf's Lake, and find there three women spinning, who can transform themselves into swans. On Christmas Eve, the King Helgi meets a witch who rides upon a wolf, having eagles for bridles.[2] Wolves eat each other; the wolf Sinfiölti becomes a eunuch; the wolf who flees before the hero is an omen of victory, as well as the wolf who howls under the branches of an ash-tree. (The howling of the wolf, the braying of the ass, the hissing of the serpent, announce the death of the demoniacal monster; this howling must necessarily take place in the morning, or the spring, when the hero has recovered his strength, as the *Edda* says that "a hero must never fight towards sunset)." If Gunnar (the solar hero) loses his life, the wolf becomes the master of the treasure, and of the heritage of Nifl; the heroes roast the

---

[1] We ought perhaps to add here the tradition cited by Cæsarius Heisterbacensis of a wolf who, biting the arm of a girl, drags her to a place where there is another wolf; the more she cries the more fiercely the wolf bites her. The other wolf has a bone in his throat, which the girl extracts; here the girl takes the place of the crane or stork of the fable; the bone may be now the moon, now the sun.

[2] In another passage in the *Edda*, the eagle sits upon the wolf. According to the Latin legend of the foundation of Lavinium, the Trojans saw a singular prodigy. A fire arises in the woods; the wolf brings dry twigs in his mouth to make it burn better, and the eagle helps him by fanning the flames with his wings. The fox, on the other hand, dips its brush in the river to put out the fire with it, but does not succeed.

wolf. All these legendary particulars relating to the wolf in the *Edda* concur in showing us the wolf as a gloomy and diabolical monster. The night and the winter is the time of the wolf spoken of in the *Voluspa;* the gods who enter, according to the German tradition, into wolves' skins, represent the sun as hiding himself in the night, or the snowy season of winter (whence the demoniacal white wolf of a Russian story,[1] in the midst of seven black wolves). Inasmuch as the solar hero becomes a wolf, he has a divine nature; inasmuch, on the contrary, as the wolf is the proper form of the devil, his nature is entirely malignant. The condemned man, the proscribed criminal, the bandit, the *utlagatus* or outlaw, were said in the Middle Ages to wear a *caput lupinum* (in England, *wulfesheofod;* in France, *teste læue*). The wolf Ysengrin, descended partly from the Æsopian wolf, and partly from Scandinavian myths, which were propagated in Germany, Flanders, and France, possesses much of the diabolical craftiness of the fox; he usually adopts against sheep the same stratagems which the fox makes use of to entrap chickens. The French proverb makes the fox preach to the fowls; the Italian proverb makes the wolf sing psalms when he wishes to ensnare the sheep. As we have seen the jackal and the fox confounded in the East, so Reinart and Ysengrin are sometimes identified by their cunning in Western tradition. A recent French writer, who had observed the habits of the wolf, says that he is "effrayant de sagacité et de calcul."[2] In the second story of the second book of

[1] Cfr. *Afanassieff*, iii. 19.

[2] Les loups, qui ont très peu d'amis en France, et qui sont obligés d'apporter dans toutes leurs démarches une excessive prudence, chassent presque toujours à la muette. J'ai été plusieurs fois en position d'admirer la profondeur de leurs combinaisons stratégiques; c'est

Afanassieff, the same wizard-wolf who knew how to imitate the goat's voice to deceive the kids, goes to the house of an old man and an old woman, who have five sheep, a horse, and a calf. The wolf comes and begins to sing. The old woman admires the song, and gives him one sheep, then the others, then the horse, next the calf, and finally herself. The old man, left alone, at last succeeds in hunting the wolf away. In the preceding story, where the animals accuse each other, the demoniacal wolf, when his turn comes, accuses God. We have already spoken of the wolf who, by the order of St Eustorgius, draws the cart instead of the mares which he had eaten. In the twenty-fifth story of the third book of *Afanassieff*, the wolf comes up to the sleeping workman, and smells him; the workman awakes, takes the wolf by the tail,[1] and kills him. Another time the same workman, when he goes with his father to the chase, after having enriched himself with money which he had taken from three brigands who had hidden it in a deserted mill, meets again with two wolves who eat the horses, but, entangling themselves in the reins, they are compelled to draw the car home again themselves; here, therefore, we have the miracle of St Eustorgius reduced to its natural mythical proportions. Here, evidently, the wolf begins to show himself as a stupid animal; the

---

effrayant de sagacité et de calcul; Toussenel, *L'Esprit des Bêtes*, ch. i.—And Aldrovandi, *De Quadrup. Dig. Viv.* ii. "Lupi omnem vim ingenii naturalem in ovibus insidiando exercent; noctu enim ovili appropinquantes, pedes lambunt, ne strepitum in gradiendo edant, et foliis obstrepentibus pedes quasi reos mordent."

[1] In Piedmont it is also said in jest, that a man once met a wolf and thrust his hand down its throat, so far down that it reached its tail on the other side; he then pulled the tail inside the wolf's body and out through its throat, so that the wolf, turned inside out, expired.

demon teaches his art to the little solar hero in the evening, and is betrayed by the hero himself in the morning; the fox cheats the solar cock in the evening, and is deceived by it in the morning; the wolf succeeds by his wickedness in the evening, and is ruined in the morning. We have already mentioned the Norwegian story of the little Schmierbock, who, put into a sack by the witch, twice makes a hole in the sack and escapes, and the third time makes the witch eat her own daughter. Schmierbock is the ram; the witch or night puts him into the sack. In the Piedmontese story,[1] and in the Russian one, instead of Schmierbock, we have Piccolino (the very little one), and the Small Little Finger (malćik-s palćik, that is, the little finger, which is the wise one, according to popular superstition). The Russian story is as follows: An old woman, while baking a cake (the moon), cuts off her little finger and throws it into the fire. From the little finger in the fire, a dwarf, but very strong son, is born, who afterwards does many wonderful things. One day he was eating the tripe of an ox in the forest; the wolf passes by, and eats dwarf and tripe together. After this,

[1] In an unpublished, though very popular Piedmontese story, Piccolino is upon a tree eating figs; the wolf passes by and asks him for some, threatening him thus: "Piculin, dame ün fig, dass no, i t mangiu." Piccolino throws him down two, which are crushed upon the wolf's nose. Then the wolf threatens to eat him if he does not bring him a fig down; Piccolino comes down, and the wolf puts him in a sack and carries him towards his house, where the mother-wolf is waiting for him. But on the way the wolf is pressed by a corporeal necessity, and is obliged to go on the roadside; meanwhile, Piccolino makes a hole in the sack, comes out and puts a stone in his place. The wolf returns, shoulders the sack, but thinks that Piccolino has become much heavier. He goes home and tells the she-wolf to be glad, and prepare the cauldron full of hot water; he then empties the sack into the cauldron; the stone makes the boiling water spurt out upon the wolf's head, and he is scalded to death.

the wolf approaches a flock of sheep, but the dwarf cries out from within the wolf, "Shepherd, shepherd, thou sleepest and the wolf carries off a sheep." The shepherd then chases the wolf away, who endeavours to get rid of his troublesome guest; the dwarf requests the wolf to carry him home to his parents; no sooner have they arrived there than the dwarf comes out behind and catches hold of the wolf's tail, shouting, "Kill the wolf, kill the grey one." The old people come out and kill it.[1] The mythical wolf dies now after only one night, now after only one winter of life. To the mythical wolf, however, bastard sons were born, who, changing only their skin, succeeded in living for a long period among mortals in the midst of civil society, preserving, nevertheless, their wolf-like habits. The French proverb says, "Le loup alla à Rome; il y laissa de son poil et rien de ses coutumes." The pagan she-wolf gave milk to the Roman heroes; the Catholic wolf, thunderstruck by Dante,[2] on the contrary, feeds upon them—

> "Ed ha natura sì malvagia e ria,
> Che mai non empie la bramosa voglia,
> E dopo il pasto ha più fame che pria.
> Molti son gli animali a cui s'ammoglia."

---

[1] Cfr. the well-known English fairy-tales of *Tom Thumb* and *Hop-o'-my-Thumb*.

[2] *Inferno*, c. i.

CHAPTER XIII.

THE LION, THE TIGER, THE LEOPARD, THE PANTHER, AND THE CHAMELEON.

SUMMARY.

Lion and tiger symbols of royal majesty.—Tvashṭar as a lion.—The hair of Tvashṭar in the fire.—Winds that roar like lions.—The lion-seducer.—The lion and the honey; the lion and riches.—Nobility of the lion.—The lion's part.—The monster lioness.—The old and sick lion; the lion with a thorn in its foot.—Monster and demoniacal lions.—The lion is afraid of the cock.—Sterility of the lion.—The story of Atalanta.—The sun in the sign Leo.—The virgin and the lion.—Çivas, Dionysos, and the tiger.—A hair from the tiger's tail; the Mantikora.—The chameleon; the god chameleon.

THE tiger and the lion have in India the same dignity, and are both supreme symbols of royal strength and majesty.[1] The tiger of men and the lion of men are two expressions equivalent to prince, as the prince is supposed to be the best man. It is strength that gives victory and superiority in natural relations; therefore the tiger and the lion, called kings of beasts, represent

---

[1] Hêraklês, Hektor, Achilles, among the Greek heroes; Wolfdieterich, and several other heroes of Germanic tradition, have these animals for their ensigns; the lion is the steed of the hero Hildebrand. Cfr. *Die Deutsche Heldensage* von Wilhelm Grimm, Berlin, Dümmler, 1867.—When Agarista and Philip dreamed of a lion, it was considered an augury, the one of the birth of Pericles, and the other of that of Alexander the Great.

the king in the civic social relations among men. The narasinhas of India was called, in the Middle Ages, the king *par excellence;* thus in Greece the king was also called leôn.

The myth of the lion and the tiger is essentially an Asiatic one; notwithstanding this, a great part of it was developed in Greece, where lion and tiger were at one time not unknown, and must have, as in India, inspired something like that religious terror caused by oriental kings.

We have already mentioned the Vedic monster lion of the West, in which we recognise the expiring sun. The strong Indras, killer of the monster, Vṛitras, is also represented as a lion. In the same way as the Jewish Samson is found in connection with the lion, and this lion with honey, and as the strength of the lion and that of Samson is said to be centred in the hair (the sun, when he loses his rays or mane, loses all his strength), so in the parallel myth of Indras we find analogous circumstances. Tvashṭar, the Hindoo celestial blacksmith, who makes weapons now for the gods and now for the demons (the reddish sky of morning and of evening is likened to a burning forge; the solar hero or the sun in this forge, is a blacksmith), is also represented in a Vedic hymn [1] as a lion, turned towards which, towards the west, heaven and earth rejoice, although (on account of the din made by him when coming into the world) they are, before all, terrified. The form of a lion is one of the favourite shapes created by the mythical and legendary blacksmith.

In the *Mârkaṇḍeya-P.*,[2] this same Tvashṭar (which the *Ṛigvedas* represents as a lion), wishing to avenge

---

[1] Ubhe tvashṭur bibhyatur ǵâyamânât pratîćî sinham prati ǵoshayete; *Ṛigv.* i. 95, 5.

[2] v.

himself upon the god Indras, who had (perhaps at morn) killed one of his sons, creates another son, Vṛitras (the coverer), by tearing a lock of hair off his head and throwing it into the fire (the sun burns every evening in the western forge, his rays or mane, and the gloomy monster of night is born). Indras makes a truce with Vṛitras (in Russian stories, heroes and monsters nearly always challenge each other to say before fighting whether they will have peace or war), and subsequently violates the treaty; for this perfidy he loses his strength, which passes into Mârutas, the son of the wind (the Hanumant of the *Râmâyaṇam.* In a Vedic hymn, the voice of the Mârutas is compared to the roar of lions),[1] and into the three brothers Pâṇḍavas, sons of Kunti (the passage of the legend from the Vedas to the two principal Hindoo epic poems is thus indicated). Thus, in the same *Mârkaṇḍeya-P.*, Indras, having violated Ahalyâ, the wife of Gâutamas, loses his beauty (in other Puranic legends he becomes a eunuch or has a thousand wombs. Indras is powerful as the sun; he is powerful, too, in the cloud, by means of the thunderbolt; but when he hides himself in the serene and starry sky, he is powerless), which passes to the two Açvinâu, who afterwards renew themselves in the two Pâṇḍavâu sons of Mâdrî, as the sons of the demons were personified in the sons of Dhṛitarâshṭras.

Tvashṭar, the creator, now of divine, now of monstrous forms, Tvashṭar the lion, must necessarily create leonine forms. In a Tuscan story, the blacksmith makes a lion by means of which Argentofo penetrates by night into

[1] Te svânino rudriyâ varshanirṇiġah sinhâ na heshakratavaḥ sudânavaḥ; *Ṛigv.* iii. 26, 5.—In the Bohemian story of grandfather *Vsievedas*, the young hero is sent by the prince who wishes to ruin him to take the three golden hairs of this grandfather (the sun).

the room of a young princess, with whom he unites himself. In the third story of the fourth book of the *Pentamerone*, the three prince brothers, when the fairy's curse is over, return home with their brides, drawn by six lions. This lion-seducer reminds us of Indras, who was also a lion and a seducer of women. A hymn tells us that Indras fights like a terrible lion;[1] in another hymn, the same lion is considered, as in the legend of Samson, in connection with honey.[2] In the twenty-second night of the *Tuti-Name*, the lion presents himself in connection with riches; flattered by a man who calls him a king, he lets him collect the riches scattered on the ground by a caravan which the lion had destroyed.[3] His royal nature is also shown in the *Râmâyaṇam*,[4] in which King Daçarathas says that his son Râmas, the lion of men, after his exile, will disdain to occupy the kingdom previously enjoyed by Bharatas, in the same way as the lion disdains to feed upon flesh which has been licked by other animals. It is perhaps for this reason that, in the fable, the lion's part means all the prey. The proud one becomes the violent one, the tyrant, and hence the monster. In the *Âitareya Br.*,[5] the earth, full of gifts

[1] Sinho na bhîma âyudhâni bibhrat; *Ṛigv.* iv. 16, 14. Cfr. i. 174, 3.

[2] Sinhaṁ nasanta madhvo ayâsaṁ harim aru haṁ divo asya patim; *Ṛigv.* ix. 89, 3.

[3] In the Greek apologue, Ptolemy, king of Egypt, wishes to send some money to Alexander in homage to him; the mule, the horse, the ass, and the camel offer themselves of their own accord to carry the sacks. On the way, they meet the lion, who wishes to join the party, saying that he too carries money; but not being accustomed to such work, he modestly begs the other four to divide his load among themselves. They consent; soon afterwards, passing through a country rich in herds, the lion feels inclined to stay, and demands his portion of the money, but as his money resembles that of the others, not to mistake, he takes by force both his own and theirs.

[4] ii. 62.

[5] vi. 5, 35.

made by the right hand—that is, by the eastern part—presented by the Âdityâs (or luminous gods) to the Añgirasas (the seven solar rays, the seven wise men, and hence the priests), attacks, in the evening, the nations with its mouth wide open, having become a lioness (sinhîbhûtvâ). In the *Râmâyaṇam*,[1] the car that carries the monster Indraǵit is impetuously drawn by four lions. In the *Tuti-Name*,[2] we have the fable of the lion, instead of the wolf, that accuses the lamb, and the lion who is afraid of the ass, of the bull (as in the introduction to the *Pañćatantram*), and of the lynx. The Western lion-sun is now monstrous, now aged, now ill, now has a thorn in his foot,[3] is now blind, and now foolish. The monstrous lion who guards the monster's dwelling, the infernal abode, is found in a great number of popular stories. In Hellenic tradition the monstrous lion occurs more than once; such is the lion that ravages the country of the King of Megara, who promises his daughter to wife to the hero that will kill it; such is the lioness who, with her bloody jaws (the purple in the dog's mouth and the meat in the dog's mouth of the myths are of equivalent import) makes Thysbe's veil bloody, so that when Pyramos sees it he believes Thysbe to be dead, and kills himself;

---

[1] v. 43. [2] i. 229.

[3] The anecdote of Androkles and the lion grateful for having a thorn extracted from his foot, is also related in almost the same words of Mentor the Syracusan, Helpis of Samos, the Abbot Gerasimos, St Jerome and (as to the blinded lion whose sight is given back to him) of Macharios, the confessor. The thorn in the lion's foot is a zoological form of the hero who is vulnerable in his feet. In the sixth of the Sicilian stories published by Signora Gonzenbach, the boy Giuseppe takes a thorn out of a lion's foot; the grateful lion gives him one of his hairs; by means of this hair, the young man can, in case of necessity, become a terrible lion, and as such, he bites off the head of the king of the dragons.

when Thysbe sees this, she too kills herself in despair (an ancient form of the death of Romeo and Juliet); such is the Nemæan lion strangled by Hêraklês; such the lion of Mount Olympos which the young Polydamos kills without weapons; such were the leonine monsters with human faces which, according to Solinus, inhabited the Caspian; such was the Chimæra, part lion, part goat, and part dragon, and several other mythical figures of the passage of the evening sun into the gloom of night.

And it is under the conception of the lion as monstrous that the ancients were unanimous in believing that he fears above all animals the cock, and especially its fiery comb. The solar cock of morning entirely destroys the monsters. In a fable of Achilles Statius, the lion complains that Prometheus had allowed a cock to frighten him, but soon after consoles himself, upon learning that the elephant is tormented by the little mosquito that buzzes in its ears. Lucretius, too, in the fourth book *De Rerum Naturâ* represents the cock as throwing seeds:—

> "Nimirum quia sunt Gallorum in corpore quædam
> Semina, quæ cum sint oculis immissa Leonum
> Pupillas interfodiunt acremque dolorem [1]
> Præbent, ut nequeant contra durare feroces."

Sometimes the hero or god passes into the form of a lion to vanquish the monsters, like Dionysos, Apollon, Hêraklês, in Greece, and Indras and Vishṇus in India.

[1] Thus, the ancients attributed to the lion a particular antipathy to strong smells, such as garlic, and the pudenda of a woman. But this superstition must be classed with that which ascribes sterility to the lioness. The women of antiquity, when they met a lioness, considered it as an omen of sterility. In the Æsopian fable, the foxes boast of their fruitfulness before the lioness, whom they laugh at because she gives birth to only one cub. "Yes," she answers, "but it is a lion;" under the sign of the lion, the earth also becomes arid, and consequently unfruitful.

In the legend of St Marcellus, a lion having appeared to the saint in a vision as killing a serpent, this appearance was considered as a presage of good fortune to the enterprise of the Emperor Leo in Africa. Sometimes, on the other hand, hero and heroine become lion and lioness by the vengeance of deities or monsters. Atalanta defies the pretenders to her hand to outstrip her in running, and kills those who lose. Hippomenes, by the favour of the goddess of love, having received three apples from the garden of the Hesperides, provokes Atalanta to the race; on the way, he throws the apples down; Atalanta cannot resist the impulse to gather them up, and Hippomenes overtakes her, and unites himself with her in the wood sacred to the mother of the gods; the offended goddess transforms the young couple into a lion and a lioness. In the *Gesta Romanorum*, a girl, daughter of the Emperor Vespasian, kills the claimant of her hand in a garden, in the form of a ferocious lion. Empedokles, however, considered the transformation into a lion as the best of all human metamorphoses. When the sun enters into the sign of the lion, he arrives at his greatest height of power; and the golden crown which the Florentines placed upon their lion in the public square, on the day of St John, was a symbol of the approach of the season which they call by one word alone, *sollione.* This lion is enraged, and makes, as it is said, plants and animals rage. The pagan legend says of Prometheus—

"Insani leonis
Vim stomacho apposuisse nostro."[1]

But the mythical lion, the sun, does not inspire the man with rage alone, but strength also.[2]

[1] Horace, *Carm.* i. 16.

[2] Sculpebant Ethnici auro vel argento leonis imaginem, et ferentes

The tiger, the panther, and the leopard possess several of the mythical characteristics of the lion as a hidden sun, with which they are, moreover, sometimes confounded in their character of omniform animals. The leopard was sacred to the god Pan, whose nature we already know, and the panther to Protheus and Dionysos, because it is said to have a liking for wine (we have seen the Vedic lion Indras in connection with honey, and Indras himself in connection with the somas), and becauses the nurses of Dionysos were transformed into panthers. Dionysos appears now surrounded by panthers, by means of which he terrifies pirates and puts them to flight, and now drawn by tigers. Dionysos is at the same time a phallical and an ambrosial god, and hence the god of wine; thus in India, Çivas, the phallical god, *par excellence*, and who is omniform like Tvashṭar and Yamas, his almost equivalent forms, has the tiger for his ensign, and is covered with a tiger's skin. It is a singular fact that in Hindoo tradition a murderous strength is attributed to the tiger's tail. A Hindoo proverb says that a hair of the tiger's tail may be the cause of losing one's life,[1] which naturally suggests to our minds the tiger Mantikora,[2] which has

hujusmodi simulacra generosiores et audaciores evadere dicebantur; idcirco non est mirum si Aristoteles (in lib. de Secr. Secr.) scripserit annulum ex auro vel argento, in quo cœlata sit icon puellæ equitantis leonem die et hora solis vagantis in domicilio leonis gestantes, ab omnibus honorari; Aldrovandi, *De Quadrup. Dig. Viv.* i.—In the signs of the Zodiac, Virgo comes after upon Leo; Christians also celebrate the assumption of the Virgin into heaven towards the middle of August, when the sun passes from the sign of the lion into that of the virgin.

[1] Cfr. Böhtlingk, *Indische Sprüche*, 2te Auflage, i. 1.

[2] Ktesias explains this word as "devourer of men," but by means of Sanskṛit it can only be explained by substituting to the initial *m* one of the words that signify man, such as *nara*, *ǵana*, *manava*, *mânusha*, &c. *Antikora* would seem to be derived from the Sanskṛit *antakara* = destroyer, who puts an end to, killer.

in its tail hairs which are darts thrown by it to defend itself, and are spoken of by Ktesias, in *Pausanias.*

Finally, having considered the tiger, the panther, and the leopard, variegated and omniform animals, and compared them with the lion, whose combat with the serpent we have also mentioned, it is natural to add a few more words concerning the chameleon, of whose enmity to the serpent and medicinal virtues Greek and Latin authors have written at such length. The *kṛikalâças* or *kṛikalâsas,* or chameleon, is already spoken of in a Vedic *Brâhmaṇam.* In the fifty-fifth canto of the last book of the *Râmâyaṇam,* we read that King Nṛigas was condemned to remain invisible to all creatures in the form of a chameleon during many hundreds and thousands of years, until the god Vishṇus, humanised in the form of Vasudevas, will come to release him from this curse, incurred for having delayed to judge a controversy pending between two Brâhmans concerning the ownership of a cow and a calf. In the stories of grateful animals, as is well-known, the hero often earns their gratitude by intervening to divide their prey into just portions, while they are disputing over it themselves. From the last book of the *Râmâyaṇam,* we learn also that the form of the chameleon is that assumed by Kuveras, the god of riches, when the gods flee terrified from the sight of the monster Râvaṇas. As Yamas and Çivas are almost equivalent forms, so between Yamas and Kuveras there is the same relation as between Pluto and Plutus. To the tiger Çivas corresponds the chameleon Kuveras; and the chameleon god of wealth, enemy of the serpent, is closely connected in mythology with the lion Indras, with the lion that kills the monster serpent, and with the lion that covets the treasure.

CHAPTER XIV.

THE SPIDER.

SUMMARY.

Tuscan superstition relating to the spider; the red sky of evening.—The night, the moon, and the aurora as weavers.—Arachnê.—Âurṇavabhas.—Dhatâ and Vidhatâ.—Golden cloths.—The spider and his prey.—The golden veil.—The lake of fire and the witch burnt.—The eagle and the spider.—The sack made of a spider's web.

THERE is in Tuscany a very interesting superstition relating to the spider: it is believed that if a spider be seen in the evening it must not be burnt, as it is destined to bring good fortune; but when seen in the morning, it must be burnt without being touched. The evening and morning aurora are compared to the spider and the spider's web; the evening aurora must prepare the morning aurora during the night. We have quoted on a previous occasion the Piedmontese proverb, "Rosso di sera, buon tempo si spera" (red at night, we hope for fine weather). If the sun dies in the west without clouds, if the luminous spider shows itself in the western sky, it augurs for the morrow a fine morning and a fine day. In the *Ṛigvedas* we have on this subject several interesting data; the aurora weaved during the night (and is therefore called vayantî;[1] sometimes she is helped by

---

[1] *Ṛigv.* ii. 38, 4.—In the fifty-fourth story of the fourth book of *Afanassieff*, the king who has no children makes the maiden seven years old manufacture a fisherman's net in the space of only one night.

Râkâ, the full moon[1]) the robe for her husband. But, in another hymn, she is entreated to shine soon, and not to stretch out or weave her work too long, in order that the sun with his rays may not fall upon it and burn it like a thief.[2] In the legend of Odysseus, Penelopê undoes in the night the work of the day; this is another aspect of the same myth: Penelopê, as aurora, undoes her web at even, to weave it again at morn. The myth of Arachnê (the name of the spider, and of the celebrated Lydian virgin whom Athenê, the aurora, according to Professor Max Müller, taught to spin, and whose father was Idmon, a colourer in purple), whom Athenê, jealous of the skill she had acquired in weaving in purple colours, strikes on the forehead and transforms into a spider, is a variety of the same myth of the weaving aurora. When the spider becomes dark, and when its web is gloomy, then the spider, or son of the spider, or Âurṇavabhas, assumes a monstrous form. Âurṇavabhas (ûrṇavâbhis, ûrṇanâbhis, ûrṇanabhas, as spider, are already spoken of in the Vedic writings) is the name of the gloomy monster Vṛitras, killed by the god Indras, the terrible monster which Indras, immediately after his birth, is obliged to kill[3] at

[1] In the German legend we have the spinner in the moon. "Die Altmärkische Sage bei Temme 49, 'die Spinnerin im Monde,' wo ein Mädchen von seiner Mutter verwünscht wird, im Monde zu sitzen und zu spinnen, scheint entstellt, da jener Fluch sie nicht wegen Spinnens, sondern Tanzens im Mondschein trifft;" Simrock, *Deutsche Mythologie*, 2te Aufl. p. 23.—Cfr. also the first chapter of this work, and that on the bear, where we read of a girl dancing with the bear in the night.—Perhaps there is also some correspondence between the Vedic word *râkâ* and *a-rachnê*.

[2] Vy ućhâ duhitar divo mâ ćiraṁ tanutha apaḥ net tvâ stenaṁ yathâ ripuṁ tapâti sûro arćishâ; *Ṛigv.* v. 79, 9.

[3] Vritram avâbhinad dânum âurṇavâbham; *Ṛigv.* ii. 11, 18.—Ǵagńâno nu çatakratur vi pṛićhad iti mâtaram ka ugrâḥ ke ha çriṇvire âd îm çavasy abravîd âurṇavâbham ahîçuvam te putra santu nishṭuraḥ; *Ṛigv.* viii. 66, 1, 2.

the instigation of his mother. In the *Mahâbhâratam*[1] we find two women that spin and weave, Dhatâ and Vidhatâ; they weave upon the loom of the year with black and white threads, *i.e.*, they spin the days and the nights. We, therefore, have a beneficent spider and a malignant one.

In the fourth story of the fifth book of the *Pentamerone*, the young Parmetella marries a black slave, who gives her as servants swans, "Vestute de tela d'oro, che, subeto 'ncignannola da capo a pede, la mesero 'n forma de ragno, che pareva propio na Regina." (The black man becomes a handsome youth during the night, perhaps as the moon; she wishes to see his features, and he disappears; this is a variety of the popular story of the wife's indiscretion.) In the fifth story of the second book of *Afanassieff*, the spider sets its web to catch flies, mosquitoes, and wasps; a wasp, being caught in the web, begs to be released in consideration of the many children that she will leave behind her (the same stratagem that is used by the hen against the fox in the Tuscan story previously mentioned.) The credulous spider lets her go; she then warns wasps, flies, and mosquitoes to keep hidden. The spider then asks help from the grasshopper, the moth, and the bug (nocturnal animals), who announce that the spider is dead, having given up the ghost upon the gibbet, which gibbet was afterwards destroyed (the evening aurora has disappeared into the night). The flies, mosquitoes, and wasps again come out, and fell into the spider's web (into the morning aurora). In the eighteenth story of the sixth book of *Afanassieff*, the beautiful girl who flees from the house of the witch that persecutes her, stretches out a veil, which, by the help of a beautiful young maiden (the

[1] i. 802, 825.

moon), she has embroidered with gold; immediately a great sea of fire springs up, into which the old witch falls and is burned; and here we come back to the popular Italian superstition that the spider must be burned in the morning.

The spider is an animal of the earth, but it weaves its web in the air; and as such—as intermediary between the animals of the earth and those of the air—supplies us with a bridge by which we may pass naturally from the first to the second part of the present work.[1] I hope that this bridge will prove as sufficient as the sack in which the young Esthonian hero carries the treasure away from hell, a sack composed of the threads of a spider, so strong that it is impossible to tear them. I wish I had, in the first book, some of the skill of the spider, and that I could weave with a few threads from the labyrinth of Âryan legendary tradition concerning animals a web which, if it be not as luminous as that of Arachnê, may be more durable than that of Penelopê.

[1] I observe, moreover, how in the Russian fables of Kriloff the same part is attributed to the spider as in the West to the wren (the regulus) and to the beetle. The eagle carries, without knowing it, a spider in its tail upon a tree; the spider then makes its web over it. Bird and spider therefore exchange places.

Second Part.

THE ANIMALS OF THE AIR.

CHAPTER I.

BIRDS.

SUMMARY.

The sky-atmosphere and the sky-tree.—The sun, the Açvinâu, Indras, the Marutas, and Agnis as birds.—Indras cuts off the wings of the mountains.—Indras and Somas as two birds hovering round the same tree of honey.—The wisdom of birds.—The birds requested to sacrifice themselves to fulfil the duties of hospitality, refuse.—The dvigas bird and brâhman.—Penitent birds.—Consolatory birds.—Presages of birds in India.—Verethraghna as a bird.—The bird's feather.—The red bird.—Grateful and prophetic birds.—The hero that understands the language of birds.—The bird and the two cypresses.—The hero becomes a bird by acquiring Solomon's ring.—The blue bird.—The bird caught by putting salt upon its tail.—The excrement of birds is propitious.—The demoniacal bird.—The bird that feeds the heroes.—Birds and poets; singers and prophets.—Auguries and auspices.—The auguries were laughed at in Greece.—Flight to right and to left.

THE sky, especially by night, is conceived now as a road on which one can walk, and where sometimes the traveller may be lost, or make others lose their way; now as the air itself, in which one flies or is carried in flight, with the risk sometimes of falling; now as a tree, in which one speaks or builds nests, with the risk of the words being sometimes sinister, or the nests falling; and now as a sea in which one navigates in peril of shipwreck.

The sky-atmosphere and the sky-tree are the world of the mythical flying birds and insects. The god, the demon, the hero, and the monster, when traversing this field, either take the forms of winged animals, or make use of them to ascend to the celestial paths, or else are conducted by them to their ruin.

The sun and the moon, the sunbeams, the thunderbolts, flashes of lightning, auroras, clouds that move and thunder, and the very shadows that move, often take in myths the forms of flying animals.

In the *Ṛigvedas*, the sun is called a bird (viḥ);[1] the Açvinâu come with the wheels of the car like a bird with feathers;[2] Indras is the well-winged red one;[3] the Marutas perch like birds upon the culm of buttered grass;[4] Agnis accomplishes the wish of the bird;[5] the well-winged ones of Agnis (*i.e.*, the thunderbolts) appear as destroyers when the black bull has bellowed (that is, when the black cloud has thundered);[6] Savitar must not destroy the woods of the birds;[7] from the house of the aurora the birds come forth;[8] the goddesses and the

[1] *Ṛigv.* i. 72, 9.

[2] Vir na parṇâiḥ; *Ib.* i. 183, 1.

[3] Aruṇaḥ suparṇaḥ; *Ib.* x. 55, 6.

[4] Vayo na sîdann adhi barhishi priye; *Ib.* i. 85, 7.

[5] Manmasâdhano veḥ; *Ib.* i. 96, 6.

[6] Â te suparṇâ aminantañ evâiḥ kṛishṇo nonâva vṛishabho yadîdam; *Ib.* i. 79, 2.

[7] Vanâni vibhyo nakir asya tâni vratâ devasya savitar minanti; *Ib.* ii. 38, 7.

[8] Ut te vayaççid vasater apaptan; *Ib.* i. 124, 12.—In the twenty-third story of the second book of *Afanassieff*, when the beautiful girl Helen, another form of the aurora, is at the king's ball, she throws bones with one hand, when birds spring up, and water with the other, when gardens and fountains spring up.

brides of the heroes are requested to come to the assistance of men with unclipt wings.[1] Finally, an interesting Vedic hymn shows us the sun and the moon, Indras and Somas, as two well-winged birds united in friendship, that continually fly round the same tree (*i.e.*, the sky); of these, one eats the sweet pippalas, the other shines without eating. Both, well-winged, sing as they safely guard the treasure of ambrosia. The honey of this tree is called pippalas: of this tree all the birds eat the honey, and on it they build their nests.[2]

The wisdom of birds is much celebrated in popular Aryan tradition. On this subject the *Mârkaṇḍeya-P.*[3] narrates a long and instructive legend.

The wise Gâiminis wishes some episodes of the great legend of the *Mahâbhâratam*, which seem obscure, to be explained to him. He has recourse to the learned Mârkaṇḍeyas; but the latter says he does not know how to enlighten him, and advises him to interrogate the birds, the best of the birds, sons of Droṇas, who know the essence of things, who meditate upon the sacred treatises, the birds Piñgâkshas, Vibodhas, Supattras, and Sumukhas, who will disperse his doubts. They live in a

---

1 Abhi no devîr avasâ mahaḥ çarmaṇâ nṛipatnîḥ aćhinnapatrâḥ saćantâm; *Ṛigv.* i. 22, 11.—If the goddesses are here the same as the nymphs, they may be the same as the clouds, and I should refer to this passage, the legend of the *Râmâyaṇam* (v. 56), according to which the lofty mountains were once winged (the clouds) and wandered about the earth at pleasure; Indras, with his thunderbolt, cut their wings, and they fell down.

2 Dvâ suparṇâ sayuǵâ sakhâyâ samânaṁ vṛiksham pari shasvaǵâte tayor anyaḥ pippalaṁ svâdv atty anaçnann anyo abhi ćâkaçîtî—Yatrâ suparṇâ amṛitasya bhâgam animeshaṁ vidathâbhisvaranti; *Ṛigv.* i. 164, 20.—Perhaps we should compare to this legend the two birds Amru and Ćamru of the *Khorda-Avesta*, of which one makes the seeds of the three mythical trees fall, and the other scatters them about.

3 Calcutta, 1851.

cave in the middle of the Vindhyâs; let him go to them and ask them. Gâiminis wonders how simple birds can possess so much wisdom. Mârkaṇḍeyas then relates to him their genealogy. A nymph, who had seduced by her song the penitent Durvâsas, was condemned to be born again in the family of the bird Garuḍas, and to spend sixteen years in the form of a bird, until, after giving birth to four sons, she should be wounded by an arrow and regain once more her primitive form in heaven. As a bird she is named Târkshî, and is married to the bird Droṇas, who is wise and instructed in the Vedâs and Vedâñgâs. Târkshî is present at the battle between the Kâuravâs and the Pâṇḍavâs; a dart strikes her in the belly, from which four eggs that shine like the moon fall to the ground. After the battle, the ascetic Çamîkas approaches the place where the four eggs lie, and hears the young birds chirping ćićîkući. The wise man marvels at seeing that they have escaped such carnage, concludes they must be Brâhmans, and thinks this a circumstance of most favourable augury and a presage of great fortune (mahâbhâgyapradarçinî). He carries the birds to his house, and places them where they run no risk of being harmed by cats, mice, hawks, or weasels. The birds are taken care of and nourished by the wise man, and grow up strong and learned, listening to the lessons that the wise man gives in school, and, being grateful to him as their deliverer, expressing their gratitude by means of words which, by exercise, they articulate clearly. Interrogated as to their previous existence, they remember that there was once a sage named Vipulâçvan, father of two children, Sukṛishas and Tumburus; these four were sons of Tumburus. Whilst they lived in the woods with their father, Indras, the king of the gods, comes to them in the form of a gigantic old bird, and demands human flesh from the hospitable sage. The wise man wonders that a bird, so old, that is, at an age in which every desire should be extinguished, should be so cruel as to wish for human flesh. Nevertheless he requests (like Viçvâmitras in the legend of Çunaḥcepas previously mentioned) his own sons to sacrifice themselves in fulfilment of this duty. They do not at first refuse this act of hospitality, but when they hear that they are to be eaten by the bird, they decisively refuse, pleading, among other arguments, the physiological, or rather, materialistic one, that if they are virtuous, their virtue too will perish with their bodies, whilst, on the other hand, in order to preserve their virtue long, they think themselves bound to prolong their existence as much as possible (we have already seen the cat adopting a similar argument to justify his fatness). Their father, indignant at this refusal after giving their promise, curses them, condemning them to be born again as animals, and then magnanimously offers himself to the famished bird. Upon which Indras reveals himself in his proper divine form, and then disappears after blessing the sage. The sons beseech their father to release them from the malediction; he takes pity upon them, but is unable to revoke his words; it is only in his power to temper the severity of the punishment. They are condemned to retain the animal form; but in that form they are to be recompensed with the gift of insight into the mysteries of being. It is for this reason that, when Çamîkas finds them, he salutes them by the name of Brâhmans. For the rest, the equivoque is easily comprehensible, when we reflect that the word *dviǵas*, or twice born, means bird (that is, born first as an egg, and afterwards as an animal), as well as Brâhman (who, by taking the sacred cord, the prætexta, and the sacrament of the holy oil, is born again). Etymology here assists our comprehension of the legend. In the same way as the Brâhman is the wisest of men, so are the dviǵâs or birds the wisest of animals. The birds, cursed by the hermit their father, go therefore to Mount Vindhyas, which is watered by many blessed streams, where they live as austere penitents. Gâiminis goes to consult them; when he approaches their abode, he hears them speaking distinctly to each other. He then comes up and sees them perched on the top of a rock. Gâiminis addresses them with amiable words; the birds answer him that, since so great a sage is come to visit them, their wish is accomplished and their curse come to an end. Then follow the questions of Gâiminis relating to Ǵanârdanas, Drâupadî, Baladevas, and the five sons of Drâupadî. The birds, before answering, sing a kind of hymn to Vishṇus, and expound his principal incarnations. In the *Mahâbhâratam*,[1] the ascetic Brâhmans go in the forms of birds to console the ṛishis Mândavyas, impaled by order of the king, for having given hospitality to the robbers of the royal booty.

Birds know everything, and hence presages are taken especially from them, whence the name *auspicium* or *augurium*, applied specifically to a presage. In the last book of the *Râmâyaṇam*,[2] the monsters are terrified by such omens as the following:—"Thousands of vultures and ducks with mouths that throw flames, which form a circle like that of the god of death upon the battalions of the monsters; the doves, the red-feet, the sârikâs (turdus salicæ) were dispersed."

In the *Avesta*, Verethraghna often appears as a bird, and as understanding the language of birds. A bird's feather, in the *Avesta*, assists Verethraghna, as in Fir-

[1] i. 4305. [2] Sixth canto.

dusi, a feather of the bird Simurg, burnt by Zal, calls up to his assistance the bird Simurg in person.[1] According to a legend of the *Khorda-Avesta*, the splendour of the old Yima, who had become proud and false-tongued (thus, in India, the celestial Yamas and the happy Çivas become infernal destroying deities), fled away in the form of a bird. According to the popular superstition of White Russia, the little bird diedka (the little one), is the guardian of treasures and has eyes of fire and a fiery beard (this is doubtless a representation of the demoniacal sun of evening, of Kuveras or of Plutos.[2]

[1] Professor Spiegel says in a note, *Khorda-Avesta*, p. 147: "Die Beschwörung vormittelst einer Feder ist gewiss eine alteranische Vorstellung."—In a story, hitherto unpublished, of the Monferrato, communicated to me by Signor Ferraro, a woman, who had gone to eat parsley in the garden of a sorceress, was obliged to give her daughter up to her as a penalty for the offence. The girl was afterwards subjected to three difficult trials; to sunder in one day a mountain of wheat and millet into the grains composing it, to eat in one day a mountain of apples, and to wash, dry, and iron in one hour all the linen of a year. In the first trial, by means of two bird's feathers, she calls up a thousand birds, who separate the grain from the millet.—In the fourth story of the fifth book of the *Pentamerone*, the birds strip themselves of their feathers to fill a mattress which the witch has ordered the young Permetella to make. In a Tuscan story, for the possession of a peacock's feather, the young brother is killed.

[2] In *Afanassieff*, v. 38, a similar little bird ravages during the night the field of a lord; the youngest of the three brothers, who is believed to be foolish, catches it and sells it to the king, who shuts it in a room under lock and key. The king's son releases the little bird, which in gratitude gives him a horse that wins battles, and a golden apple, by means of which he is able to wed a princess.—In the story v. 22, the young man who has been instructed by the devil transforms himself into a bird and tells his father to sell him, but not to give up the cage. The devil buys the bird, but does not obtain the cage; he puts the bird into a handkerchief to take it to his daughter, but when he comes home the bird has disappeared.—In the story v. 42, the king of birds releases Ivan from the witch who wishes to eat

In the *Contes Merveilleux* of Porchat, the red bird appears as a messenger.

In the legend of Sal, in Firdusi, there is a riddle about two cypresses, one withered and the other verdant, upon first the one and then the other of which a bird regularly builds his nest. The hero Sal, who solves the riddle, says that the two cypresses are the two opposite seasons

him, and takes him to his betrothed. The witch tears a few feathers off the king of birds, but does not succeed in stopping him.—In the story v. 46, the devil teaches the language of birds to the young hero.—In the story vi. 69, the wise maiden goes to take into the kingdom of darkness the bird that speaks, the tree that sings, and the water of life, with which she brings to life her two brothers, born before her, whom a witch had thrown into a fountain (the aurora delivers the Açvinâu).—In the fifth Sicilian story of Signora Gonzenbach, brother and sister go into the witch's castle to take the water that dances and the bird that speaks. The bird tells the water, in the king's presence, the story of the two young people.—In the fifth story of the second book of the *Pentamerone*, the fox teaches the young Grannonia what birds say.—In the seventh story of the fifth book of the *Pentamerone*, it is the youngest of the five brothers that acquires the faculty of understanding the language of birds.—In Pietro de Crescenzi (x. 1), we find a "rex Daucus (Dacus?) qui divino intellectu novit naturam accipitrum et falconum et eos domesticare ad prædam instruere, et ab ægritudinibus liberare."—In the legend of St Francis of Assisi, the great saint was able to make himself understood to birds, and to make the swallows be silent; the same saint made a wolf mild and tame; the miracle of Orpheus is repeated in numerous other legends.—In the sixteenth Mongol story of Siddhikür, a wise dwarf, who understands the language of birds, hears two birds, father and son, speak to each other on the summit of a tree about the king's son, who had been assassinated by the son of the minister.—In the *Edda*, Atli has a long dialogue with a bird whose language he understands.—Finally, the whole of the comedy of Aristophanes entitled *The Birds* (Ornithes) shows the wisdom and divining power of birds, and, as animals of presage, their intimate relation with the thunderbolts of Zeus.—According to the German belief, the fat of a serpent teaches how to understand the language of birds. Cfr. Simrock, the work previously quoted, p. 457.

of the year or the two sides of the sky, and that the bird is the sun.[1]

In the eighteenth Esthonian story, two birds, speaking to each other, signify where the famous enchanted ring of Solomon is to be found, which the young hero is looking for. When the hero finds the ring, he is able to transform himself at will into a bird; but the daughter of hell, in the shape of an eagle, carries it off from him. In the fourth Esthonian story, the girl of seven years of age becomes, by beneficent magic, a bird, when she is obliged to travel far. In the thirty-fifth of the stories of Santo Stefano di Calcinaia, the wife of the bird-catcher terrifies the devil in the form of an enormous and monstrous bird. In the fifth story of the fourth book of the *Pentamerone*, a fairy in the form of a bird arrests the arm of the king of Alta-Marina whilst he is about to kill his own wife Portiella. The fairy was grateful to the young woman, because, when she was asleep in a wood, Portiella had awakened her to deliver her from a satyr who was attempting to violate her.[2] The king shuts Portiella up in a tower without light; the bird makes a hole in it and brings food to her, stealing the fowls from the kitchen during the cook's absence. Portiella gives birth to a son, who is also nourished by the bird. The *oiseau bleu, couleur du temps,* of the story of Madame d'Aulnoy, who flies at night from the cypress to the window of the beautiful imprisoned Florine, is a beautiful

---

[1] "Die zwei Cypressen sind die Himmelsseiten,
Die beiden, die uns Glück und Leid bereiten;
Der Vogel, der drin nistet, ist die Sonne,
Sie giebt beim Schneiden Schmerz, beim Kommen Wonne."
—Schack, *Heldensagen von Firdusi*, p. 122.

[2] A variety of the myth of Priapos, mentioned in the chapter on the Ass.

variety of this same story. Several Russian stories end with the following refrain of an azure bird (sinićka, little azure one): "little azure one flies and says, Azure, but beautiful."[1] Inasmuch as the sun of morning, or spring, comes out of the dark-blue bird of night, or of winter, we can understand the popular Italian and German superstition, that when the excrement of a bird falls upon a man it is an omen of good luck. The excrement of the mythical bird of night, or of winter, is the sun. Considered in connection with morning or spring, the dark-coloured bird of night, or winter, is propitious; considered by itself, or in relation to the evening sun or the dying summer, it is a funereal and diabolical animal. Such is the bird Kâmek of the *Avesta*, which stretches its wings over all mankind, which carries off and hides the sun, creates darkness, keeps back the waters and devours all creatures, until after seven years and seven nights, the hero Kereçâçpa strikes it and makes it fall.

Moreover, the bird that brings food is a subject which in very popular in almost all the traditions of the Indo-European nations. Every one has heard of the bird which nourished Semiramis, abandoned by her mother in a desert and stony place, with curdled milk and cheese

[1] Sinićka letat i gavarít: Sin da charosh.—The dark-blue bird is a symbol of the azure sky of night or winter, whilst, on the other hand, the wooden bird, at which the maidens of Westphalia throw sticks on St John's Day, seems to be a phallical symbol; she who hits the bird is queen. The bird is a well-known phallical symbol; and a phallical origin must be ascribed to the popular superstition that a bird may be rendered helpless by putting salt upon its tail. The salacitas of an animal, when given way to, takes every energy from it; the ûrdhvaretas alone is strong. It was perhaps for a similar reason that in the Middle Ages, when a city was destroyed to its foundations, it was the custom to throw salt upon it, in order that it might never rise again. Salt thrown away is like seed sown in the desert, where it is fruitless.

(the moonlight), stolen from the neighbouring flocks of sheep, according to the narrative of Diodorus Siculus; and the same Persian bird nourishes, according to the legend, several other children, future heroes of Iran, who had been similarly exposed; in the legend of Romulus and Remus, the woodpecker assumes the same place and office as the nurse she-wolf. In the watery night and the watery winter, the solar child-hero, abandoned to himself, is nourished by birds. The nightingale or singer of the night sends forth his melodious notes from the nocturnal tree, predicting thus the renewal of daylight; in the tree-cloud, the thunder rumbles, the oracle speaks, and the bird prophesies. Theokritos calls poets the birds of the Muses (mousôn ornithas). The kokilas is the bird of the Hindoo poets and teaches them melody; to this bird corresponds the Hindoo Kyknos of the *Tuti-Name*, of which it is said that it has innumerable holes in its beak, from each of which a melodious sound comes forth.

The Hindoo *kavis*, the Latin *vates*, and the Hellenic *mantis* represent at once both the singer and the sage; thus the singers of the woods are at the same time omniscient prophets. They began with prophecies about the weather, as the thunder announces the storm, and finished by prophesying everything. The peasantry of Tuscany endeavour to this day to guess what weather it will be on the morrow from the songs of the birds.[1] The augures, the auguremens, the aucelli, and the aruspices were preserved even in the Middle Ages, according

[1] It is a mountaineer of the province of Siena that speaks: "I perceived by the song of the birds that the weather was about to change; their voice told me, it was so merry;" Giuliani, *Moralità e Poesia del Vivente Linguaggio della Toscana*, p. 149.

to the testimony of Du Cange.[1] As to the auguries and auspices of the ancient Greeks and Romans, I refer the reader to the numerous erudite works which treat of them in a particular manner. I must observe, however, that whilst among the Latins augury was deemed such a solemn thing that Publius Claudius and Lucius Junius were judged worthy of death for having set out on a voyage against the will of the auguries, and that whilst *ave*, that is to say, good augury, was still the solemn formula of Roman salutation, the Greeks had already turned auguries and auspices into derision. The reader remembers, no doubt, how in the *Iliad* the hero Hektor declares that he cares not whether the birds go to the right, towards the aurora and the sun, or to the left, towards the sunset. In Eusebius[2] we read that a bird was presented to Alexander, the Macedonian, when on the point of setting out for the Red Sea, in order that he might read the auguries by it according to custom; Alexander, in answer, killed the bird with an arrow; the bystanders being offended by this breach of the rules, the Macedonian hero added, "What folly is this? In what way could this bird, which could not foresee its death by this arrow, predict the fortunes of our journey?" Auguries and auspices were also taken in India. According to the *Râmâyaṇam*,[3] birds seen at a wedding to go to the left, are a sinister omen;[4] birds that fly, crying, to

[1] Cfr. among others, the words *albanellus* (haubereau) *avis auguralis species*, and *aucellus*.

[2] *De Præparat. Evang.* lib. ix.

[3] i. 76.

[4] Amongst the Romans, on the contrary, the flight to the left was an excellent omen; thus Plautus in the *Epidicus*: "Tacete, habete animum bonum, liquido exeo foras auspicio, ave sinistra." (But this change from right to left may depend upon the various positions taken by the observer in placing himself.) In the mediæval legend

the left of Râmas, announce to him a serious disaster, viz., the carrying off of Sîtâ.[1]

of Alexander, a bird with a human face (a harpy) meets Alexander and advises him to turn to the right, when he will see marvellous things.—Cfr. Zacher, *Pseudo-Callisthenes*, Halle, 1867, p. 142.

[1] *Râmây.* iii. 64.

CHAPTER II.

THE HAWK, THE EAGLE, THE VULTURE, THE PHŒNIX, THE HARPY, THE STRIX, THE BAT, THE GRIFFON, AND THE SIREN.

SUMMARY.

The bird of prey the most heroic of birds.—Indras as a hawk.—The hawk and the ambrosia; the ambrosia as sperm.—The bird of prey and the serpent.—Agnis, the Açvinâu, and the Marutas as hawks.—The place of sacrifice has the form of an eagle.—The two sons of Vinaṭâ.—Garuḍas, the bird of Vishṇus; he fights against the monsters.—Genealogy of the vultures.—Ǵâtâyus and Sampatis.—The king or the young hero who offers himself up to be devoured by the hawk or the eagle.—The grateful hawk or eagle.—Çyena and Çaena; Simurg; the feather of the bird of prey.—The birds as clouds.—The eagles as winds; Aquila and Aquilo.—The hawks as luminous birds; the eagles as demoniacal ones.—Accipiter.—The hawk as an emblem of nobility.—The hawk as the ensign of Attila.—The hawk in Hellenic antiquity.—The kite among the stars; it discharges its body upon the image of the god.—The beetle, the eagle, and Zeus.—The eagle as the thunderbolt or sceptre of Zeus.—The eagle presages supreme power and fertility; the eagle and the laurel.—The eagle carries off the robes of Aphroditê.—The eagle takes away the slippers of Rhodopê.—The eagle kills Æschilos.—Nisos and Scylla.—The vulture in ancient classical authors.—The vultures in hell.—The learned vulture.—Voracity of the vulture.—Imaginary birds.—The sun as a phœnix.—The demonaical harpies or Furiæ, canes Jovis.—Strix and striges; they suck blood.—Proca and Crane.—Bats and vampires.—The Stymphalian birds.—The birds of Seleucia.—The Gryphes and the Arimaspi.—The griffons sacred to Nemesis; the hypogriff, gryphos, logogriph, griffonage.—The Siren now as a bird, now as a fish.—Circe; a lunar myth.

The most heroic of birds is the bird of prey; the strength of its beak, wings, and claws, its size and swiftness, caused it to be regarded as a swift celestial messenger, carrier, and warrior.

The hawk, the eagle, and the vulture, three powerful birds of prey, generally play the same part in myths and legends; the creators of myths having from the first observed their general resemblance, without paying any regard to their specific differences.

The bird of prey, in mythology, is the sun, which now shines in its splendour, and now shows itself in the cloud or darkness by sending forth flashes of lightning, thunderbolts, and sunbeams. The flash, the thunderbolt, and the sunbeam are now the beak, now the claw of the bird of prey, and now, the part being sometimes taken for the whole, even the entire bird.

In the *Ṛigvedas*, the god Indras often appears in the form of a hawk or çyenas. Indras is like a hawk that flies swiftly over the other hawks, and, being well-winged, carries to men the food tasted by the gods.[1] He is enclosed in a hundred iron fortresses; nevertheless, with swiftness, he succeeds in coming out of them;[2] while flying away, he carries in his claw the beautiful, virgin, luminous ambrosia, by means of which life is prolonged and the dead brought to life again[3] (the rain, which is also confounded with the ambrosial humour of the moon.

[1] Pra çyenaḥ çyenebhya âçupâtvâ—Aćakrayâ yat svadhayâ suparṇo havyam bharan manave devaǵushṭam; *Ṛigv.* iv. 26, 4.—The somaḥ çyenâbhṛitaḥ is also mentioned in the *Ṛigv.* i. 80, 2, iv. 27, ix. 77, and other passages.

[2] Çatam mâ pura âyasîr arakshann adha çyeno ǵavasâ nir adîyam; *Ṛigv.* iv. 27, 1.

[3] Yaṁ te çyenaç ćârum avṛikaṁ padâbharad aruṇam mânam andhasaḥ—enâ vayo vi târy âyur ǵivasa enâ ǵagâra bandhutâ; *Ṛigv.* x. 144 5.

In the first strophe of the same hymn, Indus is also called ambrosia).[1] The hawk with iron claws kills the hostile demons,[2] has great power of breathing, and draws from afar the chariot with a hundred wheels.[3] However, while the hawk carries the ambrosia through the air, he trembles for fear of the archer Kṛiçânus,[4] who, in fact, shot off one of his claws (of which the hedgehog was born, according to the *Âitareya Br.*,[5] and according to the Vedic hymn,[6] one of his feathers which, falling on the earth, afterwards became a tree). After the victory gained over Ahis, the serpent-demon, Indras flees like a terrified hawk.[7] This is the first trace of the legendary and proverbial enmity between the bird of prey and the serpent. In the third book of the *Râmâyaṇam*, Râvaṇas says that he will carry off Sîtâ as the well-winged one (carries off) the serpent (suparṇaḥ pannaǵamiva).

Nor is Indras alone a hawk in the *Ṛigvedas*, but Agnis

[1] In the *Mahâbhâratam* (i. 2383), the ambrosia takes the shape of sperm. A king, far from his wife Girikâ, thinks of her; the sperm comes from him and falls upon a leaf. A hawk carries the leaf away; another hawk sees it and disputes with it for the possession of the leaf; they fight with one another and the leaf falls into the waters of the Yamunâ, where the nymph Adrikâ (equivalent to Girikâ), changed by a curse into a fish, sees the leaf, feeds upon the sperm, becomes fruitful, and is delivered; cfr. the chapter on the Fishes.

[2] Çyeno 'yopâshṭir hanti dasyûn; *Ṛigv.* x. 99, 8.—In the Russian stories the hawk and the dog are sometimes the most powerful helpers of the hero.

[3] Ghṛishuḥ çyenâya kṛitvana âsuḥ; *Ṛigv.* x. 144, 3.—Yam suparṇaḥ parâvataḥ çyenasya putra âbharat çataćakram; *Ṛigv.* x. 144, 1.

[4] Sa pûrvyaḥ pavate yaṁ divas pari çyeno mathâyad ishitas tiro raǵaḥ sa madhva â yuvate yeviǵâna it kṛiçânor astur manasâha bibhyushâ; *Ṛigv.* ix. 77, 2.

[5] iii. 3, 26.

[6] Antaḥ patat patatry asya parṇam; *Ṛigv.* iv. 27, 4.—Cfr. for this mythical episode the texts given by Prof. Kuhn and the relative discussions, *Die Herabkunft d. F. u. d. S.*, pp. 138 *seq.* and 180 *seq.*

[7] Çyeno na bhîtaḥ; *Ṛigv.* i. 32, 14.

too. Mâtariçvân and the hawk agitate, the one the heavenly fire, the other the ambrosia of the mountain.[1] The chariot of the Açvinâu is also sometimes drawn by hawks, as swift as heavenly vultures.[2] They are themselves compared to two vultures that hover round the tree where the treasure is[3] (we have seen in the preceding chapter that the tree is the sky). The Marutas are also called Gṛidhrâs or vultures (falcons according to Max Müller.[4]) In the *Ṛigvedas*, again, when the sun goes to the sea, he looks with a vulture's eye.[5] On account of this form of a bird of prey, often assumed by the solar god in the Vedic myths, we read in the *Âitareya Br.*, that the place destined for the sacrifice had the same shape. In the *Râmâyaṇam* we find, in the sacrifice of a horse, that the place of sacrifice has the form of the bird Garuḍas, the powerful mythical eagle of the Hindoos. In the 149th hymn of the tenth book of the *Ṛigvedas*, the ancient well-winged son of the sun Savitar is already named Garutman. The mythical bird is the equivalent of the winged solar horse, or hippogriff; indeed, the 118th hymn of the first book of the *Ṛigvedas*, soon after celebrating the hawks that draw the chariot of the Açvinâu, calls them beautiful flying horses (açvâ vapushaḥ pataṁgâḥ). We have observed that of the two twins, or the two brothers, one prevails over the other. Thus

[1] Anyaṁ divo mâtariçvâ ǵabhâramathnâd anyam pari çyeno adreḥ; *Ṛigv.* i. 93, 6.

[2] Â vâṁ çyenâso açvinâ vahantu—ye apturo divyâso na gṛidhrâḥ; *Ṛigv.* i. 118, 4.

[3] Gṛidhreva vṛikshaṁ nidhimantam aćha; *Ṛigv.* ii. 39, 1.

[4] *Ṛigv.* i. 88, 4.—In fact, in the hymn i. 165, 2, the Marutas are explicitly compared to hawks that fly through the air (çyenâṅ iva dhraǵato antarikshe).

[5] Drapsaḥ samudram abhi yaǵ ǵigâti paçyan gṛidhrasya ćakshasâ; *Ṛigv.* x. 123, 8.

of the two mythical vultures, of the two sons of Vinatâ, in the legend of the *Mahâbhâratam*,[1] their mother having broken the egg before the proper time, one, Aruṇas, is born imperfect, and curses his mother, condemning her to be the slave of her rival Kadrû for five thousand years, until her other son, the luminous, perfect, and powerful solar bird Garuḍas, comes to release her. Aruṇas becomes the charioteer of the sun; Garuḍas is, instead, the steed of the god Vishṇus, the solar horse, the sun itself, victorious in all its splendour. No sooner are the two birds born, than the horse Uććâiḥçravas also appears, which again signifies that solar bird and solar horse are identical. Like the hawk Indras, or the hawk of Indras, Garuḍas, the bird of Vishṇus, or Vishṇus himself, is thirsty, drinks many rivers,[2] carries off from the serpents the ambrosia, protected (as in the *Ṛigvedas*) by a circle of iron. Like Vishṇus, Garuḍas, from being very tall, makes himself very little, penetrates among the serpents, covers them with dust and blinds them; it is, indeed, on account of this feat that Vishṇus adopts him for his celestial steed.[3] The god Vishṇus goes on the back of the well-winged one to fight against the monsters;[4] indignant with them, he throws them to the ground with the flapping of his wings; the monsters aim their darts at him as another form of the hero, and he fights on his own account and for the hero.[5] When the bird Garuḍas appears, the fetters of the monsters, which compress like serpents the two brothers Râmas and Lakshmaṇas, are loosed, and the two young heroes rise more handsome and stronger than before.[6] The Nishâdâs come from their damp abodes, enter into the gaping jaws of Garuḍas

[1] i. 1078, *seq.*
[2] *Mbh.* i. 1495.
[3] *Ib.* i. 1496, *seq.*
[4] *Râmây.* vii. 6.
[5] *Ib.* vii. 7.
[6] *Ib.* vi. 26.

in thousands, enveloped by the wind and the dust.[1] (The sun of morning and that of spring devour the black monsters of night and of winter.)

Hitherto we have seen the hawk, the eagle (as Garuḍas), and the vulture exchanged for each other; even the Hindoo mythical genealogy confirms this exchange. According to the *Râmâyaṇam*,[2] of Tâmrâ (properly the reddish one; she also gave birth to Krâuńći, the mother of the herons) was born Çyenî (that is, the female hawk); of Çyenî was born Vinatâ. Vinatâ (properly the bent one) laid the egg whence Aruṇas and Garuḍas came forth (the two Dioskuroi also came, as is well known, out of the egg of Léda, united with the swan); Garuḍas was in his turn father of two immense vultures, Gâtâyus and Sampatis. In this genealogy the ascending movement of the sun appears to be described to us, like the myth of the sun Vishṇus, who, from a dwarf, becomes a giant. The vulture Gâtâyus knows everything that has happened in the past, and everything that will come to pass in the future, inasmuch as, like the Vedic sun, he is viçvavedas, all-seeing, omniscient, and has traversed the whole earth. In the *Râmâyaṇam* we read of the last fierce battle of the aged vulture Gâtâyus with the terrible monster Râvaṇas, who carries off the beautiful Sîtâ during the absence of her husband Râmas. Gâtâyus, although old in years, rises into the air to prevent the carrying off of Sîtâ by Râvaṇas in a chariot drawn by asses; the vulture breaks with his strong claws the bow and arrow of Râvaṇas, strikes and kills the asses, splits the chariot in two, throws the charioteer down, forces Râvaṇas to leap to the ground, and wounds him in a thousand ways; but at last the king of the monsters succeeds with his sword

[1] *Mbh.* i. 1337, *seq.*

[2] iii. 20.

in cutting off the wings, feet, and sides of the faithful bird, who expires in pain and grief, whilst the demon carries the ravished woman into Lañkâ.

Thus far, therefore, we always find in the bird of prey a friend of the hero and the god. Such is also, in the *Râmâyaṇam*,[1] the immense vulture that comes to place itself, and to vomit blood upon the standard of the monster Kharas, to predict his misfortunes to him; and such is the elder brother of Gâtâyus, the vulture Sampatis, who, coming out of a cavern, informs the great monkey Hanumant where Sîtâ may be found. Sampatis, after having seen Hanumant, recovers his own wings, which had been burnt by the sun's rays, once when he had wished to defend his younger brother from them whilst they were flying together too high up in the regions of the sun[2] (a variety of the Hellenic legend of Dedalus and Icarus, of that of Hanumant who wished to fly after the sun in order to catch it, and of that of the two Açvinâu).

When, in the very popular Hindoo legend of the Buddhist king who sacrifices himself instead of the dove that had looked for hospitality from him, the hawk appears as the persecutor of the dove, this apparent persecution is only a trial that Indras, the hawk, and Agnis, the dove, wish to make of the king's virtue. No sooner does the hawk see that the king offers himself up to be devoured by the hawk, who complains that the king has taken his prey, the dove, from him, than both hawk and dove reassume their divine form, and cover the holy king with benedictions.[3] Indras and Agnis, united together, are

[1] iii. 29.

[2] *Râmây.* iv. 58, 59.

[3] For the numerous Eastern varieties of this legend, cfr. the Einleitung to the *Pañćatantram*, of Prof. Benfey, p. 388, *seq.*—In the fifth story of the first book of *Afanassieff* (cfr. the sixth of the same book), Little John is carried back from the bottom of the earth into

also themselves a form of the two Açvinâu, like the two faithful doves that sacrifice themselves in the third book of *Pańćtantram.*

The wise çaena of the *Avesta* has a character nearly resembling the Vedic bird çyenas. According to the *Bundehesh,* two çaenas stay at the gates of hell, which correspond to the two crepuscular hawks or vultures of

Russia upon the wings of an eagle. When the eagle is hungry it turns its head, and Johnny gives it food; when the provisions come to an end, Johnny feeds it with his own flesh.—In the twenty-seventh story of the second book, the two young people are carried from the world of darkness into that of light on the wings of the bird Kolpalitza; when the provisions come to an end, it is the girl that gives flesh, cut off her thigh, to the bird. But the youth, who has with him the water of life, heals the amorous maiden; cfr. also *Afanassieff,* v. 23, and v. 28, where, instead of the eagle, we find the hawk.—The same sacrifice of himself is made in a Piedmontese story, recorded by me in first number of the *Rivista Orientale,* by a young prince, who wishes to cross the sea in order to see the princess that he loves; the same is done by the young hero of the following unpublished Tuscan story, which I heard from a certain Martino Nardini of Prato:—"A three-headed dragon steals during the night the golden apples in the garden of the king of Portugal; the three sons of the king watch during the night: the first two fall asleep, but the third discovers the thief and wounds him. The day after, the three brothers follow the track caused by the robber's blood: they come to a beautiful palace, in which there is a cistern, into which the third brother is lowered down, taking a trumpet with him to sound when he wishes to be taken up. Following a dark path he comes to a fine meadow, where there are three splendid palaces, one of bronze, one of silver, and one of gold; following the trace of blood, he goes to the palace of bronze; a beautiful maiden opens the gate to him, and wonders why he has come down to the world underground; the young couple are pleased with each other, and promise to marry one another; the maiden has a crown of brilliants, of which she gives him half as a pledge. The dragon comes back home, and says:—

"Ucci, ucci
O che puzzo di Cristianucci,
O ce n' è, o ce n' è stati,
O ce n' è di rimpiattati."

the Vedâs. The bird with wings that strike, into which the hero Thraetaona is transformed in the *Khorda Avesta*, whilst it reminds us of the Hindoo warrior vulture, can serve as a link to join together the Zendic çaena and the Persian Simurg. The bird Simurg has its marvellous nest upon Mount Alburs, upon a peak that touches the sky, and which no man has ever yet seen. The child Sal is exposed upon this mountain; he is hungry and cold,

---

The maiden, who has concealed the young hero, caresses the dragon and makes him fall asleep. When he is asleep, she brings the young man out of his concealment, gives him a sword and tells him to cut the three heads off at one blow. Helped by a second maiden, the young hero prepares to accomplish a second undertaking in the silver palace of the five-headed dragon. He must cut the five heads off at a blow, for if one remains, it is as if he had cut none off. After having killed the dragon, he promises to marry the second maiden too. Finally, he knocks at the gate of the golden palace, which is opened by a third maiden; she too asks, "What ever induced you to come to lose your life in the lower world? The seven-headed dragon lives here." He promises to marry her; the dragon does not wish to go to rest this night; but the maiden persuades him to do so, upon which the youths cuts off the seven heads in two strokes. The three girls, who were three princesses carried off by the dragons, are released, and take all the riches that they can find in order to carry them into the upper world. They come to the cistern, the hero sounds the trumpet, and the two brothers draw up all the riches, the three maidens, shutting up the entrance with a stone, and leaving their young brother alone in the subterranean world. The two elder brothers force the three princesses to declare that they had delivered them; they then go to the King of Portugal and boast of this feat, saying, that the third brother is lost. The three princesses are sad, at which the King of Portugal wonders. The elder brothers wish to marry the maiden who was in the bronze palace; but she declares that she will only marry him who brings to her the other half of the crown of brilliants. They send to all the goldsmiths and jewellers to find one who can make it. Meanwhile, the third brother, abandoned underground, cries out for aid; an eagle approaches the tomb, and promises to carry him into the world above, if he will allay its hunger. The young hero, by the eagle's advice, puts lizards and serpents into a

and cries out; the bird Simurg passes by, hears his cry, takes pity upon him, and carries the child to its solitary peak. A mysterious voice blesses the glorious bird, who nourishes the boy, instructs, protects, and strengthens him, and, when he lets him go, gives him one of his own feathers, saying that when he is in danger he must throw this feather into the fire, and he will come at once to assist him,[1] and take him back into the kingdom. He

sack, and calls the eagle after having made a plentiful provision of food. He fastens the sack round his neck in order to give an animal to the eagle each time that it asks for food. When they are a few arms' length distant from the upper world, the sack is empty; the youth cuts his flesh off with a knife and gives it to the eagle, which carries him into the world, when the young man asks him how he can return home. The bird directs him to follow the high road. A charcoal-seller passes by; the young man proposes himself as his assistant, on condition that he give him some food. The charcoal-seller takes him with himself for some time, and then recommends him to an old man, his friend, who is a silversmith. Meanwhile, the king's servants have been six months wandering towards the sunset, searching for a silversmith capable of making the other half of the crown, but in vain; they then wander for six months towards the sunrise till they come to the dwelling of the poor silversmith where the third brother serves as an assistant. The old man says he is not able to make the half crown; but the young man asks to see the other half, recognises it, and promises to give it back entire in eight days. At the expiration of this time, the king sends for the crown and the manufacturer, but the youth sends his master instead of himself. The princess, however, insists upon seeing the young assistant too; he is sent for and brought to the palace; the king does not recognise him, and asks what reward he wants; he answers that he wishes for what the crown cost to the princess. The latter recognises him, after which his father does so too. The young hero weds the princess to whom he had promised himself; and the two brothers are covered with inflammable gums, and used as lamps to light up the wedding.

[1] In a hitherto unpublished story of the Monferrato, communicated to me by Signor Ferraro, a king with three sons is blind; he would be cured if he could bathe his eyes in oil with a feather of the griffon-bird, which lives upon a high mountain. The third brother

only asks him never to forget his faithful and loving preserver. He then carries the young hero to his father's palace. The king praises the divine bird in the following words:—"O king of birds! Heaven has given thee strength and wisdom; thou art the assister of the needy, propitious to the good and the consoler of the afflicted; may evil be dispersed before thee, and may thy greatness last for ever." In the fifth adventure of Isfendiar, in *Firdusi*, the gigantic bird Simurg appears, on the contrary, as demoniacal as he that dims the sunbeams with his wings (in the *Birds* of Aristophanes, when a great number of birds appear, the spectators cry out, "O Apollo, the clouds!") Isfendiar fights with him, and cuts him to pieces.

In Scandinavian and German mythology, while the hawk is generally a luminous shape, preferred by the heroes, and by Freya, the eagle is a gloomy form preferred by demons, or at least by the hero or god (like Odin)[1]

succeeds in catching one, having been kind to an old woman; he brings the griffon-bird to his father, who recovers his sight and his youth.—Cfr. the third story of the fourth book of the *Pentamerone*, in which a hawk that is a princess transformed, also gives to the brother of his wife one of his feathers, which he is to throw to the ground in case of necessity; indeed, when young Tittone requires it, a battalion of hawks appear in order to free the imprisoned maiden loved by Tittone.—In the fifth story of the fifth book of the *Pentamerone*, the hawk serves as a guide to a young king to find a beautiful princess whom a witch has put to sleep, and who is believed to be dead. This princess becomes the mother of two sons, who are called Sun and Moon.—In the sixth Sicilian story of Signora Gonzenbach, a young man releases an eagle that was entangled in the branches of a tree; the grateful eagle gives him one of its feathers; letting it fall to the ground, the youth can become an eagle at pleasure.

[1] In the ninth Esthonian story it is the eagle that takes the message to the thunder-god to enable him to recover his weapon, which the devil had carried off.—In the first Esthonian story, the eagle also appears as the propitious messenger of the young prince.

hidden in the gloomy night or in the windy cloud. The *Edda* tells us that the winds are produced by the shaking of the wings of a giant, who sits in the form of an eagle at the extremity of the sky; the aquila and the wind called aquilo by the Latins, as they correspond etymologically, seem also to be mythically identical. I have observed on a previous occasion that in the *Edda* the witch rides upon a wolf, using eagles as reins. In the *Nibelungen*, Krimhilt sees in a dream his beloved hawk strangled by two eagles.

On the other hand, the swallows sing to Sigurd in the *Edda*, predicting to him his meeting with the beautiful warrior maiden who, coming forth from the battles, rides upon an eagle. But this warlike girl was, however, destined to cause the death of Sigurd.

In the chapter on the elephant, we saw how the bird Garuḍas transported into the air an elephant, a tortoise, a bough of a tree, and hermits. In the Greek variety of the same myth, we have the eagle instead of Garuḍas. In the *Edda*, three Ases (Odin, Loki, and Hönir) are cooking an ox under a tree; but from the summit of the tree, an eagle interrupts the cooking of the meat, because it wishes to have a share. The Ases consent; the eagle carries off nearly everything, upon which Loki, indignant, wounds the eagle with a stake; but whilst one end of the stake remains attached to the eagle, the other is fastened to Loki's hand, and the eagle carries him up into the air. Loki feels his arms break, and implores the eagle to have compassion upon him; the gigantic bird lets him go, on condition of obtaining, instead of him, Iduna and her apples.[1] In the twenty-third story of the

---

[1] In the story of Santo Stefano, *La Principessa che non ride*, the eaglets have the same faculty of drawing after themselves everything

fifth book of *Afanassieff*, the eagle, after having been benefited by a peasant, eats up his sheep. The name of eagles was given during the Middle Ages to certain demons which were said to appear in the form of an eagle, especially on account of their rapacious expression, and aquiline nose.[1]

The hawk, on the other hand, I repeat, usually appears as divine, in opposition to all that is diabolical. In the twenty-second story of the fifth and the forty-sixth of the sixth book of *Afanassieff*, the hero transforms himself into a hawk, in order to strangle the cock into which the devil has metamorphosed himself (a Russian proverb, however, says of the devil that he is more pleasing than the luminous hawk).[2] When they wished, in

that they touch; and, as forms of the winds (or the clouds), in which character they sometimes appear, we can understand this property of theirs; the wind, too, draws after itself everything that comes in its way, and especially the violent north wind (aquilo).—In Russian stories we have, instead, now the funereal storks, now the marvellous goose taking the place of the eagle that drags things behind it.

[1] In the tenth Sicilian story of Signora Gonzenbach, it is in the shape of a silver eagle that the king of the assassins penetrates into the room where the young wife of the king sleeps, upon whom he wishes to avenge himself.—Stephanus Stephanius, the interpreter of *Saxo Grammaticus*, writes, that among the English, the Danes, and other Northern nations, it was the custom when an enemy was defeated, to thrust a sword, as a greater mark of ignominy, into his back, in such a manner as to separate the backbone on both sides by a longitudinal wound; thence stripes of flesh having been cut off, they were fastened to the sides, so as to represent eagle's wings. (In Russian popular stories, when heroes and monsters fight, we find frequent reference to a similar custom.)

[2] Panravílas satanâ lućshe yasnavo sakalá, *Afanassieff*, vi. 16.—The proverb, however, may have another sense, viz., better the devil in person than a beautiful but diabolical shape. The devil sometimes assumed the form of a hawk, as we learn from the legend of Endo, an English man-at-arms, who became enamoured of one into which the devil had transformed himself, in Guillelmus Neubrigensis, *Hist. Angl.* i. 19.

popular Russian phraseology, to express something that it is impossible to overtake, it was said, "Like the hurricane in the field, and the luminous hawk in the sky." We know that the Latin *accipiter* and the Greek *ôküpteros* mean the swift-winged. In the seventh story of the first book of *Afanassieff*, the hawk appears in opposition to the black crow. When the young girl, disguised as a man, succeeds in deceiving the Tzar three times, she says to him, "Ah! thou crow, crow; thou hast not known, O crow, how to catch the hawk in a cage."

The hawk was one of the distinctive badges of the mediæval cavalier; even ladies kept them. Krimhilt brings up a wild hawk; Brunhilt, when she throws herself upon the funeral pyre, that she may not survive Sigurd, has two dogs and two hawks immolated along with her. On the sepulchres of mediæval cavaliers and ladies, a hawk was not unfrequently found, as an emblem of their nobility. According to a law of the year 818, the sword and hawk belonging to the losing cavalier were to be respected by his conqueror, and left unappropriated; the hawk to hunt, and the sword to fight with. In *Du Cange*, we read that in 1642 Monsieur De Sassay claimed as his feudal right, "ut nimirum accipitrem suum ponere possit super altare majus ecclesiæ Ebraicensis (of Evreux), dum sacra in eo peragit ocreatus, calcaribusque instructus presbyter parochus d'Ezy, pulsantibus tympanis, organorum loco." According to the law of the Burgundians, he who attempted to steal another man's hawk was, before all, obliged to conciliate the hawk itself by giving it to eat (sex uncias carnis acceptor ipse super testones comedat); or if the hawk refused to eat, the robber had to pay an indemnity to the proprietor, besides a fine (sex solidos illi cujus acceptor est, cogatur exsolvere; mulctæ autem nomine solidos duos). According to information supplied me by my learned friend Count Geza Kuun, the hawk (turul) was the military ensign of Attila. According to a tradition preserved in the chronicle of Keza and of Buda, Emesu, mother of Attila, saw in a dream a hawk which predicted a happy future to her, after which dream she became pregnant.

Nor was the hawk less honoured in Hellenic antiquity; according to Homer, it was the rapid messenger of Apollo; the spy of Apollo, sacred to Zeus, according to Ælianos; having after death the faculty of vaticination, according to Porphyrios (who even recommends the heart of a hawk, a stag, or a mole to any one about to practise divination). In the *Iliad*, Apollo coming down from Mount Ida, is compared to the swift hawk, the killer of doves, the swiftest of all birds. Many are the superstitious beliefs concerning the hawk collected by Ælianos; such as, for instance, that it does not eat the hearts of animals; that it weeps over a dead man; that it buries unburied bodies, or at least puts earth upon their eyes, in which it thinks it sees the sun again, upon which, as its most beloved star, it always fixes its gaze; that it loves gold; that it lives for seven hundred years; not to mention the extraordinary medical virtues which are always attributed to every sacred animal, and which are particularly considered as essential to the sacred hawk. Several of the qualities of the sacred hawk passed also into other falcons of inferior quality, the kite (milvius),[1] for instance, of which it is said that it was placed among the stars for having carried to Zeus the entrails of the monster bull-serpent, and, according to the third book of Ovid's *Fasti*, for

[1] In Plato's *Phædon*, rapacious men are transformed into wolves and kites.

having brought back to Zeus the lost ring (an ancient form of the mediæval ring of Solomon, *i.e.*, the solar disc):—

> "Jupiter alitibus rapere imperat, attulit illi,
> Milvius, et meritis venit in astra suis."

With regard to the kite, we find an apologue,[1] according to which the kite, at the point of death, asks its mother to beg grace from the neighbouring statue of the god, and especially forgiveness, for the sacrilege which it had frequently committed, discharging its body upon the image of the god (the sun upon the sky).

A richer variety of this story is found in another apologue, which illustrates a Greek proverb ("æton kantaros maicusomai"); but instead of the hawk, we have the beetle, and instead of the statue, the god himself, Zeus, with eagle's eggs in his lap. The beetle (the hostess-moon), wishing to punish the eagle, which had violated the laws of hospitality with regard to the hare (also the moon), attempts to destroy its eggs; the eagle goes and places them in the lap of Zeus; the beetle, who knows that Zeus hates everything that is unclean, lets some dung fall upon him; Zeus forgets the eggs, shakes himself, and breaks them. Here the eagle is identified with Zeus, as in the Vedic hymns the hawk with Indras. In the first of Pindar's Pythic odes, the poet speaks of the eagle as sleeping on the sceptre of Zeus (as a thunderbolt, which is the real sceptre of Zeus). The eagle of Zeus is also represented as holding the thunderbolt in its claws, which is in accordance with

[1] Cfr. Aldrovandi, *Ornith.* v.—And, moreover, in the same Aldrovandi:—"Narrant qui res Africanas literis mandarunt Aquilam marem aliquando cum Lupa coire . . . producique ac edi Draconem, qui rostro et alis avis speciem referat, cauda serpentem, pede Lupum, cute esse versicolorem, nec supercilia posse attollere."

the sentence, "Fulmina sub Jove sunt." When Zeus is equipping himself to fight against the Titans, the eagle brings his dart to him, for which reason Zeus adopted the eagle as his ensign of war. In *Dion Cassius*, the eagles let the golden thunderbolts drop out of their talons into the camp of the Pompeians, and fly towards the camp of Cæsar to announce his victory. We find very numerous examples in the ancient classics of eagles that presage now victory, now supreme power to the heroes, that now nourish, now save them, and now sacrifice themselves for them.[1] The eagle of Zeus, the royal eagle, does not feed upon flesh, but upon herbs, properly upon the moisture of these herbs, by means of which we can comprehend the rape of Ganymede, the cup-bearer of Zeus, carried off by the eagle in the same way as the hawk of Indras carries off the somas in the *Ṛigvedas*. The Hellenic eagle is generally, like Zeus, a bringer of light, fertility, and happiness. Pliny narrates of an eagle, that immediately after the wedding of Augustus it let fall, as an omen of fecundity in the family of Augustus, into the lap of Livia Drusilla a white hen, having a branch of laurel in its beak; this branch was planted, and grew into a dense laurel-grove; the hen had so many descendants, that afterwards the villa where this happened was called the Villa of the Hens. Suetonius adds that in the last year of the life of Nero all the hens died, and all the laurel plants were dried up. We also find the eagle in connection with the laurel in the myth of Amphiaraos, whose spear, carried off by the eagle and plunged into the ground, grew into a laurel plant.

[1] I recommend, to whoever wishes to find all these circumstances united, the perusal of the first volume of the *Ornithologia* of Aldrovandi, who dedicated in it to birds of prey a long and detailed study. —Cfr. also Bachofen. *Die Sage von Tanaquil*, Heidelberg, 1870.

In the first chapter of the first book, when speaking of the myth of the aurora, we mentioned the young hero who disrobes the beautiful princess on the bank of the river and carries her apparel away. In the Hellenic myth we find a zoological variety of this myth. Aphroditê (here the evening aurora) bathes in the Acheloos (the river of night); Hermês (the extreme western light, and perhaps even the moon) becomes enamoured of her, and makes the eagle (the bird of night) carry off her garments, to obtain which, Aphroditê satisfies the desire of Hermês. In *Strabo* we find a variation of the same story which reminds us of the fairy-tale of Cinderella. Whilst Rhodopê is bathing, the eagle snatches one of her slippers out of her maid's hands and carries it off to the king of Memphis, who, seeing the slipper, falls in love with the foot that wore it, gives orders to search everywhere for the girl to whom the slipper belongs, and, when Rhodopê is found, marries her. Ælianos says that this king was Psammetichos. But the Hellenic eagle is divine as long as the god Zeus, whom it represents, is propitious; when Zeus becomes the tyrant of heaven, and condemns Prometheus to be bound upon a rock, the eagle goes to gnaw at his heart. And because the poet Æschilos glorified Prometheus, making him curse the tyranny of Zeus, hence, doubtless, arose the legend that Æschilos was, when old and bald, killed by a tortoise, which the eagle, mistaking the head of Æschilos for a white rock, had let fall from the sky in order to break it and feed upon it. The eagle which, according to Theophrastos, announced death to the cutters of black hellebore, was also a funereal and demoniacal bird. In the eighth book of Ovid's *Metamorphoses*, King Nisos, the golden-haired (the sun of evening), is transformed into a marine eagle (the night or winter), when his daughter Scylla (the night, or winter), in order to give him up to his enemies, destroys his strength by cutting his hair (an evident variation of the solar legend of Delilah and Samson).

The vulture, too, is a sacred bird in the legends of ancient classical authors; Herodotos says that it is very dear to Hêraklês (the killer of the eagle that gnaws at the heart of Prometheus, who had made for the hero the cup in which he had been enabled to cross the sea); it announces sovereign dominion to Romulus, Cæsar, and Augustus. Pliny writes that burnt vulture's feathers make serpents flee; the same feathers, according to Pliny, have the property of facilitating parturition, inasmuch as, as St Jerome writes (adversus Jovinianum ii.), "Si medicorum volumina legeris, videbis tot curationes esse in vulture, quot sunt membra."[1] Two vultures (a form of the Açvinâu) eat every day, in hell, the liver that continually grows again (the *immortale jecur* of Virgil) of the giant Tityo, the offender of Latona (the moon), dear to Jupiter. (The monster of night is killed every day and rises again every night). The two youths Ægipios and Nephrôn are another form of the Açvinâu, who, hating each other on account of the love which each has for the other's mother, are changed by Zeus into two vultures, after that Ægipios, by a stratagem of Nephrôn, united himself with his own mother. Iphiklos consults the birds to have children, from the vulture downwards, who alone knew how to assign the reason why Iphiklos had no children and indicate the means of obtaining them. Philakos had tried to kill Iphiklos; not having succeeded, he fastened his sword

[1] Comparative popular medecine might be the subject of a special work which could not fail to be instructive and interesting.

on a wild pear-tree; around the sword a covering of bark grew, which hid it from the sight of men. The vulture shows the place where this tree grows, and advises Iphiklos to take the bark off, to clean the rust off the sword, and after ten days to drink the rust in a toast; Iphiklos thus obtains offspring.

The vulture, therefore, generally preserves in Græco-Latin tradition the heroic and divine character which it has in Indian tradition, although its voracity became proverbial in ancient popular phraseology. Lucian calls a great eater the greatest of all the vultures. Moreover, the special faculty of distinguishing the smell of a dead body, even before death, is attributed to him; whence Seneca, in an epistle against the man who covets the inheritance of a living person, says "Vultur es, cadaver expecta," and Plautus in the *Truculentus* says of certain parasitical servants: "Jam quasi vulturii triduo prius prædivinabant, quo die esituri sient."

Besides these royal birds of prey that become mythical, there are several mythical birds of prey that never existed, still to be noticed, such as the phœnix, the harpy, the griffon, the strix, the Seleucide birds, the Stymphalian birds, and the sirens. Popular imagination believed in their terrestrial existence for a long time, but it can be said of them all as of the Arabian Phœnix:—

> "All affirm that it exists;
> Where it is no one can tell."[1]

In point of fact, no man has ever seen them; a few deities or heroes alone approached them; their seat is in the sky, where, according to their several natures and

[1] "Come l'Araba Fenice;
Che ci sia, ciascun lo dice;
Dove sia, nessun lo sa."

the different places occupied by the sun or the moon in the sky, they attract, ravish, seduce, enchant, or destroy.

The phœnix is, beyond all doubt, the eastern and western sun; hence Petrarch was able to say with reason,

"Nè 'n ciel nè 'n terra è più d'una Fenice,"

as there is not more than one sun; and we, like the the ancient Greeks, say of a rare man or object, that he or it is a phœnix. Tacitus, who narrates, in the fourteenth book, the fable of the phœnix, calls it *animal sacrum soli;* Lactantius says that it alone knows the secrets of the sun—

"Et sola arcanis conscia Phœbe tuis,"

and represents it as rendering funereal honours to its father in the temple of the sun; Claudian calls it *solis avem* and describes its whole life in a beautiful little poem.

It is born in the East, in the wood of the sun, and until it has assumed its whole splendid shape it feeds upon dew and perfumes, whence Lactantius—

"Ambrosios libat cœlesti nectare rores
Stellifero teneri qui cecidere polo.
Hos legit, his mediis alitur in odoribus ales,
Donec maturam proferat effigiem."

It then feeds upon all that it sees. When it is about to die it thinks only of its new birth—

"Componit bustumque sibi, partumque futurum" (*Claudian*);

inasmuch as it is said to deposit a little worm, the colour of milk, in its nest, which becomes a funeral pyre,

"Fertur vermis lacteus esse color" (*Lactantius*).

Before dying, it invokes the sun:

"Hic sedet, et solem blando clangore salutat
Debilior, miscetque preces, et supplice cantu
Præstatura novas vires incendia poscit;
Quem procul abductis vidit cum Phœbus habenis,
Stat subito, dictisque pium solatur alumnum" (*Claudian*).

The sun extinguishes the conflagration, which consumes the phœnix, and out of which it has to arise once more. At last the phœnix is born again with the dawn—

"Atque ubi sol pepulit fulgentis lumina portæ,
Et primi emicuit luminis aura levis,
Incipit illa sacri modulamina fundere cantus,
Et mira lucem voce ciere novam" (*Lactantius*).

In my opinion, no more proofs are required to demonstrate the identity of the phœnix with the sun of morning and of evening, and, by extension, with that of autumn and of spring. That which was fabled concerning it in antiquity, and by reflection, in the Middle Ages, agrees perfectly with the twofold luminous phenomenon of the sun that dies and is born again every day and every year out of its ashes, and of the hero or heroine who traverses the flames of the burning pyre intact.

The nature of the phœnix is the same as that of the burning bird (szar-ptitza) of Russian fairy tales, which swallows the dwarf who goes to steal its eggs (the evening aurora swallows the sun).[1]

The solar bird of evening is a bird of prey; it draws to itself with its damp claw; it draws into the darkness of night; it has night behind it; its appearance is charming and its countenance alluring, but the rest of its body is as horrid as its nature.

Virgil and Dante ascribe women's faces to the Harpies—

"Ali hanno late e colli e visi umani
Piè con artigli e pennuto il gran ventre."

Rutilius[2] says that their claws are glutinous—

"Quæ pede glutineo, quod tetigere trahunt."

[1] Cfr. *Afanassieff*, v. 27.

[2] *Itin.* i.

Others give them vultures' bodies, bears' ears, arms and feet of men, and the white breasts of women. Servius, speaking of the name they bear of *canes Jovis*, notes that this epithet was given them because they are the Furies in person, "Unde etiam epulas apud Virgilium abripiunt, quod Furiarum est." Ministers of the vengeance of Zeus, they contaminate the harvests of the king-seer Phineus, inspired by Apollo, whom some consider to be a form of Prometheus, the revealer of the secret of Zeus to mankind, and others, the blinder of his own sons.

The bird of prey, the evening solar bird, becomes a strix, or witch, during the night. We have already noticed the popular belief that the cat, at seven years of age, becomes a witch. An ancient superstition given by Aldrovandi also recognises witches in cats, and adds that, in this form, they suck the blood of children. The same is done by the witches of popular stories,[1] and by the striges. During the night they suck the blood of children; that is to say, the night takes away the colour, the red, the blood of the sun. Ovid, in the sixth book of the *Fasti*, represents the maleficent striges as follows:

> "Nocte volant, puerosque petunt nutricis egentes,
> Et vitiant cunis corpora rapta suis.
> Carpere dicuntur lactentia viscera rostris,
> Et plenum poto sanguine guttur habent."

Festus derives the word strix *à stringendo*, from the

[1] In the first chapter of the first book we saw how the witch sucked the breasts of the beautiful maiden.—In *Du Cange*, s. v. *Amma*, we read as follows: "Isidorus, lib. xii. cap. vii. bubo strix nocturna: 'Hæc avis, inquit ille, vulgo Amma dicitur ab amando parvulos, unde et lac præbere dicitur nascentibus.' Anilem hanc fabulam non habet Papias MS. Ecclesiæ Bituricensis. Sic enim ille: Amma avis nocturna ab amando dicta, hæc et strix dicitur a stridore."

received opinion that they strangle children. The striges, in the book of the *Fasti*, previously quoted, attack the child Proca, who is only five days old—

> "Pectoraque exhorbent avidis infantia linguis."

The nurse invokes the help of Crane, the friend of Janus, who has the faculty of hunting good and evil away from the doorsteps of houses. Crane hunts the witches away with a magical rod, and cures the child thus—

> "Protinus arbutea postes ter in ordine tangit
> Fronde ter arbutea limina fronde notat.
> Spargit aquis aditus, et aquæ medicamen habebant,
> Extaque de porca cruda bimestre tenet."

The usual conjurings are added, and the incident ends thus—

> "Post illud, nec aves cunas violasse feruntur,
> Et rediit puero qui fuit ante color."

Quintus Serenus, when the *strix atra* presses the child, recommends as an amulet, garlic, of which we have seen that the strong odour puts the monstrous lion to flight.

The same maleficent and demoniacal nature is shared in by the bats and the vampires, which I recognise in the "two winged ones entreated not to suck" of a Vedic hymn.[1]

Of analogous nature were the Stymphalian birds, which

---

[1] Mâ mâm ime patatriṇî vi dugdhâm; *Ṛigv.* i. 158, 4.—In Sicily, the bat called *taddarita* is considered as a form of the demon; to take and kill it, one sings to it—

> "Taddarita, 'ncanna, 'ncanna,
> Lu dimonio ti 'ncanna
> E ti 'ncanna pri li peni
> Taddarita, veni, veni."

When it is caught, it is conjured, because, when it shrieks, it blasphemes. Hence it is killed at the flame of a candle or at the fire, or else is crucified.

obscure the sun's rays with their wings, use their feathers as darts, devour men and lions, and are formidable on account of their claws—

"Unguibus Arcadiæ volucres Stymphala colentes" (*Lucretius*);

which Hêraklês, and afterwards the Argonauts, by the advice of the wise Phineos, put to flight with the noise of a musical instrument, and by striking their shields and spears against each other. The bird of Seleucia which Galenus describes as "of an insatiable appetite, malignant, astute, a devourer of locusts," also has the same diabolical nature. If our identification of the locust with the moon be accepted, to kill the locust, its shadow alone sufficed. But inasmuch as the locusts are considered destroyers of corn, the birds of Seleucia, which come to devour them, are held to be beneficent, and the ministers of Zeus.

The gryphes are represented as of double nature, now propitious, now malignant. Solinus calls them, "Alites ferocissimæ et ultra rabiem sævientes." Ktesias declares that India possesses gold in mountains inhabited by griffins, quadrupeds, as large as wolves, which have the legs and claws of a lion, red feathers on their breasts and in their other parts, eyes of fire and golden nests. For the sake of the gold, the Arimaspi, one-eyed men, fight with the griffins. As the latter have long ears, they easily hear the robbers of the gold; and if they capture them, they invariably kill them. In Hellenic antiquity, the griffins were sacred to Nemesis, the goddess of vengeance, and were represented in sepulchres in the act of pressing down a bull's head; but they were far more celebrated as sacred to the golden sun, Apollo, whose chariot they drew (the hippogriff, which, in mediæval chevaleresque poems, carries the hero, is their exact equivalent). And as Apollo is the prophetical and divining deity, whose oracle, when consulted, delivers itself in enigmas, the word *griffin*, too, meant enigma, logogriph being an enigmatical speech, and griffonnage an entangled, confused, and embarrassing handwriting.

Finally, the siren, or mermaid, who had a woman's face, and ended now as a bird, now as a fish; and who, according to Greek grammarians, had the form of a sparrow in its upper parts and of a woman in the lower, seems to be a lunar rather than a solar animal. The sirens allure navigators in particular, and fly after the ship of the cunning Odysseus, who stuffs his ears; for which reason they throw themselves in despair into the sea. The sirens are fairies like Circe; hence Horace[1] names them together—

"Sirenum voces et Circes pocula nosti."

Pliny, who believed that they existed in India, attributed to them the faculty of lulling men to sleep by their songs, in order to tear them to pieces afterwards; they calmed the winds of the sea by their voices, they knew and could reveal every secret (like the fairy or Madonna moon). Some say that the sirens were born of the blood of Acheloos, defeated by Hêraklês; others, of Acheloos and one of the Muses; others, again, narrate that they were once girls, and that Aphroditê transformed them into sirens because they wished to remain virgins. In the sixteenth Esthonian story, the beautiful maiden of

[1] According to a Sicilian story, as yet unpublished, communicated to me by Dr Ferraro, a siren once carried off a girl, and bore her out to sea with her; and, though she occasionally allowed her to come to the shore, she secured her against running away by means of a chain which was fastened to her own tail. The brother released his sister by throwing bread and meat to the siren to satiate her hunger, employing seven blacksmiths the while to cut the chain.

the waters, daughter of the mother of the waters, falls in love with a young hero with whom she stays six days of the week; the seventh day, Thursday, she leaves him, to go and plunge into the water, forbidding the youth to come and see her: the young man is unable to repress his curiosity, surprises the maiden when bathing, and discovers that she is a woman in her upper and a fish in her lower parts—

"Desinit in piscem mulier formosa superne;"

the maiden of the waters is conscious of being looked at, and disappears sorrowfully from the young man's sight.[1]

[1] Cfr. the *Pentamerone*, iv. 7; and the legend of Lohengrin, in the chapter on the Swan.

CHAPTER III.

THE WREN, THE BEETLE, AND THE FIREFLY.

SUMMARY.

Rex and regulus.—Iyattikâ çakuntikâ.—The wren's testament.—Vasiliskos; kunigli.—The wren and the eagle.—The wren and the beetle.—The death of Cæsar predicted by a wren.—*Equus lunæ.*—Indragopas.—The red-mantled beetle.—The little cow of God in Russia.—The chicken of St Michael in Piedmont.—The cow-lady.—The Lucía and St Lucia.—The little pig of St Anthony; the butterfly as a phallical symbol.—The cockchafer.—St Nicholas.—Other popular names of the coccinella septempunctata.—The lady-cow tells children how many years they have to live.—The firefly and the refulgent glowworm.—The firefly flogged; it gives light to the wheat; the shepherd's candle.

From the largest of birds we now pass to the smallest, from the *rex* to the *regulus* (in Italian, *capo d'oro*, golden head), and to the red, golden, and green beetles (yellow and green are confounded with one another, as we showed on a previous occasion, in the equivocal words, *haris* and *harit*), which are equivalent to it, and which are substituted for it in mythology. I recognise the wren in the very little bird (iyattikâ çakuntikâ) of the *Ṛigvedas*, which devours the poison of the sun.[1] In a popular German song, the wren bewails the evils of winter, which, for the rest, it represents (in its character of the moon, it

[1] Ǵaghâsa te visham; *Ṛigv.* i. 191, 11.

absorbs the solar vapours). A popular song of Scotch children celebrates the wren's testament—

"The wren, she lies in care's nest,
Wi' meikle dole and pyne."

The wren (Greek, *basiliskos;* old German, *kunigli*), like the beetle, appears as the rival of the eagle. It flies higher than the latter. In a story of the Monferrato,[1] the wren and the eagle challenge each other to a trial of their powers of flight. All the birds are present. While the proud eagle rises in the air, despising the wren, and flies so high that it is soon wearied, the wren has placed itself under one of the eagle's wings, and when it sees the latter exhausted, comes out, and, singing victory, rises higher still. Pliny says that the eagle is the enemy of the wren: "Quoniam rex appellatur avium." Aristotle, too, relates that the eagle and the wren fight against each other. The fable of the challenge between the eagle and the wren was already known in antiquity; the challenge was said to have been given when the birds wished to procure for themselves a king. The eagle, which had flown higher than all the other birds, was about to be proclaimed king, when the wren, hidden under one of the eagle's wings, flew upon the latter's head, and proclaimed itself victorious. The wren and the beetle seem generally to represent the moon, known to be the protectress of weddings; for this reason, according to Aratos, weddings were not to take place whilst the wren was

[1] Communicated to me by Dr Ferraro.—A similar story is still told in Pomerania, Brandenburg, and Ireland, with the variation of the stork as the eagle's rival in flying: when the stork falls down tired out, the wren, which was hidden under one of its wings, comes forth to measure itself with the eagle, and not being tired, is victorious.—In a popular story of Hesse, the wren puts all the animals, guided by the bear, to flight by means of a stratagem.

hidden in the earth. We know how the full moon (a phallical symbol) was considered the most propitious season for weddings). According to Suetonius, the death of Cæsar was predicted to happen on the Ides of March by a wren, which was torn in pieces by several other birds in the Pompeian temple, as it was carrying a laurel branch away (as the eagle does; out of the wintry darkness, ruled over by the moon in particular, spring comes forth; the dark eagle represents sometimes the darkness, as the wren the moon, which wanders in the darkness).

We saw the beetle that flies upon the eagle in the preceding chapter. Pliny says of the Persian Magi that they charmed away hail, locusts, and every similar evil from the country, when "aquilæ scalperentur aut scarabei," with an emerald. According to Telesius, the Calabrians, in the Cosentino, call the gold-green beetle by the name of the horse of the moon (equus lunæ). This is the sacred beetle, which is so often represented in ancient cameos and obelisks, and in the Isiac peplums of the mummies. But there is another beetle which is yet more familiar to Indo-European tradition—viz., the little and nearly round one, with a red mantle and black spots (ladybird or cow-lady). It was already known in India, where the name of *indragopas* (protected by Indras) is given to a red beetle. In a Hindoo verse we read that the mantled red beetle falls down because it has flown too high[1] (in this myth the rising and setting both of the moon and of the sun are represented; cfr. the legends of Icaros, Hanumant, and Sampatis). In Germany the red beetle is advised to flee because its

[1] Atyunnatiṁ prâpya naraḥ prâvâraḥ kîtako yatha sa vinaçyatyasaṁdeham; Böhtlingk, *Indische Sprüche*, 2te Aufl. Spr. 181.

house is on fire.[1] In Russia the same red beetle with black spots is called the little cow of God (we have already seen the cow-moon), and children say to it—

> "Little cow of God,
> Fly to the sky,
> God will give you bread."[2]

In Piedmont the same beetle is called the chicken of St Michael, and children say to it—

> "Chicken of St Michael,
> Put on your wings and fly to heaven."[3]

In Tuscany it is called lucía,[4] and children cry out to it—

> "Lucía, lucía
> Metti l'ali e vola via."

---

[1] The same superstition exists in some parts of England, where the children address it thus:—

> "Cow-lady, cow-lady, fly away home;
> Your house is all burnt, and your children are gone."

The English names for this beetle are ladybird, ladycow, ladybug, and ladyfly (cfr. Webster's English Dictionary). The country-people also call it golden knop or knob (Cfr. Trench *On the Study of Words*).

[2] "Boszia Karóvka
Paletí na niebo.
Bog dat tibié hleba."

[3] "La galiña d' San Michel
Büta j ale e vola al ciel."

[4] Sacred, no doubt, to St Lucia. In the Tyrol, according to the *Festliche Jahr* of Baron Reinsberg, St Lucia gives presents to girls, and St Nicholas to boys. The feast of St Lucia is celebrated on the 15th of September; that evening no one need stay up late, for whoever works that night finds all the work undone in the morning. The night of St Lucia is greatly feared (the saint loses her sight; the summer, the warm sunny season, comes to an end; the Madonna moon disappears, and then becomes queen of the sky, the guardian of light, as St Lucia), and conjurings are made against nightmare, devils, and witches. A cross is put into the bed that no witch may enter into it. That night, those who are under the influence of fate see, after eleven o'clock, upon the roofs of houses a light moving slowly and assuming different aspects; prognostications of good or evil are taken from this light, which is called *Luzieschein*.

(Put out your wings and fly away.) The red beetle with black spots is also called St Nicholas (Santu Nicola), or even little dove (palumedda). When one of their teeth falls, children expect a gift from the beetle; they hide the tooth in a hole, and then invoke the little animal;[1] returning to the place, they usually find a coin there, deposited by their father or mother. The red beetle, the ladycow of the English (coccinella septempunctata), has several names in Germany, which have been collected by Mannhardt in his German Mythology; among others, we find those of little bird of God, little horse of God, little cock of Mary, little cock of gold, little animal of heaven, little bird of the sun, little cock of the sun, little calf of the sun, little sun, little cow of women (it is therefore also invoked for milk and butter), and little cock of women. German maidens, in fact, in Upland, send it to their lovers as a messenger of love, with the following verses:—

"Jungfrau Marias,
Schlüsselmagd,
Flieg nach Osten,
Flieg nach Westen,
Flieg dahin wo mein Liebster wohnt."[2]

The ladycow shows the Swedish maidens their bridal gloves; Swiss children interrogate it (in the same way as the cuckoo is interrogated) to know how many years they will live.[3]

The worship which is given to the red beetle is

---

[1] "Santu Nicola, Santu Nicola
Facitimi asciari ossa e chiova."
(St Nicholas, St Nicholas,
Make me find bone and coin.)

[2] Cfr. Menzel, *Die Vorchristliche Unsterblichkeits-Lehre.*

[3] Cfr. Rochholtz, *Deutscher Glaube und Brauch.*

analogous to that reserved for the firefly (cicindela); the firefly, however, like the German Feuerkäfer, which German children, in spring, strike in a hole and carry home[1] the luminous glowworm that hides in hedges, like the wren, called also in Italian *forasiepe*, pierce-hedge, round which glowworm the stupid monkeys of the *Pańćatantram* sit in winter to warm themselves), is not treated so well. In Tuscany the poor firefly, which appears in late spring (in Germany it appears somewhat later, whence its name of Johanniswürmchen), is menaced with a flogging, and children sing to it after catching it:—

"Lucciola, lucciola, vien da me,
Ti darò un pan del re,[2]
Con dell' ova affritellate,
Carne secca e bastonate."

(Firefly, firefly, come to me; I will give you a king's loaf of bread, with fried eggs, bacon, and a flogging.) It is said in Tuscany that the firefly gives light to the wheat when the corn begins to grow in the ear; when it has grown, the firefly disappears.[3] Children are accustomed to catch the firefly and put it under a glass, hoping in the morning they will find a coin instead of the firefly. In Sicily, the firefly is called the little candle of the shepherd (*cannilicchia di picuraru;* the shepherd, or celestial pastor, the sun; the moon gives

[1] Kuhn und Schwartz, *N. d. S. M. u. G.*, p. 377.

[2] In another Tuscan variety, the song begins—

"Lucciola, Lucciola, bassa, bassa,
Ti darò una materassa," &c.

(Firefly, firefly, down so low, I will give you a mattrass.)

[3] Pliny, too, wrote in the eighteenth book of his *Natural History:* "Lucentes vespere cicindelas signum esse maturitatis panici et milii." G. Telesius of the Cosentino wrote an elegant Latin poem upon the firefly or cicindela, in the seventeenth century.

light to the sun and shows him the way to traverse from autumn to spring, from evening to day), and is sought for and carried home to secure good luck. And inasmuch as the firefly shines by night, it is more probable that it represented the moon than the sun in popular mythical beliefs. The firefly disappears as soon as the ears are ripe, *i.e.*, with the summer; we have already seen that the winter, or cold season of the year (like the night or cold season of the day) is under the especial influence of the moon. The red beetle must flee when summer comes, in order not to be burnt; the firefly, the glowworm, or worm of fire, is flogged, and the summer sun triumphs.

I suppose that the same mythical nature belongs to the butterfly (perhaps the black little butterfly with red spots), which is called in Sicily the little bird of good news (occidduzzu bona nova), or little pig of St Anthony (purcidduzzu di S. Antoni), and which is believed to bring good luck when it enters a house. It is entreated to come into the house, which is then immediately shut, so that the good luck may not go out. When the insect is in the house, they sing to it:—

> "In your mouth, milk and honey;
> In my house, health and wealth."[1]

The butterfly was in antiquity both a phallical symbol (and therefore Eros held it in his hand) and a funereal one, with promises of resurrection and transformation; the souls of the departed were represented in the forms of butterflies carried towards Elysium by a dolphin. The butterfly was also often represented upon the seven strings of the lyre, and upon a burning torch. It dies to be born

---

[1] "'Ntr' à to vucca latti e meli,
'Ntr' à mè casa saluti e beni."

again. The phases of the moon seem to correspond in the sky to the zoological transformations of the butterfly.

Other beetles—the green beetle and the cockchafer—have also extraordinary virtues in fairy tales. In the fifth story of the third book of the *Pentamerone*, the cockchafer (scarafone; in Toscana, it is called also indovirello) can play on the guitar, saves the hero, Nardiello, and makes the princess laugh that had never laughed before. In the fifty-eighth story of the sixth book of *Afanassieff*, the green beetle cleans the hero who had fallen into the marsh, and makes the princess laugh who had never laughed before (the beetle, which appears in spring, like the phallical cuckoo, releases the sun from the marsh of winter).

CHAPTER IV.

THE BEE, THE WASP, THE FLY, THE GNAT, THE MOSQUITO, THE HORSEFLY, AND THE CICADA.

SUMMARY.

The bees and the Açvinâu.—Madhumakshas.—Indras, Kṛishṇas, and Vishṇus as Mâdhavas.—The bees and Madhuhan.—Beowulf.—The god of thunder and the bees.—Vishṇus as a bee.—The *ocymum nigrum*.—The bees as nurses.—Melissai.—Selênê as Melissa.—Souls as bees.—The bees born in the bull's dead body.—The bee according to Finnish mythology.—The bees descended from paradise as part of the mind of God.—Bee's-wax causes light.—The Bienenstock.—The madhumati kaçâ.—The bees as winds.—Apis and avis.—The mother of the bees.—The young hero as a bee.—The fairy moon as a gnat.—The fly's palace.—The flies bartered for good cattle.—Intelligence of the bee.—The wasp as a judge.—The fly, the gnat, and the mosquito.—The louse and the flea.—The ant and the fly.—The ant and the cicada.—The cicadæ and the muses.—Tithon as a cicada.—The sparrow and the cicada.—The cicada and the cuckoo.

I FIND the bee in the Vedic mythology, where the Açvinâu "carry to the bees the sweet honey,"[1] where the horses of the Açvinâu, compared to "ambrosial swans, innocent, with golden wings, which waken with the dawn, swim in the water, and enjoy themselves, cheerful," are invoked to come, "like the fly of honey,"

[1] Madhu priyam bharatho yat saradbhyaḥ; *Ṛigv.* i. 112, 21.

i.e., the bee, "to the juices."[1] The gods Indras, Kṛishṇas, and Vishṇus, on account of their name Mâdhavas (that is, born of madhus, belonging to or in connection with it), were also compared in India to bees; the bee, as making and carrying honey (madhukaras), is especially the moon; as sucking it, it is especially the sun. The name of bhramaras or wanderer given in India to the bee, is as applicable to the sun as to the moon. In the *Mahâbhâratam*[2] it is said that the bees kill the destroyer of honey (madhuhan). In the chapter on the bear, we saw how the bear was killed by the bees (cfr. the name Beowulf, explained as the wolf of bees), and how in India it personified Vishṇus. Now it is not uninteresting to learn how Madhuhan, originally the destroyer of the madhu, became a name of Kṛishṇas or Vishṇus in the *Mahâbhâratam* and in the *Bhâgavata P.*; of madhu (honey) was made a demon, killed by the god (sun and moon, sun and cloud, are rivals; the solar bear destroys the beehive of the moon and the clouds).[3]

[1] Hañsâso ye vâm madhumanto asridho hiraṇyaparṇâ uhuva usharbudhaḥ udapruto mandino mandinispṛiço madhvo na makshaḥ savanâni gaćhathah; *Ṛigv.* iv. 45, 4. Here *makshas*, in conjunction with *madhvas*, gives us the sense of *madhumakshas* and *madhumakshika*, which means bee, and not fly, as it was interpreted by other translators, and by the Petropolitan Dictionary, whose learned editors will be all the more induced to make this slight correction in the new *Verbesserungen*, as in this hymn, as well as in the hymn i. 112, the bees are considered in connection with the Açvinâu. [2] iii. 1333.

[3] The god of thunder (or Indras), in opposition to the bees, is also found in a legend of the Ćerkessians quoted by Menzel. The god destroys them; but one of them hides under the shirt of the mother of God, and of this one all the other bees are born.—According to the popular superstition of Normandy, in *De Nore*, quoted by Menzel, the bees (the same is said of the wasps and the horseflies) are revengeful when maltreated, and carry happiness into a house when treated well. In Russia it is considered sacrilege to kill a bee.

Vishṇus (as Haris, the sun and the moon) is sometimes represented as a bee upon a lotus-leaf, and Kṛishṇas with an azure bee on his forehead. When the Hindoos take honey out of a hive with a rod, they always hold in one hand the plant toolsy (ocymum nigrum), sacred to Kṛishṇas (properly the black one), because one of the girls beloved of Kṛishṇas was transformed into it.[1]

In the legend of Ibrâhîm Ibn Edhem, in the *Tuti-Name*[2] we read of a bee that carries crumbs of bread away from the king's table to take them to a blind sparrow. Melíai and Mélissai, or bees, were the names of the nymphs who nursed Zeus; the priestesses of the nurse-goddess Dêmêtêr were also called Mélissai.

According to Porphyrios[3] the moon (Selênê) was also called a bee (Melissa). Selênê was represented drawn by two white horses or two cows; the horn of these cows seems to correspond to the sting of the bee. The souls of the dead were supposed to come down from the moon upon the earth in the forms of bees. Porphyrios adds that, as the moon is the culminating point of the constellation of the bull (as a bull herself), it is believed that bees are born in the bull's carcase. Hence the name of *bougeneis* given by the ancients to bees. Dionysos (the moon), after having been torn to pieces in the form of a bull, was born again, according to those who were initiated in the Dionysian mysteries, in the form of a bee; hence the name of Bougenês also given to Dionysos, according to Plutarch. Three hundred golden bees were represented, in conjunction with a bull's head, in the tomb of Childeric, the king of the Franks. Sometimes, instead of the lunar bull we find

[1] Cfr. Addison, *Indian Reminiscences.* [2] ii. 112.

[3] Perì ton en Odüsseia tôn Nümphôn antron.

the solar lion; and the lion in connection with bees occurred in the mysteries of Mithras (and in the legend of Samson).

According to the Finnish mythology of Tomasson, quoted by Menzel,[1] the bee is implored to fly far away over the moon, over the sun, near to the axis of the constellation of the waggon, into the dwelling of the Creator god, and carry upon its wings and in its mouth health and honey to the good, and wounds of fire and iron to the wicked.

According to a popular belief (which is in accordance with the legend of the Ćerkessians), the bees alone of all animals descended from paradise.[2] Virgil, too, in the fourth book of the *Georgics*, celebrates the divine

---

[1] Die Bienen gebeten werden: "Biene, du Weltvöglein, flieg in die Weite, über neun Seen, über den Mond, über die Sonne, hinter des Himmelssterne, neben der Achse des Wagengestirns; flieg in den Keller des Schöpfers, in des Allmächtigen Vorrathskammer, bring Arznei mit deinen Flügeln, Honig in deinem Schnabel, für böse Eisenwunden und Feuerwunden;" *Die Vorchristliche Unsterblichkeits-Lehre.* In this work, to which I refer the reader, Menzel treats at length of the worship of bees, and of honey.

[2] In the Engadine in Switzerland, too, it is believed that the souls of men emigrate from the world and return into it in the forms of bees. The bees are there considered messengers of death; cfr. Rochholz, *Deutscher Glaube und Brauch*, i. 147, 148.—When some one dies, the bee is invoked as follows, almost as if requesting the soul of the departed to watch for ever over the living:—

"Bienchen, unser Herr ist todt,
Verlass mich nicht in meiner Noth."

In Germany, people are unwilling to buy the bees of a dead man, it being believed that they will die or disappear immediately after him: —"Stirbt der Hausherr, so muss sein Tod nicht bloss dem Vieh im Stall und den Bienen im Stocke angesagt werden;" Simrock, the work quoted before, p. 601.—In the East, as is well-known, it was the custom to bury great men in a tomb sprinkled over with honey or beeswax as a symbol of immortality.

nature of the bee, which is a part of the mind of God, never dies, and alone among animals ascends alive into heaven (in popular Hellenic, Latin, and German tradition, the bee personifies the soul, and this being considered immortal, the bee, too, is supposed to escape death) :—

> "Esse apibus partem divinæ mentis et haustus
> Æthereos dixere : Deumque namque ire per omnes
> Terrasque, tractusque maris cœlumque profundum.
> Hinc pecudes, armenta, viros, genus omne ferarum,
> Quemque sibi tenues nascentem arcessere vitas ;
> Scilicet huc reddi deinde ac resoluta referri
> Omnia ; nec morti esse locum ; sed viva volare
> Sideris in numerum atque alto succedere cœlo."

The wax of bees, because it produces light, and is, moreover, used in churches,[1] must also have had its part in increasing the divine prestige of bees, and the belief in their immortality, as being those that feed the fire. According to a writing of 1482, cited by Du Cange, the sacred disease or *ignis sacer* (pestilential erysipelas) was cured by wax dissolved in water.

In Germany the death of their master is announced to the bees in the little stick round which the honey is made in the hive. The hive or the Bienenstock, participates in the divine nature of the bees, and calls my attention to the madhumatî kaçâ or madhoh kaçâ of the *Ṛigvedas*, and of the *Atharvavedas*, attributed to the Açvinâu, and destined to soften the sacrificial butter, which is of a nature similar to the *caduceus* of Mercury, and to the magical rod, born of all the various elements and of none in particular, daughter of the wind, and sometimes per-

[1] Der Adel der Bienen ist vom Paradies entsprossen und wegen der Sünde des Menschen kamen sie von da heraus und Gott schenkte ihnen seinen Segen, und deshalb ist die Messe nicht zu singen ohne Wachs ; Leo, *Malberg. Glossæ*, 1842.

haps itself the wind ; the *anima*, the soul (the bee), is a breath, a breeze, a wind (anemos, anilas), which changes its place, but never dies ; it collects and scatters honey and perfumes, and passes away, changeful as the American flybird that sucks honey, the continual beating of whose wings resembles the buzzing of a bee ; the *apis* and *avis* are assimilated. In Du Cange,[1] I find an oration to the mother of the bees, to call back the dispersed ones of her family, conceived thus :—"Adjuro te, Mater aviorum per Deum regem cœlorum et per illum Redemptorem Filium Dei te adjuro, ut non te altum levare, nec longe volare, sed quam plus cito potest ad arborem venire ; ibi te allocas cum omni tua genera, vel cum socia tua, ibi habeo bono vaso parato, ut vos ibi, in Dei nomine, laboretis," &c.

In the twenty-second story of the fifth book of *Afanassieff*, a bee transforms itself into a young hero, in order to prove to the old man that he is able to fetch back his son, who has remained three years under the instruction of the devil (the moon enables the old sun to find the young one ; it helps the sun to cheat the devil of night). In the same story it is in the form of a gnat that the guardian-fairy perches herself upon the young hero, whom his father has to recognise amongst twelve heroes that bear the greatest resemblance to one another. In the forty-eighth story of the fifth book, the gnat distinguishes, among the twelve maidens that resemble each other extremely, the one whom the young hero loves, that is, the daughter of the priest, whom the devil had taken possession of, because her father had once said to her, "The devil take you." This indicatory gnat occurs in numerous fairy tales, and discharges the office of the fairy moon ;

[1] *Baluz. Capitulor.* tom. ii. p. 663, in oratione ad revocandum examen apum dispersum ex Cod. MS. S. Galli.

this is the guide and messenger of the hero. We have already seen the moon as a hostess. In the thirty-first story of the fourth book of *Afanassieff*, we have the fly that entertains in its palace (according to the sixteenth story of the third book, a horse's head) the louse, the flea, the mosquito, the little mouse, the lizard, the fox, the hare, and the wolf, until the bear comes up and crushes with one paw the whole palace of the fly, and all the mythical nocturnal animals that it contains. We have also seen the hero who barters his bull for a vegetable which brings him fortune, and we have seen above the bee that is born of the dead bull. In the seventh story of the third book of *Afanassieff*, the third brother, supposed to be foolish, collects, on the contrary, flies and mosquitoes in two sacks, which he suspends upon a lofty oak-tree, where he barters them for good cattle (the moon is the pea of good fortune, the giver of abundance). We know that the moon was represented as the judge of the departed in the kingdom of the dead, and as an omniscient fairy. The industrious bees have a singular reputation for superior intelligence.[1] In the thirteenth fable of the third book of *Phædrus*, proof of the same wisdom is given by the wasp, who sits in the tribunal as a conscientious judge between the drones and the working bees in regard to the honey which the bees had collected and stored up on a lofty oak-tree, and to which the drones had pretensions.

The fly, the gnat, and the mosquito, though small, annoy, and sometimes cause the death of, the most terrible animals; the beetle gets upon the eagle to escape the hare; the hare allures the elephant and the lion into

[1] In *Du Cange:* "Apis significat formam virginitatis, sive sapientiam, in malo, invasorem."—*Papias M. S. Bitur;* ex illo forsitan officii Ecclesiast. in festo S. Ceciliæ: "Cecilia famula tua, Domine, quasi Apis tibi argumentosa deservit," &c.

the water;[1] the moon allures the sun into the night and the winter; the moon overcomes the sun, devoid of rays; the sun is deprived of its rays, the hero loses his strength with his hair; the fly alights upon the bald head of the old man, and annoys him in every way; the old man, wishing to strike the fly, only slaps himself. In *Phædrus*, again, we find the fly quarrelling with the rustic ant; the fly boasts of partaking of the offerings given to the gods, of dwelling amidst the altars, of flying through every temple, of sitting upon the heads of kings, of the kisses of beautiful women, and that without the necessity of submitting to any labour. The ant answers the fly by referring to the certain approach of winter, during which the ant, who had worked hard, has abundant provisions, and lives, whilst the fly dies of cold and starvation. Moreover, the ant says to it in one expressive verse—

"Æstate me lacessis; cum bruma est, siles."

This same discussion is reported, with more semblance of

[1] Cfr. the chapters on the Hare, the Lion, and the Elephant. The louse and the flea have the same mythical nature as the mosquito and the fly.—In the ninth Esthonian story, the son of the thunder, by means of a louse, obliges the thunder-god to scratch his head for a moment, and thus to let fall the weapon of thunder, which is instantly carried off to hell. The lice that fall down from the head of the witch combed by the good maiden, or from that of the Madonna combed by the wicked maiden, have already been mentioned. The Madonna that combs the child is, moreover, a subject of traditional Christian painting.—In the fifth story of the first book of the *Pentamerone*, we read of a monstrous louse. The king of Altamonte fattens a louse so much that it grows to the size of a wether. He then has it flayed, orders the skin to be dirtied, and promises to give his daughter to wife to whoever guesses what skin this is. The ogre alone guesses, and carries the maiden off, whom seven heroes afterwards go to deliver towards the aurora "subito che l'Aucielle (the birds) gridaro: Viva lo Sole."

truth, by other fabulists, as having happened between the shrill and inert cicada and the silent and laborious ant.

In the preceding chapter we saw the musical beetle. We are tempted to figure the bee as a musician, from the form of the bee being sometimes attributed to the Hellenic Muses and Apollo, and the name "bee of Delphi" being given to the Pythoness (as a cloud). But according to Plato, the Muses transformed into cicadæ the men who amused themselves by singing, and were so absorbed in that occupation they forgot to eat and to drink. If this myth be not a satirical invention of Plato's against poets, the bees as Muses, and those who became cicadæ on account of the Muses, should enter into the same mythical family. According to Isidorus, the cicadæ are born of the saliva of the cuckoo; this belief figuratively expresses the passage from spring to the summer season, to the season of the harvest, to the season of abundance, in which, according to a Tuscan proverb among thieves, he is a fool who cannot make his own fortune.[1] According to Hesüchios, the ass was called at Cyprus by the name of a mature cicada (tettix prôinos); the cicada (as the sun) dies, and the ass (as the night or winter) appears. According to Philê,[2] the cicadæ feed upon the eastern dew, perhaps in reminiscence of the Hellenic myth which makes the sun Tithon the lover of the aurora. The sun feeds upon the ambrosia, and is therefore immortal; but he has not the gift of eternal youth; his members dry up; after having sung all through the laborious noisy day, through the laborious

"[1] Quando la cicala il c. batte
L'ha del m. chi non si fa la parte."

[2] *Peri Zôôn idiotêtos*, xxiv., with the additions of Joachim Camerarius.

noisy summer, he expires; for this reason the Hellenic myth represented the aged Tithon as transformed into a cicada.[1] The cicada is born again in spring of the cuckoo's saliva, and in the morning of the dew of the aurora; the two accounts correspond with one another. The cicada of summer appears, and the cuckoo of spring disappears; hence the popular belief that the cicadæ wage war to the death with the cuckoo, attacking it under its wings; hence it is supposed that the cuckoo devours its own nurse; the aurora devours the night, the spring devours the winter.

[1] Plutarch, in the *Life of Sylla*, cites among the prognostics of the civil war between Marius and Sylla, the incident of a sparrow lacerating a cicada, of which it left part in the temple of Bellona, and carried part away.

CHAPTER V.

THE CUCKOO, THE HERON, THE HEATHCOCK, THE PARTRIDGE, THE NIGHTINGALE, THE SWALLOW, THE SPARROW, AND THE HOOPOE.

SUMMARY.

The kokilas, the nightingale of the Hindoo poets.—The heron.—Kokas.—Kapiṅgalas.—The partridges.—The Vedas instead of the enchanted ring.—The partridge as a devil.—The heathcock.—The partridge and the peasant.—The pigmies ride on partridges.—Talaus becomes a partridge.—The kapiṅgalas as a cuckoo; Indras as a kapiṅgalas; Indras as a cuckoo.—Rambhâ becomes a stone.—Zeus as a cuckoo.—The laughing nightingale instead of the cuckoo.—The myth of Tereus.—The whoop, or hoopoe, announces, it divines secrets; the blind whoop and its young ones.—It buries its parents.—The cuckoo and the hawk.—The cuckoo anyapushṭas.—The phallical cuckoo.—The cuckoo as a good omen for matrimony.—The cuckoo is deceitful and a derider.—The cuckoo as the messenger of spring, and as the bringer of summer.—The death of the cuckoo.—*Cocu, coucoul, couquiol, cucuault, kokküges.*—The cuckoo announces rain; the cuckoo as a funereal bird.—The years of the cuckoo.—The cuckoo, the nightingale, and the ass.—The learned nightingales.—The nightingales predict the future.—The monster as a nightingale.—The wind as a whistler.—The nightingale as the messenger of Zeus.—Paidoletôr.—The phallical nightingale.—The nightingale as the singer of the night.—The nightingale as the messenger of lovers; he now helps them, and now compels them to separate.—The sun dries the nightingale up; a wedding custom.—The swallow; the chicken of the Lord.—The seven swallows of the *Edda.*—The swallow blinds the witch.—The birds of the Madonna; San Francesco and the swallows.—It is a mortal sin to kill them.—The swallows as guests; sacred birds.—The swallow beautiful only in spring.—The swans and the swallows sing.—The swallows as babblers.—It is a bad omen to dream of swallows.—Chelidôn, the *pudendum muliebre.*—The sparrow as a phallical bird.—The swallow as a diabolical form.

THE kokilas or Indian cuckoo is for the Hindoo poets what the nightingale is for ours. The choicest epithets are employed to describe its singing, and the one most frequently applied to it in this reference is that of ravisher of the heart (hṛidayagrahin). While I write, I have not under my eyes, nor can I have, Schlegel's edition of the *Râmâyaṇam;* but if my memory does not deceive me, in the introduction, the poet Vâlmîkis makes the first çlokas, when he hears the lamentation of a kokilas whose beloved companion has been killed. In the edition of Gorresio, instead of the kokilas, we have the krâunćas, which is the heron according to Gorresio, and the bustard (Brachvogel) according to the Petropolitan Dictionary. Kokas, a synonym of kokilas, is also mentioned in a Vedic hymn.[1] The Hindoo commentator explains it as ćakravâkas, which must be the equivalent of heron, although the dictionaries interpret it particularly as the *anas casarca.* In the forty-second and forty-third hymns of the *Ṛigvedas,* a bird occurs which partakes of the nature of both the cuckoo and the heron, or bustard. Here the bird "proclaims the future, predicts, launches its voice as the boatman his boat:" it is invoked "that it be of good augury," that "the hawk may not strike it," nor "the vulture," nor "the archer armed with darts;" in order that, "having called towards the funereal western region, it may speak propitiously with good-omened words," that it may "shout to the eastern side of the houses, propitious, with good-omened words."[2]

[1] *Ṛigv.* vii. 104, 22.

[2] Kanikradaǵ ǵanusham prabruvâṇa iyarti vâćam ariteva nâvam sumañgalaç ća çakune bhavâsi mâ tvâ kâ ćid abhibhâ viçvyâvidat.

In this prophetic bird, explained by the *Bṛihaddevatâ* as kapiṅ́galas, the Petropolitan Dictionary recognises the heathcock (Haselhuhn), of which tittiris or partridge is also a rendering. A Hindoo brahmanic tradition transforms into partridges the scholars of Vâiçampayanas to peck at the Vedas of Yâǵnavalkyas. The scholars of Vâiçampayanas are the compilers of the *Tâittiriya-Veda*, or Veda of the partridges, or else black Veda. The Vedas sometimes occupies in Eastern tradition the place of the enchanted ring. In Western tradition, the devil, or black monster, becomes a cock in order to peck at the pearl or ring of the young hero who has become wise. In St Jerome's and St Augustine's writings, we also read that the devil often assumes the form of a partridge.[1] The Indian tittiris occurs again in the Russian tieteriev (the heathcock). In a story of the second book of *Afanassieff*, the Tzar gives to a peasant a golden heathcock for a dish of kissél, made of a grain of oats found in a dunghill (a variety of the well-known fable of the chicken and the pearl). The heathcock finds the grain. In another story of the fifth book of *Afanassieff*, a heathcock sits upon the oak-tree that is to carry the peasant-hero into heaven; it falls down, struck by the bullet of a gun that goes off of itself, because a spark, coming out of the tree, fell upon the powder of the gun and made the charge explode. The partridge and the peasant often occur in connection

---

Ma tvâ çyena ud vadhîn ma suparṇo mâ tvâ 'vidad ishumân vîro astâ; pitryâmanu pradiçaṁ kanikradat sumañgalo bhadrâvâdî vadeha. Ava kranda dakshiṇato gṛihâṇâm sumañgalo bhadravâdî çakunte; *Ṛigv.* ii. 42.

[1] St Anthony of Padua said of the partridge: "Avis est dolosa et immunda et hypocritas habentes, ut dicit Petrus, oculos plenos adulterii et incessabilis delicti signa."—Partridge's foot (perdikos pous) meant, in the Greek proverb, a deceitful foot.

with each other in popular traditions. The shoes that the peasant took for partridges are proverbial. Odoricus Forojuliensis speaks in his *Itinerarium* of a man at Trebizonde who conducted four thousand partridges; as he walked on the ground, the partridges flew through the air; when he stopped to sleep, the partridges also came down. According to the *Ornithologus*, the pigmies, in the war against the cranes, rode upon partridges. An extraordinary degree of intelligence and prophetic virtue is ascribed to these birds. Aldrovandi asserts, in his Ornithology, that tame partridges cry out loudly when poison is being prepared in the house. The partridge was also called *dædala* in antiquity, both because of its intelligence, and because of the fable in which Talaus, the nephew of Dædalus, the inventor of rhyme, thrown from the citadel of Athênê, by the envoy of Dædalus, was changed into a partridge by the pitying gods.

But to return to the point we started from, that is, to the Hindoo kapiṅgalas, we must notice that Professor Kuhn,[1] has recognised in it the cuckoo rather than the heathcock. A legend of the *Bṛihaddevatâ* informs us that Indras, desirous of being sung to, and having become kapiṅgalas, placed himself at the right hand of the wise man that desired (by the merit of his praises) to rise into heaven; then the wise man having, with the eye of a sage, recognised the god in the bird, sang for psalms those two Vedic hymns of which one begins with the word *kanikradat*."[2] The god Indras is found again in

[1] *Indische Studien*, i. 117, 118.

[2] Stutiṁ tu punar evéćhanam indro bhûtvâ kapiṅgalaḥ
Risher ģigamishor âçâm vavâçe prati dakshiṇâm
Sa tam ârsheṇa saṁprekshya ćakshushâ pakshirûpiṇam
Parâbhyâm api tushṭâva sûktâbhyâṁ tu kanikradat.

the form of a cuckoo (kokilas) in the *Râmâyaṇam*,[1] where Indras sends the nymph Rambhâ to seduce the ascetic Viçvâmitras, and in order to increase her attractions, he places himself near her in the form of a cuckoo that sings sweetly. But Viçvâmitras, with the eye of asceticism, perceives that this is a seduction of Indras, and curses the nymph, condemning her to become a stone in the forest for ten thousand years.

In the first chapter of the first book we already saw the cuckoo in connection with the thundering Zeus, and as the indiscreet observer of and agent in celestial loves. In the *Tuti-Name*,[2] instead of the cuckoo, we have the nightingale. The nightingale holds the betrayed king up to ridicule, laughing at him. The king wishes to know what this laugh of the nightingale means, and Gûlfishân explains the enigma to him, not so much because he is able, as is supposed, to understand the language of birds, but because from the tower where he was imprisoned he had been the spectator of the amours of the queen with her secret lover.

In the Greek myth of Tereus we find united several of the birds hitherto named, and the swallow besides; the pheasant takes the place of the partridge, and the whoop or hoopoe that of the cuckoo. Itüs eaten by his father Tereus, without the latter's knowledge, becomes a pheasant; Tereus, who follows Prognê, becomes a whoop; Prognê, who flees from him, is transformed into a swallow; Philomela, the sister of Prognê, whose tongue had been cut out by Zeus to prevent her from speaking, took the form of a nightingale, whence Martial—

> "Flet Philomela nefas incesti Tereos, et quæ
> Muta puella fuit, garrula fertur avis."

[1] i. 66. [2] ii. 79.

With regard to the hoopoe, several beliefs are current analogous to those known concerning the cuckoo and the swallow. In several parts of Italy it is called (on account of its crest and appearance in these months) the little cock of March or the little cock of May. It announces the spring. By the ancients, its song before the vines ripened was looked upon as a prediction of a plentiful vintage and good wine. It has the virtue of divining secrets; when it cackles, it announces that foxes are hidden in the grass; when it groans, it is a prognostication of rain; by means of a certain herb, it opens secret places.[1] According to Cardanus, if a man anoints his temples with the blood of a whoop he sees marvellous things in his dreams. Albertus Magnus tells us that when an old whoop becomes blind, its young ones anoint its eyes with the herb that opens shut places, and they recover their sight. This is in perfect conformity with a Hindoo story (a variation of the legend of Lear) narrated by Ælianos, according to which a king of India had several sons; the youngest was maltreated by his brothers, who ended by maltreating and expelling their father. The youngest brother alone remained faithful to his parents, and followed them; but while they were travelling, they died of weariness; the son opened his own head with his sword and buried his parents in it; the sun, moved to pity by this sight, changed the youth into a beautiful bird with a crest. But this crested bird, instead of the whoop, may also be the lark, concerning which the Greeks had also a similar legend.

[1] Cfr. the chapter on the Woodpecker. A whoop, kept by me for some time with its young ones, had been taken with its nest from the trunk of a tree which had been cut down, and which it it had scooped out in its higher part in order to build its nest in the lowest and deepest part of the trunk.

The cuckoo is the bird of spring; when it appears, the first claps of thunder are heard in the sky, announcing the season of heat. According to Isidorus it is the kite that brings the lazy cuckoo from distant regions. In the time of Pliny, the cuckoo was supposed to be born of the sparrow-hawk, and Albertus Magnus, in the Middle Ages, asserted, "Cuculus quidam componitur ex Columba et Niso sive Sparverio; alius, ex Columba et Asture, mores etiam habet ex utroque compositos." There is nothing falser, zoologically speaking; but inasmuch as the lightning carries the thunder, the mythical hawk may well carry or produce the mythical cuckoo. Moreover, the habits of the cuckoo are very singular, and have not anything in common with those of the falcon and the dove, or indeed any other animal. It is well-known that, among the Hindoo names of the cuckoo we find anyapushṭas and anyabhṛitas, which mean nourished by another (the crow is called anyabhṛit, or nourisher of others, because it nurses the eggs of the cuckoo, which, for the rest, deposits them even in the nests of much smaller animals[1]). From this singular habit of the cuckoo, it was natural to conclude that the male cuckoo united itself in adultery with the strange female bird to which it afterwards confided the eggs, which would thus be bastard eggs of the female itself that sits on them. We have just seen Indras as a cuckoo and as a seducer of Rambhâ; Indras as an adulterer is also very popular in the legend of Ahalyâ, in which the cock (the morning sun) appears, instead, as the indiscreet betrayer of the secret amours of Indras

[1] I, for instance, kept for some time a young cuckoo which had been found in the nest of a little granivorous singing bird, which is very common in Tuscany, and is called scoperina or scopina.

(the hidden sun). In a popular song of Bretagne, the perfidious mother-in-law insinuates to her son the suspicion that his young wife betrays him, saying, "préservez votre nid du coucou."[1]

The cuckoo is the sun or solar ray in the darkness, or still oftener the thunderbolt hidden in the cloud. Dâtyuhas is one of the Indian names of the cuckoo, and also of the cloud, out of which alone the cuckoo is said to drink. As a hidden sun, the cuckoo is now an absent husband, a travelling husband, a husband in the forests, and now an adulterer in secret amorous intercourse with the wife of another. In any case, it is often a phallical symbol, and therefore delights in mysteries. Meanwhile, it sits on the sceptre of Hêrê, the protectress of marriages and childbirths, whilst Zeus himself, the thunder-striker, the thunderer, her adulterous brother, is called kokkük or cuckoo, because he had hidden himself in Hêrê's lap in the shape of a cuckoo, in order not to be recognised. Hence the song of the cuckoo was considered a good omen to whoever intended to marry. In the popular song of the Monferrato sung for the Easter eggs, the landlord is cunningly advised that it is time to marry his daughters. In Swedish and Danish songs, the cuckoo carries the wedding-nut to the nuptials. Nor was this because of its reputation as an adulterer, but because it has a phallical meaning, because it loves mysteries, and because it appears only in spring, in the season of loves. For the rest, as an adulterer, it would have been a bad omen for marriages; in the *Asinaria* of Plautus, indeed, a woman calls her husband cuculus, because he sleeps with other women. The cuckoo is therefore, properly, the deceitful husband, the adulterer,

[1] Villemarqué, *Barzaz Breiz*, sixième éd. p. 493.

the hidden lover. The cuckoo is the derider; when children play at hide and seek, they are accustomed in Germany and in Italy, as well as in England, to cry out *cuckoo* to him who is to seek them in vain, as is hoped. The Latin word *cucu*, with which the pruners of vines who came late were held up to derision, the corresponding Piedmontese motto and gesture, mentioned in the first chapter of this work, and the Italian expression *cuculiare* for to ridicule, show the cuckoo as a cunning animal. It is the first, as is said, of the migratory birds to appear, and the first to disappear. In Germany it is believed that the grapes ripen with difficulty if the cuckoo continues to sing after St John's Day. It is the welcome messenger of spring[1] in the country, where it calls the

---

[1] The old English popular song celebrates it as the bringer of summer—

"Sumer is icumen in, lhude sing cuccu."

The old Anglo-Saxon song of St Guthlak makes the cuckoo the announcer of the year (geacas gear budon). The ancient song of May in Germany welcomes it with the words—

"The cuckoo with its song makes every one gay."

The popular Scotch song caresses it thus—

"The cuckoo 's a fine bird, he sings as he flies;
He brings us good tidings, he tells us no lies.
He sucks little bird's eggs to make his voice clear,
And when he sings 'cuckoo,' the summer is near."

In Shakspeare (*Love's Labour Lost*, v. 2), the owl represents winter, and the cuckoo spring—"This side is Hiems, winter, this Ver, the spring; the one maintained by the owl, the other by the cuckoo."

In a mediæval Latin eclogue recorded in the third volume of Uhland's *Schriften* (Abhandlung über die deutschen Volkslieder), the death of the cuckoo is wept over—

"Heu cuculus nobis fuerat cantare suetus,
Quæ te nunc rapuit hora nefanda tuis?
Omne genus hominum Cuculum complangat ubique!
Perditus est cuculus, heu perit ecce meus.

peasants to their work. Hesiod says that when the cuckoo sings among the oak-trees, it is time to plough.

But inasmuch as the cuckoo seldom shows itself, inasmuch as it represents essentially the sun hidden in the clouds, and as we know that the sun hidden in the clouds has several contradictory aspects, as a wise hero that penetrates everything, as an intrepid hero that defies every danger, as a betrayed hero, as a deceived husband, a traitor, a monster or a demon, so the cuckoo also has an ungrateful and sinister aspect. The adulterer who visits in secret the wife of another, becomes the absent husband that is travelling, the husband in the forest, whilst his wife entertains guests at home; or else the husband that sleeps whilst his wife is only too watchful; whence the verse of Plautus—

"At etiam cubat cuculus, surge, Amator, i domum,"

and the French word *cocu*, and those registered by Du Cange,[1] *coucoul, couquiol, cucuault*, to express the husband of an adulterous woman. In Aristophanes, inept and inexperienced men are called kokküges. According to Pliny, a cuckoo bound with a hare's skin induces sleep

Non pereat Cuculus, veniet sub tempore veris
Et nobis veniens carmina læta ciet.
Quis scit, si veniat? timeo est submersus in undis,
Vorticibus raptus atque necatus aquis."

A popular German song shows us the cuckoo first wet, and then dried by the sun—

"Der Kuckuck auf dem Zaune sass,
Kuckuck, kuckuck!
Es regnet sehr und ward nass.
Darnach da kam der Sonnenschein,
Kuckuck, kuckuck!
Der kuckuck der ward hübsch und fein."

—Cfr. also the "Entstehung des Kukuks" in Hahn's *Albanesische Märchen*, ii. 144, 316.

[1] *s. v. cucullus.*

(that is to say, the sun hides itself, the moon appears, and the world falls asleep). When the cuckoo approaches a city, and especially if it enters it, it bodes rain (that is, the sun hidden in clouds brings rain). In *Plutarch* (Life of Aratos), the cuckoo asks the other birds why they flee from his sight, inasmuch as he is not ferocious; the birds answer that they fear in him the future sparrow-hawk. The cuckoo that placed itself upon the spear of Luitprand, king of the Longobards, was considered by them as a sinister omen, as if the cuckoo were a funereal bird. In Italy we say "the years of the cuckoo," and in Piedmont "as old as a cuckoo," to indicate great age. A mediæval eclogue ascribes to the cuckoo the years of the sun, "Phœbo comes annus in ævum." As no one sees how the cuckoo disappears (the belief that it is killed by the cicadæ not being generally received), it is supposed that it never dies, that it is always the same cuckoo that sings year after year in the same wood. And, inasmuch as it is immortal, it must have seen everything and must know everything. The subalpine people, the Germans and the Slaves, ask the cuckoo how many years they still have to live. The asker judges how many years of life he may count upon from the number of times that the cuckoo sings; in Sanskrit the varsha or pluvial season determines the new year.

We said at the commencement of this chapter that the kokilas is the nightingale of Hindoo poets and its equivalent; and we have just noticed that the cuckoo also represents the phallos. In the chapter on the ass, we saw that the same rôle is sometimes taken by it. These three animals are found in conjunction in the well-known apologue of the cuckoo that disputes for superiority in singing with the nightingale; the ass, supposed to be the best judge in music on account of his long ears, being called to decide the question, declares for the cuckoo. (In the wonderful fable of Kriloff, instead of the cuckoo, the bird preferred by the ass is the cock; the nightingale is said in it to be the lover and singer of the aurora.) Then the nightingale appeals from the unjust sentence to man, singing melodiously.[1]

A German song of the sixteenth century[2] places the nightingale in opposition to the cuckoo: "it sings, it leaps, it is always gay when the other little birds are silent."

According to Pliny, the nightingales of the young Cæsars, sons of Claudius, spoke Greek and Latin, and meditated every day to learn something new. Thus, the *Ornithologus* speaks of two nightingales which, in 1546, at Ratisbon, disputed as to which spoke German best; in one of these discussions of the nightingale, the war between Charles V. and the Protestants was predicted. In the forty-sixth story of the sixth book of *Afanassieff*, a nightingale in a cage sings dolorously; the old man who possesses it says to his son Basil, that he would give half his substance to know what the nightingale is predicting by this woful song. The boy, who understands the language of the bird, announces to his parents a prophecy of the nightingale that they will one day serve him. The father is indignant; one day when the boy is asleep, he carries him to a boat and launches it on the sea. The nightingale immediately leaves the house, and flying away, perches upon the boy's shoulder. A shipmaster finds the boy and the nightingale, and takes them; the nightingale predicts tempests and the approach of pirates. At last they

[1] Cfr. the chapter on the Peacock.

[2] Cfr. Uhland's *Schriften*, iii. 25.

arrive in a city where the royal palace is assailed by three crows, which no one who attempts it succeeds in chasing away; the king promises half the kingdom and his youngest daughter to whoever can expel them, threatening death to whoever essays the enterprise in vain. The boy, advised by the nightingale, presents himself, and tells the king that the crow, his mate, and his young one are there to be judged by him (we have seen a similar legend in the chapter on the dog); they wish to have it determined whether the young crow belongs to his father or to his mother. The king says, "To his father;" then the young crow flies away with his father, while the female crow moves off in another direction. The boy marries the princess, becomes a great lord, obtains half the kingdom, travels, and is one night the guest, without their knowledge, of his own parents, who bring him water to wash himself. Thus the prediction of the nightingale is accomplished. In the popular Russian legend of Ilia Muromietz (Elias of Murom), the monster brigand killed by the hero's dart is called Nightingale (Salavéi). He has placed his nest upon twelve oak-trees, and kills as many as come in his way by simply whistling.[1] In the *Edda* of Sömund, the dwarf Alwis says of the wind, that it is called wind by men, vagabond by the gods, the noisy one by the powerful, the weeper by the giants, the bellowing traveller by the Alfes, and the whistler in the abode of Hel, that is, in the infernal regions; the Russian demoniacal monster-nightingale would therefore appear to be the wind in the darkness.

The nightingale, like the cuckoo, is called by Sappho, in *Suidas*, by the name of messenger of Zeus (now the

[1] Cfr. *Afanassieff*, i. 12.

moon, now the wind, now the thunder which announces rain). It also assumes a sinister aspect, under the name of killer of sons (paidoletôr), given it by Euripides. In a popular song of Bretagne,[1] the nightingale laments that the month of May has passed by with its flowers. In another song of Bretagne, the nightingale seems to have the same phallical signification which it has in the *Tuti-Name.* During the night, a wife is agitated on account of the nightingale (the moon); her husband has it caught with a net, and laughs when he has it.[2] The nightingale, as its name shows in the Germanic tongues, is the singer of the night, and a nocturnal bird. Hence Shakspeare, in *Romeo and Juliet,*[3] names it, in contrast to the lark, the announcer of morning:—

"*Jul.* Wilt thou be gone? it is not yet near day;
It was the nightingale, and not the lark,
That pierced the fearful hollow of thine ear;
Nightly she sings on yon pomegranate tree:
Believe me, love, it was the nightingale.
Rom. It was the lark, the herald of the morn,
No nightingale."

And it is as a nocturnal animal, and as a bird that sings concealed, that the nightingale (as the moon does) pleases lovers, who make it their mysterious and secret messenger in popular superstition and popular songs in Germany, as in France. In the third story of the fifth book of the *Pentamerone,* the girl Betta makes a cake which has the form of a handsome youth with golden hair; by the grace of the goddess of love, the cake-youth speaks and

[1] Villemarqué, *Barzaz Breiz,* sixième éd. p. 392.

[2] "Quand il le tint, se mit à rire de tout son cœur. E il l'étouffa, et le jeta dans le blanc giron de la pauvre dame. Tenez, tenez, ma jeune épouse, voici votre joli rossignol; c'est pour vous que je l'ai attrapé; je suppose, ma belle, qu'il vous fera plaisir;" Villemarqué, *Barzaz Breiz,* p. 154.

[3] iii. 5.

walks, and Betta marries him; but a queen robs her of him. Betta goes to seek him; an old woman gives to her three marvellous things, by means of which Betta obtains from the queen the permission of sleeping during the night with her youth, who has become the queen's husband; one of these three marvels is a golden cage containing a bird made of precious stones and gold, which sings like a nightingale. In popular German songs, lovers seek to propitiate the nightingale by means of gold, but it answers that it knows not what to do with it; the nightingale (like the cuckoo, which is propitious to weddings, although an adulterer) now helps lovers, and now compels them to separate. In a popular English song,[1] two lovers go together into the shadowy forest, where the nightingale sings; the maiden is terrified by the nightingale; but when she has married her young lover, she no longer fears either the gloomy wood or the nightingale's warbling. However much poetic imagination may have adorned similar legends, their phallical origin can always be traced. A popular German song says that the sun dries the nightingale up. According to popular wedding customs, it is a great shame if the young pair let themselves be surprised in bed by the sun after the first night of their union; hence the practical joke often played upon the husband by his friends, who shut the outer shutters of the windows, in order that the rays of the morning sun may not enter the nuptial chamber. But our subject presses; let us continue.

The swallow has the same mythical meaning as the cuckoo; it is the joyful herald of spring, emerging from

[1] Dixon, *Ancient Poems, Ballads, and Songs of the Peasantry of England;* cfr. also on the traditions relating to the cuckoo and the nightingale in Russia, Ralston, *The Songs of the Russian People.*

the tenebrific winter. In the winter season, the swallow is of sinister omen; in the spring-time, on the contrary, it is propitious.

In Piedmont, the swallow is called the chicken of the Lord. In the *Edda,* the seven swallows, one after another, advise Sigurd, who is still undecided, to kill the monster that guards the treasures. Sigurd follows the advice of the swallows, finds and obtains the hidden gold, and recovers his wife (the sun marries the spring, the flowery and verdant earth, when the swallows arrive and begin to sing). In the fifth story of the fourth book of the *Pentamerone,* the swallow blinds the witch who had expelled it from its nest (the wintry season obliges the swallows to depart; the hot and luminous season disperses the wintry darkness). In Germany the swallows are called the birds of the Madonna; San Francesco called the swallows his sisters; and in the Oberinnthal it is believed that they helped the Lord God in building the sky. In Germany, as well as in Italy, the swallows are considered to be birds of the best augury; it is a mortal sin to kill them, or to destroy their nests. In Germany and in Hungary, if a man destroys a swallow's nest, his cow no longer gives milk, or else gives it mixed with blood. Hence it is advisable always to have a window open, because if a swallow enters the house it brings every kind of happiness with it; in the same way, it is believed that guests bring luck into a house, and this is a beautiful belief, which is honourable to mankind, and one of the most signal evidences of man's sociable nature. In the *Ornithes* of Aristophanes, the swallows are intrusted with the building of the city of the birds. Solinus writes that even birds of prey dare not touch the swallow, which is a sacred bird. According to Arrianos, a swallow which chirped round the head of Alexander the Great, whilst he was asleep, wakened him to warn him of the machinations in his family that were being plotted against him. In an apologue the swallow warns the hen not to sit upon the eggs of the serpent. Swallows were anciently used in time of war as messengers. According to Pliny, again, the head of a swallow that fed in the morning, was, when cut off at full moon, and tied in linen and hung up, an excellent remedy for headache.

But in an apologue where the swallow boasts to the crow of its beauty, the crow answers that he is always equally beautiful, whilst the swallow is only beautiful in spring. In another apologue, which is found in the Epistle of St Gregory of Nazianzen to Prince Seleusius, the swallows boast to the swans of their twittering for the benefit of the public, whilst the swans sing only for themselves, and that little, and in solitary places. The swans answer that it is better to sing little and well to a chosen few than much and badly to all. The Greeks, in a proverb, advise men not to keep swallows under their roofs, by which they meant to put them on their guard against babblers. The swallow here evidently begins to assume, as in the mythical tragedy of Tereus, a sinister aspect, for which reason Horace calls it—

> "Infelix avis et Cecropiæ domus
> Æternum opprobrium."

The swallow, beautiful and propitious in spring, becomes ugly and almost diabolical in the other seasons. Hence the ancients believed that it was a bad omen to dream of swallows. According to Xenophon, the appearance of the swallows preceded the expedition of Cyrus against the Scythians, and announced it to be unlucky. The same presage is made by the swallows to Darius when he moves against the Scythians, and to Antiochus, who is at war with the Parthians. It is also said that Pythagoras would have no swallows in his house, because they were insectivorous. In *Suidas*, the *pudendum muliebre* is called *chelidôn;* and it is perhaps as such that the swallow is represented in opposition to the sparrow, which is a well-known phallical symbol, sacred (like the doves) to Venus, whom it accompanied, according to Apuleius,[1] and to Asklepios. The sparrow destroys the swallow's nest, as it is said in a popular German song of Michaelstein :—

"Als ich auszog, auszog,
Hatt' ich Kisten und Kasten voll,
Als ich wiederkam, wiederkam,
Hatt' der Sperling,
Der Dickkopf, der Dickkopf
Alles verzehrt."

The swallow, moreover, is a diabolical, dark form which, by the witch's enchantment, the beautiful maiden assumes when she finds herself near the fountain (*i.e.*, near the ocean of night, or of winter).[2]

[1] Currum Deæ prosequentes, gannitu constrepenti lasciviunt Passeres; *De Asino Aureo*, vi.

[2] A woman of Antignano, near Leghorn, once told me the story of a beautiful princess who stayed upon a tree till her husband returned, who had gone in quest of robes for her. Whilst she is waiting, up comes a negress to wash clothes, and sees in the water the reflection of the beautiful princess. She induces her to come down by offering to comb her hair for her, and puts a pin into her head, so that she becomes a swallow. The negress then takes the maiden's place by her husband. The swallow, however, finds means of letting herself be caught by her husband, who, stroking her head, finds the pin, and draws it out; then the swallow becomes again a beautiful princess. The same story is narrated more at length in Piedmont, in other parts of Tuscany, in Calabria, and in other places; but instead of the swallow we have the dove, as in the *Tuti-Name*.

CHAPTER VI.

THE OWL, THE CROW, THE MAGPIE, AND THE STORK.

SUMMARY.

The funereal owl.—The owl and the vulture.—The owl and the crow.—The owls as friends of the swans and enemies of the crows.—The wise owl.—The Eulenspiegel.—The owl as the daughter of Nükteos.—The enemy of Nükteos.—An ill-omened bird.—Prophetic virtue of the owl.—The horned owl.—The owl as a weaver.—The owl and the coins.—The crow and the peacock.—The crow and the nightingale.—The crow and the swan.—*Gracculus ad fides.*—The prophetic crow.—The crow and the cheese.—The crow as the son of Indras; the Athenians swore by the crow and by Zeus.—The crow and Sîtâ.—The cunning crow.—The crow, the parrot, and the bird of prey.—The crow as the shadow of a dead man.—Yamas as a crow.—The white crow.—Go to the crows.—The rooks.—The crow as a devil.—It helps an old man to pick grains of corn up.—The crow and the cuckoo.—The crow and the waters.—The crow and the figs.—The crow and the hydromel.—The crow and the water of life and death.—The crow as the bird of light.—The crow on a mountain covered with diamonds.—The crows as brothers and sisters of the heroine and of the hero.—The crow as the messenger of St Oswald.—The crow, the maiden, and the crab.—The *corvus pica.*—The blue magpie.—The two magpies.—Huginn and Muninn.—The magpie as the bringer of the balsam herb.—The magpie sacred to Bacchus.—The magpie and the nightingale.—The daughters of Euippes as magpies.—The rook and the magpie as friends of gold.—The magpie as an infernal bird.—The malice of the magpie.—The white and black magpie.—The magpie and the guests.—The stork.—The stork and the heron.—The stork as the bringer of children.—Funereal presage of the stork.—The stork and the old

man.—Paternal and filial affection of the stork.—The presents of the stork.—The stork brother of the woodcock.—The inebriated storks.—The storks in the other world.

THE owl, the crow, the magpie, and the stork are in intimate mythical relation with each other. To give an idea of the monster that wanders in the night, the *Ṛigvedas* compares him to a khargalâ[1], which is probably an owl (also called naktaćaras); it also directs the devotee to curse death and the god of the dead (to conjure them away), when the owl emits her painful cry, and when the kapotas or dark dove touches the fire[2] (thus we read in the fragments of Menander, "if the owl should cry, we have reason to be afraid"); in the *Pańćatantram,*[3] the king of the crows also compares the hostile owl that arrives towards night to the god of the dead (the god Yamas). In Hungary the owl is called the bird of death. In the *Mahâbhâratam,*[4] the mind of the wicked which sees clearly, fishes in turbid waters, and is dexterous in foul actions, is compared to the owl, who (probably as moon) distinguishes every shape in the night. In the *Mahâbhâratam,* again,[5] the owl kills the crows by night whilst they are sleeping. In the *Râmâyaṇam,*[6] the owl (as the moon) contends with the vulture (the sun), who had usurped its nest; the two disputants appeal to Râmas, who asks each how long the nest had belonged to it; the vulture answers, "Since the earth was peopled with men," and the owl, "Since the earth was covered with

[1] Pra yâ ǵigâti khargaleva naktam apa druhâ tanvaṁ gûhamânâ; *Ṛigv.* vii. 104, 17.

[2] Yad ulûko vadati mogham etad yat kapotaḥ padam agnâu kṛiṇoti, yasya dûtaḥ prahita esha etat tasmâi yamâya namo astu mṛityave; *Ṛigv.* i. 165, 4.

[3] iii. 73.

[4] iii. 15,128, and *Hitopadeças,* iv. 47.

[5] iii. 308, x. 38.

[6] vi. 64.

trees." Râmas, with justice, decides in favour of the owl, observing that his claim is the more ancient, since there were trees before there were men, and is for punishing the vulture, but desists upon learning that the latter was once King Brahmadattas, condemned to become a vulture by the wise Gâutamas, because he had once offered meat and fish to that penitent to eat. Râmas touches the vulture, which, the malediction having come to an end, immediately resumes its human form. The third book of the *Pañćatantram* treats of the war between the owls and the crows. The birds are weary of having a useless king like Garuḍas, who thinks of no one but the god Vishṇus, and does not trouble himself to protect the nests of the little birds his subjects; they meditate electing a king, and are about to choose the owl,[1] when the crow (the dark night) comes to give its veto, of which the *Pañćatantram* says, that it is the most cunning amongst birds, as the barber among men, the fox among animals, and the mendicant friars among religious orders. The war between the owl and the crow (the moon and the dark night) is popular in Hindoo tradition; kâkâris, or enemy of the crow, is one of the Sanskṛit names of the owl, and the kâkolûkikâ or owl-like crow, as has already several times been observed by the learned men who have studied Hindoo literary chronology, is already mentioned in the Grammar of Pâṇinis.

[1] In the articles against Bernard Saget in the year 1300, recorded by Du Cange, I read—"Aves elegerunt Regem quemdam avem vocatam Duc, et est avis pulchrior et major inter omnes aves, et accidit semel quod Pica conquesta fuerat de Accipitre dicto Domino Regi, et congregatis avibus, dictus Rex nihil dixit nisi quod flavit (flevit ?). Vel (veluti) idem de rege nostro dicebat ipse Episcopus, qui ipse est pulchrior homo de mundo, et tamen nihil scit facere, nisi respicere homines."

In the thirtieth story of the fourth book of *Afanassieff*, the crow eats the eggs of the geese and the swans. The owl, out of hatred to the crow, accuses him to the eagle; the lying crow denies, but is nevertheless condemned to be imprisoned.

In the ninth book of Aristotle's *History of Animals*, I also find that the crow fights with the owl, whose eggs it destroys at midday, whilst the owl, on the other hand, eats the crow's eggs during the night. In Italian, the expression "the owl amongst the crows," is used to indicate a serious danger. In John Tzetza, we also find an apologue, according to which the crow was about to be elected king of the birds, having arrayed itself in the feathers that had fallen from the other birds, when the owl comes up (in Babrios, instead of the owl, it is the swallow that does the same), recognises one of its own feathers, and plucks it out, setting thus an example to the other birds, who in a short time despoil the crow entirely. (This is a variety of the well-known fable of the crow in the peacock's feathers, and of the same fable, in an opposite sense, contained in the *Pańćatantram*, where the crow is the wise bird, and the owl the simple one.) There are other instances of cunning ascribed to the owl in fables; for instance, it predicted to the birds that an archer would kill them with their own feathers, and advised them not to let the oak-trees grow, because on them the mistletoe grows, and birds are caught by means of it. The German Eulenspiegel, the legendary malicious buffoon, who wears a great hat, is probably of the same mythical family. The Greeks considered the owl to be a form of the daughter of Nükteus of Lesbio (according to others, of the king of the Ethiopians. Nükteus and the black Ethiopian, both being the night, correspond to each other), who, having become enamoured of her father, lay with him without his knowledge; her father wished to kill her, but Athênê took pity upon her, and transformed her into an owl, which, remembering its crime, always flees from the light (it is far from the day, like the moon). The owl was sacred to Athênê, the goddess of wisdom, inasmuch as she sees in darkness; the flight of the bird of night was, therefore, for the Athenians a sign that the goddess who protected their city was propitious; hence the owls of Athens passed into a proverb. The owl, otherwise (according to the superstition of the ancient Greeks, recorded by Pliny among the Latin writers), was the enemy of Dionysos (who loves the mysteries, which the moon and the aurora disperse); hence the prescription of ancient medicine, that the eggs of the owl, drunk for three days in wine, make drunkards abstemious. Philostratos, in the Life of Apollonius, goes so far as to say that when one eats an owl's egg, one takes a dislike to wine before having tasted it. But, even in antiquity, the owl was generally looked upon as the ignoble and ill-omened bird that it really is. It is said of Demosthenes, that before going into exile, he declared that Athênê delighted in three fear-inspiring beasts—the owl, the dragon, and the Athenian people. In *Ælianos* and *Apuleius*, the owls are spoken off as birds of ill omen. But the male owl was and is still especially considered as a bird of the worst and most funereal character in Italy, Russia, Germany, and Hungary.[1] In the

[1] Among the Tartars, according to Aldrovandi, the feathers of the male owl are worn as an amulet, probably to conjure the owl himself away, in the same way as, in the Vedic hymns, Death is invoked in order that it may remain far off. In the *Khorda Avesta* (p. 147), translated by Spiegel, the hero Verethraghna derives his strength from the owl's feathers.—We are acquainted with the funereal moon in the form of Proserpine; the Hindoos considered Manus in relation

fourth book of Virgil's *Æneid*, the song of the male owl is fatal—

> "Seraque culminibus ferali carmine Bubo
> Visa queri et longas in fletum ducere voces."

The Romans purified the city with water and sulphur when a male owl or a wolf happened to enter into the temple of Jupiter, or into the Capitol. According to Silius Italicus, the defeat of Cannes was also prognosticated by the male owl—

> "Obseditque frequens castrorum limina Bubo."

And Ovid, in the tenth book of the *Metamorphoses*—

> "Ignavus Bubo dirum mortalibus omen;
> Nam diræ mortis nuntius esse solet."

According to the fifth book of the same *Metamorphoses*, Ascalaphos was transformed by Ceres into a male owl, and condemned to predict evil, because he had accused her to Jove of having eaten a pomegranate in secret, against the prohibition.

The prophetic faculty of the owl, according to popular belief, is so great, that Albertus Magnus could seriously

with the moon, with which, moreover, it was also identified. Manus, as the first and the father of men, is also the first of the dead. Manus gives the somas to Indras. The dying sun is exchanged in the funereal kingdom for the moon; but of the moon's kingdom the souls come down, and to the moon's kingdom they return. With Manus the word *Menerva* is joined, a Latin form, as a goddess, of the Greek Athênê. The owl, the symbol of Minerva, may be equivalent to Manus as the moon. The intimate connection which exists in myths and legends between the maiden aurora and the maiden moon is well-known; they reciprocally do services to each other. Athênê may very well have represented equally the two wise maidens—the moon, who sees everything in the dark night; the aurora, who, coming out of the gloomy night, illumines everything. The head of Zeus, out of which Athênê comes, appears to be a form of the eastern sky.

write in his times—"Si cor ejus cum dextro pede super dormientem ponatur, statim tibi dicit quidquid fecerit, et quidquid ab eo interrogaveris. Et hoc a fratribus nostris expertum est moderno tempore." When the witches in *Macbeth* make the horrid mixture in the great caldron, in order to obtain from it the virtue of sinister presages, they put into it, amongst other maleficent ingredients—

"Eye of newt, and toe of frog,
Wool of bat, and tongue of dog,
Adder's fork, and blind-worm's sting,
Lizard's leg, and owlet's wing."

In Sicily, the owl that moans, the crow that caws, and the dog that howls by night near the house of a sick man, announce approaching death to him; but among owls, the horned owl (the horned moon), jacobu, or chiovu, or chiò, is especially feared. The horned owl sings near the house of a sick man three days before his death; if there are no sick people in the house, it announces to one at least of its inhabitants that he or she will be struck with squinancy of the tonsil. The peasants in Sicily, when in spring they hear the lamentation of the horned owl for the first time, go to their master to give notice of their intention of leaving his service; whence the Sicilian proverb—

"Quannu canta lu chiò
Cu 'avi patruni, tinta canciar lu pò."

The Sicilian poet Giovani Meli, in the little poem, *Pianto di Palemone*, refers to the sinister presage of the horned owl in the following verses—

"Ah! miu patri lu predissi,
E trimava 'ntra li robbi,
Ch'eu nascivi 'ntra l'ecclissi
E chiancìanu li jacobbi."

In the popular Sicilian legend, entitled *La Principessa di Carini*, when the friar goes to act as a spy, the moon envelops itself in clouds, the horned owl flies round, screeching—

"Lu jacobbu chiancennu svulazzau."

In several German popular songs, the horned owl and the common owl complain that they are alone and deserted in the forest. The owl (as the moon) is also represented in German tradition as a nocturnal weaver.[1] In the same tradition, the funereal owl is found mentioned in connection with the funereal crow.[2]

I have already mentioned, in the chapter on the Wolf, that *vṛikas*, in the Vedic hymns, may mean both wolf and crow. The crow, like the wolf, represents the dark night. The owl with yellow eyes (whence in Athens certain coins bearing the effigies of an owl were called owls, and in Italy golden coins are vulgarly called owls'-eyes) seems to represent the crepuscular bird in particular (from which we can understand why it was especially sacred to Athênê), and much oftener still the night with the yellow eye of the moon. The crow, on the other hand, seems to be the representative of the gloomy night or cloud. The owl which destroys the crow's nest, and discovers the deceit of the crow when disguised in the feathers of other birds, seems to be the same as the moon that disperses the darkness,

---

[1] "Selbst in sternloser Nacht ist keine Verborgenheit, es lauert eine grämliche Alte, die Eule; sie sitzt in ihrem finstern Kämmerlein, spinnt mit silbernen Spindelchen und sieht übel dazu, was in der Dunkelheit vorgeht. Der Holzschnitt des alten Flugblattes zeigt die Eule auf einem Stühlchen am Spinnrocken sitzend."

[2] "Wenn durch die dünne Luft ein schwarzer Rabe fleucht
Und krähet sein Geschrei, und wenn des Eulen Fraue
Ihr Wiggen-gwige heult: sind Losungen sehr rauhe."
—Rochholtz, the work quoted before, i. p. 155.

or the sahasrâkshas (the heavenly peacock), that shuts the thousand eyes of the starry sky, and makes the thousand stars of the heaven grow pale. The owl, as the king of birds (we know also the Indras-moon as Mṛigarâǵas, or king of beasts) seems generally to be the same as the moon, the mistress of the night. Indras is often the peacock-god, the azure starry sky of night; but blue and black, as we have said, are two equivalent colours (the azure god Indras becomes the azure or dark Kṛishṇas, and, on the contrary, the crow becomes a peacock), and are expressed by one and the same word; hence the black bird and the blue one are substituted for one another. According to Festus, the crow was, before the peacock, sacred to Juno. The crow-peacock has already become proverbial in the *Pańćatantram*,[1] where we read that the hasty fool takes a crow for a peacock. The voice of the peacock is as shrill as that of the crow; in the *Râmâyaṇam*,[2] the water-cock (ǵalakukkubhas, the heron, the halcyon, the duck, the swan) laughs at the peacock when striving to answer the cuckoo. Thus, the Greek proverb laughs at the crows which are more honoured than the nightingales (korakes aêdonôn aîdesimôteroi). Martial places them in contrast with the swans—

> "Inter Lædæos ridetur corvus Olores;"

and the Greek proverb turns into ridicule the rook amongst the Muses (koloios en tais mousais), and the Latin one, the "Gracculus ad fides." In a variety of the forty-sixth story of the sixth book of *Afanassieff*, the crow occupies the place of the prophetic nightingale. The fox (the spring aurora) takes the cheese (the moon) from the crow (the winter night), by making it sing. In the *Mahâbhâratam*,[3] the monster Râhus disguises himself as a god,

[1] i. 175. [2] ii. 5. [3] i. 1152.

that he may go and drink the ambrosia of the gods; the sun and the moon denounce the imposture; Râhus is recognised, and Vishṇus cuts off his head with his disc; this is an ancient variety of the fable of the crow among the peacocks. This disguise of the crow, however, will appear quite natural when we reflect that Indras is a peacock, and that in the *Râmâyaṇam*[1] a certain learned crow (pâṇḍitas) is called by Hanumant the son of Indras (putraḥ kila sa çakrasya; in the *Ornithes* of Aristophanes, I read that at Athens men swore by the crow and by Zeus). I have observed, on a previous occasion, that the Vedic Indras assumes in the Hindoo poems a sinister, and sometimes even a diabolical aspect. In the *Râmâyaṇam*,[2] a crow attacks Sîtâ with wings, beak, and claws; Râmas hurls an enchanted dart at it; the bird, by divine grace, does not die, but as it flies rapidly, between drop and drop, whilst it rains from the cloud, it sees nothing but darts and shadows of darts in the air. Then it returns to Râmas to beseech him to deliver it from this enchantment; Râmas says that the enchantment must run its full course, but that he can make it take effect in one part of the body alone; let the crow choose the part that Râmas must aim at. The cunning bird, hoping that Râmas will miss his aim, says one of its eyes; Râmas aims at it and strikes it, to the great wonder of Sîtâ, against whom the crow had begun to make war, after that Râmas had marked her forehead in red (probably after the evening aurora; the legendary husband and wife exchange the ring of recognition, now the sun and now the moon, in the evening or the autumn, in order to find themselves together again, by its means, in the morning or the spring). I have cited in the preceding chapter,

[1] ii. 105, v. 3. [2] *Ib.*

from the *Pańćatantram*, the popular Hindoo belief that the crow is the most cunning of birds, as the fox is the most cunning of animals. Aristotle says that the crow is the fox's friend; in the *Râmâyaṇam*, the stratagem adopted by the fox in the Western fable to make the cheese fall out of the crow's beak, obliging it to open its beak and let the booty fall, is advised by the rook or crow (sârikâ or *gracula religiosa*). A bird of prey holds a parrot in its claws, and a sârikâ in its beak; the rook says, "Parrot, bite the foot of the enemy whilst he is alone and in the air, and whilst his beak presses me; and as his beak is occupied and cannot bite thee, bite thou him, in order that he may let you go;" the rook thus hoped that, by opening its beak, which it did with pain, the bird of prey would let it too go. In Plautus a crafty servant is compared to a crow. The crow also personifies in Hindoo tradition the shadow of a dead man; to give food to the crows is for the Hindoos the same as to give food to the souls of the dead; hence part of their meals was always, and is still, according to all travellers in India, left for the crows. Even in the *Râmâyaṇam*,[1] Râmas orders Sîtâ to preserve the rest of the food for the crows. In the flight of the gods before the demons, described in the last book of the *Râmâyaṇam*, the god Indras hides himself in the form of a peacock, and Yamas, the god of the dead, in that of a crow (in Hellenic mythology, during the war against the giants, it is Apollo that transforms himself into a crow, but pro-

[1] ii. 105; cfr. also *Du Cange*, s. v. *corbitor.*—In the German legend of the Emperor Frederic Barbarossa, the emperor, buried under a mountain, wakens and asks, "Are the crows still flying round the mountain?" he is answered that they are still flying. The emperor sighs and lies down again, concluding that the hour of his resurrection has not yet arrived.

bably into a white one, as white crows were, according to the Greek belief, dedicated to the sun. It is said that the crow was once white, but that Apollo made it black, indignant at that animal for bringing to him the unwelcome news of having surprised in adultery his mistress, the Princess Korônis; here the crow occupies the place of the mythical cuckoo. In another Hellenic myth, the crow loses the favour of Pallas for having brought the intelligence that Erichtonios, born to Pallas by the seed of the celestial blacksmith, which had fallen upon the earth, had been found by the three daughters of Kekrops. In reward for the services of the crow, Yamas conceded to it the right of eating the funereal food, for which reason the shades of the dead, when this food is given to the crow, are enabled to pass into a better world. In the *Clouds* of Aristophanes, the Greek proverb, "Go to the crows" (ball' es korakas), means "die." Hence in India as in Persia, in Russia as in Germany, in Greece as in Italy, the crow is pre-eminently a funereal bird of sinister omen. According to Ælianos, the Venetians of ancient Hadria were accustomed to appease the rooks, in order that they should not devastate the fields, by solemnly sending to meet them two ambassadors, who presented to them a mixture of oil and flour. If the rooks accepted the offering, it was a good sign. In Lambert of Aschaffenburg, a pilgrim sees in a dream a horrid crow which caws and flies round Cologne, and which is hunted away by a splendid horseman; the pilgrim explains that the crow is the devil, and the horseman St George. In the Chronicles of the Beatified Anthony, we find described fetid and black pools "in regione Puteolorum in Apulia," whence the souls arise in the forms of monstrous birds in the evening hours of the Sabbath, which neither eat nor let themselves be caught, but wander till in the morning an enormous crow compels them to submerge themselves in the waters. In Germany, according to Rochholtz, when a crow places itself upon the roof of a house where there is a dead body, it means that the dead man's soul is damned. At Brusasco, in Piedmont, children sing to the crow this funereal verse, counterfeiting in the chorus the crow's cry—

> "Curnaiáss,
> Porta 'l sćiass (the colander);
> Me mari l'è morta
> Sut la porta.
> Qué!"

In a popular Swedish song, in the collection translated into German by Warrens, I read this verse, where the crow assumes an entirely monstrous form; men spit at it, as they do at the devil—

> "Es flog ein Rabe über das Dach,
> Hatt' Menschenfleisch in den Krallen,
> Drei Tropfen Blutes träuften herab,
> Ich spülte, wo sie gefallen."

In the thirty-ninth story of the fourth book of *Afanassieff*, an old man, having let some grain fall to the ground, says that if the sun warmed him, the moon gave him light, and the crow helped him to pick the corn up, he would give each one of his three daughters. Sun, moon, and crow listen to him, and marry the three maidens. Some time after, the old man goes to visit his son-in-law the crow, who makes him mount a never-ending ladder, carrying him in his beak; but when they are high up, the crow lets the old man drop, and he dies.

Inasmuch as Indras, or Zeus, that is, the pluvial god, takes now the shape of a cuckoo, now that of a crow, the crow, in the fifteenth story of *Siddhikür*, announces the proximity of water to the thirsty prince. Tommaso Badino of Piacenza [1] narrates an apologue which reminds us of the biblical legend of the Deluge. Phœbos sends the crow to find the lustral water for the sacrifice of Zeus; [2] but the crow, when it arrives at the fountain, sees some figs near it; instead of doing its errand, it waits till the (phallical) figs ripen. Hence the crow passed into a proverb as a procrastinator (the legend of St Athanasius, moreover, recognises the procrastinator in the crow, because it says "cras" with its voice). Nor can we accept the biblical derivation of the belief of the procrastinating crow, when we find it explicitly mentioned and illustrated in Ovid by the story of the figs and that of the corn, whose maturity the crow waits for before carrying the water. The meaning of the myth appears to me evident; the thundering and rainy clouds yield water towards the end of June, when the first figs and the grain are ripe (in Plutarch's Life of Nicias, instead of these we have the golden dates); the crow represents the pluvial god; as the cuckoo brings the rains of spring, the crow brings those of summer, and afterwards, when the later figs ripen, those of autumn, which announce the winter, dear to the crows.[3]

"Imbrium divina vis imminentum." [4]

[1] In the *Ornithologia* of Aldrovandi. The messenger crow is of frequent occurrence in legends.

[2] In Plutarch, two crows guide Alexander the Great, when he goes to consult the oracle of Zeus Ammôn.

[3] Hence the name of Avis S. Martini also given to the crow, because it often comes about St Martin's day. In Du Cange and in the *Roman du Renard* we also find indicated the auspices to be taken from the crow's flight; for the same custom in Germany, cfr. Simrock, the work quoted before, p. 546.

[4] Horace, *Carm.* iii. 27.—In *Afanassieff*, again (iv. 36), the rook is asked where it has flown to. It answers, "Into the meadows to write letters and sigh after the maiden;" and the maiden is advised to hurry towards the water. The maiden declares that she fears the

In a popular Swedish song, hydromel is offered to the messenger crow; instead of this, it solicits small grains for its young. In the fifty-second story of the sixth book of *Afanassieff*, the crow is sent to seek for the water of life and death, and to make experiments with it upon itself before bringing it.

But out of darkness comes forth light, the sun; from the black night, the clear day; from the black crow, the white one; hence, in the first of the Esthonian stories, we find the crow represented as the bird of light, in the same way as in the Hellenic myth it was sacred to Apollo. In the sixth of the Sicilian stories of Signora Gonzenbach, crows carry the boy Giuseppe, shut up in a sack made of a horse's skin dried in the sun, to a mountain covered with diamonds, and the egg of a crow thrown on the head of the monster giant kills him. In the ninth story of the fourth book of the *Pentamerone*, a king sees the blood of a crow, which had been killed, upon some white marble, and wishes for a bride who shall be white like the marble and red like the blood, and have hair as black as the crow's feathers. The foolish hero Ivan, in *Afanassieff's* story (vi. 9), calls the crows his little sisters, and pours out for them the food contained in the small pipkins which he was carrying to sell. In popular German and Scandinavian songs, where the crow often appears as the succourer of the beautiful maiden (the sun; *die Sonne* is feminine in German, as is well known), it is said to be the heroine's brother. The crow is the well-known messenger of Saint Oswald, king in Engelland (the land of the Angles). The crow often brings

crab. In this maiden, that is afraid of the crab, I think I can recognise the zodiacal sign of Virgo (attracted by the crab of the summer),—the virgin who approaches the water, the autumn and the autumnal rains; the virgin loved by the crow, who is the friend of the rains.

good luck to the heroes, even by sacrificing itself; the death of night and of winter brings round again day and spring; hence the two celebrated verses of Horace—

> "Oscinem corvum prece suscitabo
> Solis ab ortu."[1]

Several of the mythical characteristics of the crow, indeed, the principal ones, are also ascribed to the magpie (*corvus pica*). The blue magpie seems to be spoken of as a bird of evil omen, even in a Vedic hymn, in connection with the disease of consumption.[2] In the forty-sixth story of *Afanassieff*, the magpies are in relation with the mythical water; one magpie is sent for the water of life, and another for the water of speech, to resuscitate the two sons of a prince and princess, whom a witch had touched with the hand of death as they slept. These two magpies seem to correspond to the two crows, Huginn and Muninn, which the Scandinavian god Odin sent every day into the world to learn all the news there current, which they afterwards brought back and whispered in one of his ears. In a German legend given by Grimm, the magpie appears as the bringer of the balsam herb (Springwurzel). The Greeks and the Latins considered the magpie to be sacred to Bacchus, because it is in connection with the ambrosial drink; and, as drunkards are garrulous, so the magpie is famous for its garrulity. We have seen the rook amongst the Muses; in Theocritus the magpie defies the nightingale in singing; in Galenus it is proverbially emulous of the Siren; the nine daughters of Euippes were changed into magpies, because they had presumed to emulate the nine

---

[1] Horace, *Carm.* iii. 27.

[2] Sâkaṁ yakshma pra pata ćâsheṇa kîkidîvinâ; *Ṛigv.* x. 97, 13.

Muses in singing, whence Dante, invoking Calliope, wishes to continue his song—

> "Con quel suono
> Di cui le Piche misere sentiro,
> Lo colpo tal che disperâr perdono."

The reader knows, no doubt, the fable of Arnê, as given in Ovid, who, in her thirst for gold, betrayed her country to the enemy, and was changed into a rook (monedula), the friend of gold. In the tenth book of his History, Livy narrates the fable of a crow that ate the gold in the Capitol. In a popular Danish ballad, gold is offered to the messenger crow, who (like the cuckoo) answers that it knows not what to do with it, and desires rather nourishment fit for crows. The magpie, too, became proverbial as a robber of gold and silver, which it goes to hide, not so much because it likes shining metals, as because it hates too great light. The crow and the magpie hide the sun and the golden ears of corn in the rainy and wintry season. In German mythology, the magpie is an infernal bird, into which witches often transform themselves, or which is ridden by them. Hence it is also believed in Germany that the magpie must be killed during the twelve days between Christmas and Epiphany (when the days begin to lengthen again). But, inasmuch as every species of malice is learned in hell, the malice of the magpie became even more proverbial than that of the crow. The magpie makes use of this knowledge now to do evil, as a malignant fairy, now to do good to men, as a benignant fairy: the colour of the blue magpie appears now luminous, now tenebrific; the colours of white and black in the magpie (as in the swallow) represent its two mythical contradictory characters. In German superstition the magpie tells of the approach of the wolf; hence it is still believed that it is unlucky to kill a magpie. In the Russian popular song, the magpie is the punisher of the lazy little finger which would not go to the well to find water :—

> "The magpie, the magpie,
> Had cooked the gruel,
> It leaped upon the threshold,
> It invited the guests." [1]

It invites all the guests, except the little finger, which is the smallest of the fingers on account of its laziness ;—we have already mentioned the lazy little brother who refuses to go to take water, in the first chapter of the first book. In Russia, it is believed that when a magpie comes to perch upon the threshold of a house, it announces the arrival of guests ; this belief reminds me of the magpie of Petronius : "Super limen autem cavea pendebat aurea, in quâ pica varia intrantes salutabat." [2]

As the crow and the magpie are thought of, in mythology, in connection with the water, and with the funereal and infernal winter, so the stork represents especially the rainy and wintry season. The heron, already mentioned in the chapter on the Cuckoo, presents several of the mythical characteristics of the stork. In the twenty-

---

[1] Saróvka, saróvka,
Kasha varlla
Na parók skakála,
Gastiei sasziválа.

[2] The magpie is proverbial as a babbler ; hence, from its Italian name *gazza*, the name *gazzetta* given to newspapers, as divulging secrets.—In the *Dialogus Creaturarum*, dial. 80, it is written of the magpie, called *Agazia:* "Pica est avis callidissima . . . Hæc apud quemdam venatorem et humane et latine loquebatur, propter quod venator ipsam plenaria fulciebat. Pica autem non immemor beneficii, volens remunerare eum, volavit ad Agazias, et cum eis familiariter sedebat et humane sermocinabatur. Agaziæ quoque in hoc plurimum lætabantur cupientes et ipsæ garrire humaneque loqui."

ninth story of the fourth book of *Afanassieff*, the stork, tired of living alone, goes to the heron and proposes marriage to her. The heron sends him away in contempt. No sooner is the stork gone, than the heron repents, and goes in her turn to propose to the stork, who refuses out of sulkiness. He then repents of his refusal, and returns to the heron, who, sulky in her turn, rejects him. The story ends by saying that the heron and the stork continue to visit one another, but that they are not married yet. This fable, although it has a satirical meaning, also implies the intimate mythical relationship between the heron and the stork. The heron and the stork are two birds which equally love the water, and therefore serve to represent the cloudy, rainy, wintry, or gloomy sky, which, as we have already said, is often represented as a black sea. From the night, the cloud, or the winter, comes forth the young sun, the new sun, the little child-hero who had been exposed in the waters; hence the popular German belief of children that the storks carry children from the fountain.[1] However, properly speaking, as long as the stork holds the child-hero in its beak, the latter is not considered born; it is only born at the moment in which, opening its beak, it puts the child down in its mother's lap. The stork personifies the funereal sky, the sky when the celestial hero, the sun, is dead. Hence it is believed in Germany that when storks fly round, or over a group of persons, some one of them is about to die; the clouds and the shadows that collect together presage the disappearance or death of the sun.

[1] Hence the request made in the popular song to the stork, to bring a little sister; cfr. the songs of the stork in Kuhn and Schwarz, *N. S. M. u. G.* p. 452. As the bringer of children, the stork is represented as the serpent's enemy; cfr. *Tzetza*, i. 945.

In Russian stories we have a double aspect of the stork (besides the fable, probably imported, of the stork and the fox as cousins, who invite each other to supper). In the seventeenth story of the second book of *Afanassieff*, an old man begs the stork to be as his son (the reputation of the storks for their paternal and filial affection is of ancient date [1]). The stork gives to the old man a sack out of which come two young men, who cover the table with a silk tablecloth, furnished with every good thing. A godmother who has three daughters changes the old man's sack whilst he is returning home. The old man, laughed at and beaten by his wife, returns to the stork, who gives him another sack, out of which also come two young men, who flog people vigorously. By means of this sack the old man recovers the former one, and reduces his wife to obedience. In a variety of the same story, the stork makes to the foolish hero three presents—a horse which, when it is told to stop, is transformed into a heap of money, and, when it is told to go on, resumes its former shape; a tablecloth which both spreads itself and takes itself off; and a horn out of which come the two young floggers. In the thirty-seventh story of the fourth book of *Afanassieff*, the stork is said to be the brother of the woodcock, and they cut hay together, but do nothing else. We mentioned, in the chapter on the Bear, the storks that eat the harvests of a peasant who threatens to cut off their feet. They upset a barrel of wine in order to drink its contents; the indignant peasant takes and binds them to his waggon, but the inebriated storks are so strong, that they carry peasant, waggon, and horse up into the air. Here the stork assumes a

[1] Cfr. *Phile*, vi. 2; and Aristophanes in the *Ornithes*—

"Deî tous neotous t' patéra palin trephein."

diabolical aspect, as the representative of the wintry season; the chariot of the peasant is that of the sun. In the fifth story of the sixth book of *Afanassieff*, the soldier-impostor tells an old woman that he is going back to the other world, where he found her son leading storks to the pasturage. Here the storks have the funereal and infernal nature of the crows, which we have observed to be, in Âryan beliefs, one of the forms assumed by the souls of the dead.

CHAPTER VII.

THE WOODPECKER AND THE MARTIN.

SUMMARY.

The *picus* in the work of Professor Kuhn.—*Picus, corvus pica,* and *picumnus;* the Vedic word *vṛikas.*—The she-wolf and the woodpecker as the nurses of the Latin twin heroes.—*Picus* as the phallos; *picus, picumnus, pilumnus, pilum, pistor; piciu, pinco, pincio, pinson, pincone.*—The sacred herb of Indras which cleaves the mountains.—Jupiter as a *picus;* the *picus* presages rain; the herb of the woodpecker has the virtue of opening every shut place.—The woodpecker and the honey.—Beowulf and the woodpecker.—The woodpecker and the gold.—The green woodpecker.—The woodpecker as the devil.—The woodpecker in opposition to the fox.—The vengeance of the woodpecker.—The halcyon.—The martin or bird of St Martin.—*Martin piciu.*—The *yünx* in love with Zeus; it attracts lovers.—*Alküoneioi hêmerai;* the halcyon.—Robin Redbreast and its "charitable bill."—The bird of St Gertrude; the *incendiaria avis; Jean rouge-gorge.*—Sea-birds with white and black plumage and a little spot of blood on their heads.

THE woodpecker has already had the honour of being studied with great learning by Professor Adalbert Kuhn, in his excellent work upon the celestial fire and water, to which I refer the cultivated reader for the principal myths relating to the subject; that is to say, for the comparison of the Vedic hawk and the Vedic fire-bhuraṇyus with the Hellenic Phoroneus, the Latin *picus Feronius*, the *incendiaria avis*, the *picus* that carries thunder, and that which carries food to the twins Romulus and Remus,[1] and which itself enjoys wine, with King Picus, progenitor of a race, and with the corresponding German traditions. I shall only observe here the mythological relationship between *picus* and the *corvus pica* (*picumnus* was applied both to the woodpecker and the magpie), in order to return to the equivocal Vedic word *vṛikas*, which means wolf and crow, whence also arose and fostered itself the confusion between the she-wolf that nurses the Latin twin heroes, and the woodpecker which, in the same legend, offers itself as their nourisher. The woodpecker, the magpie, and the wolf, personify equally the god in the darkness, the devil, the cloud, the sky of night, the rainy season, the wintry season; from the night, and from the winter, the new sun, fed by the she-wolf, or by the funereal bird, arises; the penetrating beak of the woodpecker in the cloud is the thunderbolt; in the night, and in the wintry season, it is now the moon that disperses the darkness, now the sunbeam that comes out of the darkness. The thunderbolt, the moon, and the sun's ray, moreover, sometimes assume in myths the form of the phallos; the woodpecker as a phallos and the King Picus, progenitor of a race, seem to me to be the same. The Latin legend puts *picus* in connection with *picumnus*, *pilumnus*, the *pilum*, and the *pistor*, in the same way as a Norwegian story puts in relation with flour the cuckoo, which we already know to be a phallical symbol, properly the presser down. In the Piedmontese dialect, the common name of the phallos is *piciu;* in Italian, *pinco* and *pincio* have the same mean-

1 "Lacte quis infantes nescit crevisse ferino?
Et picum expositis sæpe tulisse cibos?"
—Ovid, *Fasti*, iii.

ing; *pincione* is the chaffinch (in French *pinson*); and *pincone* means a fool, for the same reason that the ass, as a phallical symbol, personified folly. We already know Indras as a cuckoo, as a peacock, and as a hawk. To find Indras again in the woodpecker, the *Tâittiriya-Brahmaṇam* offers us a notable analogy. In it Indras kills the wild boar, hidden in the seven mountains (the shadows of the night, or the clouds), cleaving them by the touch of the stem of a sacred luminous and golden herb (sa darbhapiṅgûlam uddhṛitya sapta girîn bhittvâ[1]), which may be the moon in the night, or else the thunderbolt in the cloud; the thunderbolt is also not seldom represented in Âryan traditions as a magic rod. It is with a golden rod that, in the seventh book of the *Æneid*, the enchantress Circe transforms the wise King Picus, son of Saturn (as Jupiter-Indras; Suidas also speaks of a Pêkos Zeus, buried in Crete) into a bird, into the *picus*, sacred to the god of warriors (Mars-Indras), whence his name of *picus martius*, the woodpecker, which is supposed to presage rain (like Zeus and Indras)—

> "Picus equûm domitor, quem capta cupidine conjux,
> Aurea percussum virga, versumque venenis,
> Fecit avem Circe, sparsitque coloribus alas."

Pliny relates that the woodpecker has the virtue of opening every shut place, touching it with a certain herb, which increases and decreases with the moon;[2] this herb

---

[1] Compare *piṅgûlas* with *piṅgalas* and *piṅjaras*.—In the hymn, x. 28, 9, of the *Ṛigvedas*, we also have the mountain cleft from afar by a clod of earth: Adriṁ logena vy abhedam ârât. This analogy is so much the more remarkable, as in the same hymn, 4th strophe, the wild boar is also spoken of.

[2] The same virtue of opening the mountain by means of an herb I

may be the moon itself, which opens the hiding-places of the night, or the thunderbolt which opens the hiding-places of the cloud. It is well known that in the Vedic hymns, Indras, who is generally the pluvial and thundering god, is frequently associated with the soma (ambrosia and moon), and even identified with it. Pliny adds, moreover, that whoever takes honey out of the hive with the beak of a woodpecker is not liable to be stung by the bees; this honey may be the rain in the cloud as well as the lunar ambrosia or the dew of the morning aurora; hence the woodpecker's beak may be the thunderbolt as well as the moonbeam, or the sunbeam. Beowulf (the wolf of the bees) is spoken of in connection with the woodpecker as well as with the bear: the *Bienenfresser* of German legends, or the *pica merops*, explains the Latin superstition and the Beowulf. Like the crow, the woodpecker, too, stays in darkness, but brings water, seeks for honey, and finds the light. In the *Aulularia*, Plautus makes woodpeckers live upon golden mountains (picos, qui aureos montes incolunt). Inasmuch as the woodpeckers announced the approach of winter, or were seen on the left, according to the well-known verse of Horace[2]—

> "Teque nec lævus vetet ire picus,

they were considered birds of evil omen. In the *Orni-*

find attributed to the little martin, in connection with Venus, in Simrock, the work quoted before, p. 415: "Schon in einem Gedichte Meister Altschwerts, ed. Holland, s. 70, wird der Zugang zu dem Berge durch ein Kraut gefunden, das der Springwurzel oder blauen Schlüsselblume unserer Ortssagen gleicht. Kaum hat es der Dichter gebrochen, so kommt ein Martinsvögelchen geflogen, das guter Vorbedeutung zu sein pflegt; diesem folgt er und begegnet einem Zwerge, der ihn in den Berg zu Frau Venus führt."

[2] *Carm.* iii. 27.

thologus, it is said that the green woodpecker (the moon, by the previously mentioned equivocalness of *haris*) presages winter (the moon, as we have said, rules over the winter). For this reason, St Ephiphanios could compare the woodpecker with the devil. According to Pliny, the woodpecker that perched upon the head of the prætor Lucius Tubero, whilst he was administering justice, announced approaching ruin to the empire if it were allowed to go free, and approaching death to the prætor if killed; Lucius Tubero, moved by love of his country, seized the woodpecker, killed it, and died soon afterwards. Hence Pliny could say with reason that woodpeckers were "in auspiciis magni."

In the twentieth story of the third book of *Afanassieff*, the woodpecker, which usually appears as a very knowing bird, lets itself be deceived by the fox, who eats its young ones, under the pretext of teaching them an art. In the twenty-fifth story of the fourth book, on the other hand, the woodpecker assumes a heroic and formidable aspect. It makes friends with an old dog, which has been expelled from its kennel, and offers its services as purveyor. A woman, is carrying some dinner to her husband, who is working in the fields. The woodpecker flies before her and feigns to let itself be taken; the woman, to run after it, puts the dinner down, and the dog feeds upon it (in a variety of the same story, the woodpecker also offers to the dog a means of getting something to drink). Afterwards the dog meets the fox; then, in order to please the woodpecker (who, perhaps, remembered the treachery of the fox who ate its little ones), it runs upon the fox and maltreats it. A peasant passes by and thrashes the poor dog, who dies. Then the woodpecker becomes furious in its desire of vengeance, and begins to peck now at the peasant, and now at his horses; the peasant tries to flog the woodpecker, instead of which he flogs the horses to death. Nor does the woodpecker's vengeance stop here; it goes to the peasant's wife and pecks at her; she endeavours to beat it, but instead of doing so, she beats her own sons (these are two varieties of the story of the mother who beats her son, thinking to beat the ass, which, as a phallical symbol, we have already said corresponds to the woodpecker. The myth of Seilenos, which we saw in connection with the ass, has also been quoted by Professor Kuhn in relation with the woodpecker. In the third book of the *Pańćatantram*, we have a bird that throws gold from behind, a characteristic of the mythical ass in fairy tales). Here the woodpecker has the same office which in another Russian story, already recorded, is attributed to the wintry, funereal, and ill-omened stork, the sun hidden in the darkness, or the cloud.

The halcyon, which announces tempests, and the bird of St Martin, the fisher martin, are of the same wintry and phallical nature as the woodpecker. In Piedmont, a fool is insultingly called by the name of Martin-Piciu (the podex and the phallos; and also the phallos martin, which reminds us of the *picus pistor*, and the *picus martius*), and the above-quoted Italian expression *pincone* is equivalent to it. The sun that hides itself in darkness or clouds loses its power. The phallical symbol is evident. Here remark the Hellenic fable of the bird Yünx tetraknamon, of the four rays, of the long tongue, always changeful (the French call it *paille en cul*). Pan is said to have been the father of a girl called Yünx, who, having attempted to seduce Zeus, was changed by the vengeance of Hêrê into a bird of the same name. In Pindar, Jason made use of this bird, the gift of Aphroditê, to gain the favour of Medea. In Theocritos, this bird is invoked by girls in love to attract their lovers into the house; women made use of this bird in their mischief-working love-mysteries.

According to the fifth book of Aristotle's *History of Animals*, the halcyon sits on its eggs in the serene days of winter, called therefore alküoneiai hêmerai; and the author cites a sentence of Simonides concerning this bird: "When Zeus, in the wintry season, creates twice seven warm days, mortals say, 'This tepid weather is nourishing the variously-painted halcyons.'" Ovid relates that Alcyon was transformed into the bird of this name while weeping for her husband, who had been drowned in the sea, whence Ariosto wrote—

> "E s'udîr le Alcione alla marina
> Dell' antico infortunio lamentarse."

This bird, the kingfisher, several kinds of woodpeckers, the wren, the crow, and the redbreast, the Scotch Robin Redbreast, also called in English ruddock and Robin-ruddock, which, "with charitable bill," according to the expression of Shakspeare in *Cymbeline*,[1] throws funereal flowers upon unburied bodies,[2] are all birds sacred to St

---

[1] "Thou shalt not lack
The flower that's like thy face, pale primrose; nor
The azured hare-bell, like thy veins; no, nor
The leaf of eglantine, whom not to slander,
Out-sweetened not thy breath; the ruddock would,
With charitable bill (O bill, sore-shaming
Those rich-left heirs, that let their fathers lie
Without a monument!), bring thee all this."
—iv. 2.

[2] Cfr. what is said on the whoop, the stork, and the lark.—Concerning the bird *gaulus*, I find in Du Cange as follows: "Gaulus

Martin, the holy gravedigger, the bringer of winter, who, according to the Celtic and German traditions, divides his own cloak with poor men, and covers them. German legends are full of incidents relating to this funereal and wintry bird, with which now the funereal Norwegian bird of St Gertrude, now the cuckoo, now the *incendiaria avis*, are assimilated. Hence the same redbreast which in German tradition is sacred to St Martin is called *Jean rouge-gorge* in the popular songs of Brittany, published by Villemarqué, and is sacred to St John; but this John may be the St John of winter, whose festival is celebrated on the 27th of December, that is, two days after the Nativity of Christ, or in the days in which the sun, the Saviour, is born again, and the light increases. Birds of the same funereal nature as that of St Martin appear in the Breton song *Bran* (or the prisoner of war):—"At Kerloan, upon the battle-field, there is an oak-tree which spreads its branches over the shore; there is an oak-tree at the place where the Saxons took to flight before the face of Evan the Great. On this oak, when the moon shines at night, birds come to meet one another, sea-birds with white and black plumage, and a little spot of blood on their heads; with them there comes an old grey crow, and with it a young crow. Both are very weary, and their wings are wet; they come from beyond the seas, they come from afar; and the birds sing such a beautiful song that the great sea is hushed and listens; this song they sing with one voice, except the old crow and the young one; now the

---

Merops avis apibus infensa, unde et Apiastra vocitatur. Papias: 'Meropes, Genus avium, idem et Gauli, qui parentes suos recondere, et alere dicuntur, sunt autem virides et vocantur Apiastræ.'"

crow has said—'Sing, little birds; sing, sing, little birds of the land; you do not die far away from Bretagne.'" The same funereal birds which have pity for the dead, like the stork, also take care of new-born infants, and bring the light forth. The cloudy nocturnal or wintry monster discovers his treasures; the funereal bird buries the dead, and brings them to life again; its beak pierces through the mountain, finds the water and the fire, and tears the veil of death; its luminous head disperses the gloomy shadows.

CHAPTER VIII.

THE LARK AND THE QUAIL.

SUMMARY.

The lark the first of animals.—It existed before the earth.—It buries its father in its own head.—The lark sings the praises of God.—Pragâpatis creates the stomas first.—The crested sun.—Christos and crista; the crested lark and St Christophoros.—Alauda the lauder.—The lark upon the father's tomb.—The mother-lark.—The lark announces morning and summer.—Bharadvâgas, the bringer of food, the bringer of good things and of sound.—Bharadvâgas as a mythical singer or poet, nourished by a lark; the son of Bṛihaspatis.—The old Bharadvâgas ascends into heaven in union with the sun.—The quail.—Vartikâ, vartakas, wachtel, perepiolka.—The quail and the wolf in the *Ṛigvedas*.—The wise girl upon a hare, with a quail tied to her hand.—Jove as a quail.—The quail sacred to Hercules.—The moon and the quail.—The quail becomes a stone.—The quail believed to eat poisonous hellebore.—The quail as a sacred bird.—The game of the quail.—The quail and the cock.—The quail as a prophetic bird.—The quail puts a price upon corn.

To the crested lark, in the *Ornithes* of Aristophanes, the name of king is given, and the same virtue of funereal charity is attributed to it which we have already seen in the redbreast of winter, in the stork, and in the crested whoop. According to Aristophanes the lark was not only the first of animals, but it existed before the earth and before the gods Zeus and Kronos and the

Titans. Hence, when the lark's father died, there was no earth to bury him in; then the lark buried its father in its own head (or in its pyramidal crest). Goropius explains the belief that the lark existed before the earth, by observing that the lark sings seven times a day the praises of God in the high air, and that prayer was the first thing which existed in the world. In Hindoo cosmogony, when Pragâpatis, the creator, wishes to multiply himself, he begins by creating the stomas or hymn.[1] The father of the lark is therefore the god himself. The crested lark is the same as the crested sun, the sun with his rays. In the legend of St Christopher, I see an equivoque between the word *Christos* and the word *crista*, and, either way, I see the sun personified. St Christopher, in the legend, carries Christ, and is associated with the lark. Goropius, when a child, on seeing a picture representing St Christopher, marvelled that the lark did not flee from the tree-staff of St Christopher, whilst the sparrows, instead, fled before him as soon as he approached; he was answered that the lark is not afraid of St Christopher, because it sees on the saint's shoulders its own creator, God. Christ, the father of the lark, dies, and the lark buries him in its crista. In the same way an equivoque in speech made of the lark (alauda) the lauder (laudatrix) of God; thus it seems to me that the equivoque between *crista* and *Christos* passed into the legend of St Christopher. In the nineteenth Mongol story, the poor young man makes his fortune when he hears a lark upon his father's tomb, which has come and placed itself upon the loom. The lark is a form of the young man himself, the young sun who from poor becomes rich; the loom upon which the

[1] *Tâittiriya Yaġurv.* vii. 1, 4.

lark perches is the sky. The Greek name of the crested lark (korüdalos) corresponds to the Latin *galerita.* The lark with the crest or with the tuft explains the custom of the Gauls, recorded by Suetonius in the Life of Julius Cæsar, of representing a crested lark upon their helmets. The Æsopian fables of the mother-lark with its young ones, and of the lark with the birdcatcher, show us this bird full of cunning and wisdom. As the larks sing the praises of God only when the sky is serene, and as they announce the morning[1] and the summer, they represent the crested sun which illumines all, which is all-luminous, all-seeing, (the Vedic *viçvavedas*), the golden sun. In the thirteenth Esthonian story, the maiden that sleeps will waken when she hears again the summer song of the larks. (Here the maiden is the earth, which wakens in the spring.)

The Hindoo name of the lark is no less interesting than the Latin *alauda.* Bharadvâǵas, or the lark, may mean the bringer of food or of goods (as the sun), as well as the bringer of sound (the singer of hymns) and the sacrificer. In this triple interpretation which can be given to the word *bharadvâǵas,* nearly all the myth of the lark seems to be contained. Bharadvâǵas, afterwards, also becomes the name of a celebrated poet, and of one of the seven mythical sages, who, according to the legend, was nourished by a lark, and who is said to be the son of Bṛihaspatis, the god of sacrifice, Fire, identified with Divodâsas, one of the favourites of the god Indras, who destroys for him the strong celestial cities of Çambaras. The *Tâittiriya-brâhmaṇam* also shows us the wise Bharadvâǵas in connection with Indras.

[1] Hence Gregory of Tours relates, in *Du Cange:* "In Ecclesia Arverna, dum matutinæ celebrarentur Vigiliæ, in quadam civitate avis Corydalus, quam Alaudam vocamus, ingressa est."

Bharadvâǵas has become old whilst travelling three degrees of the life of a studious penitent; Indras approaches the aged sage, and asks him, how, if he still had many years to live, he would employ his lifetime? The sage answers that he would continue to live in penitence and in study. In the three first degrees of his life, Bharadvâǵas has studied the three Vedâs (the *Atharva-veda* having come afterwards, or not being as yet recognised as a sacred book). In the fourth period, Bharadvâǵas learns universal science (çarvavidyâ), becomes immortal, and ascends into heaven in union with the sun (âdityasya sâyuǵyam).

The quail is also in intimate relation with the summer sun, but especially with the moon.

Vartikâ and vartakas are its Indian names, which may mean both she who is turned towards, the animated one, the ready, the swift, the watchful (cfr. the German *Wachtel*), and the pilgrim (cfr. the Russian *perepiolka*). In the *Ṛigvedas*, the Açvinâu deliver the quail from torments; they release the quail from the rage of the wolf; they liberate it from the jaws of the wolf that is devouring it.[1] In the forty-first story of the sixth book of *Afanassieff*, the wise girl comes upon a hare with a quail tied to her hand, and presents herself before the Tzar, whose riddle she must solve in order to marry him. This quail is the symbol of the Tzar himself, or the sun; the wise girl is the aurora (or the spring), who arrives near the sun upon the hare, that is, upon the moon, traversing the shadows of night (or winter). The Greeks and Latins, observing, perhaps, that the moon takes sleep

[1] Vartikâṁ grasitâm amuńćatam; *Ṛigv.* i. 112, 8.—Amuńćataṁ vartikâm aṅhasaḥ; i. 118, 8.—Âsno vṛikasya vartikâm abhîke yuvaṁ narâ nâsatyâmumuktam; i. 116, 14.—Vṛikasya ćid vartikâm antar âsyâd yuvaṁ çaçîbhir grasitâm amuńćatam; x. 39, 13.

away from the quail, believed that the quail was sacred to Latona, and relate that Jove became a quail to lie with Latona, of which union Diana and Apollo (moon and sun) were born.[1] Others also affirm that the quail was sacred to Hercules, who, by the scent of a quail, recovered his life, which had been taken from him by Tüphon. It is believed that when the moon rises, the quail cries out and is excited to agitation against it, and that the quail's head increases or diminishes according to the moon's influence. As the quail seems to represent the sun, and loves heat, it fears the cold moon. From these mythical relations of the quail was doubtless derived the fear which the ancients had for the quail, which they believed to eat poisonous hellebore during the night, and to be therefore poisonous and subject to epilepsy. Plutarch, in the *Apophtegmata*, relates that Augustus punished with death a president of Egypt who had eaten a quail which had carried off the prize in the fight; for it was long the custom to make quails fight with one another, in the same way as at Athens the game of the quail was a favourite diversion, in which several quails were placed in a circle, and he who hit one carried off all the others. According to Artemidoros, quails announced to their feeders the evils by which they would be visited from the side of the sea. The quail which agitates itself

[1] The same fable is also related in a different way: Jove cohabits with Latona, and subsequently forces her sister, Asterien, who is, in pity, changed by the gods into a quail. Jove becomes an eagle to catch her; the gods change the quail into a stone—(cfr. the stories of Indras as a cuckoo and Rambhâ, of Indras as a cock and Ahalyâ. It is a popular superstition that quails, like the crane, when they travel, let little stones fall in order to recognise on their return the places by which they passed the first time)—which lies for a long time under water, till by the prayer of Latona it is taken out.

against the moon (thus Ælianos writes that the cock excites himself and exults when the moon rises[1]) presages the bad season, the pluvial or wintry season, and makes use of its own presage to migrate to warmer regions. The quail watches, travels, and cries out during the night; from the number of times that it cries out in succession in the fields, the peasants of Tuscany infer the price of corn; as the quail generally renews its cry three, four or more times, when it cries three times they say that corn will be cheap, and that, when it cries out four or more times, it will be dear; and so they say that the quail puts a price upon corn.[2] The quail arrives with the sun in our fields in spring, and goes away with the sun in September. In the *Mahâbhâratam*,[3] when the hero Bhîmas is squeezed by an enormous serpent, a quail appears near the sun, dark (pratyâdityamabhâsvarâ), with only one wing, one eye, and one foot, horrible to the sight, vomiting blood (raktaṁ vamantî). This quail may represent either the red sky of evening, in the west, or the red heavens at the conclusion of summer.

[1] Ælianos says that the cock is in the moon's favour, either because it assisted Latona in parturition, or because it is generally believed (as a symbol of fecundation) to be the facilitator of childbirth. As a watchful animal it was natural to consider it especially dear to the moon, the nocturnal watcher.—The cock, as an announcer of news, was sacred to Mercury; as the curer of many diseases, to Æsculapius; as a warrior, to Mars, Hercules, and Pallas, who, according to Pausanias, wore a hen upon her helmet; as an increaser of the family, to the Lares, &c. Even Roman Catholic priests will deign to receive with especial favour, ad majorem Dei gloriam, the homage of cocks, capons, and chickens.

[2] This year, my quails cried out six times; and the corn in Italy is very dear, the spring having been a very rainy one.

[3] iii. 12,437.

CHAPTER IX.

THE COCK AND THE HEN.

SUMMARY.

Alektrüon, a satellite of Mars, the lover of Venus, becomes a cock.—Indras, the lover of Ahalyâ as a cock; Ahalyâ turned to stone.—Indras as a eunuch or as a ram.—Pragâpatis loves his daughter the aurora, and becomes a goat.—Ahalyâ in the ashes, like Cinderella.—The thunder and the eggs; the iron nail and the laurel in the nest.—To be made of stucco, to be turned to stone by the thunder which astonishes.—It is a sacrilege to kill cocks and hens.—The cock Parodars in the *Avesta*.—The cock chases the demons away.—The cock wakens the aurora and arouses mankind.—Christus and the cock as *cristiger*, *cristatus*, *cristeus*.—The cock sacred to St James, to St Christopher and Donar.—St James as a cock.—The hen crows like a cock.—Men turned to stone, and the cock who calls them to life again.—The cock as a devil.—The enchanted hut stands upon a hen's little feet.—Cocks killed as a form of witches.—The *lapillus alectorius;* the same enclosed in a ring.—To dream of brood-hens with chickens.—The egg is more cunning than the hen.—The golden cock on the rock; marvels come out of the rock.—The egg which becomes a girl.—The cock on the top of high buildings, to indicate the winds, and also the hours.—The black cock and the red one.—The black hen.—The cock sacrificed.—The cock, son of Mars.—Cockfights.—Auguries taken from cocks and hens; these auguries held up to derision.—The hen's egg; "Gallus in sterquilinio suo plurimum potest."—The pearl is an egg; the hen's egg in the sky is the sun.—The white hen.—Easter eggs.—The golden egg.—The cosmic egg.—It is an excellent augury to begin with the egg; "Ab ovo ad malum."—To begin *ab ovo.*

ALEKTRUON (the Greek name of the cock) was the companion and satellite of Mars. When Mars wished to spend the night with Venus during the absence of Vulcan, he placed Alektrüon to watch at the door. Alektrüon, however, fell asleep; and Mars, surprised by the returning husband, and full of indignation, transformed Alektrüon into a cock, in order that it might learn to be watchful; whence Ausonius—

> "Ter clara instantis Eoi
> Signa canit serus, deprenso Marte, satelles."

According to a Pâuranic legend, Indras, the Indian Mars, enamoured of Ahalyâ, the wife of Gâutamas, and accompanied by Ćandras (the moon), assumed the form of a kṛikavâkas (cock or peacock), and went to sing at midnight near the dwelling of Ahalyâ, whilst her husband was absent. Then, divesting himself of the form of a cock (or peacock), he left Ćandras at the door to watch, and united himself with Ahalyâ (the hen). Meanwhile Gâutamas returns; Ćandras not having warned the lovers of his approach, the saint turns Ahalyâ to stone, and scatters over the body of Indras a thousand wombs; which, being submerged in the waters, the pitying gods subsequently changed into a thousand eyes (sahasrâkshas is one of the Hindoo names of Indras and of the peacock). According to a variety of this legend,—which is analogous to the fable of the Zeus as a quail, the seducer of the sister of Latona, or of Latona herself, changed into a stone and submerged in the waters,—Indras becomes a eunuch, and obtains, as we have already seen, in compensation, two ram's testicles. In the *Âitareya Br.*, the god Brahman Praǵâpatis becomes a goat or a roebuck (ṛiçyas), in order to lie with his own daughter Aurora. In the thirty-second and thirty-third hymn of the eighth book of the

Ṛigvedas, the god Indras and the god Brahman change places. Indras is at first beautiful (çiprin); he afterwards becomes a woman (strî hi brahmâ babhûvitha). In the *Râmâyaṇam*,[1] Gâutamas condemns Indras to become powerless, and Ahalyâ to remain hidden in the forest, lying in the ashes (bhasmaçâyinî), until Ramas comes to deliver her. The ashy sky, the stony sky, the watery sky, are identical; Ahalyâ (the evening aurora) in the ashes is the germ of the story of Cinderella, and of the daughter of the King of Dacia, persecuted by her lover, her father himself.

A popular Italian belief, which has been mentioned by Pliny and Columella, says that when it thunders while the hen is sitting on her eggs, they are spoiled. To remedy this evil, Pliny advises to put under the fodder of the eggs an iron nail, or else some earth taken up by a ploughshare. Columella says that many put little branches of laurel and roots of garlic, with iron nails. These are all symbols of the sulphureous thunderbolts (because of their strong smell), and of the thunderbolt conceived of as an iron weapon; the remedy recommended is according to the principle of *similia similibus*, for the same reason as the devil is prayed to in order to keep him away. In Sicily, when a hen is setting on her eggs, they put at the bottom of the nest a nail, which has the property of attracting and absorbing every kind of noise that may be noxious to the chickens. Now it seems interesting to me to find an analogous belief in Vedic antiquity. A strophe, where the word *aṇḍâ* may be rendered eggs as well as testicles, which therefore leads us to think of oviparous birds and chickens no less than men, invokes Indras, the thunder-god, as follows:—"Do not

[1] i. 49.

harm us, Indras; do not destroy us; do not take from us our beloved enjoyments; do not break, O great one, O strong one, our eggs (or testicles); do not ruin the fruits of our bowels."[1] Indras can not only become a eunuch himself, but he can make others become eunuchs; thunder makes us astonished, and as we also say, by an analogous expression, in Italy, makes us of stucco or turn to stone.

The cock and the oviparous hen, as birds which are as egg-yielding symbols of abundance, and which personify the sun, were and are sacred in India and in Persia, where it is considered a sacrilege to kill them. Cicero, in his *Oratio pro Murena,* writes that among the ancients he who ultroneously killed a cock did not sin less than he who suffocated his own father. In Du Cange we read that Geoffrey I., Duke of Brittany, whilst he was on a journey to Rome, was slain with a stone by a woman, one of whose hens had been killed by the Duke's sparrowhawk. The same superstition about hens is still observed in Italy by a great number of housewives.

In the *Avesta* the crow of the cock accompanies the flight of the demons, wakens the aurora, and arouses mankind.[2]

---

[1] Mâ no vadhîr indra mâ parâ dâ mâ naḥ priyâ bhoǵanâni pra moshîḥ âṇḍâ mâ no maghavań ćhakra nir bhen mâ naḥ pâtrâ bhet sahaǵânushâṇi; *Ṛigv.* i. 104, 8.

[2] Der Vogel der den Namen Parodars führt, o heiliger Zarathustra, den die übelredenden Menschen mit den Namen Kahrkatâç belegen, dieser Vogel erhebt seine Stimme bei jeder göttlichen Morgenröthe: Stehet auf, ihr Menschen, preiset die beste Reinheit, vertreibet die Dâeva; *Vendidad*, xviii. 34–38, Spiegel's version.—The cock Parodars chases away with his cry especially the demon Bûshyańçta, who oppresses men with sleep, and he returns again in a fragment of the *Khorda-Avesta* (xxxix.): "Da, vor dem Kommen der Morgenröthe, spricht dieser Vogel Parodars, der Vogel der mit Messern verwundet,

Even the Christian poet Prudentius, who still sees a solar symbol in the *Christus*, compares him to the cock, also called *cristiger*, *cristatus*, *cristeus*,[1] prays to Christ to chase away sleep, to break the fetters of night, to undo the old sin, and to bring the new light, after having said of the cock—

"Ferunt vagantes dæmones,
Lætos tenebris noctium
Gallo canente exterritos
Sparsim timere et cedere.
. . . . omnes credimus
Illo quietis tempore
Quo gallus exsultans canit
Christum redisse ex inferis."

We have seen in the preceding chapter, the crested lark in connection with St Christopher. In Germany, on the 25th of July, sacred to St James[2] (the saint who

---

Worte gegen das Feuers aus. Bei seinem Sprechen läuft Bushyançta mit langen Händen herzu von der nördlichen Gegend, von den nördlichen Gegenden, also sprechen, also sagend: "Schlafet o Menschen, schlafet, sündlich Lebende, schlafet, die ihr ein sündiges Leben führt." As in the song of Prudentius, the idea of sleep and that of sin are associated together; the song of Prudentius suggests the idea that it was written by some one who was initiated in the solar mysteries of the worship of Mithras.

[1] Cfr. Du Cange, *s. v.*—And the same Du Cange, in the article *gallina*, quotes an old mediæval glossary in which *gallina* is said to mean Christ, wisdom, and soul.—The cock of the Gospel announces, reveals, betrays Christ three times, in the three watches of the night, to which sometimes correspond the three sons of the legends.

[2] According to a legend of St James, an old father and mother go with their young son on a pilgrimage to Santiago de Compostella in Spain. On the way, in an inn at San Domingo de la Calzada, the innkeeper's daughter offers her favours to the young man, who rejects them; the girl avenges herself upon him by putting a silver plate in his sack, for which he is arrested and impaled as a thief. The old parents continue their journey to Santiago; St James has pity upon them, and works a miracle which is only known to be his afterwards.

empties the bottle, as they say in Piedmont), to St Christopher, and the ancient god of thunder, Donar, cocks were made to dance, and then sacrificed. Donar carries Oerwandil on his shoulders across rivers, as the giant Christopher carries Christ.

There is a superstition which is widely diffused in Italy, Germany, and Russia, according to which a hen that begins to crow like a cock is of the worst omen; and it is the universal persuasion that it ought to be killed immediately, in order not to die before it. As the same belief exists in Persia, the discussion of Sadder with regard to it is interesting, to prove that the hen which crows like a cock must not be killed, because, if it become a cock, that means that it will be able to kill the demon, (therefore at Persian tombs they were accustomed to set a cock free). Having regard to the superstitious Eastern and European beliefs, the worthy Professor Spiegel will now find, I hope, the following passage, which appeared rather obscure to him, a little clearer:—"Qui religione sinceri sunt ludificationes expertes, quando percipiunt ex gallina vociferationem galli non debent illam

The old couple return to their country, passing by San Domingo; here they find their son alive, whom they had seen impaled, for which they there and then offer solemn thanks to St James. All are astonished. The prefect of the place is at dinner when the news is brought to him; he refuses to believe it, and says that the young man is no more alive than the roasted fowl which is being set upon the table; no sooner has he uttered the words, than the cock begins to crow, resumes its feathers, jumps out of the plate and flies away. The innkeeper's daughter is condemned; and in honour of the miracle, the cock is revered as a sacred animal, and at San Domingo the houses are ornamented with cock's feathers. A similar wonder is said, by Sigonio, to have taken place in the eleventh century in the Bolognese; but instead of St James, Christ and St Peter appear to perform miracles.—Cfr. also the relationship of St Elias (and of the Russian hero Ilya) feasted on the 21st of July, when the sun enters the sign of the lion, with Helios, the hellenic sun.

gallinam interficere ominis causa, quia eam interficiendi jus nullum habent. . . . Nam in Persia si gallina fit gallus, ipsa infaustum diabolum franget. Si autem alium gallum adhibueris in auxilium, ut cum gallina consortium habeat, non erit incommodum ut tunc ille diabolus sit interfectus." According to a Sicilian proverb, the hen that crows like a cock must neither be sold nor given away, but eaten by its mistress.[1]

In the forty-fifth story of the fifth book of *Afanassieff*, the cocks crow, and the devil's smoke disappears. In the fortieth story of the same book, the cock crows, and the devil disappears from the kingdom in which he made every man and every thing turn to stone. The son of a peasant, staying to pray all through the night with lighted candles, alone escapes from the devil's evil works; after three nights of similar penitence, all the men who were turned to stone come to life again, and the young and pious peasant espouses the king's beautiful daughter.

In the thirtieth story of the fifth book of *Afanassieff*, when the cock begins to crow, the old man becomes of a sudden at once rigid and silent. Here, perhaps, there is an allusion to the old sun of evening, and to the cock's crowing in the evening. The cock of night, therefore, assumes sometimes a diabolical form. In the twenty-second story of the fifth book of *Afanassieff*, the devil becomes a cock in order to eat the corn into which the young man who was first turned into a gold ring, has been at length transformed. But this cock of night, being demoniacal, although his crest (the sun) is always red, is of a black colour. The cock is red in the morning and in the evening; in the night it is black, with its red

[1] La gallina cantatura
Nun si vinni, nè si duna,
Si la mancia la patruna.

crest turned now to the east, now to the west; it is upon the little feet of a hen,[1] that the little movable enchanted Russian hut stands, which the young heroes and young heroines on a journey meet with in the forest, and cause to turn in the direction they came from.

In the ninth story of the second book of the *Pentamerone*, a queen gives orders to kill the cocks in the town, so that the crowing may cease, because as long as the cocks crow, she will, by a witch's enchantment, be unable to recognise and embrace her son. The witch herself evidently assumes here the form of the diabolical cock that crows in the night.[2]

---

[1] Cfr. *Afanassieff*, i. 3, ii. 30; sometimes, instead of the hen's feet we have the dog's paws; cfr. v. 28.

[2] Concerning this subject I can add an unpublished story which Signor S. M. Greco sends me from Cosenza in Calabria:—A poor girl is alone in the fields; she plucks a rampion, sees a stair, goes down, and comes to the palace of the fairies, who at sight of her are smitten with love. She asks to be allowed to go back to her mother, and obtains permission; she tells her mother that she hears a noise every night, without seeing anything, and is advised to light a candle and she will see. Next evening the girl does so, and sees a youth of great beauty with a looking-glass on his breast. The third evening she does the same, but a drop of wax falls upon the looking-glass and wakens the youth, who cries out lamentably, "Thou shalt go hence." The girl wishes to go away; the fairies give her a full clew of thread, with the advice that she must go to the top of the highest mountain and leave the clew to itself; where it goes, thither must she follow. She obeys, and arrives at a town which is in mourning on account of the absence of the prince; the queen sees the girl from the window and makes her come in. After some time she gives birth to a handsome son, and a shoemaker, who works by night, begins to sing—

> "Sleep, sleep, my son;
> If your mother knew some day
> That you are my son,
> In a golden cradle she would put you to sleep,
> And in golden swaddling-clothes.
> Sleep, sleep, my son."

In the first story of the fourth book of the *Pentamerone*, the old Minec' Aniello feeds a cock well, but being afterwards in want of money, sells it to two magicians, who, when walking back, say to each other that the cock is precious for the stone that it contains, which, enclosed in a ring, will enable one to obtain all that he wishes (the *lapillus alectorius*, which is said to be as large as a bean, to be like crystal, to be good for pregnant women, and for inspiring courage; it is alleged that the hero Milon owed all his strength to it). Minec' Aniello hears this, steals the cock, kills it, takes the stone, and by its means becomes young again, in a beautiful palace of gold and silver. When the magicians defraud him of this stone, enclosed in a ring, the young man becomes old again, and goes to seek his lost ring in the kingdom of the deep hole (de Pertuso cupo) inhabited by the rat; the rats gnaw the finger of the magician who has the ring; Minec' Aniello recovers his ring, and changes the two magicians into asses; he rides upon one ass, and then throws it down the mountains; the other ass is loaded with lard, and sent in gratitude to the rats. Here the cock appears as a nocturnal animal; the stone which, when enclosed in a ring, performs miracles, is the sun which comes out when invoked by the cock of night. According to the Sicilian belief, when one dreams

The queen then learns from the girl, that he who sings thus is the prince, who is destined to stay far from the palace until the sun rises without him perceiving it. Orders are then given to kill all the fowls in the town, and to cover all the windows with a black veil scattered over with diamonds, in order that the prince may believe it is still night and may not perceive the rising of the sun. The prince is deceived, and marries the maiden who is the fairies' favourite, and they lived happy and contented,

Whilst I, if you will believe me,
Found myself with a thorn in my foot.

of brood-hens with chickens in uninhabited and deserted houses, it is a sign that there are treasures hidden in these houses, and one must go to dig them up.

In the first of the Esthonian stories, the cock that crows is a spy over the old woman.[1] In the third Esthonian story, a woman gives her husband three eggs of a black hen to eat in order to obtain three dwarf heroes. In the twenty-second Esthonian story, the shepherds that watch over the son of the persecuted king, seeing the knowingness of the boy, recognise the truth of the proverb that "the egg is more cunning than the hen." In the ninth Esthonian story, a young man, after having made a compact with the devil, cheats him, giving him the blood of a cock instead of his own. In the fourth Esthonian story,. when three strokes are given with a golden rod upon a rock, a large golden cock comes out and perches upon the top of it; it beats its wings and crows; at each crowing a marvel comes out of the stone, a tablecloth that spreads itself and a porringer that fills itself. In the twenty-fourth Esthonian story, an old fairy gives to the queen a little basket with a bird's egg inside; the queen must hatch it for three months, like a pearl, in her bosom; first a little living doll will be born, which, when warmed in a basket covered with wool, will become a real girl; at the same time that the doll becomes a real girl, the queen will give birth to a beautiful male child. Linda, the wife of Kalew, in Finnish mythology, is also born of the egg of a woodcock or a heathcock.

In Hungry (where a dyed tin cock is placed upon the top of high buildings to indicate the direction of the

[1] Die schlaue Alte brachte bald heraus, was der Dorfhahn hinter ihrem Rücken der jungsten Tochter ins Ohr gekräht hatte; Kreutzwald u. Löwe, *Ehstnische Märchen.*

wind—this is the English and Italian weathercock; we have all heard of the cock of the tower of St Mark at Venice which makes the hours strike), it is believed that, to appease the devil, one must sacrifice a black cock to him. The red cock, on the contrary, signifies fire.[1]

In the Monferrato it is believed that a black hen split open alive in the middle, and placed where one feels the pain of the *mal di punta*, will take away the disease and the pain, on condition that when this strange plaster is taken off, the feathers be burned in the house.

The cock or fowl which, in the festive customs of Essex and of Norfolk (of which traces are preserved in the striking of the porringer by a man blindfolded at the feast of Mid-Lent in several parts of France and in Piedmont), a man blind-folded wins, if he succeeds in striking it upon the shoulders of another man (or else sometimes shut up in a porringer at the height of twelve or fourteen feet from the ground, at which projectiles

[1] In the annals of the city of Debreczen, in the year 1564, we read as follows: " Æterna et exitialis memoria de incendio trium ordinum in anno præsenti: feria secunda proxima ante fest. nat. Mariæ gloriosæ exorta est flamma et incendium periculosum in platea Burgondia; eadem similiter ebdomade exortum est incendium altera vice, de platea Csapo de domo inquilinari Stephani literati, multas domos . . . in cinerem redegit, et quod majus inter cætera est, nobilissimi quoque templi divi Andreæ et turris tecturæ combustæ sunt, ex qua turri et ejus pinnaculo, gallus etiam æreus, a multis annis insomniter dies ac noctes jejuno stomacho stans et in omnes partes advigilans, flammam ignis sufferre non valens, invitus devolare, descendere et illam suam solitam stationem deserere coactus est, qui gallus tantæ cladis commiserescens ac nimio dolore obmutescens de pinnaculo desiliendio, collo confracto in terram coincidens et suæ vitæ propriæ quoque non parcens, fidele suum servitium invitus derelinquendo, misere expiravit et vitam suam finivit sic."

are thrown [1]) is a personification of the funereal cock out of which, when struck, the daily fire is made to come. The sacrifice of a cock was a custom in India, Greece, and Germany.

In the same way as the ancients used to make quails fight against each other, so they made cocks; hence the cock was called son of Mars (Areôs neottos). We already know that the cock's crest terrifies the maned lion; the crest and the mane are equivalent; and we have also seen what heroic virtue was attributed to the *lapillus alectorius.* Plutarch writes that the Lacedæmonians sacrificed the cock to Mars to obtain victory in the battles which they fought in the open air. Pallas wore the cock upon her helmet, Idomeneus upon his shield. Plutarch says, moreover, that the inhabitants of Caria used to carry a cock on the end of their lances, and refers the origin of this custom to Artaxerxes; but it appears to be much more ancient, for the Carians wore crested helmets as far back as the time of Herodotus, for which reason the Persians gave the Carians the name of cocks. Cock-fights, which became so popular in England, are also common in India. Philon, the Hebrew, relates of Miltiades, that before the battle of Marathon he inflamed the ardour of his soldiers by exhibiting cock-fights; the same, according Ælianos, was done by Themistocles. John Goropius (who gives the extravagant etymologies of *danen* and *alanen* from *de hahnen* and *all hahnen*) relates that the Danes were accustomed to carry two cocks to war, one to tell the hours and the other to excite the soldiers to battle. Du Cange informs

[1] Reinsberg von Düringsfeld observes (*Das festliche Jahr*), that sometimes, for jest, in North Walsham, instead of the cock an owl is put,—another funereal symbol with which we are already acquainted.

us that duels between cocks were also the custom in France in the seventeenth century, and gives some fragments of mediæval writings in which these are prohibited as a superstitious custom and one which was objectionable.

It is well known that the ancient Romans, before engaging in battle, took auguries from cocks and fowls, although this custom sometimes gave occasion to derision. Of Publius Claudius, for instance, it is said that, being about to engage in a naval battle in the first Punic war, he consulted the auguries in order not to offend against the customs of his country; but that when the augurs announced that the fowls would not eat, he ordered them to be taken and thrown into the sea, saying, "If they will not eat, then let them drink."

Part of the worship which was offered to the cock and to the hen was also rendered to the egg: the Latin proverb, "Gallus in sterquilinio suo plurimum potest," shows the great value of the egg. The pearl which the fowl searches for in the dunghill is nought else but its own egg; and the egg of the hen in the sky is the sun itself. During the night the celestial hen is black, but it becomes white in the morning; and being white, on account of the snow, it is the hen of winter. The white hen is propitious on account of the golden chickens hatched by it. In the Monferrato it is believed that the eggs of a white hen laid on Ascension Day, in a new nest, are a good remedy for pains in the stomach, head, and ears, and that, when taken into a cornfield, they prevent the blight, or black evil, from entering amongst the crops, or when taken into a vineyard, they save it from hail. The eggs which are eaten at Easter and concerning which, accompanied sometimes by songs and proverbs, so many popular customs, mythologically in accordance, are current in the various countries of Europe, celebrate the resurrection of the celestial egg, a symbol of abundance,[1] the sun of spring. The hen of the fable and the fairy tales, which lays golden eggs, is the mythical hen (the earth or the sky) which gives birth every day to the sun. The golden egg is the beginning of life in Orphic and Hindoo cosmogony; by the golden egg the world begins to move, and movement is the principle of good. The golden egg brings forth the luminous, laborious, and beneficent day. Hence it is an excellent augury to begin with the egg, which represents the principle of good, whence the equivocal Latin proverb, "Ab ovo ad malum," which signified "from good to evil," but which properly meant, "from the egg to the apple," the Latins being accustomed to begin their dinners with hard-boiled eggs and to end them with apples (a custom which is still preserved among numerous Italian families).[2]

But to begin *ab ovo* also means to begin at the beginning. Horace says that he does not begin from the twin eggs the description of the Trojan war—

"Nec gemino bellum Trojanum orditur *ab ovo*,"

[1] Not only the egg of the hen is a symbol of abundance, but even the bones of fowls served in popular tradition to represent matrimonial faith and coition. In Russia, when two (probably husband and wife) eat a fowl together, they divide the bone of the neck, the English merrythought, between them; then each of them takes and keeps a part, promising to remember this rupture. When either of the two subsequently presents something to the other, the one who receives must immediately say, "I remember;" if not, the giver says to him, "Take and remember." The forgetful one loses the game. A similar game, called the verde or green, is played in Tuscany during Lent between lovers with a little twig of the box-tree.

[2] The sun is an egg at the beginning of day; he becomes, or finds, an apple-tree in the evening, in the western garden of the Hesperides.

alluding to the egg of Lêda, to which the Greek proverb, "Come out of the egg" (ex ôou exêlthen), also alludes, said of a very handsome man, and referring to fair Helen and her two luminous brothers the Dioskuroi. But here the white cock has became a white swan, of which we shall speak in the following chapter.

CHAPTER X.

THE DOVE, THE DUCK, THE GOOSE, AND THE SWAN.

SUMMARY.

White, red, and dark-coloured doves, ducks, geese, and swans.—The funereal dove; it is united with the owl; kapotas.—The doves flee from unhappy persons.—The dove and the hawk.—Two doves sacrifice themselves, one for the other; a form of the Açvinâu.—The dove and the ant.—Transformation of the hero and heroine into doves.—The two prophetic doves upon the cross-trees of the mast.—Among funereal games, that of shooting arrows at a dove which hangs from the mast of a ship.—The doves of Dodona.—The dove and the water.—St Radegonda as a dove preserves sailors from shipwreck.—A dove guides the Argonauts.—The soul of Semiramis becomes a dove.—It is sacrilege to eat a dove.—Hero and heroine become doves, in order to escape.—The dove as the bringer of joy, of light, of good; it is a symbol of the winter that ends, and of the spring which is beginning.—The daughters of Anius become white doves.—Two doves separate the barley for the girl.—The fireworks, the stove, and the car of Indras, perform the same miracles, *i.e.*, they make beautiful the girl with the ugly skin.—Zezolla benefited by the dove of the fairies.—The doves on the rosebush.—The nymph Peristera helps Aphroditê to pluck flowers.—The phallical dove.—The word *hañsas;* the guç-lebedi of Russian tales.—Agnis as a hañsas.—The Marutas as hañsâs.—The horses of the two Açvinâu as hañsâs.—The duck makes its nest upon the thief's head.—Bṛibus on the thieves' head; Bṛibus as Indras, and as a bird.—Brahman upon the hañsâs.—The sun as a golden duck.—The betrothed wife as a duck.—The arrows of Râmas as hañsâs.—Kabandhas drawn by hañsâs.—The hañsâs as love messengers.—The geese-swans and the young hero in Russian tales.—The serpent-witch and the princess as a white duck.—The golden and silver eggs of the duck.—The golden egg of the duck causes the death of the horse.—The geese of the Capitol.—The goose which, after having been cooked, rises again alive.—Geese as discoverers of deceits.—The Valkiries as swans.—Berta the Reine pédauque.—The wild goose on the bush.—The goose eaten on St Michael's Day.—The hero and the swan.—The kingdom of the San Graal.—The legend of Lohengrin; a variety of the myth of the Açvinâu; Lohengrin and Elsa's brother, the sun and the moon.—The legend of the Dioskuroi; Zeus as a swan; the Dioskuroi deliver Helen, as Lohengrin delivers Elsa.

INASMUCH as there is the white dove and the dove-coloured one,[1] the white duck and goose, the duck and the dark-coloured or fire-coloured goose, the white swan and the flamingo, the red swan and the black, these birds, dove, goose, duck, and swan, from the diversity of colour which they assume upon the earth, also assumed mythical aspects which are sometimes contradictory when translated to the sky to represent celestial phenomena. While the white ones served for the more poetical images of mythology, the red and the dark ones offered aspects now benignant, now malignant, alluring the hero now to his ruin, and now, instead, to good fortune. The red hues, for example, of the western sky appear as flames into which the witch wishes to precipitate the young hero; the roseate tints of the eastern heavens, on the contrary, are generally the pyre or furnace in which the hero burns the ill-favoured witch who endeavours to ruin him; from the dawn of morning, from the white sky, from the snow of winter, from the white earth or white swan, the golden egg (the sun) comes forth; now the beautiful maiden, now the young hero emerges from

[1] The Indian word *kapotas*, which means a dove, also indicates the grey colour of antimony, the colour of the commonest species of doves, and of those which are fed on St Mark's Place at Venice.

it—the aurora and the sun, or else the spring and the sun. The evening sun and aurora in the night, the sun and the verdant earth, which divests itself of its vari-coloured attire in autumn, veil, cover, and lose themselves; their most vivid hues become obscure in the gloom of night, or are covered by the snow of winter; the hero becomes a dark-coloured dove, or a gloomy swan which crosses the waters. I have noted more than once how the night of the year corresponds to those of the day; the sun which hides itself in the night of evening, and the sun which veils itself in the night of winter, are often represented by the same mythical images.

Let us now see under what mythical aspects the dove, the duck, and the swan appear in the East, in order to compare them with Western traditions.

The *Ṛigvedas* presents us with the funereal dove, the grey or dark-coloured dove, the messenger of the nocturnal or wintry darkness. Seeing it is joined in the Vedic hymn with the owl, it was supposed that it represented some other bird than the dove, and interpreters were fain to recognise in the Vedic kapotas the *turdus macrourus* rather than the dove; but this interpretation seems to me inadmissible, since the Vedic kapotas appears as a domestic bird, and one which approaches the dwellings of men, habits which thrushes have not, and which doves have. In the 165th hymn of the tenth book of the *Ṛigvedas*, the kapotas is exorcised as a messenger of the funereal Nirṛitis, of death, and of Yamas the god of the dead, in order that it may do no evil: "Be propitious to us," cries the poet, "be propitious to us, rapid (or messenger) kapotas; inoffensive may the bird be unto us, O gods, in the houses. When the owl emits that painful cry, when the kapotas touches the fire, honour be to

Mṛityus, to Yamas, whose messenger it is."[1] As birds of evil omen also must the doves be recognised, which flee from the unhappy in the *Pańćatantram.*[2] In the dove pursued by the hawk (the hawk has also in Sanskṛit the name of kapotâris, or enemy of doves) of the Buddhist legend concerning the king who sacrifices himself to keep his word, which has been recorded in the chapter on the hawk, the hawk is the form taken by Indras, and the dove the form of Agnis, the fire. The same legend is found again in the *Tuti-Name*, with this variation that the vulture takes the place of the falcon, and Moses that of the Buddhist king. In order to fulfil the duties of hospitality, he cuts off as much of his own flesh as the dove weighs, to give it to the vulture, who takes in jest the same part of the hero which the hatred of races and religious fanaticism make the Jew of Venice, immortalised by the genius of Shakspeare, demand with seriousness. In other Hindoo varieties of the same legend of the hero who sacrifices himself, we find two doves (in the *Pańćatantram*) which sacrifice themselves one for the other; two doves that love one another (in the *Tuti-Name*,[3] they are two turtle-doves). Here we have a form of the two Açvinâu, of the two brothers of whom one sacrifices himself for the other; the well-known fable of La Fontaine, *Les Deux Pigeons*, is a reminiscence of this Eastern legend. In the same way, a variety of the legend of the two brothers is contained in the fable of Æsop, and of La Fontaine, of the dove that throws a blade of grass into the water to the ant that is about to drown, and thus saves it, for which reason the grateful

[1] Çivaḥ kapota ishito no astu anâgâ devâḥ çakuno gṛiheshu; str. 2. —For the fourth strophe, cfr. the chapter which treats of the Owl.

[2] ii. 9.

[3] ii. 239.—Cfr. the chapter on the Eagle.

ant soon after bites the foot of the hunter who has caught the dove, so that he is compelled to let it go. In the chapter which treats of the swallow, we saw the beautiful maiden upon the tree at the fountain changed into a swallow by the witch's enchantment; numerous other legends, instead of the transformation into a swallow, give us that into a dove.[1] The stories of the maiden Filadoro and of the Island of the Ogres, in the *Pentamerone*;[2] a Piedmontese story communicated by me in 1866 to my friend Professor Alexander Wesselofski, who published it in his essay upon the poet Pucci; the thirteenth Sicilian story of Signora Gonzenbach (of which the twelfth story is a variation); the forty-ninth story of the sixth book of *Afanassieff* (a variety of which occurs at the end of the fifth of the stories of Santo Stefano di Calcinaia), and a great number of analogous European stories, reproduce this subject of the maiden transformed into a dove by the witch's enchantment: as the swallow is white and black, so does the dove into which the beautiful maiden is transformed appear now white and now black. No less numerous are the stories in which, instead of the young princess, we read of young princes transformed into doves; I publish here two unpublished Tuscan stories which refer to this subject, and which (particularly the second) are of great interest.[3]

---

[1] It appears to me that the same confusion arose between *coluber* and *columba* as between *chelüdros*, a kind of serpent, and *chelidôn*, a swallow. The beautiful maiden upon a tree occurs even in the *Tuti-Name*, i. 178, *seq.*

[2] ii. 7, and v. 9

[3] They were related to me at Antignano near Leghorn by the peasant woman Uliva Selvi:—

A gentleman had twelve sons and one daughter, who had, by enchantment, been metamorphosed into an eagle, and was kept in a cage. The father takes the twelve sons to mass every day; every day he meets an old beggar-woman and gives alms to her; one day,

Hitherto the dove has appeared as a mournful and diabolical form assumed by the hero or heroine, on com-

---

however, he has no money with him, and therefore gives her nothing; the old woman curses him, wishing that he may never see his sons again. No sooner said than done; the twelve sons become twelve doves and fly away. The despairing father and mother begin to weep; in their despair they forget to feed the eagle. Opposite the gentleman's house the king lived, who becomes enamoured of the eagle as though of a beautiful maiden; he has her stolen and replaced by another eagle. Not far thence there lived a washerwoman who had such a beautiful daughter that she never let her go out except at night. They wash at the fountain surrounded by poplar-trees; at midnight, as they wash, they hear a noise among the poplar-trees, and the maiden is afraid. One night they listen and hear the doves speaking and telling one another the incidents of the day, where they had been and what they had been doing. They then fly into a beautiful garden; the girl follows them; they enter into a beautiful palace, and the washerwoman relates what she has seen to the gentleman, who rejoices, and promises a great reward to the washerwoman if she will show him where his sons go to sleep. Both father and mother go to see; the pigeons speak, and say, "Were our mother to see us . . . "; they then fly away. The gentleman then consults an astrologer, who advises him to allure the old witch into his house by the promise of alms, to shut her up in a room, and to compel her by main force to indicate the means of turning the pigeons into youths once more, or else to kill her. The old woman gives a powder which, when scattered on the highest mountain, will make the pigeons return home. The father goes to the mountain, scatters the powder and returns home, where he finds his sons, who are inquiring after the eagle. They go to see it and do not recognise it; they complain to their mother of this. Meanwhile, the young king is always near his eagle as if making love to it; and his mother is displeased at it. The twelve brothers meet a fairy who, for some alms, tells who has their eagle, and that it will soon return home a beautiful maiden. And the eagle becomes a beautiful girl and is married by the king.

There was once a king who had a handsome son, enamoured of a beautiful princess. He is carried off with two servants by the magicians and transformed into a pigeon; the servants undergo the same metamorphosis; one becomes green, one red, and the other greyish violet (pavonazzo). They take him into a beautiful palace where he must

pulsion of external magic. Of funereal character, too, are the two doves which place themselves upon the cross-trees of the ship in which Gennariello is carrying a hawk, a horse, and a white and red bride with black hair to his brother Milluccio (a variation of the legend of the Açvinâu, and of that of the youth who sacrifices himself

stay for seven years. Each has a large basin,—one is of gold, another of silver, and the third of bronze. When they plunge into them, they become three handsome youths. The princess, meanwhile, is dying to know where her lover is gone; she goes to have her hair combed on a terrace; the three pigeons carry away her looking-glass, then the ribbon of her hair, and then her comb. A great festival occurs in this town, to which the girls of the land go by night; on the way, one of them, near the break of day, turns aside for a few minutes; she sees a golden gate, finds a little gold key on the earth, opens the door and enters into a fine garden. At the end of the path there is beautiful palace, into which she goes; she finds the three basins of gold, silver, and bronze, and sees the pigeons become young men. Meanwhile the king's daughter falls ill of grief, and is to all appearance dying; the king resolves to have her cured at any cost. The girl who had been in the place relates to the king's daughter all that she has seen; the latter is cured and goes with the girl to the palace; they find it, enter, and see a table laid for three persons; the two girls hide themselves. The prince and the princess meet with one another; but the prince, upon seeing her, is full of despair, saying that her impatience has prolonged the enchantment for seven years more, whilst it had at the time only three more days to run. He becomes a pigeon again; she must stay for seven years upon a tower exposed to all the inclemency of the seasons. Seven years pass by; the princess has become so ugly that she looks like a beast, with long hair all over her burned skin. The enchantment comes to an end for him after seven years; he goes to look for her; she says, "How much have I suffered for you!" The prince does not recognise her, and leaves her; she is left naked in a dense forest, and goes to seek her father. Night comes on, and the princess and her servant-maid do not know where to take refuge; they climb up a tree, whence they perceive a light. They walk towards it and find a beautiful little palace; a beautiful lady, a fairy, shows herself, and asks, "Is this you, Caroline?" This was the princess's name. But the fairy can give no news of the prince, and sends her on to another fairy, her

for his brother). The two doves speak to each other; one says that Gennariello is taking to his brother Milluccio a hawk which immediately after its arrival will tear out his eyes, and that he who should warn Milluccio of it, or not take the hawk to him, would turn to marble; then that Gennariello is taking to his brother Milluccio a

---

sister, with the same result; she then goes to a third fairy, walking a double distance each time. The three fairies were three queens who had been betrayed by the same young prince. The third fairy gives to the princess a magical rod; she must go to the prince and do to him what he did to her—spit in his face, to wit. She is brought in a boat before the young king's palace, and there, following the fairy's instructions, she raises, by means of the rod, a beautiful palace, a palace more beautiful than that of the king, with a beautiful fountain. The young king wishes to go and see it; he sees a beautiful princess and kisses his hand to her, but she shuts the window in his face. He then invites her to dinner, but she refuses. He sends her a magnificent diamond, which she gives to her majordomo, saying that she has many more beautiful. He then sends her a splendid dress, which can be taken in the palm of the hand; she tears it into pieces and gives it to the cook to be used for kitchen purposes. The young king becomes passionately enamoured of her, and sends to her his best watch, which she gives also to her majordomo. He falls ill of a dreadful fever and wishes to marry her; he sends his mother. The princess laughs at the prince and refuses to come, saying, "Why does he not come himself?" His mother begs again that she will come. "Let him come," she answers; and at last she consents to come if they will make from her palace to that of the king a covered way so well and thickly made that not a ray of light can enter, and which she may be able to pass through with her equipage. Half way, the covering opens, and the sunbeams enter, upon which she disappears. (Cfr. the Indian myth of Urvaçî). The king being about to die, his mother returns to the princess, who demands that they bring him to her as if dead, in a bier. The king confesses that he has betrayed four maidens, and that it is on account of the fourth that he is coming to such a miserable end. The princess laughs at him and spits twice in his face; the third time he rises again, they are reconciled and married. (The spitting of the princess, which makes the dead prince rise again, is the dew of the ambrosia, or of spring, which brings the sun to life again.)—Cfr. the stories ii. 5, iv. 8, of the *Pentamerone*, and v. 22 of *Afanassieff*.

horse which, as soon as it is ridden, will break his neck, and that he who should warn Milluccio of this, or not take the horse to him, would turn to marble; and finally, it says that Gennariello is taking to his brother a wife on whose account a dragon will devour the bride and bridegroom during the first night of their union, and that he who should warn Milluccio of this, or not take the bride to him, would turn to marble. The cunning Gennariello takes hawk, horse, and bride to Milluccio; but before he takes the hawk in his hand, Gennariello cuts off its head; before he rides the horse, Gennariello cuts its legs off; and before the dragon comes up to devour the bride and bridegroom, Gennariello shears off its head. Milluccio, who has not seen the dragon, sees his brother with a knife in his hand, and thinks that he has come to kill him; he has him bound and condemned to death. In order not to escape this fate, Gennariello reveals everything and turns to marble. Milluccio learns that by anointing the marble with the blood of his two little sons, his brother can be recalled to life; he slaughters his children; the mother, in despair, goes to the window to kill herself by throwing herself down, but she sees her father coming towards her, and shouting, "Drinto na nugola." He resuscitates her children, saying that it was to avenge himself, he had caused such bitter pain to all; on Gennariello, because he had carried off his daughter; on Milluccio, who was the cause of her being carried off; on his daughter, because she had eloped from her home. The two doves that perched upon the crosstrees of the mast were therefore messengers of death to the hero and to the heroine, as sometimes, on the other hand, they are their own funereal form. The reader will doubtless remember how, in the funeral of Patroclus in the *Iliad*, amongst the funereal games, there is that of shooting arrows at a dove hung upon the mast of a ship. (He will also remember the two prophetic doves which gave responses upon two oak-trees or beeches at Dodona, and which cried, "Zeus was, Zeus is, Zeus will be, O Zeus, the greatest of the gods!") The dove here appears in connection with funereal waters; the fable is well known of the dove that meets with its death by beating its head against a wall upon which water is painted.[1] In the legend of Queen Radegonda, the holy queen, in the form of a dove, delivers sailors from shipwreck. According to Apollonios, a dove was the guide of the Argonauts. It is said that Semiramis was transformed into one after her death. The dove also appears as a funereal symbol in Christian monuments; hence, and from its use as the symbol of the St Esprit, the superstition cherished by a great portion of the people in Italy, Germany, Holland, and Russia, to the effect that it is a sin to eat a dove. It is well-known what reverence was shown to it in antiquity, particularly in Syria and in Palestine.

Sometimes the form of a dove is voluntarily assumed by the two young lovers, to flee from the persecution of the monster; as, for instance, in the sixth of the *Novelline di Santo Stefano.* Sometimes the funereal dove (like the funereal crow) is the bringer of joy and good things to men and gods. The popular custom of the artificial dove, commonly called the dove of the Pazzi (from the name

[1] It is said of the widowed turtle-dove that it will never drink again in any fountain of limped water for fear of reviving the image of its lost companion by seeing its own in the water. The Christians pretend that the voice of the turtle-dove represents the cry, the sighing, and afterwards, for the resurrection of Christ, the joy of Mary Magdalen. Ælianos says that the turtle-dove is sacred not only to the goddess of love, and to the goddess of harvests, but also to the funereal Parcæ.

of the noble Florentine family which possessed the privilege), which, at Florence, on Holy Saturday, that is to say, Easter Eve, starts from the altar of the Cathedral, and flies at midday to light the fireworks upon the little square between Santa Maria del Fiore and the Baptistery of St John, to announce that Christ has risen to a crowd of peasants, who have flocked in from the country to augur from the dove's flight whether they will have a good harvest in the following year,—is a symbol of the end of winter, and of the commencement of spring. In the *Metamorphoses* of Ovid, the daughters of Anius, by the grace of Bacchus, change into corn, wine, and oil, whatever they touch, according to the words of the same Anius—

> "Tactu natarum cuncta mearum
> In segetem, laticemque meri, baccamque Minervæ
> Transformabantur."

Agamemnon wishes to have them with him to provision the army; the daughters of Anius refuse; Agamemnon then purposes compelling them by main force; but Bacchus takes pity upon them, and transforms them into white doves. In the thirtieth story of the sixth book of *Afanassieff*, two doves (a form of the Açvinâu) come to separate the barley for Masha or Little Mary, the black (ćornushka) or ugly or dirty little girl, the persecuted Cinderella, and then making her mount upon the stove, transform her into an exceedingly beautiful maiden, renewing thus the miracle of Indras (and of the Açvinâu), who restores to beauty the maiden of the ugly skin. The fireworks of the popular Tuscan custom, the stove, and the car of Indras perform the same miracle. In the sixth story of the first book of the *Pentamerone*, the maiden Zezolla, called at home "a cat, a cinder-girl," because she was always watching the fire, ill-treated at home by her step-mother, is benefited by the dove of the fairies of the island of Sardinia, which sends her a plant that yields golden dates, a golden spade, a little golden bucket, and a silk tablecloth. The girl must cultivate the plant, and simply remember, when she wishes for some favour, to say—

> "Dattolo mio 'naurato,
> Co la zappatella d'oro t'haggio zappato,
> Co lo secchietello d'oro t'haggio adacquato,
> Co la tovaglia de seta t'haggio asciuttato;
> Spoglia a te, e vieste a me."

The date-tree yields some of its riches to adorn the maiden. Thus, when the young king proclaims a festival, she goes disguised in regal attire, and dances with an effect that outdazzles like a sun. When she is followed by the prince the first time, she throws gold behind her; the second time, pearls; the third, her slipper; and by means of it she is recognised and espoused. In the twenty-second Esthonian story, when the young prince-lover arrives, two doves perch upon the rose-bush, in which the beautiful daughter of the gardener is enclosed by enchantment; the beautiful maiden comes out of the rose-bush, and, showing the half of her ring, weds the prince who has preserved the other half. In the Hellenic myth, Aphroditê and Love play at seeing who will pluck most flowers; winged Love is winning, but the nymph Peristera helps Aphroditê; Love indignant, changes her into the peristera or dove, which Aphroditê, to console her, takes under her protection. The doves now draw the chariot of Venus, and now (like the sparrows) accompany it. In the *Odyssey* the doves bring the ambrosia to Zeus,[1] and it is in the form of a dove that Zeus (well

[1] In the legend of St Remy it is a dove that carries to the saint the flagon of water with which he must baptize King Clodoveus.

known to be an *alter ego* of Indras) visits the virgin Phthia. Catullus, speaking of Cæsar's *salacitas*, makes mention of the *columbulum albulum*, or little dove of Venus.[1] In this passage the dove becomes a phallical symbol; and we are reminded of the well-known mythical episode of the animal, bird, or fish which laughs, by the equivocal Italian proverb, "The dove that laughs wants the bean" (said of a woman when she smiles upon her lover[2]). It is narrated of Aphroditê, that she cured Aspasia of a tumour by the help of a dove; here the dove does to Aspasia the same service as the rudder of Indras's chariot to Apalâ in the Vedic legend.

But in mythical tradition the place of the doves is sometimes taken by ducks, which are exchanged for swans.

The Hindoo word *hañsas* means now swan, now duck (anas, anser), now goose, now phænicopterus. No

---

[1] "Et ille nunc superbus et superfluens
Perambulabit omnium cubilia,
Ut albulus columbus, aut Adoneus?
Cinæde Romule, hæc videbis et feres?"

The chastity and the proverbial conjugal fidelity attributed to doves is here denied. Catullus had evidently closely observed the habits of these animals, which are sometimes, on the contrary, of a shameless infidelity. I have seen a white dove, who, in the presence of his wife, intent upon hatching her eggs, violated the nuptial bed of a gray dove, at a moment when the jealous husband was eating; the wife accepted the caresses of the husband and of the lover in the same passive attitude.

[2] We may also record here another Italian proverb, "To take two doves with one bean." In Italian anatomy a part of the phallus is called a bean (fava). The birds, and especially the thrushes and the doves, according to the popular belief, not only have the faculty of making other birds, but even plants fruitful. The words of Pliny, *Hist. Nat.* xvi. 44, have already been quoted by Prof. Kuhn: "Omnino autem satum nullo modo nascitur, nec nisi per alvum avium redditum, maxime palumbis ac turdis."

wonder then that the myths exchanged, one for another, animals which were confounded together under one and the same appellation. Russian stories call the birds goose-swans (guçlebedi) which now carry off, and now save the young hero.

In the Vedic hymns, the hansas (duck-swan or goose-swan) is represented more than once. Agnis, the fire, when entreated to arouse himself in houses with the aurora, is compared to a swan in the waters (or to the light in the darkness, to white upon black, or the sun in the azure sky[1]). The god Agnis is himself called hansas, the companion (as a thunderbolt) of the movable (waves or clouds), going in company with the celestial waters.[2] The song of the companions of Bṛihaspatis, singing hymns to the cows or auroræ of the morn, resembles the song of the hansâs.[3] The Marutas, with the splendid bodies (the winds that lighten, howl, and thunder) are compared to hansâs with black backs[4] (which reminds us of the swallows with black backs and with white ones, of black crows and white crows, black swans and white ones). The horses of the two Açvinâu are compared to hansâs, ambrosial, innocent, with golden wings, which waken with the aurora (being sunbeams), which swim in the waters, joyful and merry.[5] In the Russian stories of *Afanassieff*,[6] a duck comes to make its nest upon the head of the thief who has fallen into the waters out of

[1] Çvasity apsu hanso na sîdan kratvâ ćetishṭho viçâm usharbhut; *Ṛigv.* i. 65, 9.

[2] Bîbhatsûnâm sayuǵam hansam âhur apâm divyânâm sakhye ćarantam; x. 124, 9.

[3] Hansâir iva sakhibhir vâvadadbhir açmanmayâni nahanâ vyasyan bṛihaspatir abhi kanikradad gâ; x. 67, 3.

[4] Sasvaç cid dhi tanvaḥ çumbhamânâ â hansâso nîlapṛishṭhâ apaptan; vii. 59, 7.

[5] Cfr. the chapter which treats of the Bee.

[6] vi. 2.

the sky. The duck lays a golden egg (the sun) in its nest at morn, and a silver egg (the moon) at even. In the *Ṛigvedas*, I read that upon the head of the thieves (Paṇayas), similar to the vast forest of the Ganges, at its higher part, Bṛibuḥ went to place himself, scattering thousands of gifts.[1] I think I can recognise in Bṛibus a bird and a personification of Indras. Bṛibus is, in Çâñkhâyanas, represented as a takshan, which is explained as a constructor, an artificer, a carpenter; hence Bṛibus is supposed to be the carpenter of the Paṇayas. But this seems improbable, besides being in contradiction to the Vedic strophe. The proper primitive sense of the word *takshan* is the cutter, he who breaks in pieces; in Bṛibus, therefore, I recognise not the carpenter of the Paṇayas, but their destroyer. As we also find, in another Vedic hymn,[2] Bṛibus in connection with two other birds, viz., the bharadvaǵas (the lark) and the stokas (the cuckoo), I am induced to suppose that Bṛibus too is a bird. Finally, as I find Bṛibus in connection with Indras, I see in this bird that perches upon the head of the Paṇayas, a form of the god Indras himself. The duck, in Russian stories, deposits its egg upon the robber's head; thus Indras takes their treasures off the head of the Paṇayas. We already know of the pearls which fall from the head of the good fairy, combed by the virtuous maiden; we also know that the mythical waters are in relation with the treasures. We must record here the legend of the *Râmâyaṇam* concerning the origin of the Ganges, which, before pouring its waters upon the earth, let them wander for a long time upon the hairy head of

[1] Adhi bṛibuḥ paṇînâṁ varshishṭhe mûrdhann asthât uruḥ kaksho na gâñgyaḥ; *Ṛigv.* vi. 45, 31.—Bṛibuṁ sahasradâtamaṁ sûriṁ sahasrasâtamaṁ; vi. 45, 33.—Cfr. also the 32d strophe.

[2] *Ṛigv.* vi. 46.

the god Çivas, who is a more elevated form of Kuveras, the god of riches.[1] We know also that the pearl and the egg are the same in the myths.

The god Brahman is represented in Hindoo mythology riding upon a white hañsas.

In the *Râmâyaṇam*, the sky is compared to a lake of which the resplendent sun is the golden duck.[2] Râmas (a form of the sun Vishṇus), whose speech has the accent of the hañsas drunk with love,[3] hurls with his divine bow an arrow which penetrates through seven palm-trees, the mountain, and the earth, out of which it afterwards comes, and returns to Râmas in the form of a hañsas.[4] Kabandhas, who, when traversing the fire, is released by his monstrous form, is drawn by hañsâs whilst ascending into heaven.[5] Finally, the hañsâs are well known which served as love-messengers between the prince Nalas and the Princess Damayantî in the celebrated episode of the *Mahâbhâratam*.

In the fourth story of the first book of *Afanassieff*, little Johnny (Ivasco) is upon an oak-tree, which the witch is gnawing, to possess herself of him; three flights of geese-swans pass one after the other; Johnny begs for

---

[1] The goose is found in connection with robbers in the twenty-third story of the sixth book of *Afanassieff*. Two servants stole a precious pearl from the king; being about to be found out, they give the pearl, by the advice of an old woman, to the grey goose in a piece of bread; the goose is then accused of having stolen the pearl. It is killed, the pearl is found, and the two robbers escape.

[2] v. 55.—In the forty-ninth story of the fifth book of *Afanassieff*, a riddle occurs where the betrothed wife is represented as a duck. A father sends his son to find the wife who is predestined for him, with the following enigmatical order: "Go to Moscow; there there is a lake; in the lake there is a net; if the duck has fallen into the net, take the duck; if not, withdraw the net." The son returns home with the duck—that is to say, with his betrothed wife.

[3] ii. 46. [4] iv. 11. [5] iii. 75.

their assistance; the first flight refuse; as also the second; those of the third take Johnny upon their wings and carry him home.[1] In the nineteenth story of the sixth book, the geese-swans assume, on the contrary, a malignant aspect, carrying the little brother on their wings away from his negligent sister. The story says that these animals have had for a long time the evil reputation of carrying little children off. The geese-swans carry the boy into a fairy's house, where he plays with golden apples. The sister follows upon his track; she inquires at a stove, an apple-tree, and a brook of milk, where the goose-swans have carried the boy to, but learns nothing; at last the malicious little iosz (the sea-urchin) reveals to her the secret. The sister takes her brother and carries him home, having been followed by the geese-swans and having had to hide herself during her flight by the brook, by the apple-tree and then by the stove.

But if geese, ducks, and swans sometimes do evil, or are sometimes diabolical forms assumed by the witch's deceit, they generally produce good and conduct to good. In a variation of the forty-sixth story of the sixth book of *Afanassieff*, the geese predict the future to Ivan the merchant's son, who, having been to school under the devil, learns there, amongst other things, the language of birds. In the sixtieth story of the sixth book of *Afanassieff*, the swan, a beautiful maiden, helps the unhappy Danilo, whom the prince has ordered to sew a pelisse which must have golden lions for buttons and birds from beyond the seas for button-holes; the same swan performs other miracles for the youth whom she loves. In the forty-sixth story of the fourth book of

[1] Cfr. *Afanassieff*, vi. 17, and a variety of the vi. 19.

Afanassieff, the old serpent-witch makes the princess become a white duck during the prince's absence. The duck lays three eggs, out of which she has three sons, two handsome, and one ill-favoured, but cunning. The witch kills, during their sleep, the two handsome sons and turns them to ducks; the third escapes by means of his cunning; the white duck, anxious about her sons, flies to the prince's palace and begins to sing—

> "Krià, krià, my little sons!
> Krià, krià, little pigeons!
> The old witch has extinguished you;
> The old witch, the malignant serpent,
> The deceitful malignant serpent!
> Your own father has carried you off,
> Your own father, my husband!
> She drowned us in the rapid stream,
> She transformed us into little white ducks,
> And she herself lives in regal pomp!"

The prince has the duck caught by the wings, and says, "White birch-tree, put thyself behind; beautiful maiden, before." At this magical formula, the tree rises behind him and he finds his beautiful princess before him. He then compels the witch to bring the little children to life again.

The death of the duck sometimes makes the fortune of the hero or the heroine, on account of the egg which it produces (the sun in the morning and the moon in the evening). In the fifty-third story of the fifth book of *Afanassieff*, the young hero, by the advice of an unknown young man, goes to seek under the roots of a birch-tree a duck which lays one day (in the morning) a golden egg, and next day (in the evening) a silver one; upon its breast, the following words are written in golden letters:—"He who eats its head will become king; he who eats the heart will spit gold." He carries it to his mother when his father is absent and his mother has an intrigue with another gentleman. The gentleman reads the golden letters and advises the woman to have the duck cooked; but the two sons are before him; and whilst their mother is at mass, one eats the head and the other the heart of the duck, and meet with the adventures which are related in the chapter on the Horse.[1] The golden egg of the duck causes the death of the witch and the monster in numerous Slavonic stories. In the thirty-third story of the fifth book of *Afanassieff*, a marvellous goose, of the same nature as those that in the Capitol warned the Romans of the ambuscade of the Gauls, discovers the traitors. The wife of a rich merchant asks her husband to procure for her the marvel of marvels. Her husband buys, in the twenty-seventh world and in the thirtieth kingdom (which is the kingdom of the other night-world), from an old man,[2] a goose which, after having been cooked and eaten, all except the bones, rises again alive. The goose performs the same miracle in the merchant's house; on the morrow, when the husband is absent, his wife invites a lover of hers into the house and wishes to cook the goose to welcome him. She says to it, "Come here;" the goose obeys; she commands it to get into the frying-pan, but it refuses. The woman puts it in by force, but remains fastened to the frying-pan;[3] the lover tries to release

[1] Cfr. an interesting variety of this story in the *Griechische und Albanische Märchen* of Hahn.

[2] Thus, in a Norwegian story, the dirty cinder-girl carries silver ducks away from the magicians.—In the eighth Esthonian story, the third brother is sent to hell for the ducks and geese with golden feathers.

[3] In a Scandinavian and Italian variety of this story, instead of the goose we have the eagle and eaglets; the goose returns, in the first story of the fifth book of the *Pentamerone*, to do the same duty as in the Russian story, but with some more vulgar and less decent incidents.

her, but sticks fast also; the servants come to the rescue, and stick one to the other and all to the frying-pan, until the husband appears, hears his wife's confession, thrashes the lover and releases the woman from the goose.

In the *Pentamerone*, too, geese appear as discoverers of deceits. Marziella, when she combs her hair, scatters pearls and flower-buds about her; when she walks, lilies and violets grow up under her feet;[1] her brother Ciommo is to conduct her to the king as his wife; but the old aunt changes the bride, putting her own ugly daughter in the place of her beautiful niece. The indignant king sends Ciommo to pasture the geese; he neglects them, but Marziella, who had been carried off by a siren, comes from the bottom of the sea to feed them, "de pasta riale," and to give them "rose-water" to drink. The geese grow fat, and begin to sing near the king's palace—

"Pire, pire, pire;
Assai bello è lo sole co la luna;
Assai chiù bella è chi coverna a nuie."

The king sends a servant after the geese, and thus discovers everything; he wishes to marry the beautiful maiden, but the siren keeps her tied with a golden chain; the king, with a noiseless file, files with his own hands the chain which keeps the maiden's foot fast, and thereafter marries her.[2] It is a gooseherd who, in the

[1] The image of the legs which, when they move, make flowers grow up, is very ancient; students of Hindoo literature will remember the pushpiṇyâu ćarato ǵanghe of the *Âitareya Br.*, in the story of Çunaḥçepas.

[2] The ninth of the *Novelline di Santo Stefano di Calcinaia* is an interesting variety of this; the beautiful maiden who feeds the geese is disguised in an old woman's skin; the geese, who see her naked, cry out: "Cocò, la bella padrona ch 'i' ho," until the prince, by means of a noiseless file, makes the cook enter the room and carry the old

twentieth Esthonian story, releases the beautiful girl from the monster husband, the killer of his wives (a form of Barbebleu).

woman's skin away while she sleeps, and then weds her.—The following unpublished story, communicated to me by Signor Greco from Cosenza in Calabria, is a variation of that of the *Pentamerone* :—

Seven princes have a very beautiful sister. An emperor decides upon marrying her, but upon the condition that if he does not find her to his taste, he will decapitate her seven brothers. They set out altogether, and the mother-in-law with her daughter follow them. On the way, the sun is hot, and the elder brother cries out, "Solabella, defend me from the heat, for you must please the king." The step-mother advises her to take off her necklaces and to put them on her half-sister. The second brother next complains of the heat, and the step-mother advises her to take off her gold apparel and to put it on her half-sister. By such means the step-mother at last succeeds in making her naked; they come to the sea, and the step-mother pushes her in; she is taken by a siren, who holds her by her foot with a golden chain. The princes arrive with the ugly sister; the king weds the ugly wife and cuts off the heads of the seven brothers. When the maiden is wandering about in the sea, she asks the king's ducks for news of her brothers; the ducks answer that they have been executed. She weeps; the tears become pearls and the ducks feed upon them. This marvel comes to the ears of the king, who follows the ducks and asks the girl why she shuns the society of men; to which she answers: "Alas! how can I, who am fastened by a golden chain?" and then relates everything. Having recognised his bride, the king gives her this advice: she must ask how, after the siren's death, she would be able to free herself; and then he departs. Next day, Solabella tells the king that the siren will not die, because she lives in a little bird, enclosed in a silver cage which is shut up in a marble case, and seven iron ones, of which she has the keys, and that if the siren died, a horseman, a white horse, and a long sword would be necessary to cut the chain. The king brings her a certain water, which he advises her to give the siren to drink; she will then fall asleep, and the girl will be able to take the keys and kill the little bird. When it is killed, the white horse plunges into the sea, and the sword cuts the chain. Then the king takes his beautiful bride to his palace, and the old step-mother is burned in a shirt of pitch; the seven brothers are rubbed with an ointment which brings them to life again, each exclaiming, "Oh! what a beautiful dream I have had!"

In the Russian story, the fairy maidens (in German traditions, the Virgin Mary too) sometimes take, in order to cross the waters, the form of geese-swans; thus in the *Eddas*, three Valkyries spin on the shores of the lake, with their swan forms close behind them. "The maidens," sings the poem of Völund, "flew from the south across Mörkved, in order that the young Allhvit might be able to accomplish his destiny. The daughters of the South sat down upon the shore to spin the precious cloth. One of them, the most beautiful maiden of the world, was clasped to the white bosom of Egil; Svanhvit, the second, wore swan's feathers; the third embraced the white neck of Völund."[1] To the Bertha of popular German tradition, only the foot of the white goose or of the swan of the Valkyries has remained; hence her name of Foot-of-goose and of *Reine pédauque*, in the same way as the swan's foot alone has remained to the goddess Freya.

When the form of a duck, a goose, or a swan is destroyed, the young hero or the young heroine alone remain. In a German tradition, quoted by Simrock in his *German Mythology*, we find an enchanted hunter who strikes a wild goose on the flight, and which falls into a bush; he comes up to take it, and instead of it (in the same way as we saw above, the rosebush on which the doves perch) a naked woman rises before him. The custom of eating a goose in England on St Michael's Day, is referred by tradition to the times of Queen Elizabeth, who, on St Michael's Day, received the news of the defeat of the Invincible Armada, when she had

[1] The old ogress of the ninth story of the fifth book of the *Pentamerone*, who keeps three beautiful maidens shut up in three citron-trees, and who feeds the asses which kick the swans upon the banks of the river, is a variety of the same myth.

just eaten a goose. But inasmuch as, according to Baron von Reinsberg-Düringsfield, the custom of eating a goose on St Michael's Day dates from the times of Edward IV., we must admit that Queen Elizabeth conformed to a popular custom which already existed in England.[1] St Michael's goose announces the winter like the halcyon. It is eaten as an augury of the termination of the rainy and wintry season, inasmuch as when the aquatic bird, the halcyon, the goose, the duck, or the swan, finds no more water, when the sea of night, or the snow of winter dries up, when the aquatic bird is wounded, or is eaten, or dies, the golden egg is found, the sun comes out, the aurora returns, the winter appears again, the young hero and the beautiful maiden come forth. When the hero or heroine becomes an aquatic bird,[2] when he becomes a swan, is drawn by a swan, or rides upon it, it means that he is traversing the sea of death, and that he is returning to the kingdom of the San Graal. When he comes on the swan to meet the beautiful maiden, no one must ask him whence he came. The swan awaits him and will draw him once more under its magic power, and into its gloomy kingdom, as soon as this kingdom is remembered by the living. The imagination of the Celtic and Germanic nations has, in a cycle of numerous and fascinating legends, invested with solemn

[1] Instead of geese, swans were also solemnly eaten; a popular mediæval German song in Latin offers the lamentation of the roasted swan; cfr. Uhland's *Schriften*, iii. 71, 158.—In the *Pańćatantram*, we have the swan sacrificed by the owl. In order to allure the swan, the funereal owl, who wishes to kill it, invites it into a grove of lotus-flowers, only, however, to decoy it subsequently into a dark cavern, where the swan is killed by some travelling merchants, who believe it to be an owl.

[2] In the *Eddas*, when the hero Sigurd expires, the geese bewail his death.

mystery this myth, to which the inspired and classical music of Richard Wagner has, in Lohengrin, imparted a new attractive magic. Lohengrin, the *recens natus*, the hero born of himself, arrives in a boat drawn by a swan, into which a sorceress has transformed Elsa's young brother: he comes to deliver the Princess Elsa, and is about to marry her, but he does not forget that as long as he remains with her, so much the longer will the torment of her brother endure, so much the longer will he suffer in the shape of a swan; woe to him if any one asks who he is, whence he came, or what that swan is, for he would then be obliged to remember that the swan waits for him to deliver it. Lohengrin must either renounce his love for Elsa, or betray his cavalier's faith to the swan, of whose mysterious nature he is cognisant; he bids a funereal farewell to Elsa, reunites her with her young brother, and mournfully disappears on the gloomy waters, over whose moonlit depths he had come. This is the legend of the two brothers, raised to its utmost poetic and ideal power by Northern genius. The sun and the moon appear in turns before the dawn and the spring. They are separated, and one delivers the other in the legends inspired by the good genie of man, as in others inspired by his evil genie, one persecutes and deceives the other. We have, even in the Vedic hymns, the Açvinâu, the divine twins, identified now with the twilights, now with the sun and the moon, drawn by swans; Lohengrin is the sun; Elsa's brother is the moon. When the evening aurora, when the autumnal earth, loses the sun, it finds the moon; when the morning aurora or the vernal earth loses the moon, the sun takes its place; the lovers change places. One swan causes the birth of the other, carries the other, dies for the other, like one dove for the other, and as the Dioskuroi lay down their lives for each other. And, in truth, the legend of the Dioskuroi is, in some points, in marvellous accordance with the Northern legends of the rider of the swan. Zeus becames a swan and unites himself with Leda, wife of Tyndareos, and generates by her the sun and the moon, Polüdeukes and Helen; according to Homer Helen alone is Zeus's daughter, and Polüdeukes and Kastor are sons of Tyndareos; according to Herodotos, Helen, on the contrary, is the daughter of Tyndareos, and this is in accordance with Euripides, who tells us that the Dioskuroi are sons of Zeus. In the *Heroides* of Ovid, where the primitive tradition has already been altered, Leda, after having united herself to the swan Zeus, gives birth to two eggs; Helen comes out of one, Kastor and Polüdeukes out of the other. Evidently *tot capita tot sententiæ*; but these contradictions, far from excluding the myth of the sun, the moon, and the aurora (or of the spring) confirm it. It is always difficult to determine the paternity of a child who is born in an irregular manner, and the birth of Helen and her two brothers was certainly extraordinary. What is important here is that we have the swan which generates sons in Leda; these sons, who are partly of the nature of the bird, and partly of that of the woman, must assume a double form, and now become swans like their father, now shine in their mother's beauty; when, moreover, we think that only one of the brothers was, with Helen, born of the swan, it becomes natural to think of the other brother who may love Helen without being guilty of incest.[1] Before becoming famous by the varied fortunes of Troy,

[1] Cfr. also, with regard to this subject, the twenty-fourth Esthonian story of the princess born in the egg, of whom her brother, born in a more normal manner of the queen, becomes enamoured.

Helen, as a girl, had her adventures; Theseus seduced her and carried her off. The Dioskuroi come to deliver her in the same way as Lohengrin comes upon the swan to deliver Elsa, whilst her seducer is about to effect her ruin. Finally, the adventures of the two Dioskuroi, of whom one sacrifices himself for the other, correspond to the legend of the Schwanritter, the brother, or brother-in-law, who, on account of the swan offers up his own life. Thus India, Greece, and Germany united, in various forms, the figure of the swan with the story of the two brothers, or of the two companions; India created the myth, Greece coloured it, Germany has imbued it with passionate energy and pathos.

CHAPTER XI.

THE PARROT.

SUMMARY.

Haris and harit; harayas and harî; green and yellow called by a common name.—The moon as a green tree and as a green parrot; the parrot and the tree assimilated.—The wise moon and the wise parrot; the phallical moon and the phallical parrot, in numerous love stories.—The god of love mounted on the parrot.—The parrot and the wolf pasture together.

THE myth of the parrot originated in the East, and developed itself almost exclusively among the Oriental nations.

I mentioned in the chapter on the Ass, that the words *haris* and *harit* signify green no less than fair-haired, and hence gave rise to the epic myth of the monsters with parrot's faces, or drawn by parrots. The solar horses are called harayas; harî are the two horses of Indras; Haris is a name of Indras himself, but especially of the god Vishṇus; but there are more fair-haired figures in the sky then these; the golden thunderbolt which shoots through the cloud, and the golden moon, the traveller of the night, are such. Moreover, because green and yellow are called by this common name, all these fair ones, and the moon in particular, assumed the form, now of a green tree, now of a green parrot. A very interesting Vedic strophe offers us an evident proof of this. The solar horses (or the sun himself, Haris) say that they have imparted the colour haris to the parrots, to the pheasants (or peacocks.[1] Benfey and the Petropolitan Dictionary, however, explain *ropaṇâkâ* by drossel or thrush), and to the trees, which are therefore called hârayas. As the trees are green, so are the parrots generally green (sometimes also yellow and red, whence the appellation haris is always applicable to them).[2] The moon, on account of its colour, is now a tree (a green one), now an apple-tree with golden branches and apples, now a parrot (golden or green, and luminous). The moon in the night is the wise fairy who knows all, and can teach all. In the introduction to the *Mahâbhâratam*, the name Çukas or parrot is given to the son of Kṛishṇas, *i.e.*, of the black one, who reads (as moon) the *Mahâbhâratam* to the monsters. In the chapter on the Ass, we saw the ass and the monster of the *Râmâyaṇam* with parrots' faces. But inasmuch as the ass is a phallical symbol, the parrot is also ridden by the Hindoo god Kâmas, or the god of love (hence also called Çukavâhas). The moon (masculine in India) has already been mentioned, in the first chapter of the first book, as a symbol of the phallos; in the same way as the thunderbolt pierces the cloud, the moon pierces the gloom of the night, penetrates and reveals the secrets of the night. Therefore, the parrot

---

[1] The parrot is sung of by Statius in connection with the same birds in the second book of the *Sylvæ*—

> "Lux volucrum plagæ, regnator Eoæ
> Quam non gemmata volucri Junonia cauda
> Vinceret, aspectu gelidi non phasidis ales."

[2] A pathetic elegy in Sanskṛit distiches, of a Buddhist character, of which I do not now remember the source, presents us the çukas, or parrot, who wishes to die when the tree açokas, which has always been his refuge, is dried up.

being identified with the night in the *Çukasaptatî*, and in other books of Hindoo stories, we see the parrot often appearing in love-stories, and revealing amorous secrets.

Some of the stories concerning the parrot passed into the West; no doubt, by means of literary transmission, that is to say, of the mediæval Arabic and Latin versions of the Hindoo stories.[1]

Some of the Hindoo beliefs concerning the parrot had already passed into ancient Greece, and Ælianos shows himself to be very well acquainted with the sacred worship which the Brâhmans of India professed for it. Oppianos, moreover, tells us of a superstition which confirms what we have said concerning the essentially lunar character of the mythical parrot; he says that the parrot and the wolf pasture together, because the wolves love this green bird; this is the same as saying that the gloomy night loves the moon. One of the Hindoo epithets applied to the moon, moreover, is rağanîkaras, or he who makes the night.

[1] Such as, for instance, the following unpublished story, communicated to me by Dr Ferraro, which is related in the Monferrato, and of which I have also heard, in my childhood, a variation at Turin:—A king, going to the wars, and fearing that another king, who is his rival, will profit by his absence to seduce his wife, places by her side one of his friends transformed into a parrot; this friend warns her to remain faithful every time that the rival king sends to tempt the queen by means of a cunning old woman. The queen pays attention to the parrot's advice, and remains faithful till the husband's return. This is, in a few words, the contents of the seventy Hindoo tales of the parrot, of which the *Tuti-Name* is a Persian version.—In the story which I heard at Turin, the wife is, on the contrary, unfaithful and covers the parrot's cage that it may not see; she then fries some fishes in the guest's honour; the parrot thinks that it is raining. The fish and the rain remind us of the myth of the phallical and pluvial cuckoo.

CHAPTER XII.

THE PEACOCK.

SUMMARY.

The starry sky and the rayed sun.—The peacock becomes a crow; the crow becomes a peacock.—Peacock and swan; the dove and the peacock.—The kokilas and the peacock.—Indras now a peacock, now a cuckoo.—The peacock's feather.—Indras's horses have peacock's feathers and peacock's tails.—Skandas rides upon the peacock.—Argus becomes a peacock.—The peacock as the *avis Junonia*; Jove is the bird of Juno.

WE end our mythical journey in the kingdom of winged animals with the bird of all the colours.

The serene and starry sky and the shining sun are peacocks. The calm, azure heavens, bespangled with a thousand stars, a thousand brilliant eyes, and the sun rich with the colours of the rainbow, offer the appearance of a peacock in all the splendour of its eye-besprinkled feathers. When the sky or the thousand-rayed sun (sahasrânçus) is hidden in the clouds, or veiled by the autumnal waters, it again resembles the peacock, which, in the dark part of the year, like a great number of vividly-coloured birds, sheds its beautiful plumage, and becomes dark and unadorned; the crow which had put the peacock's feathers on then returns to caw amongst the funereal crows. In winter the peacock-crow has nothing remaining to it except its disagreeable and shrill cry, not dissimilar to that of the crows. It is commonly said of the peacock that it has an angel's feathers, a devil's voice, and a thief's walk. The crow-peacock is proverbial.[1]

The peacock hides itself when it becomes ugly; so does the sky, and so does the sun when the autumnal clouds cover it; but in the summer clouds the thunder rumbles, and thunder made upon the primeval races of men the impression of an irresistible, much-loved, and wished-for music, resembling the song of the melodious kokilas (the cuckoo), or of the watercock (the heron, the halcyon, the duck, or the swan).[2] In the *Râmâyaṇam*, as we observed in the chapter on the Cuckoo, the peacock and the kokilas appear as rivals in singing; although the watercock laughs at the peacock for its pretentiousness, this rivalry is no slender proof upon which to admit the mythical identity of two rival birds.[3]

---

[1] Cfr. the chapter on the Crow.

[2] "Wie wir den Hugschapler sogar auf den Pfauen schwören sehen, legten sie die Angelsachsen auf den Schwan ab (R. A. 900), den wir wohl nach den obigen Gesange Ngördhs, S. 343 als den ihm geheiligten Vogel (ales gratissima nautis, Myth. 1074) zu fassen haben, &c." Simrock, the work quoted before, p. 347.—A Hindoo proverb considers the dove in connection with the peacock; it says, "Better a pigeon to-day than a peacock to-morrow" (Varamadya kapoto na çvo mayûraḥ). According to the *Ornithologia* of Aldrovandi, the peacocks are the doves' friends, because they keep serpents and all venomous animals at a distance.

[3] The Russian fable of Kriloff presents to us the ass as a judge between the nightingale (the kokilas of Western poets) and the cock in a trial of singing; in Sanskṛit *çikhin*, or crested, means cock and peacock; besides mayûras, peacock, we have mayûraćaṭakas, the domestic cock. Mayûras is also the name of a Hindoo poet.—In the chapter on the Cuckoo we saw the cuckoo and the nightingale as rivals in singing; the kokilas and the peacock are the equivalents of the nightingale and the cuckoo; we have also identified the cuckoo with the swallow, and seen the swallows as rivals of the swans in singing; cfr. the chapter on the Crow.

The Hindoo myth, in fact, shows us the god Indras (now sky, now sun) as a peacock and as a cuckoo (like Zeus). When the sky is blue, serene, and starry, or when the sun shines with its thousand rays, and in the colours of the rainbow, the sahasrâkshas, or thousand-eyed Indras, is found as a peacock; when the sky or the sun in the cloud thunders and lightens, Indras becomes a kokilas that sings. In the twentieth of the stories of Santo Stefano di Calcinaia, two brothers steal a peacock's feather from their younger brother, and kill him (that is, they kill the peacock, in the same way as in the Russian story the red little boots are stolen from the little brother, and he is killed). Where the little brother of the peacock's feather is killed and buried, a sapling grows up; a stick is made out of the sapling, and out of the stick a pipe, which, when played upon, sings the dirge of the little brother who was killed for a peacock's feather. When the luminous sky or the sun is hidden in the clouds, when the luminous feathers of the peacock are torn off,[1] when the peacock is buried, the tree which is its tomb (the cloud) speaks, at the return of spring, like the cornel-tree of Polidorus in *Virgil*, and the trunk of Pier delle Vigne in Dante's *Inferno;* the tree becomes a cane, a magic flute, a melodious kokilas. Indras-kokilas remembers Indras-peacock, Indras whose horses, even in the Vedic hymns, have "peacocks' feathers,"[2] and "tail (or phallos) of peacocks."[3] We have already seen that the

[1] Hence Aldrovandi writes with reason, that the smoke of the burnt feathers of a peacock (that is, of the celestial peacock), when taken into the eyes, cures them of their redness.

[2] Â mandrâir indra haribhir yâhi mayûraromabhiḥ; *Ṛigv.* iii. 45, 1.

[3] Â tvâ rathe hiraṇyaye harî mayûraçepyâ; viii. 1, 25.—Klearchos relates in Athênaios, that a peacock in Leucas loved a maiden so much, that when she died it also immediately expired.

body of Indras was, after intercourse (as sun) with Ahalyâ in adultery, covered with a thousand wombs (waves or clouds; cfr. the equivoque *sahasradhâras*, given to the solar disc, properly because it has a thousand darts that wound), which were already a thousand eyes (stars or sunbeams), whence his names of Sahasradṛiç, Sahasranayanas, Sahasranetras, and Sahasrâkshas, which are equivalent. The long refulgent tail of the peacock took a phallical form. According to the Petropolitan Dictionary, mayûreçvaras (or Çivas-peacock), is the proper name of a liñgam or phallos, the well-known emblem of Çivas, which also calls our attention to Mayûrarathas, Mayûraketus, Cikhivâhanas, and Çikidhvaǵas, names of Skandas, the god of war, who is also a phallical god, like Mars, the lover of Venus, and like the Hindoo Kâmadevas, or god of love, who rides upon the parrot, and which therefore brings us back to the lunar phallical symbol.[1] The sky with the sun, as well as with the moon, is superseded by the sterile sky with the stars of the night or the clouds of autumn; the phallos falls; the impotent sky remains—Indras the eunuch, Indras with a thousand wombs, Indras plunged into the waves of the spotted clouds, Indras a ram, the pluvial or autumnal Indras, Indras lost in the sea of winter, Indras the fish, Indras without rays, without lightning, and

[1] According to the *Pańćatantram* (i. 175), in the very house of Çivas (the phallical god), the animals make war against each other; the serpent (the night) wishes to eat the mouse (which seems here to be the grey twilight); the peacock (here, perhaps, the moon), wishes to eat the serpent (cfr. the preceding notes; according to Ælianos, a certain man who wished to steal from the King of Egypt a peacock, supposed to be sacred, found an asp in its stead); the lion (the sun) wishes to eat the peacock. (The Hindoo name of mayûrâris, or enemy of the peacock, given to the chameleon, is remarkable; the animal which changes its colour is the rival of the bird which is of every colour; gods and demons are equally viçvarûpâs and kâmarûpas.)

without thunder, Indras cursed, he who had been beautiful and resplendent like a crested peacock (çikhin), Indras as the peacock enemy of the serpent (ahidvish, ahiripus), into which form he returns by the pity of the gods. According to the *Tuti-Name*, when a woman dreams of a peacock, it presages the birth of a handsome son.

The Greeks were also acquainted with the myth of the peacock, and amplified it. In the first book of Ovid's *Metamorphoses*, Argus, with the hundred eyes, who sees everything (Panoptês and son of Zeus), by the order of the goddess Juno, the splendid and proud wife of Jove, to whom the peacock is sacred (and therefore called *avis Junonia, ales Junonia;* the peacock of Juno is Jove himself, as we have already seen that Jove's cuckoo is himself; Argos the son of Zeus is Zeus himself), whilst two eyes rest (perhaps the sun and the moon), watches with the others (the stars) Io (the daughter of Argus himself, priestess of Juno, identified with Isis the moon, loved by Jove). Mercury, by means of music, puts Argus to sleep, and kills him as he slumbers. The eyes of the dead Argus pass into the tail of the peacock (that is, the dead peacock rises again). The peacock, which annually loses and renews its various colours and splendours, and is fruitful in progeny, served, like the phœnix, as a symbol of immortality, and a personification of the fact that the sky is obscured and becomes serene again, that the sun dies and is born again, that the moon rises, is obscured, goes down, is concealed, and rises once more. It is said of Pythagoras that he believed himself to have once been a peacock, that the peacock's soul passed into Euphorbos, that of Euphorbos into Homer, and that of Homer into him. It was also alleged that out of him the soul of the ancient peacock passed into the poet Ennius, whence Persius—

"Postquam destituit esse
Mæonides quintus pavone ex Pythagoræo."

If the peacock be Zeus, if Zeus be Dyâus, if Dyâus be the luminous and splendid sky, the divine light, which of my readers would disclaim the Pythagorean belief? The dream of being the sons of the divine light, and destined to return to the heavenly fatherland, certainly is much more consoling than the dreary conclusion of modern science, which reduces us, in our origin and final lapse, into unconscious vegetables upon the surface of the earth. The only drawback is, that this same heretical mythology, which often, even in its grossest forms, such as the animal ones, opens up to our incredulous reason a ray of hope in the immortality of the soul, that this mythology which resuscitates and transfigures into new living forms all its dead, does not permit us to believe in an eternity of joy in heaven; heaven, like earth, is in perpetual revolution, and the gods of Olympus are no more secure on their divine throne than our royal automata that sit upon their earthly ones. The metempsychosis does not end when the soul goes to heaven; on the contrary, it is in heaven that it is fated to undergo the strangest and most diverse transformations; from the heroic form we have seen it pass into that of a quadruped and a biped. Nor is its curse yet come to an end; the deity or the hero must humble himself yet more, and assume in the zoological scale the most imperfect of organisms; the animal god will lose his speech in the form of a stupid fish; he will creep like a serpent or hop grotesquely like a filthy toad.

Third Part.

THE ANIMALS OF THE WATER.

CHAPTER I.

FISHES, AND PARTICULARLY THE PIKE, THE SACRED FISH OR FISH OF ST PETER, THE CARP, THE MELWEL, THE HERRING, THE EEL, THE LITTLE GOLDFISH, THE SEA-URCHIN, THE LITTLE PERCH, THE BREAM, THE DOLPHIN, AND THE WHALE.

SUMMARY.

Why Indras, the fearless hero, flees after having defeated the serpent; the fish causes the death of the fearless hero.—Çakrâvatâras and the fisher.—The stone and the fish.—Adrikâ, Girikâ, the mother of fishes.—The matsyâs as a nation.—Çaradvat.—Pradyumnas.—Guhas.—The fishes laugh.—The fish guards the white haoma.—The water of the fish drunk by the cook.—The devil steals the fishes.—The dwarf Andvarri and the pike as the guardian of gold and of a ring.—The goldfish and the pike.—The dwarf Vishṇus as a little goldfish.—The legend of the Deluge.—Vishṇus as a horned fish draws the ship of Manus; the sea-urchin or hedge-hog of the Ganges, the little destroyer.—The dolphin with the horned bull draws the chariot or vessel of the Açvinâu.—The little turbulent perch.—The thorns of the sea-urchin compared to a hundred oars.—The whale as a bridge or island; the whale devours a fleet.—The pike.—The bream.—The phallical fishes; the phallos and the simpleton.—Why fishes are eaten in Lent, that is, spring; and on Friday, the day of Freya or Venus.—The *poisson d'avril.*—The herring.—The eel.—The bream cleans the workman.—The phallical and demoniacal eel; *anguilla* and *anguis.*—The eel and the cane; *ikshus* and *Iskshvâkus.*—Diabolical fishes.—The red mullet.—The bream and the ring.—Cimedia.—The whale vomits out the vessels; the whale as an island.—The little perch finds the ring and draws the casket by the help of the dolphins.—The war of the little perch with the other fishes.—The eel pout.—The perch.—The sturgeon.—The little perch is the fox of fishes.—The words *matsyas*, *matto*, *mad*, *matt*, *mattas*, *madidus*.—The drunken pike.—The three fishes.—Çakuntalâ, the pearl and the fish.—The genera *cyprinus* and *perca*; *lucius*, *lucioperca sandra*; the lunar horn.—The dolphin.—The carp.—The fish *Zeus Chalkeus*, the fish *faber*, the fish of St Peter; the fish of St Christopher; the equivoque of *crista* and *christus* again in conjunction with the legend of St Christopher.

THE god Indras, in the *Ṛigvedas*, after having killed the monster, flees in terror across the ninety-nine navigable rivers; the pluvial god, after having lightened, thunder-stricken and thundered, is terrified by his own work; the Vedic poet asks him what he has seen, but the god passes on and answers not; killing the monster, he has unchained the waters; the pluvial god has wounded himself while wounding his enemy; the monster's shadow or his own shadow pursues him; the waters increase and threaten to drown him. The god Indras fears the very waters he has caused to flow. The god Indras was condemned to remain hidden in the waters (of night and winter) during the period of his malediction, for defiling in adultery the nuptial bed of Ahalyâ. The god shut up in the waters, the wet god, is his most infamous and accursed form.[1] The celestial metamor-

[1] Indras, as a warlike god, does not know fear, or rather, he kills fear (the hymn says, "Aher yâtâram kam apaçya indra hṛidi yat te ǵaghnuso bhîr agaććhat; *Ṛigv.* i. 32, 14), and lets himself be terrified by a trifle, which may be either a nightly shadow (the dark man of fairy tales), or the terror caused to him by some fish (the moon) which leaps upon him in the waters which he himself has set free.—In the twenty-second of the Tuscan stories published by me, the young hero who passed through all the dangers of hell without being afraid, dies at the sight of his own shadow. (We have also referred to this when treating of the dog and the lion who meet with their death, allured by their own

phosis into a fish is perhaps the vilest transmutations of animal, and therefore the most feared; the fish lives especially in order to reproduce itself; to represent, therefore, the decadence of the god after a phallical crime of his, he is condemned to lie down in the waters. We know that the fisher, in the *Çakuntalâ*, lives at Çakrâvatâras (that is, the fall of Indras). We have seen the sister of Latona, and Rambhâ and Ahalyâ, after having transgressed, the one with Jupiter and the others with Indras, become stones in the waters. The fish, rendered powerless and stupid, becomes inert and motionless like a stone (sun and moon pass into sky or cloud). We already find the image of the stone with the honey brought, in the *Ṛigvedas*,[2] into close affinity to that of the fish which lies in shallow water, or of the fish made powerless and deprived of its vital qualities.

The legend of the nymph Adrikâ (from the word *adris*, which means a stone, a rock, a mountain, or a cloud) presents the same analogy between the stone-cloud, that is, the stone in the waters, and the fish. By a divine malediction, Adrikâ is transformed into a fish, and lives in the Yamunâ. Being in these waters, she picks up a leaf upon which had fallen the sperm of King Uparićaras, enamoured of Girikâ (or of Adrikâ herself, the two words *adrikâ* and *girikâ* being equivalent); this

shadow.)—In the forty-sixth story of the fifth book of *Afanassieff*, the merchant's son, who did not know fear, who feared neither darkness nor brigands nor death, is terrified and dies when he falls into the water, because the little perch entered into his bosom whilst he was sleeping in his fishing-boat.—It is also easy to pass from the idea of Indras, who inebriates himself in the *soma* to that of the fish, when we consider that the Hindoo word *matsyas*, the fish, properly means the inebriated, from the root *mad*, to inebriate and to make cheerful.

[2] Açnâpinaddham madhu pary apaçyam matsyaṁ na dîna udani kshiyantam; *Ṛigv.* x. 68, 8.

leaf had been let fall into the waves of the Yamunâ by the bird çyenas, that is, by the hawk. Having fed upon this sperm, the nymph fish is caught by fishermen, and taken to King Uparićaras; the fish is opened, and the nymph resumes her heavenly form; of her a son and a daughter are born, Matsyas the male fish, and Matsyâ the female one.[1] The male afterwards becomes king of the matsyâs or fishes, which some authorities have, in vain, as I think, endeavoured to identify with a historical nation; for it is not enough to find them named as a people in the *Mahâbhâratam*, to prove their real historical existence, when we know that the whole basis of the *Mahâbhâratam* is mythological. Moreover, when we find the Matsyâs in the Vedic hymns, it is one more argument from which to infer the mythical nature of the peoples named in the *Ṛigvedas* in connection with the waters. In another legend of the *Mahâbhâratam*, the semen of the penitent Çaradvat (properly the autumnal or the pluvial one), provoked by the sight of a beautiful nymph, falls upon the wood of an arrow; the wood of the arrow splits in two, and two sons are born of it, who are given to the king; a variety of this legend will be found further on in the Western traditions connected with the story of the fish.[2]

To the ninety-nine or hundred cities of Çambaras (the clouds) destroyed by Indras, correspond the ninety-nine rivers which Indras crosses. In the *Vishṇu P.*,[3] a fish receives the hero Pradyumnas (an appellation of the god

---

[1] *Mbh.* 2371–2392.

[2] *Mbh.* i. 5078–5086.—In another variety of the same myth, the semen of the wise Bharadvâǵas comes out at the sight of a nymph; the sage receives it in a cup, out of which comes Droṇas, the armourer and archer *par excellence*; i. 5103–5106.

[3] v. 27.

of love), thrown into the sea by Çambaras, and enables him to recover and wed Mâyâdevî.

King Guhas (the hidden one ? the dark one ?) the king of the black Nishâdâs, the king of Çriñgaveras (in which we have already recognised the moon), who, during the night, receives Râmas on the banks of the Ganges, hospitably entertains him, offering him beverages, meat, and fishes.[1]

In the *Çukasaptatî*, and in the *Tuti-Name*, the fishes laugh at the prudery of an adulterous servant-girl; we have already shown, in the first chapter of the first book, the phallical signification of the fish that laughs.

In the *Khorda Avesta*, we find a fish with acute eyesight (Karo-maçyo, the posterior Khar-mâhî), which guards the white haoma, that is, the ambrosia (with which sperm was also identified).

In the *Pseudo-Callisthenes*, Alexander, having arrived at the luminous fountain which scatters perfumes, asks his cook for something to eat; the cook prepares to wash the fish in the refulgent water; the fish returns to life, and disappears from his sight; but the cook drinks some of the water of the fish, and gives some to Alexander's daughter Une, who becomes, by the curse of Alexander himself, a nereïd or marine nymph, whilst he fastens a stone to the cook's neck, and orders him to be thrown to the bottom of the sea. It is unnecessary for me to demonstrate the analogy between this legend and the myth of Indras, or to insist upon the phallical meaning of the myth.

We already know that phallical images and demoniacal ones sometimes correspond; hence, in the ninth Esthonian story, the devil steals the fishes from the fishermen; hence, in the *Eddas*, the brigand Loki now assumes the

[1] *Râmây.* ii. 92.

form of a salmon, and now catches the pike, into which the dwarf Andvarri has transformed himself. The pike is the guardian of gold and of a ring which is taken from him; the fish enters into the stone, and predicts that gold will be the cause of the death of the two brothers. The ambrosial rain which comes out of the cloud, and the ambrosial dew, are the water in which the fish is washed, and the ambrosial dew is the water or seed of the fish; the fair-haired and silvery moon in the ocean of night is the little gold fish, and the little silver fish which announces the rainy season, the autumn, the deluge. Out of the cloudy, nocturnal, or wintry ocean, comes forth the sun, the pearl lost in the sea, which the gold or silver fish brings out.

The little goldfish of our aquariums, the *cyprinus chrysoparius*, the *cyprinus auratus*, the *cyprinus sophore* (the Hindoo *çapharas*, in the feminine *çapharî*), and the luminous pike, like the moon, can expand and contract. We are already acquainted with the sea-monster which, in the *Râmâyaṇam* (like the siren fish), allures from the sea the shadow of Hanumant, and can make itself now small, now large; we have seen the dwarf Andvarri of the *Eddas*, who hides himself in the form of a pike; we are familiar with the god Vishṇus or Haris, who, from being a dwarf, becomes a giant (Haris means fair-haired or golden, and refers now to the sun, now to the moon); Vishṇus, in his incarnation as a fish, first takes the form of the little golden fish, the çapharî; and, in this form, the god Vishṇus is especially identified with the moon, the ruler of the rainy season. As the moon (which we have already seen as a little learned puppet) grows by quarters, and from being exceedingly small, becomes large, so, in the Hindoo legend of the Deluge, narrated in the Vedic commentaries, in the *Mahâbhâratam*, and in the Pâuranic legends, the god Vishṇus or Haris begins by being an exceedingly small fish, a çapharî, which beseeches the penitent Manus to be taken out of the great river, the Ganges, where it is afraid of being devoured by the aquatic monsters. Manus receives the little fish in the vase of water in which he performs his ablutions (a Hindoo proverb says that the çapharî is agitated from petulance in water an inch deep, whilst the rohitas, a kind of carp, does not become proud even in bottomless depths[1]); in one night (evidently in its character as the moon) the fish grows so much that it can no longer remain in the vase; Manus carries it into a pool, afterwards into the Ganges; finally, the fish increases so much in size that Manus, recognising Vishṇus in it, is obliged to give it entire liberty in the sea. Then the grateful fish announces that in seven days the waters will inundate the world, and all the wicked will perish; he orders him (as the biblical God does Noah) to build a ship: "Thou shalt enter into it," says Vishṇus to him, "with seven sages, a couple of every kind of animal, and the seeds of every plant. Thou shalt wait in it the end of the night of Brahman; and when the vessel is agitated by the waves, thou shalt attach it by a long serpent to the horn of an enormous fish, which will come near thee, and will guide thee over the waves of the abyss." On the appointed day, the waters of the sea came up over the surface of the earth; the fish made its appearance to draw the ship in order to save Manus. The ship stopped upon the horn, that is, upon the peak of a mountain. Now this little goldfish, in which Vishṇus is incarnate, when it becomes horned to draw the ship of Manus, assimilates itself to another interesting

[1] Cfr. Böhtlingk, *Indische Sprüche*, i. 59.

sea animal, the sea-urchin or hedgehog of the Ganges, (çiṅçumâras, which is also one of the names of the dwarf Vishṇus (we have already seen Vishṇus as a wild-boar), and which means properly the little destroyer. The eighteenth strophe of the precious 116th hymn of the first book of the *Ṛigvedas*, shows us the çiṅçumâras or sea-urchin, which, together with another horned animal, the bull (we have already seen the moon as a horned bull) draws the chariot of the Açvinâu, full of riches;[1] we know that the chariot of the Açvinâu is often a vessel. Çiṅçumâras also means in Sanskṛit the dolphin;[2] and the dolphins and the fish called jorsh (the little perch), with its little horns, thorns, and thin shape, sharpened at one end like a pole ending in a point, called in Russian stories the turbulent one (kropaćishko), are in relation with each other, as they draw the casket away; the jorsh takes the place of the "little destroyer," of the çiṅçumâras, of the sea-urchin, concerning which there is a very interesting Sicilian verse, which compares the stings of the sea-urchin to a hundred oars, with which it must row, carrying its little invokers; after having caught it, Sicilian children scatter a little salt over it, and sing—

"Vócami, vócami, centu rimi,
Vócami, vócami, centu rimi."

---

[1] Revad uvâha saćano ratho vâṁ vṛishabhaç ça çiṅçumâraç ća yuktâ.

[2] Our readers will not be astonished at seeing the dolphin, the whale, and the sea-urchin classed here with fishes. We are not treating of natural history according to the classifications of science, but of the gross classifications made by impressionable popular imaginations. Thus, amongst the animals of the water we shall find the serpent described, although it be amphibious, because popular belief makes the dragon watch over the waters.

(Row for me, row for me, hundred oars). Then it moves, and the children are delighted. In the Russian little poem, *Kaniok Garbunok*, of Jershoff, already mentioned by us in the chapter on the Horse, Ivan must seek, for the sultan, a ring shut up in a casket which has fallen into the sea (the evening or the autumnal sun). Ivan upon his crook-backed horse arrives in the middle of the sea, where there is a whale which cannot move because it has swallowed a fleet, that is to say, the solar vessel. The part played here by the whale is the same as that of the sea-monster who swallows Hanumant in the *Râmâyaṇam*, to vomit him out again, as in the case of the biblical Jonah (the night devours the sun, or carries it into its body). Hanumant enters into the fish by its mouth, and comes out at its tail; however, in the narrative given of it in the fifty-sixth canto of the fifth book by Hanumant himself, he says that the sea-monster having shut its mouth, he came out of it by the right ear. When the night is with the moon, instead of swallowing the hero, the bull-moon or fish-moon carries him or serves as a bridge for him. In Russian fairy tales the brown pike (which, on account of its colour, is called the chaste widow) [1] is now a form assumed by the

[1] The pike becomes in spring of an azure or bluish or greenish-blue colour; hence the name of *golubbi—però* (that is, of the azure or bluish fins; in German, the bluish colour is called *echt-grau*—that is, grey of pike; in the nineteenth of the Russian stories of *Erlenwein*, golden fins are ascribed to the pike), which is also given to it in Russia. *Golub*, or brown, violet and azure, is a name given in Russia to the dove; so in Italy we say, that the dove is *pavonazzo* (properly the colour of the peacock, which is generally blue and green). But in Sanskṛit, amongst the names of the peacock there is that of *haris*, a word which represents both the moon and the sun. By the same analogy, the bluish or greenish pike may represent the moon. But another analogy, caused by a similar conception, is found again in the

devil in order to eat the young hero, who has become a little perch,[1] and now an enormous fish with great teeth, which slaughters the little fishes.[2] Now, instead, it serves as a bridge for Ivan Tzarević, who is seeking for the egg of the duck which is inside the hare under the oak-tree in the midst of the sea;[3] now it is caught in the fountain (as the moon, soma, in the well) by the foolish and lazy Emilius, and because Emilius saves its life, it makes him rich by performing several miracles for him, such as that of the barrels full of water, of the trees of the forest, of the waggons or the stoves which move off by themselves, and finally that of the cask thrown into the sea, into which Emilius is shut with the beautiful daughter of the Tzar, and which comes to shore and breaks open.[4] Now the phallical pike with the golden

word *çyâmas*, which means black, azure, and also silvery; whence it serves to represent the *convolvolus argenteus* (we must remember that the Latin name of the pike is *lucius;* the Greek, *lükios*—that is, the luminous one). The pike takes the colour of the water in which it lives, and the waters are dark, black, azure, greenish, silvery; as being azure, or greenish, or silvery, the pike represents the moon; as being dark, the tenebrific night, the cloud, the wintry season.—In the thirty-second story of the fourth book of *Afanassieff*, the little perch relates that the pike was once luminous (that is, in spring), and that it became black after the conflagration which took place in the Lake of Rastoff from the day of St Peter (June 29) to the day of St Elias (July 20), or in the beginning of summer. As we learn in the *Pseudo-Callisthenes*, near the black stone, which makes black whoever touches it, there are fishes which are cooked in cold water, and not at the fire, I recollect here also that the *Hecht-könig*, or king of pikes, is described as yellow and black-spotted.

[1] *Afanassieff*, v. 22.

[2] *Afanassieff*, i. 2.—Cfr. the eleventh of the *Novelline di Santo Stefano di Calcinaia;* a monstrous fish devours the princess; the fish is said to be a shark (pesce cane); and v. 8 of the *Pentamerone.*

[3] Cfr. *Afanassieff*, ii. 24.

[4] Cfr. *Afanassieff*, v. 55, vi. 32.—It is the same fish which, saved by the girl who is persecuted by her step-mother, comes to her assistance,

fins[1] is caught, washed, quartered, and roasted; the dirty water is thrown away and drunk by the cow (in *Afanassieff*) or by the mare (in *Erlenwein*); a portion of the fish is eaten by the black slave, whilst she is carrying it to table, the rest by the queen; hence three young heroes, considered as brothers, are born at the same time to the cow (or mare), to the black maiden, and to the queen. Now the pike (as in the satirical fable of Kriloff) draws the car in company with the crab and the heron; and here, it would appear, these two animals are rather stupid than intelligent, inasmuch as, whilst the pike draws the car into the water, the crab draws it back on the earth and the heron essays to mount with it into the air. Here we have the usual correspondence between the phallical figure and that of the simpleton. Thus, in the Piedmontese dialect, the phallos and the stupid man is called *merlu* (blackbird). From the word *merlo* (Lat. *merula*) was derived the name of the fish called *merluccio* or *merluzzo* (*gadus merlucius*, the melwel or haddock), called *asellus* by the Latins and *onos* by the Greeks. The ass is a well-known phallical symbol, and Bacchus being also a phallical

separates the wheat from the barley for her (like the Madonna, the purifying moon-fairy, the nightly cleanser of the sky), and gives splendid robes to her, in vi. 29.—In the story v. 54, instead of the pike as a fœcundator we find the bream, which is also called "of the golden fins" (szlatopioravo), of which the colours are the same as those of the pike.

[1] In the nineteenth Russian story of *Erlenwein*, and in a variety of the same in the last book of Afanassieff's stories.—In an unpublished story of the Monferrato, communicated to me by Dr Ferraro, a fisherman catches a large fish which says to him, "Let me go, and you will always be fortunate." The wife of the fisherman opposes this, roasts and eats the fish, from whose bones are born to the fisherman three sons, three horses, and three dogs. Evidently the story has been corrupted.

god, we read in Pliny, "Asellorum duo genera, Callariæ minores, et Bacchi, qui non nisi in alto (in the deep) capiuntur." The Italian name *baccalà*, given to the cod-fish, seems to me to be derived from the union of the two names Bacchus and Callaria. In the Piedmontese dialect, a stupid man is also called by the name of *baccalà*. There is also a fish called *merula*, of which the ancients describe the extraordinary salacity, by indulging which it literally consumes itself away and perishes.[1] In Italy we find the following phallical proverbs: "The blackbird has passed the Po," and "The blackbird has passed the river;" to denote a woman or a man exhausted, to impotence. The ancients wrote of the fish called *chrüsofrüs* by the Greeks, and *aurata* by the Latins, that it would let itself be taken in children's and women's hands, and (according to Athenaios) it was sacred to Aphroditê. Aphroditê, Venus, goddess of love, especially, represented in myths the aurora and the spring (hence in Lent and on Friday, the day of Freya, *dies Veneris*, we eat fishes); therefore the *gemini pisces*, the two fishes joined in one, were sacred to her, and the joke of the *poisson d'Avril*, as I have already mentioned in the first chapter of the first book, is a jest of phallical origin, which should be abandoned.[2] Aphroditê and Eros, pursued by Typhon, transformed themselves into fishes and plunged into the Euphrates. The Hellenic Eros was also represented riding (instead of the phallical butterfly) on a dolphin; according to other accounts, he rides upon a swan with dolphins before him. In an epigram of the *Anthologia Græca*, the dolphin, moreover,

---

[1] Cfr. Salvianus, *Aquatilium Animalium Historiæ*, Romæ, 1554.

[2] At Berlin, children sing on the first of April—

> "April! April! April!
> Man kann den Narren schicken wohin man will."

carries a weary nightingale. In several parts of Alsace, on the evening of St Andrew's Day, girls eat herrings to dream during the night of the husband who is to quench their thirst.[1] The fish *julis* of Pliny, or Julia, is called *donzella* (damsel) in Italian, and *menchia di re* (king's phallos) at Naples and in Venetia, and other fishes also take their name from the organs of generation.[2] The phallos is called *u pesce* at Naples, and, in Italian, *nuovo pesce* (a new fish) signifies a stupid man. An essentially phallical character, moreover, is possessed by the eel, which, according to Agatharchides, quoted by Hippolitus Salvianus, the Bœotians crowned as a victim and sacrificed solemnly to the gods, which, according to Herodotos, the Egyptians venerated as a divine fish, and which Athenaios pompously calls the Helen of dinners. The eel became proverbial; the Italian proverbial expressions, "To take the eel," "To hold the eel by its tail," "When the eel has taken the hook it must go where it is drawn," are all equivocal. The Germans also have a proverb concerning the eel, which reminds us of the story of the cook who steals the fish from Alexander, and, together with Alexander's daughter, drinks its water.[3] The phallos

[1] Another custom concerning herrings is described by Baron von Reinsberg, relating to Ash-Wednesday, when people return from church in Limburg: "Begiebt man sich zuerst nach Hause, um nach gewohnter Weise den Häring abzubeissen. Sobald man nämlich aus der Kirche kommt, wird ein Häring, nun muss jeder mit geschlossenen Beinen, die Arme fest an den Leib gedrückt, in die Höhe springen und dabei suchen, ein Stück abzubeissen." And Karl Simrock, the work quoted before, p. 561, writes: "In der Mark muss man zu Neujahr Hirse oder Häringe essen, im Wittenbergischen Heringssalat, so hat man das ganze Jahr über Geld."

[2] Cfr. Salvianus, *ut supra.* The habit certain fishes have of ejecting froth from the mouth may have suggested a phallical image.

[3] Bei Hans Sachs, Nürnberger, Ausgabe von 1560, ii. 14, 96, Eine Frau und Magd essen den für den Herrn bestimmten Aal; eine Elster

discovers secrets, and therefore, in a German legend,[1] the faculty of seeing everything which is under the water is ascribed to a woman who had eaten an eel (a variety of the story of the fish that laughs, which, in the ninth story of the third book of *Afanassieff*, enriches whoever possesses it, and the fish *silurus* (the bream), so called from the Greek words *sillô* and *oura*, because it shakes its tail, which, in the fifty-eighth story of the sixth book of *Afanassieff*, cleans the workman who had fallen into the mud, and makes the princess laugh who had never laughed before). In the eighteenth story of Santo Stefano di Calcinaia, a fisherman catches an eel with two tails and two heads, which is so large that he has to be assisted in carrying it. The eel speaks, and commands that its two tails be planted in the garden, that its intestines be given to the bitch, and its two heads to the fisherman's wife. Two swords are born of the tails in the garden (in the Hindoo legend we saw two sons born of the wood of Çaradvat's arrow), two dogs are born of the intestines to the bitch, and two beautiful young men of the heads to the wife (the two Açvinâu, drawn, as we have seen in the Vedic hymn, by the sea-urchin). In the chapter on the Dove, we saw the two young lovers, when pursued, take the form of doves. In the fourteenth Sicilian story of Signora Gonzenbach, the young man and the maiden pursued by the witch transform themselves first into church and sacristan, then into garden and gardener, then into rose

schwatzt es aus; um sich zu rächen, rupfen die Weiber ihr den Kopf kahl. Daher man sprichwörtlich von einem kahlen Mönche sagt: der hat gewiss vom Aale ausgeschwatzt; Menzel, *Die Vorchristliche Unsterblichkeits-Lehre.*

[1] In the same: "So erzählt Gilbert bei Leibnitz Script. rer. Brunsw. i. 987. Ein Frauenzimmer, welches Aal gegessen, habe plötzlich Alles sehen können was unter Wasser war."

and rosebush, and finally into fountain and eel. In the first volume of the *Cabinet des Fées*, the fairy Aiguillette is taken in the form of an eel. In the fourth of the stories of Santo Stefano di Calcinaia, the beautiful maiden is asked by the servant-maid of the priest (that is, by the servant-maid of the black man, by the black woman or the night), who went to wash clothes at the fountain, to come down from the tree. The maiden descends, is thrown into the fountain and devoured by an enormous eel. The fishermen catch the eel and take it to the prince; the witch has it killed and thrown into a canebrake. The eel is then transformed into a large and beautiful cane, which is also carried to the prince, who, cutting it gently with a penknife, makes his beautiful girl come out (this legend is a variety of that of the wooden girl).[1] This form of a diabolical eel has a close relationship with the monster-serpent; the *anguilla* reminds one of the *anguis;* hence, in the ninth story of the first book of the *Pentamerone*, instead of the eel as a fœcundator, as in the eighteenth Tuscan story, we find the fish called *draco marinus* (in Italian, *trascina*), of which it is curious to read, what Volaterranus writes, that—"Si manu dextra adripias eum contumacem renitentemque experieris, si læva subsequentem,"—as if he meant to imply that the left hand is the hand of the devil. Thus Oppianos describes the wedding of the muraina eel (the *murana*) with the serpent (the viper according to Ælianos and Pliny). Other fishes have assumed an essentially diabolical character, such as the

[1] It is well known that the word *ikshvâkus* has been referred to the word *ikshus*, the sugar-cane. In the fortieth canto of the first book of the *Râmâyaṇam*, one of the two wives of Sagaras gives birth to a son who continues his race; the other wife gives birth to an ikshvâkus (gourd or cane) containing 60,000 sons.

fish called *alôpêx* (Lat. *vulpes, vulpecula*), of which Ælianos relates that it swallows the hook and then vomits it out with its own intestines; the *rana piscatrix*, also called the marine devil; the *trügôn* (Lat. *pastinaca*, It. *bruco*), which, according to Oppianos, kills men with its dart (fame reports that Ulysses was killed with the bone of a *trügôn*) and dries up trees (although it is strange that to cure one's self from such a fatal wound, as it was supposed by the ancients to be venomous, Dioscoris only recommends a decoction of sage). The sea-scorpion (whose wounds, according to the ancients, were cured by means of the *trigla*, the red mullet—Lat. *mullus*—sacred according to Athenaios and Apollodorus to Artemis, or to Diana Trivia, the moon; Plutarch writes that it was sacred to Diana as a hunting fish, because it kills the marine hare, noxious to man; but we have seen that the mythical hare is the moon itself), the bream, or *silurus, glanis*, or *piscis barbatus*, which, in Hungary, according to Mannhardt (Manardus, quoted in the sixteenth century by Ippolito Salviano), had the reputation of attacking men, so much so, that it is said that one of these fishes, which are, in fact, very voracious, was once found with a man's hand, covered with rings, in its intestines. But these rings in the fish's body (like the gem called cimedia,[1] which, according to the popular belief, is found in the brain of a great number of fishes) recall us to the interrupted poem of Jershoff, to the little perch, the dolphins, the whale, and the ring fallen into the water and found again by the fish, which is perhaps the most interesting subject of legends in the mythical cycle of the fishes, and, if I may say so, their epic exploit.

[1] Cfr, Du Cange, *s. v.*, and Salvianus, the work quoted before.

Ivan, therefore, has come with his hump-backed little horse into the midst of the sea near the whale which has swallowed a fleet;[1] upon the whale a forest has grown; women go to seek for mushrooms in its moustaches. Ivan communicates his wish, and the whale calls all the fishes together, but no one can give information except one little fish, the little jorsh, or little perch, which, however, is at the time engaged in chasing one of its adversaries. The whale sends ambassadors to the jorsh, which unwillingly desists for an instant from the fight, in order to search for the casket; it finds it, but is not strong enough to lift it up. The numerous army of the herrings come and try, but in vain; at last two dolphins come and raise the casket. Ivan receives the wished-for ring; the whale's malediction comes to an end; it vomits the fleet forth again, and is once more able to move about, whilst the little perch returns to pursue its enemies. This war of the little perch with its adversaries has had in popular Russian tradition its Herodotuses and its Homers, who

[1] In the thirteenth story of the first book of *Afanassieff* (of which the Bohemian story of *Grandfather Vsievedas* is a well-known variety), the whale complains that all the footmen and horsemen pass over it and consume it to the bones. It begs the hero Basilius to ask the serpent how long it has still to undergo this fate; the serpent answers, when it has vomited forth the ten vessels of the rich Mark.—In the eighth story of the fourth book of the *Pentamerone*, the whale teaches Cianna the way to find the mother of time, requiring her, in recompense, to be informed of the way in which the whale may be able to swim freely to and fro in the sea without encountering rocks and sandbanks. Cianna brings back for answer, that it must make friends with the sea-mouse (*lo sorece marino*, perhaps the same as the sea-urchin), which will serve as its guide.—In the eighth story of the fifth book of the *Pentamerone*, the little girl is received in the sea by a large enchanted fish, in whose belly she finds beautiful companions, gardens, and a beautiful palace furnished with everything. The fish carries the girl to the shore.

have celebrated its praises both in prose and verse. Afanassieff gives in the third book of his stories, from a manuscript of the last century, the description of the judgment of the little perch (jorsh) before the tribunal of the fishes. The bream (leçć) accuses the little jorsh, the wicked warrior (as the sea-urchin is the little destroyer; the confounding of the sea-urchin with the little perch is all the easier in Russian legends, inasmuch as the former is called josz, and the latter jorsh), who has wounded all the other fishes with its rough bristles, and compelled them to forsake the Lake of Rastoff. The jorsh defends itself by saying that it is strong in virtue of its inherent vigour; that it is not a brigand, but a good subject, who is known everywhere, highly prized and cooked by great lords, who eat it with satisfaction. The bream appeals to the testimony of other fishes, who give witness against the little perch, who thereupon complains that the other fishes, in their overweening importance, wish, by means of the tribunals, to ruin him and his companions, taking advantage of their smallness. The judges call the perch, the eel-pout, and the herring to give witness. The perch sends the eel-pout, and the eel-pout excuses itself for not appearing, pleading that its belly is fat, and it cannot move; that its eyes are small, and its vision imperfect; that its lips are thick, and it does not know how to speak before persons of distinction. The herring gives witness in favour of the bream, and against the little perch. Among the witnesses against the jorsh, the sturgeon also appears; it maligns the jorsh, alleging that when he attempts to eat it he must spit more out than he can swallow, and complains that when it was one day going by the Volga to Lake Rastoff, the little perch called him his brother and deceived him, saying, in order to induce him to retire from the lake, that he had once also been a fish of such size that his tail resembled the sail of a ship, and that he had become so small after having entered Lake Rastoff. The sturgeon goes on to say that he was afraid, but remained in the river, where his sons and companions died of hunger, and he himself was reduced to the last extremities. He adduces, moreover, another grave accusation against the jorsh, who had made him go in front, in order that he might fall into the fishermen's hands, cunningly hinting that the elder brothers should go before the younger ones. The sturgeon confesses that he gave way to this graceful flattery, and entered into a weir made to catch fish, which he found to be similar to the gates of great lords' houses—large when one goes in, and small when one goes out; he fell into the net, in which the jorsh saw him, and cried out, deriding him, "Suffer for the love of Christ." The deposition of the sturgeon makes a great impression upon the minds of the judges, who give orders to inflict the knout upon the little jorsh, to impale it in the great heat, as a punishment for its cheating; the sentence is sealed by the crayfish with one of his claws. But the jorsh, who has heard the sentence, declares it to be unjust, spits in the eyes of the judges, jumps into the briar brake, and disappears from the sight of the fishes, who remain lost in shame and mortification.

In the thirty-second story of the fourth book of *Afanassieff*, we find two varieties of this zoological legend.

The turbulent jorsh enters into Lake Rastoff, and possesses himself of it. Called to judgment by the bream, it answers that from the day of St Peter to that of St Elias, the whole lake was on fire; and cites in proof of this assertion that the roach's eyes are still red from its effects, that the perch's fins are also still red, that the pike became dark coloured, and that the eel-pout is black in consequence. These fishes, called to give witness, either do not appear, or else deny the truth of these assertions. The jorsh is arrested and bound, but it begins to rain, and the place of judgment becomes muddy; the jorsh escapes, and, from one rivulet to another, arrives at the river Kama, where the pike and the sturgeon find him, and take him back to be executed.

The jorsh, arrested and brought to judgment, demands permission to take a walk for only one hour in Lake Rastoff; but after the expiration of the appointed time, it neglects to come out of the lake, and annoys the other fishes in every way, stinging and provoking them. The fishes have recourse for justice to the sturgeon, who sends the pike to look for the jorsh; the little perch is found amongst the stones; it excuses itself by saying that it is Saturday, and that there is a festival in his father's house, and advises him to take a constitutional in the meanwhile, and enjoy himself; on the morrow, although it be Sunday, he promises to present himself before the judges (the analogy between the actions of the jorsh and those of Reincke Fuchs is very remarkable). Meanwhile, the jorsh makes his companion drunk. The Sanskṛit name of the fish, *matsyas*, from the root *mad*, we know to mean drunk and joyous, properly damp (Lat., *madidus*); in Italian, *briaco* and *folle* are sometimes equivalent; in the Piedmontese dialect, *bagnà* (wet) and *imbecil* (idiot) are expressions of the same meaning. Drunkenness is of two forms: there is a drunkenness which makes impotent and stupid; it is a question of quantity and of quality of beverages, as well as constitution. Thus, there are two kinds of madness; that which makes a man infuriated, to cope with whom the strait-waistcoat is necessary, and that which ends by exhausting all a man's strength in prostration and debility. Indras, when drunk, becomes a hero; the pike when drunk is a fool (cfr. the Italian *matto*, English *mad*, which means insane, crazy, with the German *matt*, which means cast down, exhausted[1]). When the jorsh has made the pike drunk, it shuts it in a rick of straw, where the inebriated fish is to die. Then the bream comes to take the little perch from among the stones, and to bring him before the judge. The jorsh demands a judgment of God. He tells his judges to put him in a net; if he stays in the net, he is wrong; if he comes out, he is right; the jorsh jerks about in the net so much that he gets out. The judge acquits him, and gives him entire liberty in the lake; then the jorsh begins his numerous revenges upon the little fishes, proving his astuteness in continual efforts to ruin them.

As the drunkard and the fool now intensify their strength and now lose it, so they now double and now lose their intelligence. Hence, among mythical fishes we find very wise ones and very stupid ones. The story is very popular of the three fishes of different intelligence, of which the lazy and improvident one allows himself to be caught by the fishermen, whilst his two companions escape; it is found in the first book of the *Pańćatantram.* In the fifth book of the *Pańćatantram*, a variety occurs: we read of a fish which has the intelligence of a hundred (Çatabuddhis), of one which has the intelligence of a thousand (Sahasrabuddhis), and of the frog which has the intelligence of one (Ekabuddhis); but that of the two fishes is not intelligence, but pre-

[1] If I am not mistaken, the German words *Narr*, fool, and *nass*, wet, are in connection with each other by the same analogy which gives us the Sanskṛit *mattas*, drunk, and the Latin *madidus*, damp, from the root *mad.*

sumption; the one intelligence of the frog is better than the hundred and the thousand of the fishes. The frog escapes, but the two fishes fall into the hands of the fishermen.

The little sea-urchin (and the dwarf Vishṇus and the dolphin are equivalent to it, the word *çiñçumâras* being equivocal in Sanskṛit) in the *Ṛigvedas* draws the chariot of riches; in the *Eddas*, a dwarf in the form of a pike (in Greek *lükios*, in Latin *lucius*) watches over gold, and guards the ring; in Russian legends, the little jorsh (formidable, like the josz, by its sharp quills), united with the dolphins, draws out of the sea the casket containing the sultan's ring. The horn of the moon, which appears in the sea of night, belongs now to the bull which carries the fugitive hero, now to the fish çapharî, which, having become large, takes in tow the ship of Manus, and saves it from the waters, that it may not be wrecked. Now it is the solar hero or heroine that takes the form of a fish to save himself or herself; now the fish helps the solar hero or heroine in their escape; now the little golden or luminous fish plunges into the sea, or into the river, to seek the pearl or ring for the hero or heroine who had let it fall, the ring without which King Dushyantas cannot recognise his bride Çakuntalâ; now it vomits out from its mouth or its tail that which it has swallowed—the hero, the pearl, the ring (the solar disc).

In the sixth act of *Çakuntalâ*, the fisherman finds in the stomach of a fish (the *cyprinus dentatus*), the pearl enchased in the ring which King Dushyantas had given to Çakuntalâ, in order to be able to recognise her when they should come together again. The genera *cyprinus* and *perca*, as the thorny or wounding ones in the order of fishes, have supplied the greatest number of heroes to mythology; the sea-urchin is identified to them on account of its darts; the names *hecht, brochet, pike,* given to the *lucius* in Germany, France, and England, express its faculty of stinging, or cleaving with its flat and cutting mouth (the fish *lucioperca sandra* is an intermediate form between the perch and the pike). The lunar horn, the thunderbolt, the sunbeam, have the same prerogative as these fishes; the dolphin, on account of the two scythe-shaped fins which it has on its anterior extremity, or of its fat and curved dorsal fin, as well as on account of its black and silvery colour, might well serve to represent the two lunar horns and the moon's phases. Thus the pike and the bream, dark or bluish on their backs, are white underneath. The dolphin also has a flat mouth and sharp teeth, like the pike.[1] The lunar horn announces rain; thus the scythe-shaped fin of the dolphin, appearing on the waves of the sea, announces a tempest to navigators, warns them, and saves them from shipwreck; hence, as a çiñçumaras, it may, like the sea-urchin, have saved or drawn the chariot, that is, the vessel of the Açvinâu, laden with riches. The dolphin which watches over Amphitritê, by order of Poseidôn, in the Hellenic myth, is the same as the dolphin, the spy of the sea, or the moon, the spy of the nocturnal and wintry sky. Inasmuch as the sky of night or winter was compared to the kingdom of the dead, both the dolphin and the moon, according to the Hellenic belief, carried the souls of the dead.

The *cyprinus, par excellence,* the carp (Lat. *carpus*),

[1] A superstitious belief quoted by Pliny concerning the cramp-fish merits being recorded here: "Mirum quod de Torpedine invenio, si capta cum Luna in Libra fuerit, triduoque asservetur sub dio, faciles partus facere postea quoties inferatur."

is celebrated, in connection with gold, in an elegant little Latin poem of Hieronimus Fracastorus. Carpus was the name of a ferryman of the Lake of Garda, who, seeing Saturn fleeing, took him for a robber who was carrying gold away, and endeavoured to despoil him of this gold; then Saturn cursed him and his companions in the following manner:—

> "Gens inimica Deum dabitur quod poscitis aurum:
> Hoc imo sub fonte aurum pascetis avari.
> Dixerat: ast illis veniam poscentibus et vox
> Deficit, et jam se cernunt mutescere et ora
> In rictum late patulum producta dehiscunt,
> In pinnas abiere manus; vestisque rigescit
> In squamas, caudamque pedes sinuantur in imam;
> Qui fuerat subita obductus formidine mansit
> Pallidus ore color, quamquam livoris iniqui
> Indicium suffusa nigris sunt corpora guttis;
> Carpus aquas, primus numen qui læsit, in amplas
> Se primus dedit et fundo se condidit imo."

From the comparisons which we have made hitherto, it is impossible not to admit that the enterprise of the fish who seeks the gold or the pearl, who finds it, or who contains it in himself, is a very ancient Âryan tradition. In the Vedic hymns we see now Indras, now the Açvinâu, saving the heroes from shipwreck, and bringing riches to mankind; we have also seen the çiñçumâras (sea-urchin, dolphin, or Vishṇus) draw the chariot of the Açvinâu, who are bringing riches. The Greeks called a fish of a strange shape by the name now of Zeus, now of chalkeüs (the name given to Hêphaistos, or Mulciber, or Vulcanus, the worker in metals), or blacksmith, whence the name of *Zeus faber*, by which it was known to the Latins. This fish is of a really monstrous shape. Its back is brownish, with yellow stripes; the rest of its body is of a silvery-grey colour; on its sides it has two spots of the deepest black. Its dorsal fin opens like a fan, with rays going out on all sides, and furnished with strong quills, which make this prominence resemble a crest. We remember that the cock and the lark were compared to Christ and to Christophoros, on account of their crest; the same happened in the case of the Zeus faber.[1] The Italian legend says that those two black spots (which make the fish's body resemble a forge, whence its name of blacksmith) were caused by the marks left upon it one day by St Christopher, while carrying Christ upon his shoulders across the river. The fish which wears the crest and Christopher are here identified with each other. But this is not all; at Rome, at Genoa, and at Naples, this same fish is called the fish of St Peter, because it is said to be the same fish which was caught by St Peter in the Gospels, in the mouth of which (as a blacksmith or chalkeüs, it must have known well how to coin money), by a miracle of Christ's, St Peter found the coin which was to serve for the tribute. Is it probable that the legend of the fish with gold in its mouth, so common in Âryan legends, was current in Judea? I do not think so; inasmuch as *petrus* and the *petra*, upon which Christ makes a bad Græco-Latin pun, in connection with the fish, is another mythical incident which calls me back to the Âryan world, and tears me away from the Semitic world, and from childish faith in the Judaic authenticity of the evangelical story, though without prejudice to my belief in the holiness of the doctrine.

[1] *s. v. citula*, Du Cange writes concerning the fish faber or Zeus: "Idem forte piscis, quem Galli doream vocant ab aureo laterum colore, nostri et Hispani Galli Baionenses jau, id est gallum, a dorsi pinnis surrectis veluti gallorum gallinaceorum cristis." The fish Zeus lives in solitude; hence it appears to me to be the same sacred fish, called anthias, of which Aristotle, in the ninth book of the *History of Animals*, says that it lives where no other animal is found.

CHAPTER II.

THE CRAB.

SUMMARY

The riddle, how it is a fish, and not a fish.—The crab appears and the sun goes back; the crab-moon draws the solar hero back.—The crane and the crab.—The crab kills the serpent and releases the solar hero.—The crab draws the chariot.—Palinurus.—The crabs prick and waken the hero.—The race between the crab and the fox.—The prince becomes a crab to release his beloved from the waters.—The nightingale, the stag, and the crab as awakeners.—The crab as an antidote for the venom of the toad, and as a remedy for the stone.

In the eighth Esthonian story, a husband beats his wife because she is unable to solve the riddle which he proposes, to provide him a fish to eat, which is not a fish, and which has eyes, but not in its head. The third brother, the cunning one, recommends his mother to cook the crab, which lives in the water like a fish, and which has eyes, but not in its head.

When the sun seems to enter, in the month of June, into the tropic which bears the sign of the crab (Lat. *cancer;* Gr. *karkinos;* Sanskṛit, *karkaṭas, karkas, karkaṭakas;* the Hindoo constellation of the crab is called *karkin,* or furnished with the crab, in the same way as the leaping moon, furnished with the hare, is called *çaçin*), it is said to come back again; on the first day of summer the days begin to shorten, as on the first of winter they begin to lengthen; the sun in the month of June was therefore compared to a crab, which retraces its steps, or was represented as drawn by a crab, which, in this case, is particularly the moon. We all know the myth of Hêraklês, who, when combatting the hydra of Lerne, was caught and drawn back by the crab, which Hêra, therefore, transformed into the celestial constellation of the crab. In the *Pseudo-Callisthenes*, Alexander returns in terror from his journey to the fountain of immortality, when he sees that the crabs draw his ships back into the sea. In the same work, we find a crab caught which contains seven precious pearls; Alexander has it shut up in a vase, which is enclosed in a large cage, fastened by an iron chain; a fish draws the cage a mile out to sea; Alexander, half dead with terror, thanks the gods for the warning, and so saving his life, persuading himself that it is not fit to attempt impossible undertakings. In the seventh story of the first book of the *Pańćatantram*, the old crane, on the other hand, terrifies the crab and the fishes by threatening them with a visitation of the gods in the chariot of Rohinî, the red wife of the Lunus, that is, in the constellation of the Wain or the Bulls (the fourth lunation of the moon), in consequence of which the rain will cease to fall, the pond will be dried up, and the crabs and fishes will die; the fishes allow themselves to be deceived by the crane, who eats them on the way; but the crab, on the contrary, when it has got half way, perceives the deceit of the crane, kills it, and returns back again. Professor Benfey has found a variation of this story in the Buddhist sacred and historical books of Ceylon. In the Æsopian fables, the crab kills the serpent. In the twentieth story of the first book of the *Pańćatantram*, the crab causes, at the same time, the death of the serpent and the crane, by means of the ichneumon; the crab, which walks a little backwards and a little forwards, when transported into the sky, causes now the death of the solar hero and now that of the monster, now delivers the solar hero from the monster and now drags it into the waters. In the fifteenth and last story of the fifth book of the *Pańćatantram*, the young hero Brahmadattas takes, for his companion in his journey, the crab, who, whilst he sleeps in the shade of a tree, kills the serpent which comes to kill him. This mythical crab, this red animal which kills the serpent, is sometimes the sun, but, perhaps, oftener it may be compared to the horned moon, which increases and diminishes, and releases the solar hero, asleep in the shadow of the night and of the winter, from the black serpent who endeavours to turn his sleep into death; Brahmadattas, when he wakens, recognises the crab as his deliverer. Thus we have already seen the moon considered more than once, in several forms, as the saviour of the solar hero and heroine. When the sun falls in the evening, in the west, it must necessarily go back like the crab, to reappear in the morning on the same eastern side from whence it came; when the sun goes back and the days grow shorter, after the summer solstice, the crab, in the Zodiacal cycle, retraces its steps. When the sun goes back, the moon either rules the darkness of the frigid night, or in autumn brings on the autumnal rains; the horns of the moon, and those of the crab, serve now to draw the hero into the waters (in the evening, and after solstice of June), now to draw him out of the waters (towards dawn and towards spring). The sun is now represented as having transformed himself into the moon, and now as having been deceived or saved by the moon. The sun which retraces its steps is a crab; the moon which draws back, or draws out, is also a crab, and, in this respect, seems to hold the same place as the sea-urchin with the hundred oars, or of the dolphin with the scythe-shaped fin, which draws the chariot of the solar hero, or the solar hero himself. In the fable of Kriloff, the crab draws the chariot with the pike and the heron (the latter taking the place here of the crane, which we have seen above in connection with the crab, and which is also called in Sanskṛit by the same name as the crab, that is, karkaṭas). It it well known that the sea-crab, *Palinurus vulgaris*, took its name from the pilot Palinurus, who fell into the sea. In the fourteenth story of the first book of *Afanassieff*, the crabs prick and waken the young hero Theodore (gift of God, an equivalent of Brahmadattas, given by the god Brahman), put to sleep by the witch; they are grateful to the hero, because he divided the caviare into equal parts among the crabs who were disputing for it.

We have seen the challenge to a race with the hare and the locust, the hare and locust both seem to lose the race. Afterwards we saw the challenge to a trial of flight of the beetle and the wren with the eagle, in which the animal that symbolises the moon, on the other hand, wins the race. Thus, in the same way, as to spring succeeds June or the month of the crab, we find represented in the fifth story of the fourth book of *Afanassieff* a race between the fox (which, as it symbolises the twilights of the day, represents also the equinoxes in the year) and the crab (it is well known that the crab, *Palinurus vulgaris*, was called by the Latins by the name of *locusta*). The crab fastens itself to the fox's tail; the latter arrives at the winning-post without knowing of the crab's presence; the fox then turns round to see whether his opponent is far off, upon which the crab, letting go the fox's brush and dropping quietly on the ground, looks up and placidly remarks that it has been waiting for some time.

In the first of the Esthonian stories, the young prince, in order to release from the waters his beloved, who had become a water-rose, by the eagle's advice takes off his clothes, covers himself with mud, and holding his nose between his fingers, snivels out, "From a man, a crab;" then he instantly becomes a crab, and goes to draw the water-rose out of the water, to bring it to shore near a stone, at which, when arrived, he says, "From the water-rose, the maiden; from the crab, the man." (This myth appears to represent the amours of the sun as a female, with the moon as a male.) I observe that among the Sanskṛit meanings of the word *karkaṭas*, which means a crab, there is that of a heap of water-roses, or a heap of lotuses.

We have already seen the nightingale and the stag as images representing the moon; here we also find a crab as a lunar figure. The moon is the watcher of night; either it sleeps with its eyes open like the hare, or it is watchful like the stag, or, as a nightingale, it justifies the Greek proverb of the watchers who sleep less than the nightingales (oud' hoson Aêdones üpnôousin), or, as crab, it wakens up with its claws those who are asleep and menaced by any danger.[1] In Pliny we find the nightingale, the stag, and the crab in concord; he in-

[1] We know that lynx's eyes, or lynx-like eyes, mean very sharp-sighted ones; ancient physicians recommended against the stone or the disease of the gravel, now the lyncurium, the stone which was supposed to be made of the urine of the lynxes, given by India to Bacchus, according to Ovid's expression, and now crab's eyes. The moon destroys with its light the stone-sky, the sky of night; hence crab's eyes are recommended against the disease of the stone. When the moon is not in the sky of night, the stone is there.

forms us that crab's eyes, with the nightingale's flesh, tied up in a stag's skin, are useful to keep a man awake. The moon, in fact, not only herself watches, but makes men watch, or prolong their vigils ; we know, moreover, of the excitement with which her presence agitates the quail, which cannot sleep when the moon shines in the sky. Pliny also recommends the river-crab, cut in pieces and drunk, as a remedy against any poison, but especially against the venom projected by the toad. In the *Heisterbac. Hist. Miracul.*, we read of a man named Theodoric, and surnamed Cancer, that the devil persecuted him in the form of a toad ; he kills the diabolical toad more than once, but it always rises again ; then Cancer, recognising the devil in this form, forms a heroic resolution, uncovers one of his thighs, and lets himself be bitten ; the thigh inflames, but he is cured at last, and from that day forward he is and continues a holy man. German superstition, therefore, combines with Græco-Latin to consider the crab as an enemy of the monster ; but as in Græco-Latin beliefs, besides the crab which awakens, there is also, as we have seen, the crab which seeks to ruin the solar hero, so in Germanic mythical tradition, the death of the solar and diurnal hero Baldur takes place, when the sun enters the Zodiacal sign of Cancer.

CHAPTER III.

THE TORTOISE.

SUMMARY.

Equivoque between the words *kaććhapas* and *kaçyapas* (by the intermediate form, *kaçapas*).—Explanation of the myth of the production of the ambrosia, by means of the mandaras.—Mantharas as a tortoise.—Kûrmas.—Kaććhapas the lord of the shores.—The tortoise and the elephant.—Kaçyapas as Pragâpatis.—Somas and Savitar.—Kaçyapas and the thirteen daughters of Dakshas; Dakshagâ.—The funereal tortoise and the frog.—The tortoise and the lyre; the Schild-kröte; the shields of the Kureti; kaććhâs, kaććhapî; kûrmas as a poet and as a wind.—The tortoise and the warriors.—The shields fallen from the sky.—The demoniacal tortoise.—The tortoise as an island.—The hare and the tortoise.—The tortoise defeats the eagle.

Of the three principal Hindoo names of the tortoise, *kûrmas, kaććhapas*, and *kaçyapas*, the third alone, in connection with the second, seems to have any importance in the history of myths. The expression *kûrmas* is the word usually employed to designate the real tortoise, whilst the expression *kaçyapas* gave rise to mythical equivoques, which deserve to be observed.

We know of the famous incarnation of Vishṇus as a tortoise, treated of in the *Kûrma P.* The problem was to stir up the ocean of milk to make ambrosia; the sea had no bottom, inasmuch as the earth had as yet no existence; to stir up the waters of the ocean, something of colossal size was needed; the gods had recourse to the mandaras, which was made to serve for the purpose, as the king of the rods, *kaçapas;* the gods and the demons shook the rod, and the ambrosia came forth; no sooner was the ambrosia produced, than the world of animated beings began to be created. The character of this cosmogony is preternaturally phallical; the white froth of the sea (born of the genital organs of Ouranos, castrated by his son Kronos), whence Aphroditê rises, and the cosmic ambrosia, being nothing else than the genital sperm. At a later period a mountain was seen in the mandaras, and the words *kaçapas* and *kaććhapas* (subsequently changed into *kaçyapas*) being confused, the king of the rods or phallos, *par excellence*, was converted into a tortoise. The mandaras (from the root *mand-mad*, to inebriate, to make joyful), however, might mean the agitator, that which makes joyful; but as from *mad* is derived the word *matsyas*, the fish now drunken, now stupid, so the word *mandaras* also has, for its proper meanings, slow and large, and is closely connected with mandas, which, besides slow, lazy, soft, also means drunken; with mandakas, foolish; and with mandanas, merry; and, as such, we can understand how there was in the celestial Paradise, in the mandanas or making joyful, the tree mandaras, the inebriating. Finally, it is connected with manthanas, the agitator, and identified with mantharas, which also means the agitator, the slow, and the lazy. But there is also another analogy which offers us the means of understanding how the equivoque of kaçapas, confused with kaććhapas, and which afterwards became kaçyapas or tortoise, became popular, just through the word *kûrmas*, which, as we have said, means a tortoise. When the mandaras or mantharas was conceived of as a producer of ambrosia, they soon identified the mantharas itself (the slow, the late, the curved) with the tortoise; in fact, *mantharas* is the name given to a tortoise in the *Hitopadeças*, and the name *mantharakas* is applied to another in *Somadevas* and in the *Pańćatantram*. Considered simply as the slow and the curved, the thought of the tortoise, which answers this description, naturally arose in connection with the name; the primitive myth became complicated, and the mandaras and the kaçapas, which were originally one and same, were at length distinguished from each other, the kaçapas, at first a kaçyapas or kaććhapas or tortoise, and, *vice versa*, the mandaras or mantharas also; the words in course of time lost their primitive meaning, the mandaras (as the slow one) became a mountain (which does not move), and the kaçapas a tortoise, supporting the mountain, at once vast, ponderous, and inert. As it often happens in mythology that two distinct personalities spring out of two names at first applied to the same mythical object or being, and both being names which indicate something heavy, it was surmised that the one heavy thing carried the other, and that the heavy tortoise, into which the god Vishṇus transformed himself, sustained the weight of the heavy mountain placed upon it by his *alter ego* Indras. The ideas of weighty and curved being united in both the mandaras and the kaçapas, the tortoise, as kûrmas, serves well for this office of a carrier, an assertion I venture to make, inasmuch as in *kûr-mas* I think I can recognise the same root which appears in the Sanskṛit *gur-u-s*, fem. *gur-v-î*, superlat. *gar-ishṭh-a-s* (Lat. *gra-v-is*, from *garvis*), and in the Latin *curvus*.[1]

As for the name of kaććhapas, to which the equivocal

[1] Cfr. the Sanskṛit roots, *kar*, *kur*, *gur*, *gûr*.

Hindoo epithet of kaçyapas, applied to the tortoise, should be referred, it properly means the lord, the guardian of the shores, he who occupies the shores, and is a perfectly apt designation for the tortoise, and an expression *à propos* to what is related of it in the legend quoted by us in the chapter on the elephant. Both animals (sun and moon) frequent the banks of the same lake, and have conceived a mortal dislike one for the other, continuing in their brutal forms the quarrel which existed between them when they were not only two men but two brothers. As the elephant and the tortoise both frequent the shores of the same lake, they mutually annoy each other, renewing and maintaining in mythical zoology the strife which subsists between the two mythical brothers, who fight with each other for the kingdom of heaven, either in the form of twilights, or of equinoxes, or of sun and moon, or of twilight and sun, or of twilight and moon, in any of the various interpretations which can, all with same basis of truth, be given to the myth of the Açvinâu, according to their appearance among celestial phenomena, which, although distinct, have nevertheless a great resemblance. In this particular mythical struggle between the tortoise and the elephant, terminated by the bird garuḍas, who carries them both up into the air in order to devour them, the tortoise and the elephant seem, however, especially to personify the two twilights of the day and the two twilights of the year—that is, the equinoxes, or the sun and the moon in the crepuscular hour, the sun and the moon in the equinoctial day, upon the banks of the great heavenly lake.

But, in the legend contained in the *Mahâbhâratam*[1] of the tortoise and the elephant carried into the air by

[1] i. 1353–1456.

the Vishṇuitic bird, there is still another interesting circumstance or variation, which corroborates the cosmic interpretation of the myth of the tortoise now proposed by me. The divine Kaçyapas is mentioned in it; he desires to have a son, and therefore has himself served by the gods (since it is the gods who make the mandaras, the producer of ambrosia, turn round) in the sacrifice adapted to produce children. The phallical Indras carries on his shoulders a mountain of wood, which evidently corresponds to the mandaras or kaça-pas, and, on the way, offends the dwarf hermits born of the hairs of the body of Brahman, that is, the hairs themselves; to this Kaçyapas, the name of Pragâpatis or lord of generation is given. We here again meet with the monstrous phallos which produces the ambrosia (or the Somas to which corresponds Savitar, the generator and the lord of the creatures[1]) and generates living beings in the world. Kaçyapas being considered as the generator, he was therefore placed in relation with the movements of the moon and the sun, who are also generators (as Somas and Savitar); and it is in this respect that Kaçyapas also appears as the fœcundator of the thirteen daughters of Dakshas, who correspond to the thirteen months of the lunar year (Dakshagâ is the name of a lunar asterism and of the wife of a phallical Çivas, and dakshagâpatis one of the Hindoo names given to the moon; Dakshas is also identified with Pragâpatis; whence Kaçyapas must have united himself, probably as the phallical moon, with his own daughters, or with his thirteen lunations). Of the thirteen wives made fruitful by Kaçyapas, everything that lives was born,—gods, demons, men, and beasts,—so

[1] Savitâ vâi prasavânâmiço.—*Âit. Br.* The story of Cunahçepas; he appears evidently as a form of Pragâpatis.

that in the cosmogony of the mandaras, of the Kaçapas, and hence of the tortoise, the mandaras, when shaken, produced the phallical ambrosia, of which all animated things were spontaneously generated.

But the tortoise, taken in connection with the moon, sometimes also had a funereal signification. The souls of the dead go into the world of the moon, into the sky of night, and the souls of the living descend from the world of the moon, that is, from the night; Çivas, the god of Paradise, becomes the destroying god; Plutus and Pluto are identified. Thus, in a note of Professor Haugh to the *Âitareya Br.*, I think I can recognise the tortoise, as representing in particular the dying moon, the burnt-up moon, which has the fire of spring for its tomb, round whose corpse the moon also moves in the here equivalent form of a frog (being *haris*, which means both yellow and green), and who is herself afterwards turned out. We know how Haris or Vishṇus now represents the sun and now the moon (the sun and the moon, as Indras and Somas, were called together rakshohanâu or monster-killers), is identified now with the tortoise, now with the bird garuḍas, the enemy of the tortoise. Here is, however, the note of Professor Haugh: "At each Atirâtra of the Gavâm ayanam the so-called Chayana ceremony takes place. This consists in the construction of the Uttarâ Vedi (the northern altar) in the shape of an eagle. About 1440 bricks are required for this structure, each being consecrated with a separate Yaǵusmantra. This altar represents the universe. A tortoise is buried alive in it, and a living frog carried round it and afterwards turned out." According to Pliny, the blood of a tortoise is an antidote to the venom of a toad (in the same way as the hare and a stag's horn is also recommended as of similar efficacy on the old principle of *similia similibus;* the hare is the moon, the stag's horn the moon's horn; the blood of the killed tortoise would appear to represent the moon itself as in a manner chasing the gloom of night away). The tortoise is also found in connection with frogs in a fable of Abstemius; the tortoise envies the frogs, who can move rapidly, but ceases to complain when it sees them become the prey of the eel.

One of the ten stars of the constellation of the tortoise, situated in the northern heavens—that is, in the cloudy and gloomy autumnal sky, and therefore especially ruled by the moon—was called the lyre by the Greeks, and it was fabled that the tortoise of which Hermês had made the lyre, had been transfigured into it. I may remark here that the German name for the tortoise is Schild-kröte (toad with shields), that the Koribantes[1] produced their noisy music, and accompanied their Pyrrhic dances with kettledrums and the sound of arms, and that the Kureti, in order to conceal from Kronos the birth of Zeus, struck their shields with their lances. It is interesting to observe, that in Sanskṛit also, kaććhâs is the name given to the little shields of the tortoise or kaććhapas; that kaććhapî is the term applied to the noise of the thundering Sarasvatî, or the thunder; that several Vedic poets are called Kaçyapas; that Kûrmas (another designation of the tortoise) is also the name of the Vedic poet, the son of Gṛitsamadas, and also an epithet applied to the *flatus ventris,* which is compared to a clap of thunder (Cfr. the roots *kar, kur, gar, gur*). In the

[1] The Koribantes remind us of the Salii of the Latins, to whom Numa gives the arms and the words, to be sung leaping. According to Ovid's distich—

> "Jam dederat Salii (a saltu nomina ducunt)
> Armaque et ad certos verba canenda modos."
> —*Fasti,* iii. 389.

chapter on the ass, we saw this *flatus* compared to the noise of a trumpet or a kettle-drum; here we have the thunderbolts that strike upon the shields, the spots of the celestial tortoise, of the rainy moon, upon the clouds, attracted by or formed from the moon's spots, that is, which produce the thunder. According to the Hellenic myth, the tortoise obtained from Zeus himself—that is, from the pluvial god, from the god of the clouds, the god in connection with the shield-clouds which concealed his birth, and we may add, from the god tortoise,—the power of concealing itself under shields, and of carrying its house along with it. The Romans were accustomed to bathe new-born babes in the concavity of a tortoise, as if in a shield. It was predicted that Clodius Albinus would one day attain to sovereign power, because, when he was born, an enormous tortoise was brought to his father by some fishermen. The tortoise protects Zeus, the new-born warrior-god; the tortoise, on account of its shields, makes the new-born child a warrior, and predicts dominion to him; my well-informed readers will remember how a shield, fallen from the sky, presaged to the Romans the glories they should achieve as a warlike people, according to Ovid's verses—

> ". . . Totum jam sol emerserat orbem:
> Et gravis ætherio venit ab axe fragor.
> Ter tonuit sine nube Deus, tria fulgura misit.
> Credite dicenti: mira sed acta loquor.
> A media cœlum regione dehiscere cœpit:
> Submisere oculos cum duce turba suo.
> Ecce levi scutum versatum leniter aura
> Decidit: a populo clamor ad astra venit."

Under this aspect the tortoise becomes the dark moon, in opposition to the luminous one, the slow moon, in opposition to the jumping one. Being slow or tardigrade, in the myths the tortoise is the moon, but the winter one; and sometimes it becomes also now the cloud, now the earth, now even the darkness (as such it appears demoniacal in a German legend, where two devils who have assumed the forms of monstrous tortoises, prevent the foundations of the cathedral church of Merseburg from being laid; the tortoises are exorcised, and their bodies slain, in memory of which circumstance it is said that the cups of these tortoises are preserved, hung up in the church; in the fourteenth fargard of the *Vendidad*, too, the tortoises are, as demoniacal, to be killed). We have seen in the first chapter of the first book, the hare-moon passed over and crushed by the cow's waggon, suggesting to us the cloud (as the moon, now a bridge, now an island of the sky, as sea), which passes over the moon, but he perhaps, again, of the eclipse of the moon by the means of the earth, which is also called a cow in Sanskṛit. In Sanskṛit, the earth, which comes out of waters—an island[1] (as the moon and the cloud)—is also called by the name of kûrmas, *i.e.*, a tortoise (properly the

[1] It is interesting in this connection to find in the translation of Lane a passage from the *Ágáïb-el-Makhlooḳát* (*Marvels of Creation*), a work of the thirteenth century: "The tortoise is a sea and land animal. As to the sea tortoise it is very enormous, so that the people of the ship imagine it to be an island. One of the merchants relates as follows regarding it: 'We found in the sea an island elevated above the water, having upon it green plants, and we went forth to it, and dug [holes for fire] to cook; whereupon the island moved, and the sailors said, "Come ye to your place, for it is a tortoise, and the heat of the fire hath hurt it, lest it carry you away." By reason of the enormity of its body,' said he [*i.e.*, the narrator above mentioned], 'it was as though it were an island, and earth collected upon its back in the length of time, so that it became like land, and produced plants.'" Evidently here the tortoise occupies the same place as, in popular tradition, the lunar whale recorded by us in the chapter on the Fishes. Cfr. Lane, *The Thousand and One Nights*, London, 1841, vol. iii. chap. xx.

curved, the humped, the eminent, the prominent; mantharas is a name given to the tortoise, and Mantharâ is the name of the humpbacked woman who causes the ruin of Râmas in the *Râmâyaṇam*). Hence we also have in the West, besides the fables of the leaping hare (the moon) and the cow, of the leaping locust (the moon) and the ant, the apologue of the hare and the tortoise who run together; the hare, relying on its swiftness, falls asleep and loses, while the tortoise by steady perseverance wins the race.

We have already seen the tortoise in the Hindoo legends as the rival of the eagle or the Vishṇuitic bird Garuḍas. The two are now identified and now fight against each other (we must remember that it was by the advice of Kaçyapas that the bird Garuḍas ravished the ambrosia from the serpents). In Greece, the proverb of the tortoise which vanquishes the eagle, was already diffused; now it is the eagle which carries the tortoise into the air, or rather makes it fly, now it is, on the other hand, the tortoise which defies the eagle to arrive first. It is interesting to compare with this the Siamese apologue published by A. Bastian in the *Orient und Occident*, of evidently Hindoo origin. The bird Khruth, no doubt a limited and particular form of Garuḍas, wishes to eat a tortoise (here perhaps the moon) which lies upon the shore of a lake. The tortoise consents to be eaten, under the condition that the Khruth accepts a challenge to a trial of speed, and arrives soonest on the other side of the lake, the bird to go through the air, and the tortoise through the water. The bird Khruth accepts the wager;

n. 1 and 8, p. 80 *seq.*—Grein, *Bibliothek der angelsächsischen Poesie*, Göttingen, 1857, 1, 235, the Celtic legend of St Brandan and the *Pseudo-Callisthenes*.

then the tortoise calls together millions and millions of tortoises, and places them all in such a way that they surround the lake, each distant a few steps from the water. Then it gives the signal to the bird to commence the race. The Khruth rises into the air, and flees to the opposite bank; wherever he essays to alight, he finds the tortoise has been there before him. (This myth represents, perhaps, the relation of the sun to the lunations).

CHAPTER IV.

THE FROG, THE LACERTA VIRIDIS, AND THE TOAD.

SUMMARY.

The mâṇḍukâs or frogs as clouds in the *Ṛigvedas.*—Bhekas.—The frog announces the summer; the *canta-rana* announces Christ.—The serpent, the hero, and the frog.—The frog and the ox.—Dionysos and the frogs.—Indras and the frogs.—The dumb frogs.—Proserpina and the frog.—Rana cum gryllo.—The frog finds the sultan's ring.—The frog and the rook.—The frog as the serpent's daughter.—The demoniacal frog.—The yellow and the green frog.—The beautiful maiden as a frog.—The demoniacal toad.—The sacred toad.—The beautiful maiden as a toad.—The toad in Tuscany, in Sicily, and in Germany.—The handsome youth as a toad.—Women who gave birth to toads.—The venomous and the alexipharmic toad.—Kröte and Schildkröte.—The toad swallows the dew.—The stone of the frog.—The horned lizard.—Eidechse, hagedisse.—Apollo as sauroktanos.—The lizard on St Agnes's Day.—The little lizards must not be killed in Sicily, being intercessors before the Lord.—The amphisbhæna.—The *lacerta viridis.*—The *couleuvre* as a good fairy.

I AM sorry to be unable to concur entirely in the opinion of the illustrious Professor Max Müller, when, in translating a hymn of the *Ṛigvedas,* in his *History of Ancient Sanskṛit Literature,* he remarks, "The 103d hymn, in the seventh Maṇḍalam, which is called a panegyric of the frogs, is clearly a satire on the priests." It is possible that at a later period, in deriding a brâhmanic school similar to that of the mâṇḍûkâs, a satirical sense would have been ascribed to this hymn, but it does not seem to me that the intention of the author of the Vedic hymn was such. Professor Max Müller has shown well in his History how the Vedic hymns have suffered in the hands of the Brâhmans, by means of their arbitrary interpretations; the interesting story of the hypothetical god Kas is a very convincing proof of it; it is, therefore, possible, and even probable, that attempts were made to use this Vedic hymn as an arrow for satire; but if I am not mistaken, no trace of a satirical meaning can be found in the hymn itself. Above all, I must observe that the Anukramaṇikâ of the *Ṛigvedas* properly calls the hymn only parǵanyastutis, or hymn in honour of Parǵanyas, the hymn of the tempest; secondly, it scarcely seems possible that a satirical hymn, intended to caricature the priests, should be inserted in the seventh book, which is attributed to Vasishṭas, the most religious of all the legendary Brâhmans, and he who, for the glory of Brâhmanism and the rights of the sacerdotal caste, maintained such a protracted and disastrous war against Viçvâmitras, the champion of the warrior race; hence, if a satirical hymn against priests had been found in the third book of the *Ṛigvedas,* ascribed to the wise Viçvâmitras, I should not have thought it so strange, whilst it would be misplaced in the hymns said to be written by Vasishṭas. To me it seems rather that, when speaking of frogs, the hymn does not allude to the frogs of the earth, but to the clouds, the cloud-frogs, attracted by the pluvial moon, whilst the tempest is at its height. We know that in the *Ṛigvedas,* the wives of the gods weave hymns in honour of the lightning and thundering god Indras, who has killed the monster serpent which kept back the waters of the heavenly cloud; we have also, in the first chapter of the first book, heard the cows lowing and exulting joyfully before their deliverer Indras, who lets his seed drop in the midst of them as soon as they are released from the cave where they were imprisoned. In the seventh book, the hymns 101 and 102 are sung in honour of Indras as Parǵanyas; the hymn 103 is also sung in his honour, but by the clouds of the sky themselves, by the celestial frogs, inasmuch as the frog which croaks, when transported into the sky, is nought else then the thundering cloud; in fact, in Sanskṛit the word *bhekas*, which means frog, has also the meaning of cloud. We have seen that the cuckoo who sings in spring, and admonishes the tillers of the soil to begin their work, personifies the thunder in the sky: the frog has the same office; it, like the thunder, announces the approaching tempest. And because, when the first claps of thunder are heard, it is the summer which announces its coming, so the frog that croaks and the frog that sings served specially to announce the summer. I remember that, a few years ago, there still existed at Turin, among children, the custom of sounding in the Holy Week (in order to greet the approaching festival of the resurrection of Christ, who died amongst flashes of lightning and peals of thunder) a wooden instrument, which emitted a sharp squeak resembling the croaking of a frog, and which was therefore called *canta-rana* (the frog sings). It was also the custom on Easter Eve to strike all the doors violently with sticks, as if to reproduce under another form the sound of the *canta-rana*. According to Pliny, the frogs die in winter, and are born again in spring; when the frogs ask for a king, and obtain, in the Greek fable[1] a serpent, and in the Russian

[1] Cfr. the first story of the fourth book of the *Pańćatantram*, where the king of the frogs invokes the help of a black serpent to avenge himself upon certain frogs who are his enemies, and, instead of this, draws down death upon all the frogs and upon his own son.

fable of Kriloff a heron, the serpent and the heron symbolise the autumnal and wintry seasons. Indras, Zeus, and Christ are born and born again amid the noise of musical instruments, shields, arms, winds and thunder, among the lowing of cows, the bleating of goats, the braying of asses, and the croaking of frogs, called by Aristophanes *philôdon genos*. In the 103d hymn of the seventh book of the *Ṛigvedas*, one maṇḍûkas (frog or cloud) lows like a cow (gomâyus); another like a goat (aǵamâyus); one is pṛiçnis, or variegated; another haritas, or fair-haired, golden, red (the cloud born by the lightning and the violence of the wind), and, as a frog, green or grey; the maṇḍûkas or frog being transported into the sky, or identified, as a ǵomâyus, with the cow, it is no wonder that, in the fable, the frog has the presumption of thinking it can inflate itself to the size of an ox; but when the little cloud has become a large one, it ends by bursting, and so does the frog in his attempt to distend himself and become as large as the ox. (In the eighteenth Esthonian story, we find a monster who has a body like that of an ox, and feet like those of a frog.) When Indras and Zeus have accomplished their work in the celestial cloud, when the cloud has passed away and dispersed, when the frogs are drunk with water, they cease their croaking; thus, in the *Frogs* of Aristophanes, when Dionüsos (nüseios Dios) has passed the Stygian marsh, they stop croaking; whilst Zeus, on the other hand, floods the earth with water, they (Dios pheugontes ombron) retire into the depths of the waters to dance in chorus (as the ap-saràs). On the other hand, before the pluvial god satisfies their desires, before it rains, they croak incessantly; the thunder always makes itself heard before the rain, and at the outbreak of the tempest; hence, in the *Ṛigvedas* itself, Indus (the moon), as a bringer of rain (or the rain itself), is implored to run and plead with Indras, the pluvial god, to satisfy the desire of the frog.[1] Here, therefore, it is especially Indus who satisfies the frogs' desire for rain. Indus, as the moon, brings or announces the somas, or the rain; the frog, croaking, announces or brings the rain; and at this point the frog, which we have seen identified at first with the cloud, is also identified with the pluvial moon. Another characteristic of the frog made this identification all the more natural, and that was, its green colour (harit). By the word *harit* (which, as we, several times, have remarked, means yellow and green in Sanskṛit) not only the moon, but the green parrot was designated, and also the frog. The identification having been effected, the Greeks could then relate fables concerning the frog of the Island of Seriphos (batrachos ek Seriphou), which was dumb; so in the Lives of St Regulus and St Benno, we read that when these two saints, as they preached the Christian faith, were annoyed by the croaking of the frogs, they ordered the frogs to be silent, and they became dumb for ever. In truth, the frogs are silent (and even die, according to Pliny) in winter, which is under the especial dominion of the silent moon; the frog and the moon are exchanged one for the other. In *Ovid*, the metamorphosis of the frog is made to enter into the lunar myth, that is, into the myth of Proserpina; it was the form of the frog which certain peasants of Lycia assumed who dirtied the water of which Ceres and Proserpina wished to drink; their croaking (coax) is the punishment to which the goddesses condemned them, because in those waters they had emitted a vile sound from

[1] Vâr in maṇḍûka iĉhatîndrayendo pari srava; *Ṛigv.* ix. 112.

their mouths.[1] Another proof of the identity of the frog with the moon is the Latin proverb, "Rana cum gryllo," which afterwards served to represent two opposite things, but which, in fact, are the same, on account of their shrill voice, their way of hopping, and their common mythical connection with the leaping moon. We are reminded of the moon and the cloud in the war waged between the frogs and the mice, who are mutually destroying each other until the falcon comes with impartiality to annihilate both. We are, moreover, reminded of the little goldfish, the fair-haired moon, and the pike, in the frog which, in the *Tuti-Name*, finds the sultan's ring, which had fallen into the river, for the young hero, in gratitude to him for having saved it from the serpent who was about to devour it; it is said that both the frog and the serpent were two fairies who, freed from their curse, united themselves to protect the young hero (the new sun). In the twenty-third Mongol story, the golden frog (the moon) is dancing; the rook (the night) carries it off to eat it; the frog recommends it to wash it in water; the rook is taken in, and the frog, like the jorsh of Russian stories, succeeds in escaping; this frog is said to be the daughter of the prince of the dragons, who watches over the pearl. As the daughter of a serpent, the golden frog (the moon), when it is darkened, itself appears as a diabolical serpent or pythoness, and is more like a toad than a frog; then it becomes, according to Sadder, a meritorious service to kill the frogs: "Ranas si interfecerit aliquis quicunque fortis eorum adversarius, ejus quidem merita propterea erunt mille et ducenta. Aquam eximat eamque removeat et locum siccum faciat

[1] A similar tradition was current concerning the tarantula (stellio). Ceres, being thirsty, wished to drink; the boy Stelles prevented her, and the goddess transformed him into a *stellio*. According to Ulpianus, from the *stellio* was derived the *crimen stellionatus*.

et tum eas necabit a capite ad calcem. Hinc Diaboli damnum percipientes maximum flebunt et ploratum edent copiosissimum."

In the second Calmuc story of Siddhikür, two dragons who keep back the river which irrigates the earth and makes it fruitful, and who eat a man every year, assume the form of frogs (one yellow and the other green), and speak to one another of the way in which they can be killed. The king's son understands their language, and kills them, helped by a poor friend of his, with whom he enriches himself, but only to encounter (like the two mythical brothers) the most dangerous adventures afterwards.

But the diabolical form of a frog is sometimes assumed by the beautiful maiden (or else by the handsome youth) as the effect of a malediction or an enchantment. Thus it is in the interesting twenty-third story of the second book of *Afanassieff*. There is a Tzar who has three sons; each son must shoot an arrow; where the arrow falls, each brother will find his predestined wife. The two eldest brothers marry in this way two beautiful women; the arrow of the youngest brother Ivan, however, is taken up by a frog, whom he is oblige to marry. The Tzar wishes to see which of the three brides makes the handsomest present to her husband. All three give their husbands a shirt, but that of the frog is the most beautiful; for whilst Ivan sleeps (that is, in the night), she casts her skin, becomes the beautiful Helen (generally the aurora, but here, it would seem, the same transformed into the good fairy moon), and orders her attendants to prepare the finest shirt possible; she then again becomes a frog. The Tzar (a truly patriarchal Tzar) then wishes to see which of his three daughters-in-law bakes bread best; the first two brides know not what to do, and send secretly to see what the frog does; the frog, who sees all, understands the trick, and bakes the bread badly on purpose; afterwards, when she is alone and Ivan asleep, she again becomes the beautiful Helen, and orders her attendants to bake a loaf such as those which her father ate only on feast-days. The loaf of the frog is pronounced the best. Lastly, the Tzar wishes to see which of his daughters-in-law dances best. Ivan is sorrowful, thinking that his bride is a frog; but Helen consoles him, sending him to the ball, where she will join him; Ivan rejoices to think that his wife has the gift of speech, and goes to the ball; the frog takes her robes off, becomes the beautiful Helen once more, dresses herself splendidly, comes to the ball, and all exclaim as they pass by her (as to the Homeric Helen), "How beautiful!" They first sit down to table to eat; Helen takes bones in one hand, and water in the other; her sisters-in-law do the same. Then the ball begins. Helen throws water from one hand, and groves and fountains spring up; and bones (we remember a similar virtue in the bones of the cow) from the other, from which birds flutter upward (the same is narrated in a story I heard in Piedmont when a child). Meanwhile, Ivan runs home to burn the frog's skin. Helen returns home, can no longer become a frog, and is sorrowful; she goes with Ivan to bed, and awakening at morn, says to him, "Ivan Tzarević, thou hast not been patient enough; I would have been thine; now, as God wills it, Farewell! Seek me in the twenty-seventh earth, in the thirtieth kingdom" (*i.e.*, in my opinion, in hell, in the night into which the moon and the aurora descend, and whence the moon comes out again and renews itself after twenty-seven days; the Russian story is evidently a variety of the fable of Cupid and Psyche).[1] She then disappears. Ivan goes

[1] Cfr. also *Afanassieff*, vi. 55; Masha (Mary), the wife of Ivan, at first appears as a goose, afterwards as a frog, a lizard, and a spindle.

to seek his bride at the dwelling of the frog's mother, who is a witch; he takes from her the spindle which spins gold, throws part of it before him, and the rest behind. Helen appears once more, and the pair flee away upon the carpet which flies by itself. Here the helped aurora and the helping moon are assimilated.

But in popular stories the hero and heroine assume by witchcraft, instead of the form of a dark frog, that of a toad, and sometimes that of a horned lizard,[1] whence the verse of Mehun—

> "Boteraulx et couleuvres, visions de deables."

Inasmuch as the toad is a form proper to the demon, it is feared and hunted; inasmuch as, on the contrary, it is considered as a diabolical form imposed by force upon a divine or princely being, it is respected and venerated as a sacred animal. In Tuscany it is considered by the peasants a sacrilege to kill a toad. A low Tuscan song heard by me at Santo Stefano di Calcinaia records the transformation of the beautiful maiden into a toad; the mother toad speaks to her daughter to console her, inspiring her with the hope of being soon married to the king's son—

> "Botta, gragna,[2]
> Il figlio del re che poco ti ama
> Se non t'ama, t'amerà,
> Quando per isposa lui t'avrà."

---

[1] In the eighth story of the first book of the *Pentamerone* it is a lacerta cornuta (horned lizard, the moon) which watches over the destiny of the girl Renzolle (the aurora).

[2] It was thus that I heard it recited, but it should, as it appears to me, be corrected both in rhyme and sense, and *gragna* changed into *grama*, unless *gragna* is a verb and stands for *grandina* (hail); in Italy, there is a superstitious belief that the toads are generated of the first large drops of rain which fall into the dust at the beginning of a tempest.

(Wretched toad! the king's son, who little loves thee, if he love thee not, will love thee when he has thee for his wife.) The prince weds the toad, which is immediately transformed into a beautiful maiden. With regard to the superstitions concerning the toad current in Sicily, it is interesting to note what my friend Giuseppe Pitrè writes to me—"The toad brings fortune; he who is not fortunate must provide himself with a toad and feed it in his house[1] upon bread and wine, a consecrated nourishment, inasmuch as it is alleged toads are either 'lords' or 'women from without,' or 'uncomprehended genii,' or 'powerful fairies,' who have fallen under some malediction. Hence they are not killed, nor even molested, lest when offended they should come at night to spit water upon the offender's eyes, which never

[1] A similar superstition is current in Germany, as I find in Rochholtz, the work quoted before, i. 147: "Auch die Hauskröte, Unke, Muhme genannt, wohnt im Hauskeller und hält durch ihren Einfluss die hier verwahrten Lebensmittel in einem gedeihlichen Zustand. Dadurch kommt Wohlstand ins Haus, und das Thier heisst daher Schatzkröte. In Verwechslung mit dem braunschwarzen Kellermolch wird sie auch Gmöhl genannt und soll eben so oft ihre Farbe verändern, als der Familie eine Veränderung bevorsteht."—The various popular superstitions concerning the salamander are well known,—viz., that it resists the power of fire, that it lives in fire, that it becomes like fire: "immo ad ignem usque elementarem orbi lunari finitimum ascendere" (according to Aldrovandi), and that, devoid of hairs itself, it causes the hairs of others to fall out by means of its saliva, whence Martial, cursing the baldness of a woman's head—

"Hoc salamandra caput, aut sæva novacula nudet."

Pliny therefore recommends against the poisonous venom which is ascribed to the salamander, the seeds of the hairy and stinging nettle, with broth of a tortoise (which it resembles by its yellow spots). The salamander of popular superstition seems to me to represent the moon which lights itself, which lives by its own fire, which has no rays or hairs of its own, and which makes the rays or hairs of the sun fall.

heal, not even if he recommend himself to the regard of Santa Lucia." Hence the poet Meli, in his *Fata Galanti*, writes that he prevented a peasant from killing a toad—

> "Jeu ch'avia 'ntisu da li miei maggiuri
> Che li buffi 'un si divinu ammazzari,
> Fici in modu chi l'ira e lu rancuri
> A ddu viddanu cci fici passari."

As a recompense for having saved its life, the toad soon afterwards appears to him in the shape of a very beautiful woman, and promises to assist him all the days of his life—

> "Oh picciotti furtunatu!
> Eu ti prutiggirò d'ora nn' avanti,
> Jeu su' dda buffa, chi tu, gratu e umanu
> Sarvasti antura da l'impiu viddanu."

In Piedmont, I have heard a popular story [1] related

---

[1] It was narrated to me by a peasant woman who heard it at Cavour in Piedmont:—

A man who is paralytic has three daughters, Catherine, Clorinda, and Margaret; he sets out on a journey to consult a great doctor, and asks his daughters what they wish him to bring them when he returns; Margaret will be content if he bring her a flower. He arrives at his destination, a castle; everything is prepared to receive him, but the doctor is not to be found; he sets out to return home, but on the way he recollects the flower, which he had forgotten; he goes back to the garden of the castle and is about to pluck a daisy (margherita), when a toad warns him that he will die in three days if he does not give it one of his daughters to wife. The father informs his daughters of this, upon which the two eldest refuse; but the youngest, in order to save her father's life, consents. Her father is cured, and the wedding takes place; during the night the toad becomes a beautiful youth, but warns his bride never to tell any one, for if she does, he will always remain a toad, and he gives her a ring by means of which she will obtain whatever she wishes for. The sisters have an inkling of some mystery, and make her confess; the toad falls ill and disappears; she calls him with the ring, but in vain; seeing this, she throws the ring, as useless, into a pond, upon which the beautiful youth steps out, and never becomes a toad again; their happiness together thereafter is unbroken.

in which the toad is, on the other hand, the diabolical form assumed by a handsome youth; in Aldrovandi,

In an unpublished Tuscan story, related to me by Uliva Selvi at Antignano near Leghorn, instead of the toad we have a magician of frightful aspect. The father of the three daughters is a sailor; he promises to fetch a shawl to the first, a hat to the second, and a rose to the third. When the voyage is over, he is about to return, but, having forgotten the rose, the ship refuses to move; he is compelled to go back to look for the rose in a garden; a magician hands the rose with a little box to the father to give it to one of his daughters, whom the magician is to marry. At midnight, the father, having returned home, relates to his third daughter all that happened. The little box is opened; it carries off the third daughter to the magician, who happens to be king of Pietraverde, and is now a handsome young man. He shows her, in the palace, three rooms, of which one is red, one white, and another black. They live together happily. Meanwhile, the eldest sister is to be married; the magician conducts his wife into the red room; she wishes to go to the wedding, and the magician consents, but warns her not to say either who he is, or aught she knows of him, if she does not wish to lose him, as to recover him again she would have to wait till she should wear out as many shoes as there are in the world. He gives her a dress which, as she goes, is heard rustling a long way off; and he tells her, if her pin should drop, to let the bride pick it up and keep it; warning her, moreover, not to drink or to eat of anything they may offer her. All this she observes to the letter. The second sister is about to be married; the magician leads his wife into the white room and repeats the same instructions, only, instead of the pin, she is to let her ring of brilliants drop. The father dies; the magician then takes his wife into the black room, the chamber of melancholy. She wishes to go to the funeral, and is permitted, after the usual warnings; the magician, moreover, gives her a ring; if it become black, she will lose him; she forgets the warning and loses him. She wanders about for seven years, and no one can give her any news of the king of Pietraverde; she then disguises herself as a man, and arrives at a city where the king's hostler takes her into his service; no sooner does she touch the carriages than they become clean. The queen passes by and wonders at the personal appearance of the youth; she engages him to work in her kitchen, then to serve at table, and finally to be her *valet de chambre*. The queen falls in love with him, and wishes to have him at any cost; in vain; she then accuses him of designing to

several things are narrated of women who gave birth to toads.[1]

take her life. The king, although unwillingly, has him put in prison; soon he has pity upon him and lets him free. The fictitious youth continues to wander about; he arrives at the city, and asks for news of the king of Pietraverde; they tell her that he has long been dead, and point her to a room where his bier is supported by columns of wax, or candles; he will not awake until the candles are consumed. She goes up and weeps; the king takes three hairs from his beard and recommends her to preserve them carefully. She continues her wanderings, still dressed as a man, and is engaged by other hostlers of a king as assistant. The news of her bravery reach the king, who takes her into his kitchen. The queen sees him and falls in love with him; in vain; she accuses him to the king, who puts her in prison; she is condemned to death, and the guillotine is prepared. While going to execution, she remembers the three hairs, and burns one; an army of warriors appear, sent by the king of Pietraverde; they terrify all the king's people, whom they compel to postpone the execution till next day. The next day she does the same with the same result. The third day she brings out the third hair; the cavalry appear again, commanded this time by the king of Pietraverde in person, dressed so that he shone like a brilliant, that he appeared like a sun; he releases the youth from the execution; the king of Pietraverde has the young girl dressed as a princess; she is tried in a court of justice; her innocence is established; the queen's head is cut off.

[1] "Suessanus tradit, quod bufonem quempiam obviam fieri felicissimum augurium fuisse antiquitas existimavit.—Anno 1553, in villa quadam Thuringia ad Unstrum, a muliere bufo caudatus natus est, quemadmodum in libro de prodigiis et ostentis habetur. Nec mirum, quia Cœlius Aurelianus et Platearius scribunt mulieres aliquando cum fœto humano bufones et alia animalia hujus generis eniti. Sed hujus monstrosæ conceptionis causam non assignant. Tradit quidem Platearius illa præsidia, quæ ad provocandos menses commendantur, ducere; etiam bufonem fratrem Salernitanorum quemadmodum aliqui lacertum fratrem Longobardorum nominant. Quoniam mulieres Salernitanæ potissimum in principio conceptionis succum apii et porrorum potant, ut hoc animal interimant, antequam fœtus viviscat. Insuper mulier quædam ex Gesnero, recens nupta cum omnium opinione prægnans diceretur, quatuor animalia bufonibus similia peperit et optime valuit."—Aldrovandi also reads: "apud Heisterbacensem in historia miraculorum," that some monks found a living toad inside a

From the double and contradictory aspect in which the toad was regarded, popular medicine, although believing that the humour which the toad, when provoked, ejects from behind, is fatal, and that the toad not only poisoned men, but even all the plants over which it passed, still recommends the wearing of dried toads under the armpits as amulets against plague and poison. The same alexipharmic virtue was also ascribed to the stone called and believed to be toad's-stone (or bufonite), which was said to change colour when its wearer was poisoned. The bufonite was supposed to be taken out of a toad's head, but science has demonstrated that the bufonite, sold by quacks is made of the tooth of a fossil fish.[1] Out of the toad, the dark animal of the night, the gloom or winter, the solar pearl comes; thus popular German stories regard the *Schild-kröte* (or toad with the shield) as sacred, on account of the pearl supposed to be contained in its head. In Hungary it is said that the toad swallows the dew in the dry season; it is believed, moreover, that the frog, like the serpent, vomits forth, in spring, a precious stone called the stone of the serpent or the stone of the frog. According to what Count Geza Kuun writes to me, in the testament of a citizen of Kaisa three golden rings are mentioned, one of which contained a "frog's stone."

I have observed above that the toad's place is sometimes taken in popular tales by the horned lizard; the lizard also represents the demoniacal shape, the shape of a witch. On this subject there was an interesting dis-

hen in place of intestines. In the same author, a priest finds an immense toad at the bottom of a jar of wine; whilst he is wondering how such a large toad should have been able to enter by such a small orifice, the toad disappears.

[1] Cfr. Targioni Tozzetti, *Lezioni di Materia Medica*, Florence, 1821.

cussion by Karl Simrock upon the word *Eidechse* (the lizard in German), derived from the ancient form *Hagedisse* which is the same as *Hexe* or witch. It is as a witch that the lizard is killed, in the Greek myth, by Apollines, whence its name of *sauroktanos.*[1] But, inasmuch as the lizards appear in spring and announce the fine season, they are considered (according to Porphyrios) sacred to the sun, and therefore of good augury. A Bolognese proverb says, "Sant' Agnes, la luserta cor pr' al paes," to indicate that the season is beginning to improve, inasmuch as with the appearance of the lizards on the Day of St Agnes, which is in the beginning of March, spring begins to make itself felt. In Sicily it is believed that the little lizards called San Giuvanni must not be killed, because they are in the presence of the Lord in heaven, and light the little lamp to the Lord (as we have already seen the firefly give light to the grain). And when they are killed, in order that they may not curse one, one must say to the tail which is shaking, that it was not the real killer, but the dog of St Matthew who committed the crime,

"Nun fu' ieu, nun fu' ieu :
Fu lu cani di San Matteu."

They are believed to be powerful intercessors before the Lord, for which reason Sicilian children warm them in

[1] Some extraordinary lizards of which Aldrovandi speaks are of a half sacred and half monstrous nature: "Præter illud memorabile, quod Mizaldus recitat accidisse anno Domini 1551, mense Julii in Hungaria prope pagum Zichsum juxta Theisum fluvium nimirum in multorum hominum alvo lacertas naturalibus similes ortas fuisse. Interdum contingit, ut animadvertit Schenchius, lacertam viridem in cæti magnitudinem excrescere, qualis aliquando Lutetiæ visa est. Sæpe etiam lacertæ duobus et tribus caudis refertæ nascuntur, quas vulgus ludentibus favorabiles esse nugatur."

their bosoms, and feed them on crumbs of bread soaked in water.

But an especially sacred character is ascribed to the *lacerta viridis* (It. *ramarro*; Sicilian, *vanuzzu*, a diminutive of Giovanni) and to the *amphisbhæna*, of which the ancients believed that it had two heads (like the Hindoo ahîraṇis), its tail being taken for one. The *amphisbhæna* is still held sacred and revered in India.[1] The green lizard of popular superstition is partly solar and partly lunar; the firefly and the quail, as summer animals, are sacred to the sun; as watchers by night, to the moon. Thus the green lizard, as a summer animal which hunts away the serpent of winter, appears particularly in relation with the sun; but inasmuch as there is also the serpent of night, the green lizard or green *ramarro* takes the place of the crab-moon, that is, it wakens the young solar hero who sleeps in the night, and wakens the sleeping man lest the serpent should bite him. The moon of winter wakens the sun of spring, the moon of night wakens the sun of day; the moon-lizard, like the moon crab, hunts the serpent or black monster away. In Piedmont, Tuscany, and Sicily, the green lizard is believed to be the friend of mankind; indeed, it is called *guarda omu* in Sicily, where it is believed to cure from

[1] In the *Mahâbhâratam*, i. 981–1003, it is said that the serpents amphisbhænæ (duṇḍubhâs, duṇḍavas, nâgabhṛitas, the same, I think, as the mannuni of Malabar,) being good, must not be killed; an amphisbhæna relates that it had once been the wise Sahasrapâd (properly of the hundred feet; the amphisbhæna appears to be a lizard without feet, and with a tail the same size as its head, for which reason the belief arose that it had two heads; it seems to be another personification of the circular year, like the serpent), and that it became a serpent by a curse, because it had once frightened a Brâhman with a fictitious serpent made of grass; at the sight of the wise Kurus, the amphisbhæna is released from its malediction.

incantations, perhaps on account of the yellow cross which the people think they can see upon its head. At Santo Stefano of Calcinaia it is said that the green lizard hisses in the ears of Christians like a Christian when the serpent approaches a man; they even relate several cases of shepherds or peasants who, being asleep, were saved by the green lizard passing over them (Aldrovandi speaks of a similar superstition). It is, moreover, believed that the green lizard, if caught and put in a vase full of oil, will produce the oil of a *ramarro*, which is said to be good against wounds and poisons. In the *Contes Merveilleux de Porchat*, a fairy protects the poor Laric and brings fortune to him in the shape of a grateful *couleuvre*, which he, in winter, found frozen and warmed in his bosom. The *couleuvre* makes radiant coins fall to Laric from the beaks of certain partridges, enables him to find whatever he is in need of, and puts a golden chain round the neck of his wife. Thus the myths of the golden (or green) fish, the golden (or green) frog and the golden (or green) lizard, correspond to each other in the beautiful myth of the good moon-fairy, who protects the solar hero or heroine in the nights both of the day and the year.

CHAPTER V.

THE SERPENT AND THE AQUATIC MONSTER.

SUMMARY.

The feet and the tail; the serpent is the favourite form of the demon; the devil is betrayed by his tail.—The serpent and the waters; the dragon as the keeper back of the waters, and as the guardian of the treasures; the devil evoked from the waters.—The otter. —The chief enterprise of Indras is the killing of the serpent.—The names of the Vedic serpent; *arbuda* and *reptilis.*—Description of the Vedic serpent.—The wives of the demons and the wives of the gods; Indras wounds the wife of the demon in the *yonis*, and the demon himself in the eggs; the serpent's death consists in the broken egg; broken eggs, skins, vases, boxes, and testicles.—The god as a serpent; the python.—Gods and demons, birds and serpents dispute the possession of the ambrosia.—The phallical Anantas of cosmogony; the two *phalloi.*—Nâgalatâ; the game of the serpents, nâgas, nâgapadas, nâgapaças.—The caduceus.—Kaçyapas Pragâpatis, father of the birds and of the serpents.—Kumbhakarnas.—The hero dies as soon as he touches the serpent.—The funereal rope of Yamas is a serpent; the collar of Hêphaistos.—The serpents carry Sîtâ on their heads.—The city of Bhogavatî.—The hero becomes an aquatic monster in consequence of a curse.—The serpent released from the fire.—The wisdom of the serpent passes into the hero.—The three-headed serpent.—The serpent sacred in India and in Germany.—The stone of the serpent.—The serpent and the tree.—The tree and the phallos.—The cypress.—The tree, the maiden, and the serpent at the fountain.—The tree of the cross.—The serpent is wholly diabolical in Persian tradition.—The serpent is a mythical animal, both physically and morally amphibious.—The hero, the frog, and the serpent.—The grateful serpent.—Dialogue between two little serpents in a variety of the legend of Lear.—The serpent burnt.—Serpents and worms.—The serpent as the beautiful maiden's husband.—The heads of the serpent.—The serpent of the Black Sea.—The serpent-fairy gives eyes back to the blind woman.—The avenging serpent.—When the serpent is asleep.—The serpent in the garden of the Hesperides.—The serpent-wizard.—The serpent's kiss.—The serpent that whistles.—The wings of the serpent wet; the Vedic myth once more.

THE mythical animal with which I conclude the study of traditional zoology is perhaps the most popular of the whole series. The omniform demon makes the god or hero who falls under his power assume the most diverse zoological forms, the power of transforming into which he holds in possession, of which he holds the secret; but he almost always reserves for himself as his most favourite and privileged form that of the serpent. The devil, says the popular proverb, is known by his tail; and to show that women know more than the devil, it adds that they also know where the devil secretes his tail, or where he keeps his poison, for his poison and power to harm are in his tail. A devil without a tail would not be a real devil; it is his tail which betrays him; and this tail is the serpent's tail.[1] In the forty-fifth story of the fifth book of *Afanassieff*, the devil-serpent comes every night to visit the young widow in the form of her deceased husband, eats with her and sleeps with her till morning; she grows thinner every night, like a candle before the fire; but her mother counsels her to let a spoon drop when she is sitting at table, that, in lifting it, she may scrutinise the guest's feet; instead of his feet, she only sees his tail. Then the widow goes to the church to be

[1] St Augustine, *Hom.* 36, says of the devil: "Leo et draco est; Leo propter impetum, Draco propter insidias;" in Albania, the devil is called *dreikj*, and in Romania, *dracu*.

purified.[1] In the *Eddas*, too, the serpent Lokis, who has taken the form of a horse, betrays himself by his feet.

The serpent-devil appears in special connection with the infernal waters (darkness of night and of winter, and cloudy sky), which conceal treasures, the pearl, the solar hero or heroine with the waters of youth and life. The serpent-devil draws to himself every beautiful thing, now to swallow them, now to preserve and guard them like a miser. The dragon became the symbol of the keeper back of the waters, of the guardian of the treasures, who devours or attracts to himself everything that shines. In Du Cange, the name of *dracus* is given to "species dæmonum qui circa Rhodanum fluvium in Provincia visuntur forma hominis, et in cavernis mansionem habent." In ancient Latin manuscript comments given by the same Du Cange, the devil is called by the name of *hydros* or aquatic serpent. Hincmarus Remensis believes that the devil is evoked from the waters,[2] and according to St Augustine, it was from the waters and from the illusions created in the water by demons that Numa derived his inspirations.[3] Hence the custom, so

[1] A proverb of the *Râmâyaṇam* says, that "only a female serpent can distinguish the feet of a male serpent (v. 38): Ahireva hyaheḥ pâdâu viǵâniyânna saṁçayaḥ). The feet of the serpent, like those of the devil, which is the tail (or the phallos of the male) can be perceived by a female alone; women know where the devil has his tail.

[2] Tom. i., "Sunt qui in aquæ inspectione umbras dæmonum evocant, et imagiones vel ludificationes ibi videre et ab iis aliqua audire se perhibent."

[3] In the seventh book *De Civitate Dei*, the saint writes: "Ipse Numas ad quem nullus Dei propheta, nullus Sanctus Angelus mittebatur, Hydromantiam facere compulsus est, ut in aqua videret imagines deorum vel potius ludificationes dæmonum, a quibus audiret, quid in sacris constituere atque observare deberet quod genus divinationis idem Varro a Persis dicit allatum."

frequent in German and Slavonic countries,[1] of blessing the water to chase the monsters away from it; hence, also, the custom which I have observed in several parts of Russia, where the children, before they bathe in the rivers, and as soon as they put their feet in the water, make profound inclinations and the sign of the cross; hence, according to Du Cange, the god of the waters, Neptunus, in the Middle Ages, becomes under the name of *Aquatiquus,* a personification of the devil;[2] hence, also, the otter (enüdris) assumes a diabolical character in the *Edda,* where the Ases take its skin off and fill it with the gold taken from the dwarf-pike Andvarri, and in the sixth story of the first book of *Afanassieff,* where it destroys the beasts of the menagerie of a Tzar, and finally drags the third son of the Tzar Ivan under an enormous white stone (the snowy winter) in the lower world, where there are palaces of gold and silver and three beautiful girls, sisters of the monster otter, who sleeps in the sea, and snores so that he pushes the waves to a distance of seven versts, until Ivan, after having drunk the water of strength, cuts the monster's head off at a blow, after which it falls into the sea.

But to proceed in the order which we have hitherto generally followed, let us examine before all the tradition of the aquatic monster, the dragon or serpent, in Hindoo mythology.

---

[1] It also exists in Roumania, where the new solar year is celebrated by the benediction of the waters, as if to exorcise the demons that inhabit them.

[2] *Codex Reg.,* 5600 ann. circ. 800, fol. 101, in Du Cange: "Sunt aliqui rustici homines, qui credunt aliquas mulieres, quod vulgum dicitur strias, esse debeant, et ad infantes vel pecora nocere possint, vel dusiolus, vel Aquatiquus, vel geniscus esse debeat." Neptunus, vel aliquis genius, quia quis præest designari videtur.

The most important of the heroic undertakings accomplished by the Vedic god Indras is, as already remarked, that of killing the monster; and the enterprise of Indras against the monster is the theme of all the great popular Indo-Persian, Græco-Latin, Turko-Slavonic, Franco-Germanic, and Franco-Celtic epic poems, as also of the greatest number of the popular stories which are the real epic material of the new epopees. Indras, Vishṇus, Ahura-Mazda, Feridun, Apollo, Hêraklês, Kadmos, Jason, Odin, Sigurd, and several other gods and heroes, are celebrated for the undertaking of killing the serpent. Now, in the Vedic hymns the black monster (kṛishṇas), the growing monster (râuhin),[1] the full-grown monster (piprus), the monster coverer (vṛitras), the monster that dries up (çushṇas), the monster that keeps back (namućis), generally appears with the name and shape of a serpent, or if it has not always the form of a serpent, it is assimilated to it, and certainly inclines to become so from its office of a constrictor, its black colour, and other characteristics which it possesses in common with the serpent (Ahis).[2]

The monster killed by Indras, the monster with the horrid voice which Indras strikes upon the head with a thunderbolt, is, like the serpent, deprived of feet, deprived both of hands and shoulders.[3] But the serpent is also

[1] The monsters which mount into heaven by magical deceits, killed by Indras, are said to creep like serpents: Mâyâbhir utsisṛipsata indra dyâm; *Ṛigv.* viii. 14, 14.

[2] The name of *Arbudas*, given to the monster which Indras, the ram (meshas), crushes (for *ni-kram* seems to me to have this meaning) under his foot while it is lying, is nothing else than a serpent; moreover, he, whose people is the *sarpâs* or serpents, is the king of the serpents. To *arbud-as* I would refer the Latin words *rep-ere, rept-are, reptil-is.*

[3] Apâd ahasto apṛitanyad indram âsya vaǵram adhi sânâu gaghana;

often explicitly named in the *Ṛigvedas* as a monster which keeps back the waters, and which is killed by Indras. The serpent, the first-born of the serpents, was lying in the mountain;[1] he was lying under his mother,[2] he was keeping the waters, his wives, shut up, as a miser his treasure, or a robber the stolen cows;[3] a miser or rich robber[4] resembling a magician, he staid enclosed in a cavern, and kept the waters in it;[5] he lay down and perhaps slept;[6] he lay near the seven torrents;[7] Indras arouses him;[8] in another hymn, however, the serpent, making a loud noise, provokes Indras, and comes against him.[9] When Indras kills the serpent with the thunderbolt, or else crushes it under his foot, or burns it, he opens the torrent of the waters and causes it to flow out

---

Ṛigv. i. 32, 7.—Yo vyaṅsaṁ ǵahṛishâṇena manyunâ yaḥ çambaraṁ yo ahan piprum avratam; i. 101, 2.—Apâdam atram mahatâ vadhena ni duryoṇa âvṛiṇañ mṛidhravâćam; v. 32, 8.

[1] Ahann ahim parvate çiçṛiyâṅam; i. 32, 2.—Ahann enam prathamaǵâm ahînâm; i. 32, 3.

[2] Nîćâvayâ abhavad vṛitraputrendro asyâ ava vadhar ǵabhâra—uttarâ sûr adharaḥ putra âsîd dânuḥ çaye sahavatsâ na dhenuḥ; i. 32, 9. Properly speaking, the verse speaks here of Vṛitras, and not of Ahis; but the coverer and the constrictor being equivalent, it seems to me that there are not here two beings distinguished, in the same hymn, by two analogous appellations.

[3] Dâsapatnîr ahigopâ atishṭhan niruddhâ âpaḥ paṇineva gâvaḥ; i. 32, 11.—The reader will remember the discussion concerning the proverb of shutting the stable after the oxen are stolen, in the first chapter of the first book.

[4] Avâdaho diva â dasyum uććâ; i. 33, 7.

[5] Guhâhitaṁ guhyaṁ gûḷham apsu apîvṛitam mâyinaṁ kshiyantam uto apo dyâm tastabhvâṅsam ahann ahiṁ çura vîryeṇa; ii. 11, 5.

[6] Âçayânam ahim vaǵreṇa maghavan vi vṛiçćaḥ; iv. 17, 7.

[7] Sapta prati pravata âçayânam ahiṁ vaǵreṇa vi riṇâ aparvan; iv. 19, 3.

[8] Sasantaṁ vaǵreṇâbodhayo 'him; i. 103, 7.

[9] Navantam ahiṁ saṁ piṇag ṛiǵîshin; vi. 17, 10.

towards the sea; he makes the sun be born, and finds the cows;[1] he destroys the machinations of the sorcerer, generates the sun, the day, and the dawn, removes every enemy to a distance,[2] makes the serpent's trunk fall to the earth, like a tree cut down by axes, or torn up by the roots,[3] and (as in Russian stories the hero, after having cut the monster's head off, throws his trunk into the sea) over the killed monster, now fallen, the waters which make joyful pass;[4] the gods, who have given Indras three hundred oxen to eat (according to another hymn, only one hundred), and three lakes of ambrosia to drink, that he might be able to vanquish Ahis, are joyful at the victory gained by Indras over the serpent, with their wives and with the birds; not only this, but the women, the wives of the gods, compose on this occasion a hymn to Indras.[5]

We have already seen several times in the course of this work how, by killing his monstrous form, the hero or heroine enclosed in this is set at liberty; the waters, or rainy clouds, which are the monster wives of the demons, as long as the monster keeps them in the

---

1 Sa mâhina indro arṇo apâm prâirayad ahihâćhâ samudram aǵanayat sûryaṁ vidad gâh; ii. 19, 3.—Sṛiǵaḥ sindhûṅr ahinâ ǵagrasânân; *Ṛigv.* iv. 17, 1.—Ahann ahim anv apas tatarda pra vakshaṇâ abhinat parvatânâm; i. 32, 2.

2 Yad indrâhan prathamaǵâm ahînâm ân mâyinâm aminâh prota mâyâḥ—ât sûryaṁ ǵanayan dyâm ushâsaṁ tâdîtnâ çatruṁ na kilâ vivitse; i. 32, 4.

3 Ahan vṛitraṁ vṛitrataraṁ vyaṅsam indro vaǵrena mahatâ vadhena skandḥaṇsîva kuliçenâ vivṛiknâhiḥ çayata upapṛik pṛithivyâḥ; i. 32, 5.—Ud vṛiha rakshaḥ sahamûlam indra vriçća madhyam praty agraṁ çṛinîhi; iii. 30, 17.

4 Çayânam mano ruhânâ ati yanty âpaḥ; i. 32, 8.

5 Anu tvâ patnîr hṛishitaṁ vayaç ća viçve devâso amadann anu tvâ; i. 103, 7.—Asmâ id u gnâç ćid devapatnîr indrâyârkam ahihatya ûvuḥ; i. 61, 8.

darkness, become the radiant wives of the gods when they are released; the same may be said of the aurora, kept in ward by the gloomy or watery monster of night, or of the spring detained in the dreary realm of winter; as long as they are in the power of the black demon, they are black and monstrous, and live with him in the infernal kingdom; when delivered from this kingdom, however, they become beautiful maidens, or princesses of dazzling splendour. When the monster fights with the god or solar hero of the thunderbolt, he arms his women too, and makes use of them as powerful helpers;[1] hence Indras also aims at them and lacerates the black-wombed witches,[2] being afterwards himself condemned to become Sahasrayonis. In popular Âryan tradition, however, it is often the daughter, wife, or sister of the monster that reveals to the hero the way of killing the monster. In Russian stories, one of the ways oftenest recommended to ensure the death of the monster, is to take the egg contained in the duck which is under the tree in the midst of the sea, and crush it upon the monster's forehead, who immediately dies; with the monster's death the two young lovers,—the daughter, wife, or sister of the monster, and the young hero,—marry each other. We have just seen that when Indras has killed the monster serpent, the waters pour out, and the sun ap-

[1] Striyo hi dâsa âyudhâni ćakre; *Ṛigv.* v. 30, 9.

[2] Sa vṛitrahendraḥ kṛishṇayonîḥ puraṁdaro dâsîr âirayad vi; ii. 20, 7.—Vṛitras the killer of Piprus, Indras *puraṁ-daras*, properly, who wounds the full one, who cleaves the full or the swollen one, and hence who wounds, the city, and Indras the lacerator of the witches with the black wombs are equivalent; cfr. what was said concerning the thunderbolt as a phallos, in the first chapter of the first book, where the cuckoo is spoken of, and in the chapter on the Cuckoo in the second book.—In the hymn, i. 32, 9, Indras also wounds underneath the mother of the monster: Indro asyâ ava vadhar ǵabhâra.

pears. In another Vedic hymn we also find the interesting accompaniment of the egg, which reminds us, on the one hand, of the subject of Russian popular stories, and on the other of the belief described by us in the chapter on the Hen, to the effect that the thunderbolt breaks its eggs : Indras, with his strength, breaks the eggs of the monster that dries up the waters, and wins the luminous waters ;[1] crushing the eggs, or wounding the testicles of the gloomy monster, he makes the sun come out of them, and thereupon the monster dies.[2] The symbolical representation of the solar year in the form of a serpent biting his tail is equivalent to the myth of the monster-serpent who dies when his eggs are broken, that is, when the light comes out of its tenebrous envelope.

Inasmuch, moreover, as from the monster serpent, the cloud and the darkness, come forth flashes of lightning, thunder-bolts, sunbeams, tongues of fire, even serpents sometimes assume a divine nature in the Vedic hymns. The

[1] Uto nu ćid ya oǵasâ çushṇasyâṇḍâni bhedati ǵeshat svarvatîr apaḥ ; *Ṛigv.* viii. 40, 10.—In the hymn i. 54, 10, it is said that the cloud-mountain is found amongst the intestines of the coverer ; one might say that the serpent binds the cloud in the form of bowels. The reader will recollect what we observed concerning the intestines, the heart, and the liver, of the sacrificed victim in the first chapter of the first book.

[2] In the twentieth story of the fifth book of *Afanassieff* we find a singular variety, which is of some importance in the history of mythology and language. A princess asks the serpent, her husband, by what his death can be caused. The serpent answers that his death can be brought about by the hero Nikita Kaszemiaka, who, in fact, comes up and kills the serpent by submerging him in the sea. Nikita is called, it is said, Kaszemiaka, because his occupation was that of tearing skins. The torn skins (cfr. here also the *Jupiter Aegiocus*) take here the place of the duck's egg broken upon the serpent, and of the eggs of the monster broken by Indras. In Italian, *coccio*, means a piece of a broken vase, and also, in botany, the skin of a seed ; *incocciarsi* signifies to be angry. In Piedmont, it is said of one who annoys people, that he breaks the boxes, and, more vulgarly, that he breaks the testicles.

Vedic god of fire, Agnis, the born of the waters (napâtam apâm), called Ahir-budhnyas, has already been compared to the Greek *püthôn ophis*, the python. Agnis is also compared to a serpent with a golden mane,[1] which reminds us of the horned monster that dries up, spoken of in another hymn as killed by Indras.[2] Indras himself is called he who has the strength of the serpent.[3] The Marutas have the serpent's anger;[4] and as the Marutas are resplendent with golden attire and ornaments, so the monsters appear adorned with gold and pearls.[5] In the *Âitareya Br.*,[6] the serpent Arbudas has even become a ṛishis, a wise poet, as the python becomes the oracle of wisdom in Greece; and the serpents oppose a Vedas of their own (the Sarpavedas) to the Vedâs of the gods. In the same *Âitareya Br.*,[7] we have the description of a struggle between the gods and a venomous serpent, whose greedy eye gazes at the somas, of which he desires to be possessed. The gods bandage his eyes; the serpent sings a verse in praise of the somas; the gods, as an antidote, sing several verses, and counteract the effect of the serpent's verse. And the witch (âsurî) of the long tongue (Dîrghaǵihvî) is no doubt a serpent, who in the *Âitareya Br.*,[8]

[1] Hiraṇyakeço 'hiḥ; *Ṛigv.* i. 79, 1.

[2] Vi çriñgiṇam abhinaǵ ćhushṇam indraḥ; i. 33, 12.

[3] Ahiçushmasattvâ; v. 33, 5.

[4] Ahimanyavaḥ; i. 64, 9.

[5] Ćakrâṇâsaḥ parîṇaham pṛithivyâ hiraṇyena maṇinâ çumbhamâ-nâḥ; i. 33, 8.

[6] vi. 1, 1.

[7] The passage cited before.

[8] i. 3, 22.—In Russian stories, we frequently find the incident of a serpent, or witch, who endeavours to file, or pierce through, with her tongue the iron doors which enclose the forge in which the pursued hero has taken refuge; he, from within, helped by divine blacksmiths, draws the witch's tongue in with red-hot pincers and causes her death; he then opens the gates of the forge, which represents now the red sky of evening, now the red sky of morning.

again, licks the morning libation of the gods, and makes it inebriating. In the *Râmâyaṇam* it is recorded that the long-tongued witch (Dîrghaǵihvâ), the devourer, is killed by Indras. The struggle between the gods and the serpents for the possession of the ambrosia is the subject of a long episode of the first book of the *Mahâbhâratam*.[1] The serpent loves dampness, water, ambrosia, and rain. When Bhîmas, the son of the wind, is thrown into the waters of the Ganges, he falls into the kingdom of the serpents, who give him the water of strength to drink.[2] In the *Mahâbhâratam*, the mother of the serpents, who have been burned by the sun, invokes the rain to bring them to life again; Indras, to please her, veils the sky with clouds.[3] In the *Râmâyaṇam*, instead of the serpents, the monkeys are resuscitated by means of the rain. The rains of spring also waken the earth, which is in the *Âitareya Br.*[4] called by the name of Sarparaǵnî, and was at first, like the serpents, bald, that is, devoid of vegetation; invoking the heavenly cow, it became covered with trees. In the Hindoo cosmogony, which we described in the chapter on the Tortoise, a very interesting account is given of the way the great stick or phallos, the generator of the world, is made to turn round. The serpent Anantas (the infinite) or Vasukis,[5] who makes the mountain revolve, is twined round it;

[1] i. 792, *et seq.*—Cfr. also the second Esthonian tale, where the young hero, in the kingdom of the serpents, drinks milk in the cup of the king of the serpents himself.

[2] *Mbh.* i. 5008, *et seq.* [3] i. 1283–1295. [4] v. 4, 23.

[5] Cfr. *Râmâyaṇam*, i. 46, and *Mahâbhâratam*, i. 1053, 1150.—In the *Râmâyaṇam* (vi. 26), the arrows of the monsters are said to bind like serpents; the bird Garuḍas appears and the serpents untie themselves, the fetters are loosed; Râmas and Lakshmaṇas, supposed to be dead, rise again stronger than before.

the mountain and the serpent are synonymous;[1] they are two phalloi, which rub each other, and produce the seed (nâgalatâ or climbing serpent, serpent-creeper, is one of the Hindoo names of the phallos; in Piedmont it is said of a man in the venereal act, that he "climbs upon the woman;" and in Sanskṛit nâgas, nâgapadas, nâgapaças, nâgapâçakas, denotes union in the manner of serpents, who apply their bodies to each other in their entire length,[2] in the same way as fire is produced by the friction of two pieces of wood—the araṇî. Anantas, or Vâsukis, and Mandaras, or Kaçapas, and hence Kaçyapas, are identified with one another;) and this is all the more probable as Kaçyapas is also called by the name of Vasukas, and as Kaçyapas himself, in another cosmogonic legend of the *Mahâbhâratam*, appears as having made fruitful two wives, Kadrû, properly the dark one, and Vinatâ,[3] properly the concave, the curved or swollen one

[1] As we have seen that *mandaras* is equivalent to *mantharas*, a name of the tortoise which, according to the cosmogonic legend, sustains the weight of the mountain, or enormous stick which produces the mountain, so Anantas, in another Hindoo legend (cfr. *Mbh.* i. 1587–1588) sustains the weight of the world.—The rod of pearls which when placed in fat enables the young prince to obtain whatever he wishes for, seems to have the same originally phallical meaning as the mandaras; it is the king of the serpents who presents it to the young prince. The fat may, in the mythical sky, be the milk of the morning dawn, or the rain of the cloud, or the snee, or the dew; as soon as the thunderbolt touches the fat of the clouds, or of the snee, or as soon as the sunbeam touches the milk of the dawn, the sun, riches, and fortune come forth.

[2] The *coitus* is also called a game of serpents in the *Tuti-Name.* Preller and Kuhn have already proved the phallical signification of the caduceus (*tripetêlon*) of Hermês, represented now with two wings, now with two serpents. The phallical serpent is the cause of the fall of the first man.

[3] *Vinatâ* is also the name of a disease of women; and, as far as we can judge from the passage of the *Mahâbhâratam* (iii. 14,480), which

(two appellatives by which the *yonis* appears to be equally represented), from one of which is produced the egg from which serpents are hatched, and especially the nâgâs serpents, with human faces, like the devils, and from the other, that which generates Aruṇas and Garuḍas (a form of the Açvinâu). Whilst, in the *Mahâbhâratam*, the serpent Vasukis rubs itself against the Mandaras and makes it turn round, it keeps blowing wind, smoke, and flames out of its mouth, which form clouds, with the water of which the creator gods are afterwards refreshed. Although this last particular shows the serpents intent upon the welfare of the gods, they hold in Hindoo tradition the same place as Anhṛomainyu, or Ahrimanes, in Persian; whilst one phallos gives birth to luminous phenomena and good beings, the other produces gloomy phenomena and wicked beings.

Among the productions of the phallical and serpentine genie of darkness are the clouds. In the *Râmâyaṇam*,[1] the monster Kumbhakarṇas sleeps for sixth months; no number of drums, trumpets, nor any noise is able to awaken him; he is struck with hammers, but feels nothing; elephants pass over him, but he does not move: at last the tinkling of the golden ornaments of beautiful women suffice to rouse him. He rises; his arms resemble two great serpents, and his mouth the mouth of hell. He yawns, and that yawn alone sends forth a wind which resembles a rushing wind that shall usher in the end of the world. The aspect of Kumbhakarṇas when he rises is like that of an immense cloud swelled out with

---

refers to it, it is the malignant genius who destroys the fœtus in the womb of the pregnant mother. He is defined as *çakunigrâhî*, properly the seizer of the bird. Kaçyapas, the universal phallos, the Pragâpatis, certainly unites himself to Vinatâ in the form of a phallos-bird, as to Kadrû in that of a phallos-serpent.

[1] vi. 37–38, 46.

rain towards the end of summer; he is horned like a mountain, and bellows like a thunder-cloud. No sooner is he born, than, inasmuch as by the curse of Brahman he can waken but one day in the year (that is in the autumn), he asks for food, and devours buffaloes, wild boars, men and women; he once swallowed even the ten nymphs, or Apsarasas (the clouds that blow over the waters), of the god Indras; he finds that the world is not provided with animals enough to satiate his hunger. When Kumbhakarṇas moves to battle against the monkeys of Râmas, he draws his enemies to himself to devour them, he draws and receives the shock of whole mountains, but is not shaken. Râmas cuts one of his arms off, and the arm cut off (or the serpent, or the cloud cut off, like the stick of fairy tales which beats of itself) continues to massacre the monkeys. Râmas cuts Kumbhakarṇas's other arm off, which supports with its hand the whole trunk of a robust shorea; but arm and trunk continue to slaughter the enemies on their own account.[1] At last Râmas shoots him in the mouth and heart; the monster falls, and crushes as he falls two thousand monkeys under his immense body. Here, therefore, we again see the monster and the serpent in relation with the clouds and waters. To touch the serpent, that is, the rainy season or the night, is for the solar hero or heroine the same as to die. In the *Mahâbhâratam*[2] the girl Pramadvarâ falls dead to the ground, having inadvertently pressed a serpent with her foot on the way; Rurus brings her to life again by renouncing half of his own life. In this legend the year or the day personifies life; summer sacrifices itself to winter, winter to summer, day to night,

[1] Cfr. for this subject the first and second chapters of the first book.
[2] i. 949, 974.

night to day, the sun to the moon, and the moon to the sun. In the beautiful legend of Savitrî, the wife sacrifices herself and offers herself to Yamas, the god of the dead, in order to be faithful to her husband. In the same *Mahâbhâratam*,[1] the King Parîkshit falls into the power of Takshakas, the king of the serpents, a form of Yamas the god of the dead (also called Anantas), because he had thrown a dead serpent on the shoulders of a Brâhman. In the *Râmâyaṇam*,[2] it is said that a man who has, when asleep, fallen into the hands of the god of the dead, Yamas, is bitten by a venomous serpent. The very rope with which Yamas the god of the dead binds men is a serpent. To the rope-serpent of Yamas we must refer the fatal collar with seven serpents and seven pearls (a symbol of the year, half luminous, half gloomy) which Hephaistos gave to Harmonia and Kadmos on the occasion of their wedding. Kadmos and Harmonia become serpents, and are taken into heaven by the gods. The daughters of Kadmos all come to an unhappy end. The collar is afterwards possessed by Erüphilê, for which reason evils befalls Amphiaraos, and subsequently also Alkmeôn. When Sîtâ,[3] in order to escape from the unjust suspicions of her husband and the perverse evil-speakings of the vulgar, wishes to disappear from the sight of men and to descend under ground, the serpents (pannagâs, who go not with feet) carry her upon their heads (as in Christian tradition the Virgin crushes the head of the serpent-seducer), and from the depths of the earth a voice is heard saying : " Difficult to be acquired is the sight of this woman, who resides in the three worlds ; staying down here, she is honoured by

---

[1] i. 1671, 1980, *et seq.*

[2] iv. 16.

[3] *Râmây.* vii. 104, 105.

the serpents (pûǵyate nâgâiḥ), and, in the world of the mortals, by mankind ; nectar of the higher blessed ones, she is the satiator of the immortals." The kingdom of the nâgâs, or the city of Bhogavatî (an equivocal word, which means both furnished with serpents and furnished with riches), is full of treasures, like the hell of Western tradition. This infernal world went definitively under ground when the gods, having fallen, took humbler forms upon the earth and upon the waters of the earth ; the lower world became the kingdom of the serpents and of the devils of the Vedic cloudy and gloomy heavens (devils and serpents, which Jewish tradition therefore represents with great justice as fallen angels). The riches of heaven, concealed by the cloudy or gloomy monster of night or winter, passed into the earth ; the observation of heavenly phenomena helped this conception. The true mythical treasures are the sun and the moon in their splendour ; when they go down they seem to hide themselves underground ; the solar hero goes underground, he goes to hell, after having lost all his treasures and all his riches ; he undertakes in poverty his infernal journey ; when the sun rises from the mountain, it seems to come out from underground ; the solar hero returns from his journey through hell, he returns resplendent and wealthy ; the infernal demon gives back to him part of the treasures which he possesses, having carried them off from him, or else the young hero recovers them by his valour. But this hell was once the watery, wintry, nocturnal heaven itself, from which now the sun, now the moon emerges ; the hero or the god was obscured or eclipsed, and assumed a gloomy form in the sky itself, and, as we have already said,[1]

[1] Cfr. concerning this subject in particular, the first chapter of the first book, the chapter on the Wolf and that on the Frog.

he who destroys, lacerates, or kills this form, does a service to the poor and cursed wandering Jew who wears it. We are reminded of the aquatic monster, in the *Râmâyaṇam*,[1] by the gandharvas[2] Tumburus, who assumed, under a curse, the form of the monster Virâdhas who carries Sîtâ off from Râmas, with the sole design that Râmas may kill him and deliver him from the malediction, so that he may be able to reascend in happiness to heaven. In a similar manner, Hanumant delivers from her curse the ogress of the lake, the seizer (grâhî) and devourer, who was once a nymph.[3] The body of the old ṛishis Çarabhañgas also gives us the idea of a serpent's body. Çarabhañgas desires to deliver himself from it, as a serpent casts off its old skin. He then enters the fire; the fire burns him; Çarabhañgas, arising from the conflagration, comes forth young, splendid, and as brilliant as fire.[4] In the celebrated episode of Nalas in the *Mahâbhâratam*,[5] the serpent Karkoṭakas, surrounded by the flames, asks Nalas, on the other hand, to deliver him from the flames; the serpent makes himself small in order that Nalas may be able to carry him away; Nalas does so, and the serpent bites him; he then

[1] iii. 8.

[2] Cfr. the discussion concerning the gandharvâs in the chapter on the Ass.

[3] *Râmây.* vi. 82.—This nymph becomes grâhî, because she had once struck a holy Brâhman with her chariot. The same reason is assigned for the malediction which falls upon King Nahushas, who became an enormous serpent; this serpent squeezed the hero Bhîmas in its mortal coils; his brother, Yudhishṭhiras, runs up, and answers in a highly satisfactory manner to the abstruse philosophical questions addressed to him by the serpent, which then releases Bhîmas, casts off its skin, and ascends in the form of Nahushas to heaven; *Mbh.* iii. 12, 356, *et seq.*

[4] *Râmây.* iii. 8.

[5] iii. 2609, *et seq.*

loses his shape, which passes into that of the serpent. In this new diabolical form Nalas becomes invulnerable and invisible. The diverse action taken by fire in legends can be comprehended by reference to the solar hero, now in the morning, now in the evening, now in spring, now in autumn : in the morning and in the spring the serpent of night enters the flames and becomes a handsome youth again ; in the evening and in the autumn the serpent comes out of the flames of the evening aurora, or of the summer, and becomes the moon, after having made the sun disappear, or rendered it invisible or invulnerable. In the forty-seventh story of the sixth book of *Afanassieff*, a hunter (the hunting solar hero) is about to heat the stove ; a serpent is lying in it, and promises, if he will draw it out of the fire, to render him happy, and teach him the language of all animals. He tells the hunter to put the end of his stick into the fire, by which means it will be enabled to make its escape ; the hunter complies, but is warned that he will die himself should he reveal that secret to any one.

The serpent, therefore, is not only monstrous and maleficent in Hindoo tradition, but also at once the learned one, and he who imparts learning ; it sacrifices itself to let the hero carry away the water of life, the water of strength, the health-giving herb or the treasure ; it not only often spares, but it favours the predestined hero ; it destroys individuals, but preserves the species ; it devours nations, but preserves the regenerative kings ; it poisons plants, and throws men into deep sleep, but it gives new strength in its occult domain to the sun, who gives new life to the world every morning and every spring. In the Vedic heavens the serpent is a magician expert in every kind of magic ; in the kingdom of the serpents the young lost hero recovers his splendour, wisdom, and victorious power. Hence the worship in India of the serpent, who is revered as a symbol of every species of learning. We have, on a previous occasion, found the horned or crested serpent who personifies, in the *Ṛigvedas*, fire or the god Agnis, and by this we must understand the crest or mane of the sun, which comes out of the darkness ; thus the god Haris or Vishṇus lies upon a crested serpent or a many-headed serpent. Three-headed serpents or dragons, such as are famous in fairy tales, occur in the *Harivaṅças*,[1] and correspond to the Vedic monster Triçiras, that is, three-headed. The crest of the serpent is the god Vishṇus himself, as a solar deity who comes out of the serpent's body. Hence the hooded-serpent, called Nalla Pâmba in the Malabar,[2] is especially revered in India. " The sudden appearance of one of these serpents," wrote Lazzaro Papi from India, " is considered to presage some future good or evil. It is the divinity himself in this form, or at least his messenger, and the bringer of rewards or chastisement. Although it is exceedingly venomous, it is neither killed, molested, nor crushed in the house which it enters, but respected, and even caressed and adored by the more superstitious. They give it milk to drink, and the accommodation to which it is accustomed ; they construct little huts for it, and prepare receptacles and nests for it under large trees. This reminds me of the ancient inhabitants of Prussia, who nourished several serpents with milk in honour of Patriumpho or Patrimpos, their deity. The family in which one of these serpents takes up its abode esteems itself fortunate and secure from

[1] Triçîrshâ iva nâgapotâs ; 12, 744.

[2] Cfr. Papi, *Lettere sulle Indie Orientali*, Lucca, 1829 ; it is the *cobra de capello* of the Portuguese.

poverty and other misfortunes; and if some one, as it not seldom happens, is bitten by them and dies, the victim of his own credulity, it is, they say, a punishment of God that has overtaken him for some crime." It is nearly the same belief as that which we found in the preceding chapter concerning the toad and the amphisbhæna. In Hungary, as Count Geza Kunn informs me, some fairies are said to be born with a serpent's skin, and to resume their form after this serpent's skin has been shed. It is said that a precious stone can be found under a serpent's tongue. When the serpents warm themselves in the sun of spring, they blow out the stone (or the sun itself), and subsequently conceal it under the tongue of a still larger serpent, the king of the serpents.

The serpent is supposed to protect and preserve the lost riches, and to guard the soul of the dead hero; hence serpents, like crows amongst birds, are revered in India as embodied souls of the dead. In Germany,[1] the white serpent (that is, the snowy winter), according to the popular legend, gives to whoever eats of it (or who is licked by it in the ears) the gift of understanding the language of birds, and of universal knowledge (it is in the night of Christmas, that is, in the midst of the snow, that those who are predestined to see marvels can comprehend, in the stables, the language of the cattle, and, in the woods, the language of the birds; according to the legend, Charles le Gros, in the night of Christmas, saw heaven and hell open, and was able to recognise his forefathers). Thus in Greece, Melampos, Cassandra, and Tiresias became seers by their contact with the

[1] Cfr. Simrock *Deutsche Mythologie*, pp. 478, 513, 514, and Rochholtz *Deutscher Glaube und Brauch*, i. 146.

serpent, symbolised at a later period in the python and the pythoness, as the depositaries of all the oracles of wisdom. In Scandinavian mythology, Odin also assumes the form of a serpent (ormr), and the name of Ofnir, in the same way as Zeus becomes a serpent in Greek mythology when he wishes to create Zagreus, the bull-headed, another Zeus or another Dionüsos. In Rochholtz and Simrock, we find indications of the same worship as that given to the serpent in India, where it is regarded as a good domestic genie. Milk is given to certain domestic little snakes to drink; they are put to watch over little children in their cradles, with whom they divide their food; they bring good luck to the children near which they stay; it is therefore considered a fatal sacrilege to kill them. It is fabled, moreover, that a serpent is sometimes born with a child entwined round its neck, and that it and the child are thenceforth inseparable (an image of the year and of the day, half luminous and half tenebrous, inseparable the one from the other). It guards the cattle in the stables, and procures for good and beautiful maidens husbands worthy of them. According to a popular legend, two serpents are found in every house (a male and a female), which only appear when they announce the death of the master and mistress of the house; when these die, the snakes also cease to live. To kill one of these serpents is to kill the head of the family. Under this aspect, as a protector of children, as a giver of husbands to girls, and identified with the head or progenitor of the family, the serpent is again a phallical form. From the gloomy serpent of night, the tenebrous serpent of winter, even the nocturnal and wintry heavens illumined by the moon, and from the white moon, emerges the diurnal sun, the sun of spring, the day and the warm and luminous season. The ogre, dragon, or serpent keeps back the waters in the cloud and the waters in the rivers, occupies the fountains, lies at the roots of the tree which yields honey, of the ambrosial tree, of the tree in the midst of the lake of milk; the tree and the phallos are again identified. The Phrygian Attis, loved by Cybele, is deprived of his phallos, and expires; Cybele transforms him into a pine tree (which is cone-bearing and evergreen, which resists, like the moon, even the rigours of winter), in which the funereal and regeneratory phallos is personified; the cypress (cone-bearing and evergreen), which the three brothers of the fairy tales must watch during the night, and which only the youngest brother succeeds in delivering from the dragon or serpent which carries it away, is also represented in Persian tradition as in the middle of a lake of ambrosia. The serpent steals this tree, as in the Hindoo myth it steals the ambrosia from the gods; it knows well that in it consists the regeneratory strength of the hero, whom the serpent has bitten; sometimes it steals the tree from him, and sometimes guards over it. Out of the golden apple, or out of the orange of the tree guarded by the dragon, in popular tales, the beautiful maiden comes; the dragon keeps her back a second time on the way, making her mount upon a tree, or throwing her into the fountain, near which the beautiful maiden becomes a dark fish or a dark bird (a swallow or a dove), in order to come out again from the fish or the bird in the form of a beautiful girl. The love of the young princess for the young hero, in Russian stories, comes out of the duck's egg taken under the tree, and the death of the serpent-dragon is caused by it. Here the gloomy monster of the night and winter, the monster serpent, appears, in guardianship of the moon, the protectress of marriages, as an ambrosial and evergreen tree, and, like the cypress, a funereal tree, which is at the same time symbolical of immortality. From the moon of winter and of night, the solar hero of spring and the day, the maiden spring and the maiden aurora come forth. The serpent, like the toad, the frog, the fish, and the bird, now desires the moon of winter and of night for itself, and now presents it to the young hero, whom it protects. The moon appears when the diurnal sun goes down in the west; hence the garden of the Hesperides, as the word denotes, was supposed to be situated in the west; the moon rules the northern heavenly region, the cold season of the year; for this reason Apollodorus placed this same garden of the Hesperides in the north, amongst the Hyperboreans, where the tree of oblivion also grew according to Ælianos. In India, the ambrosial tree, the tree of immortality, the tree of Brahman's paradise, like the moon and Çivas (the god of paradise and of hell, the phallical and destroying god), was also placed in the north, on Mount Merus, the phallical and primeval mountain, near the sea of oblivion, guarded by a dragon; but because the dragon or serpent represents evil oftener than good, because Çivas, the moon, and the cypress, have a double aspect, phallical and funereal, paradisiacal and infernal, because Kaçyapas, the great primitive phallos, created opposite things in the form of a bird and in that of a serpent, two trees are also represented upon Mount Merus, one of good and one of evil, one of life and one of death, which reminds us of the Jewish and Mahometan traditions. The legends concerning the tree of the golden apples or figs, which yields honey or ambrosia, guarded by dragons, in which the life, the fortune, the glory, the strength, and the riches of the hero have their beginning, are numerous among every people of Âryan origin; in India and in Persia, in Russia and in Poland, in Sweden and in Germany, in Greece and in Italy, popular myths, poems, songs, and fairy tales amplify with a great variety of incidents, partly unconscious of their primitive signification, this strange subject of phallical cosmogony.[1]

[1] Cfr. again the legend of Adam and Eve, of the tree and the serpent, and the original sin. In the mediæval comedy *La Sibila del Oriente*, Adam when dying says to his son, "Mira en cima de mi sepulcro, que un arbol nace." In Russian stories the young hero will be fortunate, now because he watched at his father's tomb, now because he defended the paternal cypress from the demon who wished to carry it off. In the legend of the wood of the cross, according to a sermon of Hermann von Fristlar (cfr. Mussafia, *Sulla Leggenda del legno della Croce*), the tree upon the wood of which, made into a cross, Christ died, is said to have been a cypress. The same mediæval legend describes the terrestrial paradise whence Adam was expelled, and where Seth repairs to obtain for Adam the oil of pity. The tree rises up to heaven, and its root goes down to hell, where Seth sees the soul of his brother Abel. On the summit there is a child, the Son of God, the promised oil. The angel gives to Seth three grains which he is to put into Adam's mouth; three sprouts spring up which remain an arm's-length in height till the time of Moses, who converts them into miraculous rods, and replants them before his death; David finds them again, and performs miracles with them. The three sprouts become one plant which grows proudly into a tree. Solomon wishes to build the temple with this wood; the workmen cannot make use of it; he then has it carried into the temple; a sybil tries to sit upon it, and her clothes take fire; she cries out, "Jesus, God and my Lord," and prophesies that the Son of God will be hanged upon that wood. She is condemned to death, and the wood thrown into a fish-pond, which acquires thaumaturgic virtue; the wood comes out and they wish to make a bridge of it; the Queen of the East, Saba, refuses to pass over it, having a presentiment that Jesus will die upon that wood. Abia has the wood buried, and a fish-pond appears over it.—Now, this is what an author, unsuspected of heresy, writes concerning the symbol of the serpent (Martigny, *Dictionnaire des Antiquités Chrétiennes*): "Les ophites, suivant en cela les nicolaïtes et les premiers gnostiques, rendirent au serpent lui-même un culte direct d'adoration, et les manichéens le mirent aussi à la place de Jésus Christ (S. Augustin. *De Hæres.* cap. xvii. et xlvi.) Et nous devons regarder comme ex-

The Persian cosmogony is of a less material character than the Hindoo, but its principle is the same. Ahuramazda and Anhromainyu, who occupy the first place as the creators of the world, are also two males in opposition to one another. From Ahuramazda descends Thrætaona or Feridun, the killer of the serpent (azhi) Dahâka, or Dahak, or Zohak, the three-headed dragon which Anhromainyu created to destroy the beautiful in the world, as the strongest of monsters.[1] In Hindoo tradition we find the bird Garuḍas on the side of the gods, and the Nâgas or serpent on that of the demons; so, in Persian tradition, the bird Simurg is on the side of the gods, and the serpent or sea-monster on that of the demons. It is in the midst of the waters that the hero Kereçâçpa finds the great serpent Çruvara, who devours men and horses, and who ejects a venom as large as a man's thumb. Taking him probably for an island,[2] he has food cooked

trêmement probable que les talismans et les amulettes avec la figure du serpent qui sont arrivés jusqu' à nous, proviennent des hérétiques de la race de Basilide, et non pas des païens, comme on le suppose communément." To the continuers of the admirable studies of Strauss and Renan will be reserved the office of seeking the sense hidden in this myth, made poetical by the evangelical morals. When we shall be able to bring into Semitic studies the same liberty of scientific criticism which is conceded to Âryan studies, we shall have a Semitic mythology; for the present, faith, a natural sense of repugnance to abandon the beloved superstitions of our credulous childhood, and more than all, a less honourable sentiment of terror for the opinion of the world, have restrained men of study from examining Jewish history and tradition with entire impartiality and severity of judgment. We do not wish to appear Voltairians, and we prefer to shut our eyes not to see, and our ears not to hear what history, studied critically and positively, presents to us less agreeable to our pride as men, and to our vanity as Christians.

[1] Cfr. *Yaçna*, ix. 25–27; cfr. also Prof. Spiegel's introduction to the *Khorda Avesta*, pp. 59, 60.

[2] Cfr. the chapter concerning the Fishes and that on the Tortoise.

upon it; the serpent feels the heat, and begins to move; it then throws Kereçâçpa, the courageous Kereçâçpa, over backwards. There seems to be some analogy between this myth of the Yaçna of the *Avesta* and the story of the fearless hero of the Russian story, who, being asleep in a boat, falls into the river when terrified by the little fish which had jumped upon him. (The serpent appears also as the enemy of fire in the *Khorda-Avesta.*)[1] The serpent causes the diseases which Thrætaona is requested to cure; it poisons whatever it sees and touches; and, according to the *Khorda-Avesta,*[2] the wicked are condemned to feed upon poison after death. In the *Shah-Name* the sun disappears, devoured by a sea-monster or crocodile. In the third adventure of Isfendiar, the hero is almost inebriated by the venomous smoke and the pestilential breath of the dragon which he has victoriously combated; and, after having won, he falls to the ground as if dead; thus Indras, after having defeated the monstrous serpent, flees in terror over the rivers, like a madman attacked by hydrophobia, terrified by the shadow, the smoke, or the water of the dead serpent, because this shadow, which is perhaps his own, and not his enemy's, menaces to submerge him in those poisoned waves, and to transform him into a sea-monster, assimilating him thus to his enemy; inasmuch as the god sends to make man like himself, so also does the demon. In Persia, therefore, the serpent is generally considered as a demoniacal and monstrous animal, the personification of evil. If it is prayed to, it is to conjure it away, to induce it to go far distant, as the Arabs and the Tatars particularly do to expel the devil. The Persian genius has

[1] Cfr. Prof. Spiegel's introduction to the *Khorda-Avesta*, p. 60.
[2] xxxviii. 36.

not the mobility, the plasticity, and elasticity of the Hindoo; its mythical images are more severe and less multiform; hence the serpent remained in Persian tradition the demoniacal animal *par excellence*. In the *Tuti-Name*, on the contrary, which is of Hindoo origin, the serpent has a double aspect. The serpent wishes to eat the frog. (In the fifteenth story of the third book of the *Pańćatantram*, the frogs ride upon the serpent, and leap upon it in delight, like Phædrus's frogs upon King Log, which was sent to them in derision by Jove; the serpent and the rod are assimilated.) The hero saves the frog, upon which the serpent reproves him, because he thus takes its food from it; the hero then cuts off some of his own flesh to give it to the serpent;[1] the serpent protects the hero ever afterwards, and cures with an ointment the king's daughter, who had been bitten by another serpent; the king gives his daughter, on her recovery, to the hero who had satisfied the serpent's hunger. In the tenth story of the third book of the *Pańćatantram*, two little serpents, who talk to each other, both work their own ruin and make the fortune of the hero and of the heroine. A king's son has a serpent in his body without knowing

[1] A variety of the Hindoo legend of the hawk (Indras), of the dove (Agnis), and of King Çivis, who, to save the dove from the hawk, his guest, gives some of his own flesh to the hawk to eat. Here the serpent is identified with the hawk or eagle; in the Mongol story, however, the dragon is grateful to the man who delivered him from the bird Garuḍas; the king of the dragons keeps guard over the white pearls, arrives upon a white horse, dressed in white (probably the snow of winter, or the moon); the king of the dragons rewards the hero by giving him a red bitch, some fat, and a string of pearls.—In the sixth story of the *Pańćatantram*, we have the serpent and the crow, one at the foot of a tree, the other on the summit; the serpent eats the crow's eggs, and the crow avenges itself by stealing a golden necklace from the queen and throwing it into the snake's hole; the men go to seek the necklace, find the serpent and kill it.

it, and becomes ill; he abandons in despair his father's palace, and goes begging; he is given, in contempt, the second daughter of another king to wife, who had never said amiable things to her father, like her eldest sister (a variation of the legend of Cordelia and Lear); whilst one day the young prince has fallen asleep with his head upon an ant-hill, the little serpent which is in his body puts out its head to breathe a little fresh air, and sees another serpent coming out of the ant-hill;[1] the two little serpents begin to dispute and call each other names; one accuses the other of tormenting the young prince by inhabiting his body, and the accused responds by charging it with hiding two jars full of gold under the ant-hill.[2] Continuing their quarrel, one says how easy it would be to kill the other; a little mustard would suffice to settle the first, and a little hot oil the second (the serpent is killed by being burned; the rich uhlan-serpent of the Russian story is burned in the trunk of an oak-tree, in which it had taken refuge out of fear for the fire and the lightning); the hidden wife listens to everything, delivers her husband from the little serpent in his body, and kills the other serpent to take out the treasure which it keeps hidden.[3] In the fourteenth of the stories of Santo

[1] We have seen in the chapter on the Ant how the ants make serpents come out of their holes; in Bavaria, according to Baron Reinsberg von Düringsfeld, the work quoted before, p. 259, an asp (*natter*) taken in August must be shut well up in a vase in order that it may die of heat and of hunger; then it is placed upon an ants' nest, that the ants may eat all its flesh; of what remains, a sort of pater-noster is made, which is supposed to be very useful against all kinds of eruptions upon the head.

[2] Cfr. the interminable riches of the uhlan-serpent in the story vi. 11, of *Afanassieff*.

[3] Here we have a serpent which expels and ruins another. In a similar manner, before the times of San Carlo Borromeo, a bronze serpent, which had been carried from Constantinople by the Arch-

Stefano di Calcinaia, the third of the young daughters, in order to save her father from certain death, consents to marry the serpent, who carries her upon his tail to his palace, where he becomes a handsome man called Sor Fiorante, of the red and white stockings. But she must reveal the secret to no one. The maiden (as in the fable of Cupid and Psyche) does not resist the temptation of speaking of it to her sisters, on which her husband disappears; she finds him again after having filled seven flasks with her tears; breaking first a walnut, then a hazel-nut, and finally an almond, of which each contains a magnificent robe, she recovers her husband, and is recognised by him.[1] In a variety of the same story in my

bishop Arnolfo in the year 1001, was revered in the basilica of St Ambrose at Milan; some said that it was the serpent of Æsculapius, others that of Moses, others that it was an image of Christ; for us it is enough to remark here that it was a mythical serpent, before which Milanese mothers brought their children when they suffered from worms, in order to relieve them, as we learn from the depositions of the visit of San Carlo to this basilica: "Est quædam superstitio de ibi mulierum pro infantibus morbo verminum laborantibus." San Carlo put down this superstition.

[1] These marvels are always three, as the apples are three, the beautiful girls three, the enchanted palaces in the kingdom of the serpents which they inhabit three (cfr. *Afanassieff*, i. 5). The heads of the dragon are in this story and generally three, but sometimes also five, six (cfr. *Afanassieff*, v. 28), seven (cfr. *Pentamerone*, i. 7, and *Afanassieff*, ii. 27; the serpent of the seven heads emits foul exhalations), nine (iii. 2, v. 24), or twelve (cfr. *Afanassieff*, ii. 30).—In the twenty-first story of the second book of *Afanassieff*, first the serpent with three heads appears, then that with six, then that with nine heads which throw out water and threaten to inundate the kingdom. Ivan Tzarević exterminates them. In the twenty-second story of the same book the serpent of the Black Sea, with wings of fire, flies into the Tzar's garden and carries off the three daughters; the first is obtained and shut up by the five-headed serpent, the second by the seven-headed one, and the third by the serpent with twelve heads; the young hero Frolka Sidieu kills the three serpents and liberates the three daughters.

little collection, a good serpent fairy advises the blind princess, and gives her the hazel-nut, the almond, and the walnut; each of the three gifts contains a marvel; by means of the first marvel the young princess regains one eye from the false wife; by means of the second marvel, the other eye, which the serpent puts in its place;[1] and by means of the third, which is a golden hen with forty-four golden chickens (perhaps forty-four stands for forty times four, or a hundred and sixty, which might represent the luminous and warm days of the year, from the first of April to the end of August), she finds her lost husband again. In an unpublished Sicilian story communicated to me by Dr Ferraro, a serpent presses the neck of King Moharta to avenge a beautiful girl whom the king had forsaken, after having violated her; in order to release himself from the serpent, the king is compelled to marry the beautiful girl whom he had betrayed. In the sixteenth of the Tuscan stories published by me, the three sons of the king go to get the water which jumps and dances, and which is guarded by a dragon who devours as many as approach it; the dragon sleeps from twelve to two o'clock, and sleeps with its eyes open, which signifies, if we interpret twelve o'clock as twelve o'clock of the day, that the dragon is asleep when the sun watches, and if, on the contrary, as twelve o'clock at night, that it sleeps when the moon, compared to the hare which sleeps with its eyes open, shines in the sky.[2] In an ancient Neapolitan vase ex-

[1] Cfr. also, for the legend of the blind woman, the first chapter of the first book.

[2] When the mythical serpent refers to the year, the hours correspond to the months, and the months during which the mythical serpent sleeps seem to be those of summer, in contradiction to what is observed in nature.

plained by Gerhard and Panofka, we find a tree and a fountain, a serpent (the same as that which gnaws at the roots of the tree Yggdrasill in the *Eddas*), three Hesperides, and Hêraklês. One Hesperis is giving the wounded serpent some beverage in a cup, the second is plucking an apple, the third is about to pluck one, and Hêraklês has also an apple in his hand. The myth and the story of the ogre and the three oranges correspond perfectly to one another.[1] The maiden was at first identified with the serpent, as the daughter of the dragon, and as a female serpent; she lays aside her disguise on the approach of the young hero, and recovers all her splendour. In an unpublished story of the Monferrato, communicated to me by Dr Ferraro, a beautiful girl, when plucking up a cabbage (a lunar image), sees under its roots a large room, goes down into it, and finds a serpent there, who promises to make her fortune if she will kiss him and sleep with him; the girl consents. After three months, the serpent begins to assume the legs of a man, then a man's body, and finally the face of a handsome youth, the son of a king, and marries his young deliverer. In popular tradition, we also have the con-

[1] In the fifth story of the second book of the *Pentamerone*, a serpent has itself adopted, as their son, by a man and woman who have no children, and then asks for the king's daughter to wife; the king, who thinks to turn the serpent into ridicule, answers that he will consent when the serpent has made all the fruit-trees of the royal garden become golden, the soil of the same garden turn into precious stones, and his whole palace into a pile of gold. The serpent sows kernels of fruits and egg-shells in the garden; from the first, the required trees spring up; from the second, the pavement of precious stones; he then anoints the palace with a certain herb, and it turns to gold. The serpent comes to take his wife in a golden chariot, drawn by four golden elephants, lays aside his serpent's disguise, and becomes a handsome youth.

trary form of the same myth, that is, the beautiful maiden who becomes a serpent again. In a German legend,[1] the young hero hopes to deliver the beautiful maiden by three kisses:[2] the first time he kisses her as a beautiful girl; the second time as a monster, half woman half serpent; the third time he refuses to kiss her, because she has become entirely a serpent.

When the day or the summer dies, the mythical serpent shows himself (in absolute contradiction to what we are taught by Natural History, one would almost say that when the serpent ceases to creep along the ground and to devour the animals of the earth, it goes to creep and to devour the animals of the sky); then the north winds begin to whistle,—and the serpent, particularly the mythical serpent, is a famous whistler. Isidorus[3] even identifies the basilisk and the serpent, called a *regulus* with the whistle itself: "Sibilus idem est qui et Regulus: sibilo enim occidit antequam mordeat vel exurat." In the twenty-fifth story of the fifth book of *Afanassieff*, the gipsy and the serpent challenge one another to see who will whistle loudest. When the serpent whistles or hisses (that is, in autumn) all the trees lose their leaves. The gipsy defeats the serpent by a cheat; he makes it believe that it will be unable to resist the effects of his whistle if it does not cover its head, and then beats it without pity, so that the serpent is convinced of the gipsy's superiority, and says that it reveres him as its elder brother.[4] I cited in the first chapter of the first

[1] Cfr. Mone, *Anzeig.* iii. 88.

[2] Cfr. on this subject the stories recorded in the first and second chapters of the first book.

[3] *Origines*, xiv. 4.

[4] Cfr. the same, *Afanassieff*, vi. 10, where the cunning workman, in reward for having vanquished the little devil in whistling, and for having made it believe that he could throw a stick upon the clouds, obtains the money which can remain in a hat which never fills.

book the Russian story of Alexin the son of the priest, or the divine Alexin, who fights against Tugarin, the son of the serpent, or the demon-serpent, and begs the Virgin to bathe the monster's wings with the rain of the black cloud : the monster's wings being heavy with water, force it to fall to the ground. Here we return again to the simple yet grandiose Vedic myth, the most remote of all, from which we started ; we return to lyrical poetry, inspired, spontaneous, ingenuous, full of agreeable or fearful surprises, of naïve enthusiasms, of creative impulses, the unconscious originator of a new civilisation and a new faith, as yet undefiled with phallical cosmogonies, as yet unruptured and unimpoverished by the sterile dreams of eunuch-like metaphysics.

CONCLUSION.

> "E come quei che con lena affannata
> Uscito fuor del pelago a la riva
> Si volge all 'onda perigliosa e guata,
> Cosi l'animo mio che ancor fuggiva
> Si volse indietro a rimirar . . ."

and the shadows of the mythological monsters rise again before me, and occupy my fearful thoughts. During these months of my solitary sojourn on Olympus, have I only been the victim of a horrible nightmare, or have I apprehended aright the reality of the changeful figures of the sky in their animal forms? The ancient mythology, which used to be taught to us at school, was filled with the incests of Jove, of Mars, and of Venus; but they were classical myths, and the adulterers were called gods; and our good fathers, in the vain search for symbolical meanings, tortured their ingenious brains to extract from each scandal of Olympus a moral lesson for the instruction of youth. Hence it was permitted to art to represent Jove as a bull, an eagle, a swan, a seducer in an animal form, without offending decency or violating the sanctity of the schools; and the young scholars were encouraged to write their rhetorical exercises in Italian or Latin verse upon the favourite themes of classical mythology, inasmuch as with symbols and moral allegories the vile matter could all be made divine. Platonic or metaphysical love not requiring the vehicles of sense to communicate itself, the animal forms of the god were for our old masters nothing else than symbols and allegories, conceived and intended to veil an elevated educational wisdom. But we have rocked ourselves long enough in the cradle of this infantile fantasy, and must now discard from this and kindred themes all such idle dreams. It is at last necessary to summon up the courage to front the problems of history with the same frankness and ardour with which naturalists approach the mysteries of Nature, and pierce the veil; nor is this attempt so hazardous, since, in order to demonstrate entirely our historical theses, we have certain and positive data provided for us in speech and in legend by comparative oral and written tradition. We do not invent; we simply accumulate, and then put in order the facts relating to the common history of popular thought and sentiment in our privileged race. The difficulty consists only in classifying the facts; the facts themselves are many and evident. It is very possible to be deceived in their arrangement, and hence also in their minute interpretation; and I am, for my part, not without apprehension that I may have here and there made an unlucky venture in interpreting some particular myths; but if this may, in some degree, reflect discredit on my intelligence, which is perhaps imperfectly armed, and without sufficient penetration, this can in nowise prejudice the fundamental truths which permit comparative mythology to constitute and install itself as a positive science, that may henceforth, like every science, instruct and edify with profit. The principal error into which the students of the new science are apt to fall, and into which I may myself have sometimes been betrayed in the course of this work, is that of confining their observations to one special favourite mythical point or moment, and referring almost every myth to it, and not taking sufficient account of their mobility and their separate history, that is, of the various periods of their manifestation. One sees in the myth only the sun, another only the moon in its several revolutions, and their amours with the verdant and resplendent earth; one sees the darkness of night in opposition to the light of day, another the same light in opposition to the gloomy cloud; one the loves of the sun with the moon, another those of the sun with the aurora. These diverse, special, and too exclusive points of view, from which the myths have hitherto been generally studied by learned men, have afforded ill-disposed adversaries an opportunity of ridiculing the science of Comparative Mythology as a science which is little serious, and which changes its nature according to the student who occupies himself with it. But this opposition is disarmed by its own weapons. For what does the concord of all learned men and scholars in this department prove? It proves, in my opinion, but one thing, and that is, the reproduction and confirmation of the same natural myths under multiplex forms, the representation by analogous myths of analogous phenomena, and that the variations met with in fairy tales are also found in myths. The sun chases away the darkness in the day, the moon the darkness in the night; both are called haris, or fairhaired, golden, luminous. Indras is haris; as haris, he is now in relation with the sun that thunders in the cloud (Jupiter Tonans), now with the ambrosial moon which attracts rain (Jupiter Pluvius); Zeus gives up the field to his son Dionüsos, and, be it as the sun, be it as the moon, he is always Zeus the refulgent one, Diespiter or the father of light; in the first case, he pierces through the cloud, and in the second through the darkness. Even when the moon or the sun is hidden, when Zeus or Dionüsos lives in his august mystery, they prepare new luminous phenomena. Thus Vishṇus is haris, and as haris he is identified now with the sun, now with the moon; or, to speak with more precision, the sun haris and the moon haris are confounded in one sole mythical personage, in one god, who represents them both in various moments, that is to say, in Vishṇus. It is desirable that the entirety of the myths should be studied with full comprehension of the whole field which the myth may have enriched, and of the whole period in which the myth may have been developed; but this does not prevent, in special studies, a learned man from addressing himself (as Professors Kuhn, Müller, and Bréal have done) to one special point to prove one special mythological thesis. To this point he applies his lever; he might, perhaps, use it somewhere else; but this causes no prejudice to the essential truth, by bringing his demonstrations to the highest degree of clearness in one point alone. The excess of demonstration can easily be corrected, and meanwhile from these special studies, in which investigation becomes every day more profound, the myths come out in brighter colours. It would be an exaggeration to ascribe to all the myths one unvaried manner of formation, as also to think absolutely that all myths began by a simple confusion of words. Equivocalness, no doubt, played a principal part in the formation of myths; but this same equivocalness would not always have been possible without the pre-existence, so to speak, of pictorial analogies. The child who even now, gazing on the sky, takes a white cloud for a mountain of snow, certainly does not yet know that *parvatas* meant both cloud and mountain in the Vedic language; he continues, however, to elaborate his elementary myth by means of simple analogies of images. The equivoque of words usually succeeded to the analogy of external figures as they appeared to primitive man. He had not yet named the cloud as a mountain, and yet he already saw it. When the confusion of images took place, that of words became almost inevitable, and only served to determine it, to give it in the external sound a more consistent form, to manifest it more artistically, and to constitute it into a sort of trunk upon which, with the help of new particular observations, of new images, and of new equivoques, an entire tree of mythical genealogies was to sprout out.

It has fallen to me to study the least elevated department of mythology. In the primitive man, who created the myths, the same twofold tendency shows itself which we observe in ourselves—the instinct by which we are allied to the brutes, and the instinct which lifts us to the comprehension and sentiment of the divine or the ideal. The ideal was the portion of few; material instinct that of many: the ideal was the promise of human progress; material instinct represented that inert resisting matter which still acts in opposition to progress. Hence images full of elevated poesy by the side of others, vulgar and gross, which remind us of the relation of man to that petulant and lascivious brute from which it is supposed that he descends. The god who becomes a brute cannot preserve always intact his divinity; the animal form is that of his *avatâras* or of his decadence, of his fall; it is usually the form assumed by the god or the hero in consequence of a curse or a crime. The Hindoo and the Pythagorean beliefs considered the disguise of the animal as the purgatory of a guilty man. And the god-beast, the hero-beast, the man-beast cannot restrain themselves from brutish acts. The proud and ferocious King Viçvâmitras, the Indian Nebuchadnezzar, when he wanders through the forest in the form of a monster, takes the nature of the forest-rakshasas, the devourer; the beautiful celestial nymphs become sea-monsters, devour the heroes who approach their fountain. Only when the animal form is killed, when the matter is shaken off, does the god or hero assume his divine goodness, beauty, and excellence. Here mythology is not in contradiction to physiology; the character of the mythical personages is the result of their corporeal forms, of their organism, until the natural destiny changes, and a new physical transformation taking place in the species, even its moral characteristics are modified; light is good, darkness is evil, or good only inasmuch as it is supposed to enclose light in its body. From the dark wood rubbed and shaken, from the dark stone struck and dilated, comes forth the spark which causes conflagrations; from the body when exercised and made agile comes forth the splendour of look, of speech, of affection, of thought; the god breaks forth. Substance is dark, but when it is agitated it produces light; as long as it is inert, it is evil, and it is still evil as long as it attracts to itself, as if to a centre of gravity, everything that lives. In as far as the monster swallows beautiful things, it is evil; in as far as it lets them radiate and go forth, it is good. Disperse the cloud, disperse the darkness, dilate and expand the matter which tends to grow narrow and to become inert, to absorb life, and the divine light will come out of it, the splendid intelligent life will appear; the fallen hero, the hero turned to stone, who has become inert substance, will ascend again, agile and refulgent, into the divine heavens.

Certainly, I am far from believing that this was the intention of the myth. Morals have often been an appendix of fables, but they never enter into the primitive fable itself.

The elementary myth is a spontaneous production of imagination, and not of reflection. When the myth exists, art and religion may make use of it as an allegory for their æsthetic and moral ends; but the myth itself is devoid of moral conscience; the myth shows, as I have said, only more or less elevated instincts. And if I have sought to compare several physiological laws with the myths, it is not because I attribute to the myth a wisdom greater than that which it contains in reality, but only to indicate that, much better than metaphysics, the science of nature, with the criteria of positive philosophy, can help us to study the original production of myths and their successive development in tradition. I have had to prove in mythology its most humble aspect, that is to say, the god enclosed in the animal; and inasmuch as amongst the various mythical animals which I have endeavoured to describe, several preserve the propitious character and resplendent form of the god, they are generally considered as the form which the deity assumes either to feed secretly upon the forbidden fruit or to fulfil a term of punishment for some former fault of his; in any case, these forms never serve to give us a superlative idea of the divine excellence and perfection. Instead of ascribing to the god all the attributes of beauty, goodness, and strength at once, instead of associating in one all the gods, or all the sympathic forces and figures of Nature, a new divine form was created for each attribute. And because the primitive man was not so much inclined to make abstractions as comparisons (to represent strength, for instance, he had recourse to the image of the bull, the lion, or the tiger; to represent goodness, he figured it in the lamb, the dog, or the dove; to represent beauty, he chose the gazelle, the stag, the peacock, and so on), in the primitive speech of mankind no conjunctions existed by means of which to unite the two terms of a comparison: hence a strong king became the lion, a faithful friend the dog, an agile girl the gazelle, and so on. We sometimes hear our women, in their moments of tenderness for a distant person, or in their impatience to go where their heart calls them, or in their curiosity to know what is going on at such a moment in such a place, say, "I wish I could become a bird to go there." In reality they envy only the bird's wings, in order to fly, to arrive there sooner, and for this desire alone they would renounce all the precious privileges which distinguish them as women. The same sacrifice of their own luminous forms to obtain some determinate end happens in the mythical sky. The god humbles himself in order to make use of some quality which he needs to manifest especially. Thus Indras, to put the generosity of King Çivis to the proof, finds it necessary to follow, in the shape of a hawk, the god Agnis, who had become a dove, and taken refuge with the king. Primitive man does not ascribe to the god any other form than those which he sees round him, and which he knows: the god cannot have wings of his own, divine wings; he must become a bird in order to be winged. Thus, to draw a chariot, or to carry a hero through the air, he must become a hippogriff, that is, horse and bird; and when he falls into the sea, he must enter a fish's body to escape drowning.

The god can therefore exercise his divine power only on the condition of entering into the forms of those animals which are supposed to have the privilege of the qualities which the god is in need of in a special mythical occurrence. But in this animal form in which the god displays in a transcendent manner some particular quality, he dims at the same time a great part of his divine splendour. Having, therefore, surprised the deity in this strange and unlucky moment, the reader will not, I hope, impute to me the poor figure which the deity has had to make in many pages of this work ; nor will he think evil of me if I have deprived him, perchance, of some illusion in compensation for some imperfect, but perhaps not useless revelation.

INDEX.

(*This Index is compiled at the instance of the Publisher, and is not by the Author.*)

ABSALOM and his hair, i. 334.
Achilleus, horses of, i. 351.
Acheloos, horn of, i. 266.
Açvinâu, the, i. 18, 19; friendship for Tritas, 25; awakening of, 27; and the aurora, 30; eyes to the blind, feet to the lame, 32, 36; and Kabandhas, 63; the sons of, 78; as the two ears of Vishnus, 81; 285-287, 300-302, 304, 306-308, 310, 315, 319, 321, 327, 370; ass of, 371.
Adam and Eve, legend of, ii. 411.
Aditis and the cow, in Vedic literature, i. 5, 6; 23, 70, 74.
Adonis, ii. 14-16.
Adrikâ, the nymph-fish, ii. 331; son and daughter of, 332.
Æschylos, fabled death of, ii. 197.
Æsculapius, i. 353.
Afrasiab, i. 114, 116, 117.
Agas and synonyms, i. 402.
Agnis, as the fire-god, 10; adjutant to Indras, 13; 299, 301.
Agnus Dei, sacrifice of the, i. 423.
Ahalyâ, legend of, i. 414.
Ahura Mazda, i. 97, 109.
Aiêtas, bulls of, i. 267.
Ai-Kan, story of, i. 146.
Alexander the Great, i. 119; and augury, ii. 178; and the fish, 333; and the crab, 355.
Allwis, the dwarf, i. 207, 225, 260, 261.
Amalthea, i. 430.
Amazons, the, i. 211, 212.
Ambrosia, i. 5; giver of, 18; the milk which forms, 52, 54; contest for, 53; the demons and, 53; Gandharvas, guardians of, 53; 81; of the cow, 275, 276; the origin of, ii. 361; the phallical reference of, 361, 365.
Ampelos, i. 267.
Amphisbhæna, the, ii. 386.
Anantas, the serpent, ii. 398, 399.
Angadas, i. 337.
Animals, gradation of, for sacrifice, i. 44; substitutes for, in sacrifice, 44; battles of tame and savage, 186; inviolability of the mysteries of, 246; mythical identification of, ii. 123; colours of, in mythology, 295, 296.
Ansumant, i. 332.
Antony, St, the Vedic, i. 47; and the hog, ii. 6.
Antelopes and the Marutas, ii. 83, 84; king disguised as an, 86.
Ants, the, and the serpent, ii. 44; and the shepherd's son, 45; and the grain, 47; and the horses, 50; Indian, 50, 51; that dig up gold, 51; the monster, 51.
Apâlâ, Indras, and the somas, ii. 3; and her ugly skin, 5.
Aphroditê, i. 394; and Hermes, ii. 197.
Apollo, and Laomedon, i. 279; Smintheus, ii. 68; and the crow, 254.
Apple-tree, the legend of, i. 251; the mythical, 405; and the goat, 405.
Aquila and Aquilo, ii. 191, 192.
Arabs, the, saying of, ii. 11.
Arachnê, ii. 163.
Arcadia, i. 387, 390.
Ardshi-Bordshi Khan, the history of, i. 120; stories from, 134, 139.
Ardvî Çûra Anâhita, the Persian, i. 99, 100.
Argos panoptes, i. 418.
Argus, ii. 327.
Argunas, i. 79, 104.
Ariadne, i. 212.
Arkas, ii. 118.
Arnê, ii. 259.
Artemis and Aktaion, ii. 86; the huntress, 87; and hind, 88.
Arunas, i. 292.
Ases, the three, and the eagle, ii. 191.
Ashis Vaguhi, i. 108, 109.
Ass, the, among the Greeks and Romans, i. 259, 260; in the East, 360; in the West, 360; mistakes about, 361; Christianity powerless to redeem, 361, 362; hymn in honour of, 361, 362; treatment of, by the Church, 363; down-trodden condition of, 363; in the Rigvedas, 364; names of, 364, 365; of Apuleius, 366; which carries mysteries, 367; and flight into Egypt, 367; of the Açvinâu, 371; of Indras, 371; phallic nature of, 372, 373; chastisement of, for phallic offences, 372, 373; fall of, in the Rigvedas, 372, 374; the demoniacal, 374, 376; slowness, 374; the golden, 375, 376; the Hindoo, 377; and the jackal, 377, 378; -lion, 378, 379;

-musician, 378, 379; three-legged, braying, 379; and lion, 380; braying of, and the merchants, 380; and Vesta, 384; and the Trojans, 386; ears of, 386; skin of, 388; that throws gold from its tail, 388; and the waters of Styx, 390; horned, of India, 390, 391; horn of the Scythian, 390, 391; and Silenos, 391, 392, 394; and Bacchus, 392; and the talisman, 393; skin of, 394; proverbs about, 394; the combed, 395; shadow and nose, 395; golden, of Apuleius, 395; uncontainedness, 396; that brays, 397, 398; in hell, 398; knowledge of, 398.

Assassins, story of the king of the, ii. 35.

Atavism in mythology, i. 199.

Atli, i. 226.

Attis, the Phrygian, ii. 409.

Audhumla, the cow, i. 224.

Aulad, the warrior, i. 112, 113.

Aurora, the cow, process of re-creating, i. 20; cow of abundance, 26; relations to Indras, 27; the milk of, 27; and her cows, 25, 29; the girl, the swift one without feet, 30, 31; the evening, perfidy of, 32; as a sorceress, 33; persecutions of, 34; the saviour, 35; once blind, now seeing and sight-giving, 36; and the night, 36–38; the sisters, 38; the younger, 38, 39; nuptials of, and its conditions, 39; fruit of the nuptials of, 39, 40; and Rakâ, 50; characteristic form of, 50; as a cow, 51; mother of the sun, 51; rich in pearls, 56; and the moon, 56, 65; the Persian, 100–102, 121–125, 146; awakener of, 163; 170; amours of, 324; the two, and the fox, ii. 124.

Avesta, the, i. 109, 110.

BACCHUS and the asses, i. 392.

Bâlin and Sugrîvas, i. 312, 313; ii. 100, 101.

Barrel, the mythical, i. 197.

Basiliça, story of, i. 298, 299.

Batrachomyomachia, the, ii. 71.

Battos the shepherd, i. 279.

Bear, at blind-man's-buff with the maiden, ii. 69; and Vicvâmitras, 109; king of the bears, 109; in the forest of honey, 109; eater of honey, 110; and peasant, 110–112; duped by the peasant, 112; and the fox, 113; king and the twins, 114, 115; the demoniacal, and the two children, 115, 116; disguises of, 117; woman in the den of, 117, 118; half bear half man, 118; as musician, 118, 119.

Beaver, the, ii. 79, 80.

Bees and the Açvinâu, ii. 215; Vedic gods as, 216; as moon, 217; from the bull's carcase, 217; in Finnish mythology, 218; spiritual and immortal, 218–220; wax of, 219; and young hero, 220; as musician, 223.

Beetle, the, and eagle, ii. 209; the sacred, 209; red, 209, 210; names of the red, 210, 211; and first teeth of children, 211; worship of the red, 211, 212; green, 214.

Bellerophontes, i. 305, 338.

Berta, i. 85; the Russian Queen, 218; Queen, legend of, 251–257; large-footed, 253.

Betta and the cake-youth, ii. 238, 239.

Bharatas, King, ii. 85.

Bharadvâgas, ii. 275, 276.

Bhîmas the terrible, i. 77–79, 104.

Bhogavatî, city of, ii. 403.

Bhrigus and Cyavanas, ii. 10.

Binding, vanquishing by, i. 106, 107.

Birds, language of, i. 151, 152; the mythical impersonations of, ii. 168, 169; the wise, story of, 169–172; virtue of feathers of, 172; the language of, 174; story of, and the queen, 175; excrement of, 176; the blue, 176; Semiramis and, 176; as diviners, 177; auguries from, 178; the, of Bretagne, 271, 272.

Bitch, the mythical, ii. 19–25; as spy, 35.

Blind lame one, the, i. 31, 32.

Blue Beard, the Esthonian, i. 168.

Boar, the, of Erymanthus, ii. 9; of Meleagros, 9; the monster wild, in the Rigvedas, 9, 10; Indo-European tradition of, 13; tusks of, 15.

Brahmadattas and the crab, ii. 356.

Brahmanâs, the, i. 414.

Bréal, M., i. 263.

Bribus, ii. 308.

Bridge, the mythical, i. 228.

Brian, the Celtic hero, i. 239, 240.

Brother, the third, i. 79, 83; the Turanian, and his dream, 139–142; the riddle-solving eldest Turanian, 142; the third, in quest of the lost cow, 155, 156; journey to hell, 157; as counsellor, 156, 159; royal, as peasant, 162; awakener of the princess of the seven years' slumber, 162, 163; who mounts to heaven, 176; and the tree-purchaser, 176; endeavour of, to milk the bull, 177; who snaps his fingers, 184; ascent into and descent from heaven of, 189, 190; who steals from the other two, 194; and the flying-ship, 205; in bronze, silver, and gold, 291.

Brothers, the three, i. 77, 80, 82, 104; the Persian, 105; the two, 107, 108, 120; the three, 109, 111, 125, 128; the four, and the pearls, 127; the six, Calmuc story of, 128, 129; the two, Calmuc story of, 130; the two Calmuc, rich and poor, 131, 132; the two (lion and bull), and the fox, 134; the three, 148, 153, 156, 161; the three dwarf, story of, 161, 162; the two rich and poor, and magic stone, 177; the three, of the purse, whistle, and mantle, 288, 289; the two, who go one to the right and the other to the left, 317, 319; 327.

Brünhilt, i. 212.

Brutus, the first, i. 199.

Bufonite, ii. 384.
Buhtan and the fox, ii. 134, 135.
Bull, the sun a, i. 4; the, fecundator of the cow, 5; the great bellowing, 7-10; the horns of, 9; a symbol of royalty, 44; of the Persians, 95; the excrement of, 80, 95; disembodied soul of, 97; ambrosial, 99; capacity of, for drinking, 175; in the council of animals, 185; which comes out of the sea, 222, 223; which carries the maiden, 223; about to be sacrificed, 270; without entrails, 270, 271.
Buri, i. 224.
Butterfly, the mythical, ii. 213, 214.
Butter-ears, the cat, ii. 53, 54.
Bucephalus, i. 338.

Cabala, i. 73.
Cacus, i. 280, 281.
Caduceus of Mercury, ii. 219, 220.
Çakuntalâ, i. 219.
Calf, the, as marriage-priest, i. 257.
Çambaras, cities of, i. 13.
Çantanus, myth of, i. 67, 68.
Canicula, the, ii. 33.
Çaoka, i. 98.
Çaradvat, ii. 332.
Çarmishthâ, the witch, i. 83, 84.
Carp, the, ii. 351, 352.
Carpus, ii. 352.
Cat, the white, ii. 42; penitent, 54; fox, and fattened mouse, 56; and sparrow, 56; dog, and ring, 56, 57; and dog and supposititious child, 57; and moon, 58; and Diana, 58; and St Martha, 58; and Freya, 59; and St Gertrude, 59; the chattering, 59; and fox, 59; and cock, 59; and lamb, 60; the grateful, 60; the white, Blanchette, 61; and the house, 62.
Cats, the enchanted, ii. 62; the black, 62, 63; ill-omened apparitions of, 63; and witches, 63, 64; the two, 64.
Çavarî, i. 64, 66, 69.
Cerberi, the, i. 49.
Cerire, i. 117.
Chameleon, the, ii. 161.
Charlemagne, tradition of, i. 161; and Orlando, 256.
Children, king of, story of, i. 135, 136.
Chimæra, the, ii. 158.
Chinese, the, and Little Tom, i. 336.
Christ and Prometheus, ii. 40.
Christopher, St, and Christ, ii. 57; and lark, 274; and the cocks, 284.
Chrysaor, i. 305.
Cianna and the grateful ant, ii. 46.
Cicada, the, ii. 223, 224.
Cienzo and Meo, story of, i. 329, 330.
Cinderella, origin of the legend of, i. 31; 101, 126, 161; the Russian, 196, 197; ii. 5, 197, 281, 304.
Circe and the ass's head, i. 366; and the companions of Odysseus, ii. 6.
Çivas, the *deus phallicus*, i. 44, 59; ii. 160.
Claudius, Publius, and the auguries, ii. 291.
Clodoveus and St Martin, i. 356.
Clouds, the, i. 6-9; mythical conceptions of, 11, 12; sky with, as a forest, 14; as mountains, 61; battles in, 62; as barrels, 63.
Cock, the mythical functions of, ii. 278; and Mars, 280; Indras, the paramour of Ahalyâ, as a, 280; and hen in India and Persia, and sacredness of the, 282, 284; crowing of, 282, 285, 286; Christus invoked as a, 283; in the Gospels, 283; the miraculous, 284; of night, 285; and Minee' Aniello, 287; Esthonian legends of, 288; hitting the, 289; as a symbol, 290; -fights, 290; the Danes and, 290; auguries from, 291.
Coition, mythical, i. 348.
Cornucopia, Scandinavian, i. 225.
Cosmogony, the Persian, ii. 412.
Cosimo and the fox, ii. 135, 136.
Cow and the Bull, the, origin and meaning of the myth, i. 3, 4; respect paid to, in the family, 46.
Cow, the infinite, celestial, i. 5, 6; son of the, 5; -child, the spotted, 6, 14; as monster, 15; -moon, 19; -aurora, 19, 20; of abundance, 26, 95; hide of, as symbol of fecundity, 46, 47; sour milk of, as favourable to generation, 47; milk-yielding, of night, 48; invocation of the spotted, 50; the sacred, of the Persians, 97; purification by the excrement, 99; pearl excrement of, 129; the black, 167; and the weather, 174; Vedic, double aspect, 175; filled with straw and sparrows, 187; of abundance, Scandinavian, 224; red, 228; German proverbs relating to, 229; and dwarf Allwis, 260; testicles of, and the jackal, 233; the, that spins, 250; the Sabine, 268; the sacrificed, 269; the ashes of, 276.
Cow-cloud, the, i. 14, 15, 74.
Cow-moon, the, i. 274, 275.
Cows, the, of night, i. 17; the two, 27; that do not cover themselves with dust, 28, 31; seen in dreams, 47, 48; coming forth of, 50.
Cowherd, the hero disguised as, i. 168, 169.
Cox, Mr, i. 262, 263.
Crab, the, in the riddle, ii. 354; celestial, in June, 354; in the myth of Herakles, 355; and Alexander, 355; and the deceiving crane, 355; and the serpent, 356; sun and moon as, 356; and fox, 357; "from a man, a," 358; as a charm, 359; Cancer, the, 359.
Crescentia, the Persian, i. 121.
Cross, the, ii. 411; of paradise, 411.
Crow, the, in borrowed feathers, ii. 246; mythical significance, 250, 251; and cheese, 251; disguised, 251, 252; the enchanted, and Râmas, 252; cunning of, 253; Râmas and Apollo as, 253;

and Pallas and Yamas, 254; of evil omen, 254; the giant, 255; and the dead, 255; and the old man, 255; the procrastinating, and Phœbus, 256; as messenger, 257; the egg, 257; brood, 257.
Cuckoo, the, and Zeus, i. 248; its mythical congeners, ii. 226; Indras as a, 228, 229, 231; birth of the, 231; a phallical symbol, 232; and Hêra and Zeus, 232; and marriage, 232; as mocker, 233: harbinger of spring, 233: sinister aspect of, 234; as cuckold, 234; as a bird of omen, 234, 235; immortal and omniscient, 235; and nightingale, 235.
Çunahçepas, i. 35; story of, 69-72, 74.
Cupid and Psyche, i. 368, 369; ii. 378.
Cypresses, riddle of the two, ii. 174.
Cyrus, legend of, i. 110, 118
Cyzicene, the, i. 275.

DÆDALUS and Icarus, ii. 186.
Dadhyanć, the head of, i. 303, 304.
Dadhikrâ, the solar horse, i. 337.
Dakshas, ii. 364.
Danaidæ, the, i. 265.
Daphnê, i. 170, 273.
Darius Hystaspes, myth of, i. 346.
Daughter, the third, and the toad, i. 381; and the magician, 382, 383.
Dawns, the two, i. 27.
Dejanira, i. 212.
Delilah, counter-types of, i. 212.
Deluge, the Vedic, ii. 335.
Demons, mountain of, i. 96.
Demosthenes on Athênê, ii. 247.
Devayânî, the nymph, i. 83, 84.
Devil, the, as a bull, i. 184; and the waters, ii. 390, 391.
Dhâumyas, three disciples of, i. 79.
Diana (Hindoo), ii. 43.
Dead, the, good luck brought by, i. 198.
Dionysos, ii. 217; and the panther, 160.
Dioskuroi, i. 304, 305; the legend of, 318.
Dîrghatamas, i. 84, 85.
Dog, the, and cat, ii. 56, 57.
Dolphin, the, ii. 351.
Dominic, St, and the dog, ii. 40.
Domitian and the astrologer, ii. 39.
Dove, in the Rigvedas, ii. 297; Agnis as, 297; Moses and the flesh of, 297; self-sacrificing, 297; and the ant, 298; stories of the maiden (and prince) transformed into, 298; story of the twelve sons changed into, 298, 299; of the prince and servants changed into, 299-301; the two, and Gennariello, 300-302; the funereal, 303; as announcer of the resurrection, 304; the daughters of Anius changed into, 304; the two, and Little Mary, 304; and Zezolla, 305; doves and the rosebush-maiden, 305; Peristera changed into, 305; and Venus, 305; the laughing, 306; and Aspasia, 306; infidelity of, 306.
Drinking, trial of, i. 206.
Drusilla, Livia, and the white hen, ii. 196.
Duck, swan, or goose, the, Agnis as, ii. 307; the Marutas, and the horses of the Açvinâu as, 307; and golden egg, 308; the sun as, 309; in the lake, 309; the white, and her three sons, 311; death of, 311; that lays a golden and a silver egg, 311, 212.
Drunkenness, and madness, ii. 348, 349.
Dundus, i. 75, 76.
Dundubhis, the cloud-monster, i. 75.

EAGLE, the, and Zeus, ii. 195-197; and the classic heroes, 196; the Hellenic, 196; and Aphroditê, 197.
Earrings, theft and recovery of the, of Karnas, i. 80, 81.
Eel, the, as phallical, sacrificial, and divine, ii. 341; proverbs about, 341; eating, 342; with two heads and two tails, 342; transformation into a fountain and an, 343; the maiden changed into an, 343; and monster-serpent, 343; diabolical, 344; the epic exploit, 344.
Eggs, hatching of, and thunder, ii. 281; worship of, 291; the golden, 292; beginning with, 292, 293.
Elephant and the hare, ii. 77; mythical qualities of, 91; general mythical significance, 92; Airavanas, 92; the white, overcome by the monkey, 93; in the lake, 93; that supports the world, 92, 93, 95; and the tortoise, 93-95; the Vedic, 94.
Emilius, the lazy, and the grateful pike, i. 195-198.
Empusa, i. 367.
Endymion, i. 429.
Epics, the, killing of the serpent the theme of all, ii. 392.
Eros as a fish, ii. 340.
Esmeralda and Quasimodo, loves of, i. 421.
Eulenspiegel, ii. 246.
Eurôpê, i. 264, 265, 272.
Exchanges, tales of unfortunate, i. 176.

FARQUHAR II., death of, ii. 14.
Fecundity, symbols of, i. 49.
Feridun, episode of old age of, i. 111.
Finger, the knowing little, i. 166; Small Little, story of, ii. 151, 152.
Finns, the, the epopee of, i. 150.
Firefly, the, ii. 212, 213.
Firud, i. 117.
Fish, the laughing, i. 249; symbolic meaning of, 249; the April, 250; and the man's seed, 250; celestial metamorphosis into, ii. 331; become a stone, 331; laughing, 333; Alexander and the, 333; the little gold, 334; Vishnus as a, 334, 335; and Aphroditê,

340; phallical, 341; wise and stupid, 349; and the ring, 350; the heroic, 350, 351; and pearl, 352; sacred, 353.
Fly, the, and bear, ii. 221; and ant, 222.
Flies, ii. 221.
Fleece, the golden, i. 146, 429.
Flute, the magic, i. 161, 195.
Fool, the fortunate, 195; the would-be, fortune-making, i. 240.
Fox, the, and the bear, ii. 113; mythical significance, 122; and jackal, 123; double aspect of legendary, 123, 124; the wolf and honey, 128, 129; and the old man whose wife is dead, 129, 130; as weeper, 130; and tail, 131; and four hungry animals, 131; the hungry, and bird, 131; and wolf, 132, 133; and lost girl, 133; and the cheese, 133; as go-between, 134; and Buhtan, 134, 135; and Cosimo, 135; and hare, 136, 137; and cock, 137, 138; knaveries and cunning, 139: and other animals, 139, 140; the sick, and lion, 140; human antitype, 140; Lycaon, 147.
Formicola, Captain, and the shepherd's son, ii. 45.
Freya, i. 212; the foot of, 253.
Frog, the, and mouse, ii. 71, 72.
Frogs, the, in the sky, ii. 373; imitating the sounds of, 373; and the serpent or heron, 374; in the 103d hymn of the Rigvedas, 374; and Indras and Zeus, 374; and the moon, 375–377; the dumb, 375; and Proserpina, 375; and serpent, 376; and rook, 376; the diabolical, 376, 377; two dragons in the form of, 377; the maiden changed into, 377–379.

Gahs, the, i. 98.
Galanthis, ii. 53.
Galathea, i. 421, 422.
Gandhamâdanas mountains, i. 52, 55.
Gandharvas, the, i. 52, 53, 149, 160, 311; appetites of, 365; 367, 369, 370, 379.
Ganeças, ii. 68.
Gangâ, the nymph, i. 68.
Ganges, the, ii. 308.
Ganymede, rape of, ii. 196.
Garatkarus, the wise, i. 68, 69.
Gardabhas, i. 365, 369.
Gargantua, at birth, i. 259.
Garudas, the bird, and elephant, ii. 94, 95; and the monsters, 184; and the birds, 245; 363.
Gâtâyus, the omniscient vulture, ii. 185.
Gazelle, the misleading, ii. 84.
Gefion, voyage of, i. 222.
Gemshid, legend of, i. 95.
Geneviève, the Persian, i. 121; 219.
Gennariello and Milluccio, ii. 300–302.
Geusurva, the, i. 98, 99.
Gerion, the oxen of, i. 273, 277.
Ghoshâ, the leprous, ii. 3, 5,
Giant-monster, the, and dwarf, i. 148, 149.
Giovannino, the fearless, i. 202, 388.
Girl, the, persecuted, i. 121; affianced to three, 123; in the chest, Calmuc story of, 131; seven years old, Esthonian story of, 153; wise, of the wood, 154; the poor, and the lady of the waters (Esth.), 154; the beautiful, and the witch, 218.
Giuseppe, the boy, and the ant's leg, ii. 45, 46.
Gnat, the, ii. 221.
Goat, the, triple aspect of, i. 401; the cloud as, 402; the he-, 402, 403; Açvinâu as, 403; and apple-tree, 405; and walnut-tree, 405; kids of, and wolf, 406, 407; revenge of the goat, 406, 407; mythical meaning, 407; he-, and merchant's daughter, 410; the sacrificed he-, 415, 416; as all-seeing, 418; with seven eyes, 419; with twelve eyes, 419; constellation of the, 421; as rain-bringing, 421; milk of the, 421, 424; blood of the he-, 422; stones, 422; sacrifice of he-, 423; cunning of the she-, 424; the witch and the boy goat-herds, 425; and the peasants of Sicily, 426; and the goatherd of Val di Formazza, 426; and the god Thor, 426; in the Scandinavian mythology, 427; the horned, 427, 428; lust of, 427, 428; in Greek mythology, 428.
Gods, the cheating of, i. 44, 45.
Gold, hand of, ii. 32.
Goose, the, and pearl, ii. 309; the miraculous, 312; foot of, 315; the disenchanted, 315; eating of, on St Michael's Day, 316.
Gorgons, the, ii. 9.
Godiva, the Mongol, i. 138.
Grasshopper, the, the wedding of, with the ant, ii. 48, 49; as diviner, 48; song of the wedding, 49.
Griffins, the, ii. 204, 205.
Gudrun, i. 226.
Guhas, i. 58.
Guhas, King, ii. 333.

Halcyon, the, phallical nature of, ii. 269; the Greek, 270.
Hansas, the, ii. 306, 307, 309.
Hanumant in quest of the herb of health, i. 52; 57–59, 61, 64, 78, 89; the monkey, ii. 101, 106.
Haoma, the ambrosial god, i. 97, 104.
Harayas and Haritas, i. 376.
Hare, the mythical, ii. 76; habitat and king, 76; and the elephant, 77; and hungry lion, 77; and the lion, 78; and dying eagle, 78; and cave of the wild beasts, 79; and lamb, 79; transfigured by Indras, 79; and parturition, 80; that sleeps with eyes open, 80; and bear, 81; and a wedding procession, 81; and the girl that rides on it, 82.
Hariçcandras, i. 69–72.
Haris and hari, meanings of, i. 376; ii. 99, 320.
Harpies, the, ii. 201, 202.

Hawk, mythical meaning of, ii. 192, 193; as a badge of knighthood, 193; sacredness of, 193; and Attila, 194; and the Greek gods, 194; superstitious beliefs about, 194.
Heads, exchange of, i. 303, 304.
Health, herb of, i. 52–54; Gandharvas, guardians of, 53.
Heaven, cup of, i. 8; battle in, 10, 11.
Hedgehog and wolf, ii. 11, 12.
Helen, the Argive, i. 170, 212; ii. 318.
Hen, the crowing, ii. 284, 285; dreaming of the brood of the, 288.
Herakles and Augeias, i. 143; and Cacus, 232, 235, 266, 267; and the golden cup, 273; and the oxen of Gerion, 277; competes with the he-goat, 428; and the boar, ii. 9.
Hermes and Admetos, i. 279; and Sârameyas, ii. 22.
Hermits, the dwarf, ii. 364.
Hero, the solar, riddle of, as a wonderful cowherd, i. 29; maiden helper, 209; concealed, 237; in the night, 326; saved by a tree, 334, 335.
Heroes, the, hunger and thirst of, i. 8; chief arena of, 15; weapons of, 62; mountain of, 97; biblical, 118; disguise of, ii. 2; noises at the birth of, 373.
Heroines, perverted, i. 211, 212.
Hesperides, garden of the, i. 274; ii. 410, 418.
Hippolytos, the legend of, i. 345.
Hippomenes and Atalanta, ii. 159.
Hog, as guise of the hero, ii. 2; the skin of, 5; bristles of, 5; dedicated to St Anthony, 6; lust of, 6; as Vishnus, 7, 8; and wolf, 11.
Holda, the dark, i. 251, 252.
Hoopoe, the, ii. 230.
Horse, the, of the sun, i. 290, 291; black, 291, 292, 295; the three, 291, 296; tail and mane, 295; and the cat, 317; the myth of, 330, 331; fat of, 332; the strength of Indras, 336; the symbolic meaning of head of, 339; the hero's, 340; binding of, 341; the neighing of, 346, 347; tears of, 349, 350; mythical, 349; the foam of, 352; the hoofs of, 353, 354; and the gods, 355.
Husband, the wicked, i. 124.
Husbands, exchange of, i. 317.

IDOL, the wooden, Æsop's fable of, i. 177.
Ichneumon, the, ii. 51–53.
Iliad, the, most solemn moment of, i. 16.
Ilvalas and Vâtâpis, legend of, i. 414.
Indras, the rôle of, i. 7, 15; appetite and food, 8; horns of the bull, 9; as the fire-god Agnis, 10; his fields of battle, 12, 15; great exploits of, 12; threefold victory, 13, 14; weapons of, 14; companion of Somas, 18, 19; the triple, 20; moments of, 20, 23; special function, 27; relations to the aurora, 27; and the blind lame one, 32; destroyer of the witch Aurora, 33; lover of the aurora, 35; personified in Râmas, 59–61; slays Viçvarûpas, 76; fall of, 76; protector of Utankas, 80, 81; transformation, 89; quarrel of, with the Marutas, 106; horses of, 351; as a ram, 403; with the thousand eyes, 418; the rudder of, ii. 7; as a wild boar, 8; and the dwarf hermits, 95; and Vishnus, 99, 100; and the monkeys, 101; and Vritras, 154, 155; deprived of strength and beauty, 155; as a hawk, 181; and Ahalyâ, 280, 281, 330; impotent, 326; unchaining the waters, 330; drunk, 349; and the monster, 393, 394; killing the monster, 394, 395.
Indus, i. 18.
Io, i. 264, 265, 271, 272.
Iphiklos, ii. 198, 199.
Isfendiar, seven adventures of, i. 118.
Iskander, legend of, i. 119.
Ivan, three essays of, i. 301, 302; (and Mary), with horse, dog, and apple-tree, ii. 28; resuscitated, 29; the three, sons respectively of the bitch, the cook, and the queen, 29; and the ring, 345; and his frog-bride, story of, 377–379.
Ivan Tzarević and the serpent, i. 177; and Helen and the bear, 178; and Princess Mary, 179–182; and the demoniacal cow, 181; and the magic apples, 182; and the witch in the balance, 183; and the hero Nikanore, 184; and the theft of the black bull, 186; son of the black girl, 188; and his brothers, killing the serpents, 191; and the rescue of the three sisters, 194; of the dog, 194; the drinker, 194; and the dead body of his mother, 198, 199; courage of, 201; variations of, 202–204; horse of, 340.
Ivan Durak and the humpbacked horse, i. 293, 294; and the fire-breathing grey horse, 296; who, mounted, three times kisses the princess through twelve glasses, 297.
Ivanushka and little Helen, i. 409.

JACK and the beanstalk, i. 244.
Jackal and the ass, i. 378; the perfidious, ii. 125; friend of the hero, 125; in borrowed feathers, 126; the, inquisitive and vile, 126; and the parrots, 127.
Joan lou Pec, i. 397.
John, little, and his red shoes, i. 195, 196.
Johnny and the goose-swans, ii. 309, 310.
Jonah (the Hindoo), ii. 337.
Jorsh, the, ii. 336-345; trial by the fishes of, 346–349; and Reinecke Fuchs, 348.
Julius Cæsar, horse of, i. 338, 350.
Jupiter Ammon, i. 429.

KABANDHAS, the monster, i. 62–64.
Kaçapas, the, ii. 362.
Kaçyapas, the fecundator, ii. 364.
Kadmos, i. 265, 272.
Kai Khosru, the hero, i. 117, 118.
Kan Pudai, Altaic story of, i. 144, 145.

Kapilas, ravisher of the sacrificial horse, i. 331.
Kapis, ii. 98, 99.
Katoma and the hero's horse, i. 340, 341.
Kâuçalyâ, i. 332.
Kawus, King, i. 112, 113, 115, 116.
Kentaurs, the, i. 367-369.
Ker lupta and the third brother, i. 290.
Kereçâçpa, the Persian hero, i. 106, 108; myth of, 313, 314, 335.
King's son, the, and the peasant girl, i. 163-166.
Kishmar, cypress of, i. 96.
Krimhilt, i. 212.
Krishnas, celebration of birth of, i. 51; father of, 75.
Kruth, the bird, and tortoise, ii. 369, 370.
Kuhn, A., i. 263.
Kumbhakarnas, the monster, ii. 400, 401.

LAKSHMANAS, i. 55; and Râmas, 62, 63, 66, 77; ii. 85.
Lame, the, and the blind, i. 217.
Lapillus Alectorius, ii. 287.
Lanka, three brothers of, i. 77.
Lark, the, in cosmogony, ii. 273, 274; and St Christopher, 274; the crested, 275; Bharadvâgas, 275.
Leaf, the magic, i. 155, 156.
Lear, King, in embryo, i. 85; ii. 230.
Lêda, ii. 185.
Lion, the, and the bull, i. 278; (and tiger) symbol of strength and majesty, ii. 153; Indras as a, 154; virtue of hair of, 155; lion's share, 156; -sun, the western, 157; sign of, 159; Androcles and, 157; the Nemæan, 158; afraid of the cock, 159.
Lizard, the, as witch, ii. 385; as omen, 385; the little, 385; the green, 386, 387; and poor Laric, 387.
Locust, the nocturnal, ii. 47.
Lohengrin and Elsa, the legend of, ii. 317-319.
Loki, i. 226, 227; and the pike, ii. 333, 334.
Louse, the, stories of, ii. 222.
Lucia, St, the Vedic, i. 36, 254; feast of, ii. 210.
Lucius, of Apuleius, i. 366.
Lunus. i. 58; the god, 139, 324.
Lynx, the, ii. 54.

MADONNA the old, and the maiden who combs her head, i. 180.
Magician, the, of the seven heads, ii. 36.
Magpie, the, in mythology, ii. 258, 259; as a robber, 259; knowledge and malice of, 259; bird of omen, 260.
Mahâbhâratam, the, most solemn moments of, i. 16.
Mahrusa, i. 125.
Maiden, the enchanted, and her hair, i. 146; Esthonian story of the prince and persecuted, 151-153; and the golden slipper, 208; that by a puppet weaves a shirt for a prince, 208; the, and the apple-tree, 251; the fairies' favourite, and the enchanted prince, ii. 286, 287.
Man and woman, the old, with the nine cows, i. 132 133; the old, who essays heaven in vain with his wife, 190; and the cabbage, beanstalk, &c., 190, 191; the old, and the beanstalk, 243.
Man-bull, Calmuc tale of, i. 129.
Mandaras, the, ii. 361, 362.
Manus, ii. 248; and Vishnus as a fish, 335.
Mansûr, i. 315.
Marcellus, St, the legend of, ii. 159.
Mare's head and the two girls, i. 298.
Mârgâras, ii. 42, 43.
Marîças, the stag, i. 64; ii. 85.
Mars and the wild boar, ii. 14.
Martin, St, and birds of, ii. 270.
Marutas, or winds, i. 5-7, 10, 12; kindred of, 17, 59; ii. 7; horses of, 83, 84; as monkeys, 99.
Marziella and the geese, ii. 313.
Mary and the cow's ear, and the stepmother with three daughters, i. 179-182; little, and the slipper, 196, 197.
Matsyâs, the, ii. 332.
Mâyâvin, the monster, i. 313.
Max Müller, i. 262, 263; and the panegyric of the frogs, ii. 371, 372.
Medea, of the Vedas, i. 33, 35.
Medea, i. 212.
Medusa, i. 305.
Menas, ii. 87.
Merchant, synonymous with miser, i. 184; son of the, who transforms himself into a horse, 342; the, and his three daughters, 410.
Mercury, i. 335; legend of, ii. 23.
Merdi Gânbâz, the faithful, i. 120.
Merhuma, the story of, i. 120, 121; 315.
Merula, the fish, ii. 340.
Metempsychosis, ii. 328.
Mice and the dead, ii. 67; apparitions of, 67; men transformed into, 67; presages from, 67, 68; and lion and elephant, 68; war of, with the frogs, 72.
Michael, St, i. 183.
Midas, myth of (the Mongolian), i. 381; (the Phrygian), 382, 383; as musical critic, 385; ears of, 386; as a miser, 389; the progenitor and judge, 390.
Milky-sea, the, i. 52; -way, the, 228.
Millstone, the devil under the, i. 114.
Milôn of Kroton, ii. 113, 147.
Minotaurus, the Calmuc, i. 129; 265.
Minućehr, the hero, i. 112.
Mithra, the solar god, i. 95, 102, 103; bow of, 107.
Mitras, the sun, a witch at a riddle, i. 30, 31; 52.
Mole, the, ii. 73, 74.
Monkey, original home of myth of, ii. 97; equivalents, 97, 98; and Vishnus, 99; mythical significations, 99; king of, 100, 101; Hanumant, 101-106; mistaken for a man, 103; tail of, 107

divination from, 107; and Jove, 108; as stupid, 108; musician, 119.
Monster, the celestial, i. 10, 12; subdued by Indras, 12-14; that keeps back the waters, ii. 393; killing of, 394, 395; and the egg of the duck, 395; the eggs of, 396; the aquatic, 404.
Moon, the mythical nature and office of, i. 18; as a pearl, 54; as a good fairy, 56, 57; as a bull, 58; Indian, ii. 87.
Mother of gold and her three dwarf sons, i. 153; story of the, who recovers her hands and son by throwing her arms into a fountain, ii. 31; and the hands of gold, 31.
Mouse, transformed by the penitent into a beautiful maiden, ii. 65, 66; and the mountain 66; and maiden, 69; the grateful, 70; and sparrow, 70, 71; the, Psicharpax, 71.
Muses, the, and the bee, ii. 223.
Mûsh (mûshas, &c.), ii. 43.
Music in the heavens, sorrow-inspired, i. 149.
Mythology, the Greek, i. 262; mobile nature of the objects of, 319, 320; allegorical treatment of, 421, ii. a Semitic, 412; the science of, 422; principal error in the scientific study of, 422, 423; concord of the learned in, 423; way to study, 424; animal, 425; product of imagination, 427.
Myths, the central interest and most splendid moments of, i. 15, 16; development of objects in the, into personalities with relationships, 320, 321; the negative as a factor in the formation of, 322; the uncertain subjective in, 323; entrance of variety into, 324; interpretation of, 323-326.

NAKULAS, i. 311; ii. 43, 51, 52.
Nalas, ii. 404.
Neptune, i. 430.
Netherworld, the, ii. 403.
Nibelungen, the, most solemn moments of, i. 16; 257.
Night and the aurora, i. 36, 37.
Nightingale, as prognosticator, ii. 236; whistling of, 237; propitious to lovers, 239.
Nisos and Scylla, ii. 197.
Noah, the Vedic, ii. 335.
Nose, the bleeding, Calmuc story of, i. 131.
Nükteus, ii. 246, 247.
Numbers, sacred, i. 6, 76, 77; ii. 416.

ODIN, i. 224, 226, 227.
Odysseus, i. 266.
Oidin-oidon, i. 398, 399.
Okeanos, the bull-headed, i. 267.
Onokentaurs, i. 367-369.
Orpheus, i. 149, 160.
Otter, the monster, ii. 391.
Owl, the, as the bird of death, ii. 244; as an evil genius, 244; and vulture, 244, 245; and the crows, 245, 246; cunning, 246; and Athênê, 247; eggs of, 247; the male, 247, 248; prophetic faculty of, 249; horned, 249, 250.
Ox, the speaking, i. 247; and Zeus, 248; as priest, 258.

PALLAS and the war of the frogs and mice, ii. 72; and the crow, 254.
Pan and Midas, i. 385; and the ass, 387, 391; god of shepherds, 387; at Marathon, 389; 428, 429.
Panayas, the, ii. 19, 20.
Pândavas, the five brothers, i. 77-79.
Pandora, i. 34.
Pandus, ii. 84.
Paravrig, the blind-lame, i. 32.
Parîkshit, King, ii. 84.
Parrot, the, myth of, ii. 320; and the colour haris, 321; as çukas, 321; lunar character of, 322; as counsellor, 322.
Partridge, the devil as, ii. 227; Talaus changed into, 228; and peasant, 228;
Pasiphaë, myth of, i. 237; 266.
Peacock, the mythical equivalents of, ii. 323; the hiding of, 324; as rival of the cuckoo, 324; and dove, 324; Indras as, 325, 326; feather of, and the younger brother, 325; tail of, 326, 327; as a symbol of immortality, 327.
Pearl, the ambrosial, i. 54.
Peasant, riddle-solving, i. 142.
Pêgasos, and Hippocrene, i. 176; 291, 305, 338.
Penelope, i. 428; and he-goat, ii. 163.
Pepin, the times of, i. 252; King, 255, 256.
Peirithoos and Trikerberos, ii. 39.
Perrault, story of, i. 367.
Perrette, the Calmuc, i. 134, 135.
Peter, St, and the dog, ii. 27.
Phaethôn, i. 277; the bull, 277; 343, 344.
Phalaris, the bull, i. 239.
Phineus, ii. 74.
Phrixos and Helle, the Russian, i. 409; 429.
Phœnix, the, mythical significance of, ii. 200, 201; death of, 200.
Piçâcâs, the ass, i. 375, 376.
Piccolino, ii. 151.
Picus, King, ii. 265, 266.
Pike, the luminous, ii. 334; the brown, 337, 338; and Emilius, 338; the phallical, 339; and crab and heron, 339; drunk, 349.
Pimpi, the stupid, and the hog, ii. 10.
Pipetta and the sackful of souls, i. 388.
Pipkin, the miraculous, i. 126; the stories of, 243-245.
Piran and Pilsem, i. 314.
Poem, an epic, i. 141.
Polyphêmos, i. 266.
Porcupine, the, ashes and quills of, ii. 12, 13.
Pork, virtues of, ii. 10, 11.
Porringer, the enchanted, i. 126.

Portugal, third son of the King of, and the dragons, ii. 187-189.
Poseidôn, i. 266.
Pragâpatis, i. 47.
Pretiosa, disguised as a bear, ii. 117.
Priapos, i. 394, 396; and Silenos, 384.
Priçnayas, the, i. 6, 16, 17.
Prince, the, and princess of the bird's egg, i. 170; who three times wins the race, 291; and enchanted mantle, 411.
Princess, three-breasted, i. 86, 122; in the chest, Celtic story of, 241; and the pups, 412.
Proserpina, the Teutonic, i. 252, 260.
Proverb, the, of shutting the stable after the cow is stolen, i. 231; of shutting Peppergate, 231; recovering the cow's tail, 232; of the cow's tail wagging but never falling, 234; of the egg-hatching cow, 238; of the cow and the hare, of the cow and the moon, 241, 242; of hunting by blowing a horn, 242; of the blind cow finding the pea, 243; of the laughing cow, 245; of the spinning cow, 250, 251; of the cow-maid that spins, 250.
Proverbs, German, relating to the cow, i. 229; mythical, 230, 231.
Puppets, the three, i. 207.
Purse, the enchanted, i. 126.
Purûravas, myth of, i. 67.
Pûrus, i. 84.
Pûshan, i. 409.
Pyramos and Thysbe, ii. 157.
Pythagoras once a peacock, ii. 327; the belief of, 328.

QUAIL, the, in Rigvedas, ii. 276; as symbol of the Tzar, 276; and Hercules and Latona, 277; and moon, 277; the game of, 277; as a bird of omen, 277, 278.
Queen, the blinded, and her servant, i. 218, 219.
Queen-mother, the, and her wicked sister, i. 412.

RAHUS, ii. 252.
Râkâ, i. 50, 56.
Ram, the rain-cloud as a, i. 402; Indras, 403; Indras and testicles of, 414; devourer of, 415.
Râmas, the sun, i. 55, 57-59; *alter ego* of Indras, 59-62; and Lakshmanas, 63, 77, 311, 312, 315; ii. 24, 85; and Kabandhas, i. 64-66, 81, 86; and Bharatas, 374.
Râmâyanam, the, most solemn moments of, i. 16.
Râvanas, the monster, i. 76, 77; asses of, 375.
Rebhas, i. 299.
Reinardus Vulpes, ii. 141.
Renart, Procession du, ii. 140, 141.
Resurrection, offerings symbolic of, i. 48, 49; faith in, 339.
Rhodopê and her slipper, ii. 197.
Ribhavas, the brothers, work and workmanship of, i. 20, 21, 46; names and relationships, 21, 22; identification with Indras as Agohyas, 22; the third of, 20-26; in Hindoo tradition, 25; protectors of the cow, 27; and the evening aurora, 33; the three, in search of the earrings, 79; 81, 125.
Riddles, propounding, i. 82, 102, 112; solving of, 143; identification by solving, 206, 207.
Rigrâçvas, the red horse, i. 415, 417.
Rigvedas, the, i. 4, 40; 28th hymn of 10th book, ii. 77, 78; the 103d hymn of, 371-373.
Rikshas, ii. 98.
Ring of recognition, i. 55; of Dushyantas, ii. 350.
Rocco, San, and dog, ii. 27.
Rohitas, i. 69-72.
Romeo and Juliet, i. 125.
Romulus, i. 118; and Remus, ii. 177.
Round table, the, poems of, i. 257.
Rudras, i. 5, 47, 89; ii. 7.
Rustem, the myth of, i. 112-116; and the ass, 379; horse of, and the lion, 380.

SACK, the, the hero in, i. 237, 239, 240; the dwarf in, 238; and the hero cut in pieces, 295.
Sailors, the, saved in the buffalo's hide, i. 239.
Saints, i. 355, 356.
Sal, the hero, i. 112.
Salamander, the, ii. 380.
Sampo, the Finnish cup of abundance, i. 150.
Samson, i. 236; the Hindoo, ii. 104-107; and the lion, 154-156.
Samvaranas, i. 86, 87.
Saramâ, i. 57, 58, 97; and the Panayas, ii. 19-22; and the cows in the rock, 19; impersonation of the moon, 21; sons of, 22; and Sarameyas, 24.
Sarameyas, ii. 22-24.
Savitar, i. 54, 65.
Saranyû, i. 347.
Schmierbock, the cunning, i. 413, 416; ii. 151.
Schwanritter, the, ii. 319.
Scylla, ii. 34
Sea-urchin, the, ii. 336, 350.
Sefid, the demon, i. 113.
Selênê, ii. 217.
Serpent, as the privileged demoniac form, ii. 389; tail of, as betraying the devil, 389; the devil, and the young widow, 389; -devil, and the waters, 390; the killing of, the theme of all epics, 392; in the Rigvedas; 393-396; that bites its tail, 396; Agnis as, 397; Indras, the Marutas, 397; the wisdom of, 397; and the Somas, 397, 398; the phallical. 399; Anantas, 399; Vasukis, 400; and the cloud-monster, 400, 401; the funereal, 401, 402; -rope, of Yamas, 402; collar of, 402; and Sitâ, 402;

and riches, 403; and the lower world, 403; Karkotakas, and Nalas, 405; and hunter, 405; as a wise magician, 405; the crested, 406; three-headed, 406; skin and tongue of, 407; and lost riches and the dead, 407; the white, 407; worship of, 408; and children, 408; and the heads of the family, 408; and the tree, 409; and moon, 410; tree guarded by a, 410; symbol of, 411; the, in the Persian mythology, 412, 417; the Çruvara, 412, 413; the breath of, 413; and frog, 414; the two talking, 415, 416; the three headed, 416; fairy, and three gifts, 417; and king who has betrayed the maiden, 417; the sleeping, with eyes open, 417; and the king's daughter, 418; as whistler, 419.
Sheep, the, triple aspect of, i. 401.
Shepherd's son, ii. 45; and Giuseppe, 45.
Shepherdess, the, who proves herself a queen, i. 209-211.
Siddhi-Kûr, stories of, i. 120; Mongol and Calmuc stories of, 128-135.
Sîfrit, i. 213, 214; and Brünhilt, 329, 330; horse of, 339.
Sijavush, i. 116.
Simurg, the bird, and the child Sal, ii. 188, 189.
Sirens, the, i. 149, 205, 206.
Sister, triple, i. 85.
Sisters, the three, i. 105; Calmuc story of, 130.
Sitâ, the dawn, i. 26, 55-60, 62, 65, 66; fire sacrifice of, 67, 69; and Saramâ, ii. 21; and the serpents, 403.
Sky, the glowing, a fire, i. 69; stone of, 96; by night, ii. 167; winged animals of, 168.
Slipper, the lost, i. 31; enchanted, 126; origin of throwing the, 196.
Snail, the, ii. 74, 75.
Sohrab, son of Rustem, i. 114, 115.
Solabella and her seven brothers, ii. 314.
Solomon, ring of, and the hero, i. 167; story of the ring of, ii. 175.
Somas, the, i. 8, 18; as a bull, and a stallion, 19; 104.
Son, the, who sacrifices his mother, i. 124.
Sons, three, rape and restoration of the, ii. 57; transformation of, into doves, 57.
Sperm as ambrosia, ii. 181.
Spider, the, and its web, ii. 161, 163, 165; and the wasp, 164.
Squirrel, the, and fox, ii. 73; in the Edda, 73.
St James's Way, i. 422; Day, 422, 423, 430.
Stag, the mythical, ii. 83; the golden, 85; the hero, 86; at the fountain, 86; Eikthyrner, 87; and Telephos, 88; as nourisher of heroes, 88; silver images of, in churches, 88; disguise of, 88, 89.
Stone, mountain of, i. 314; the man turned to, ii. 285.
Stork, the, and heron, ii. 261; and children, 261; mythical meaning of, 261; and the old man, 262; and the peasant, 262.
Strix, the, ii. 202, 203.
Stymphalian, the, birds, ii. 204.
Styx, the, i. 390.
Sudabe, i. 116.
Sudeshnâ, Queen, i. 85.
Sugrîvas, ii. 109.
Sun, the, as a god, i. 7; as a bull, 8; relations of, to aurora, 27; as a cowherd, 29; child of night and aurora, 37; the, in relation to the aurora, 27; as a lame hero, 31, 32; persecuted by, and persecutor of, the aurora, 33; as born of aurora, 51; the pearl, 54; and the aurora, 56, 65; and moon, 65; light of the, and Ssaran, intrigue of, 138; firing at, 344; the, in the cloud, 394.
Sundas and Upasundas, the inseparable, i. 310.
Sunlight and Moonlight, i. 315, 316.
Superlatif, i. 259.
Suramâ, i. 57, 58.
Sûryâ, i. 65; husband of, 307.
Svaçvas, i. 343.
Svetazor and his brothers, i. 192-194.
Swallows as birds of omen, ii. 240; the seven, and Sigurd, 240; and the Lord, 240; of good augury, 240; and the crow, 241; and swan, 241; as babblers, 241; dreaming of, 241.
Swan, the, and the prince, ii. 311; hero as or on, 316.
Swineherd, the, and the hogs' tails, i. 234.
Sword, the enchanted, i. 126.

Tail, the, value of recovering, i. 235, 237; the fox's, 236.
Takshakas, king of serpents, i. 80, 81.
Tapatî, legend of the loves of, i. 86, 87.
Tâtos, the Hungarian horse, i. 288, 296.
Tehmime and Rustem, i. 114.
Telephos and the stag, ii. 88.
Tereus, the myth of, ii. 229.
Theodore, the hero, i. 296.
Thief and the pigs, i. 200, 201; the, in the myths, 333.
Thomas, little, and the priest's horse, i. 234; the ass, 362.
Thor, and the serpent of Midgard, i. 225; his appetite, 226; and the goat, 426; the vessel of, 426; ii. 6.
Thraetaona, i. 101, 103-106.
Three, the number, ii. 416.
Thrita, i. 103-105.
Thunder, son of, thunder-god and devil, story of, i. 159, 160.
Thunderbolt, the, i. 9, 14; symbolic meaning, 250.
Tiger, tail of, ii. 160.
Tistar, i. 98.

Toad, the, as demon and as a diabolic form, ii. 379; the maiden changed into, 379, 380; fortune-bringing, 380; sacredness of, 381; and the third daughter, 381; -births, 383; the dried, as an amulet, 384; the -stone, 384.
Tom, little, blind of an eye, and his brothers, i. 335, 336.
Tortoise and the elephant, ii. 93–95; the incarnation of Vishnus as a, 360–362; originally, 361; names of, 361, 362; and mountain, 362; and elephant, 363–364; the funereal, 365; buried, 365; blood of, 365; and frogs, 366; changed into the lyre, 366; the shields of, 366; and Zeus, 366, 367; and new-born children, 367; mythical meaning, 368; German legend of, 368; the island, 368; and the hare, 369; and the eagle, 369; and the bird Kruth, 369, 370.
Tree, the ambrosial, guarded by a dragon, ii. 410, 411.
Triçankus, i. 72–74.
Triçiras, i. 76, 77.
Trigatâ, i. 57.
Trinity, Indian, dispute for pre-eminence, ii. 8.
Tritas, i. 8; horse of, 23; character and relationships, 23; why called stupid, 23; in the well, 24, 25; and his brothers, 25.
Turn-little-Pea and his brothers, story of, i. 191, 192.
Tuti-Name, the, i. 119.
Tvashtar, i. 21, 34; the Hindoo Vulcan, ii. 154, 155.
Twilights, the two, i. 18, 27.
Tyrant, the, and the bleating lamb, i. 416, 417.
Tzarevic, Ivan, and his Medea sister Helen, i. 212–214; and his penitent sister, 214–216; and his perfidious mother, 216; and his perfidious wife, 216, 217; and his wife Anna, 217.

Uccaihçravas, the horse, i. 288, 289.
Uddâlakas, i. 80.
Ukko, the Finnic thunder-god, i. 147.
Upamanyus, i. 79.
Ursula, St, ii. 118.
Urvaçi, the myth of, i. 39; 67, 84, 170, 273, 365, 369.
Ushâ, i. 26.
Utankas, myth of, i. 80, 81, 95; 331, 333.

Vadhrimatî, ii. 32.
Väinämöinen, dwarf-god, i. 147, 148; harp of, 149.
Valkyries, the, and their swan forms, ii. 315.
Valmîkam, ii. 43.
Vamrî, ii. 43.
Vamras, ii. 44.
Varunas, i. 52, 69–72, 107.
Vasavas, the, i. 68.
Vasishtas, cow of, i. 72–74, 87, 88; vain attempt at self-destruction, 88, 99.
Valas, the grotto of, i. 13; as a cow, 15.
Vâyus, i. 5–7.
Vedas, i. 80.
Vegetables, as symbols of generation, i. 164.
Veretraghna, the bull, i. 103, 104.
Vespasian and the horse's dung, i. 389.
Vesta, i. 384.
Viçvamitras, myth of, i. 72–74, 88.
Viçvarûpas, with the three heads, i. 76.
Vikramâdityas, the history of, i. 136, 137.
Vishnus, i. 20, 24, 26, 54, 57; personified in Ramâs, 59; three steps of, 301, 302, 334; as a wild boar, ii. 8, 9; and Hiranyakshas, 8; and the monkeys, 99, 100; as haris, 424.
Vivasvant, i. 34.
Vouru-Kasha, sea of, i. 96.
Vulcan, the Vedic, i. 21; the Christian, ii. 40.
Vulnerability of the hero or monster, i. 82.
Vulture, the, in the classics, ii. 198; feathers of, 198; and the immortal liver, 198; voracity, 199.
Vultures, the twin, ii. 184.

Walchelm, the priest, i. 293.
Walnut-tree, and goat, i. 405.
Wasp, wisdom of, ii. 221.
Way, the Milky, i. 421; and she-goat, 422.
Weasel, the, ii. 52, 53.
Wedding-ring, the, i. 169.
Whale, the mythical, ii. 337; and the fleet, 345.
Wife, the, and the bewitching voice, i. 137.
Willimar and his vow, i. 356.
Wind, Persian god of, i. 105.
Winds, the, as bulls, i. 7, 12.
Wise men, the seven (Angirasas), i. 17, 28.
Wolf, the, and goat's kids, i. 406, 407; mythical meaning of, 408; the monster, 408; the, and the devotee, ii. 142; impersonations of, 142; and dog, 143; heroic forms of, 144; the she-wolf, 144; transformation into, 145; sent by God as instrument of vengeance, 146; hide and teeth of, 146, 147; the demoniacal, 147; as omen of death, 147; Sköll and Hati, 147; disguises of, 147–149.
Woman, made of wood, story of, i. 137; the old, and her older sister, ii. 6.
Women, knowledge of, i. 246, 247.
Woodman and painter, the, Calmuc story of, i. 130.
Woodpecker, the mythical meaning of, ii. 265; and King Picus, 265; beak of, 267; and Beowulf, 267; of evil omen, 267, 268; and dog, 268, 269.
Wren, the, in mythology, ii. 207; and the eagle, 208; and beetle, 208; and death of Cæsar, 209.

YAMAS, i. 23, 71, ii. 25; kingdom of, 48, 49; son of, 78, 95, 107.
Yayâtis and the girl in the well, i. 83. 84.
Yggdrasil and the four stags, ii. 87.
Ysengrin, the wolf, ii. 141, 149.
Yudhishthiras, i. 77-79, 82.
Yünx, the bird, ii. 269.

ZAFARANA, ii. 10.
Zeus and Hera, i. 247, 248; the beetle, and the eagle's eggs, ii. 195; eagle of, 195, 196; and Latona, 277, 280; and Lêda, 318; and Io, 327; Faber, 352, 353.
Zezolla, the maiden, and the dove, ii. 304, 305.

THE END.

www.ingramcontent.com/pod-product-compliance
Lightning Source LLC
Chambersburg PA
CBHW022142300426
44115CB00006B/303